Mountain Echoes

COLLECTED STORIES & INTERVIEWS

FROM THE DICKENSON STAR

1984 - 2011, Vol. 2

Mountain Echos available at
Mountain Gifts, Haysi, VA
and Amazon.com

Anita Belcher

PREFACE TO MOUNTAIN ECHOES VOLUMN II

~ Wayne Rogers ~

We are excited to bring you Mountain Echoes, Volume II! We have been able to collect over 100 more stories about you, your kin, your family, your friends, your neighbors, and your community from *The Cumberland Times* and *The Dickenson Star*! This is more than simple biographies! This is Appalachian Mountain history and life!

You will notice there are many gaps in the articles that we have not been able to locate or print. We have tried the Library and *The Dickenson Star* archives but their format has made it virtually impossible to use. What we need are newspapers! If you have old newspapers of Anita's "Mountain Echoes" that we have not included we would love to have them for Vol. III!

WHAT ARE YOUR ROOTS?

What is your heritage, your family, and your future? Again, you are probably related at least to some of the people and families mentioned here in Volume II (Remember Vol. I as well). In the end we are all related; we are all related to Adam and Eve, Genesis 1-3! The Bible says that we are all fallen and guilty of sin through our relationship with Adam.

Romans 5:12–21 says, "Wherefore, as by one man sin entered into the world (Adam), and death by sin; and so death passed upon all men, for that all have sinned:"

Jesus was fully human also, a son of Adam, Luke 3:23-28! But he was also a son of Abraham and David, Mat. 1:1, "The book of the generation of Jesus Christ, the son of David, the son of Abraham." God had promised to them that they would have a child, a seed, who would be a blessing to all nations! This was fulfilled in Jesus, the Son of God!

Jesus was not only truly and fully human, but the eternal and divine Son of God, born of the virgin Mary, without sin, so that He could die and pay the price of sin for all who come to him in truth and faith, with repentance, and to follow Him as Disciple and Lord.

"….But not as the offence, so also is the free gift. For if through the offence of one (Adam) many be dead, much more the grace of God, and the gift by grace, which is by one man, Jesus Christ, hath abounded unto many."

"….or if by one man's offence death reigned by one (Adam); much more they which receive abundance of grace and of the gift of righteousness shall reign in life by one, Jesus Christ."

"Therefore, as by the offence of one (Adam) judgment came upon all men to condemnation; even so by the righteousness of one (Jesus Christ) the free gift came upon all men unto justification of life....For as by one man's disobedience many were made sinners, so by the obedience of one shall many be made righteous."

"....as sin hath reigned unto death, even so might grace reign through righteousness unto eternal life by Jesus Christ our Lord."

Therefore, while we are all related to Adam, fallen in Adam, guilty of sin, under God's just judgment and wrath, we are not all (the "many")related to Jesus as Savior and Lord!

Matthew 11:28–30, "Come unto me, all ye that labor and are heavy laden, and I will give you rest. Take my yoke upon you and learn of me; for I am meek and lowly in heart: and ye shall find rest unto your souls. For my yoke is easy, and my burden is light."

MOUNTAIN ECHOES

VOL. II – COLUMNS BY ANITA BELCHER

THE DICKENSON STAR

SELECTED ARTICLES FROM 1984-2011

Volume I consist of newspaper clippings, scans, and documents from The Dickenson Star from 1984-2011. Vol II (and perhaps Vol. III) will consist of more articles from these same years as well. I'm certain you will find yourself, your kin, your neighbors, and your community in these articles. Don't fail to read one of the articles just because you don't recognize someone's name. Every article, like a book of short stories, has a story to tell which will delight you!

Gathering these articles has been a quite challenge. We have had to flatten old wrinkled newspapers with an iron, cut, clip, paste, align, trim, and glue to try to fit the pages together by hand! Please be patient and bear with us as you read, remember, and celebrate your history, your family, your friends, and your community!

We have approximately 250 more articles for Vol. II, the Lord willing (and perhaps Volume III!). So, if you don't see yourself in here, your kin, or your neighbors in one of these articles, surely you eventually will.

We have not been able to locate all the "Mountain Echoes" published, however, if you have or know of, or have saved some of these old newspapers, we would love to have them.

PS-some of the articles end with "cont'd next week;" however, we may not have the cont'd article for next week! Every article, however, is a story on its own, I assure you!

Wayne Rogers
wrogers892@gmail.com

TABLE OF CONTENTS

ARTICLES

Keepers of old tradition

By Anita Belcher

Mr. and Mrs. Henry Rasnick
Haysi, Virginia
(Baker Photo)

In the year of 1910, a short while after the huge chestnuts had showered down their harvest and the wind was racing through the tree tops proclaiming the on-coming winter, a small sturdy mountain woman gave birth to her eighth and last child. She had not been alone in her travail, for Dr. "Tiv" Sutherland, not long out of medical school had returned to his native mountains to care for his beloved people. Thus it was that Elihu J. and Malvina Powers Rasnick welcomed their small son into the world at Tiny, Va., November 13th. They named him Henry Stuart, and today Henry loves to share with others stories of his youth and his ancestry.

Henry's father, Elihu, was the son of Napoleon B. and Margaret Rasnick. Margaret was the daughter of Jonas and Rachel LaForce Rasnick, who came into the Tiny area somewhere close the time that "Fightin' Dick Colley" came to Sandlick. Jonas and Rachel homesteaded at the mouth of Russell Fork River and lived there until after the birth of their first three children, then returned to what is now Russell County, near Cleveland.

Before leaving Dickenson County, Jonas "staked out" and paid tax on about 1,500 acres of land, later giving each of his five children three hundred acres.

Margaret met and married Napoleon B. Rasnick in Russell County. Here they settled down and raised their family. One of their sons, Elihu, made frequent trips back into Dickenson County, to visit with relatives who had settled here, and to help them hand cut the large fields of wheat at harvest time. While traveling back and forth between the counties, and spending much time on Lick Creek and Frying Pan, Elihu decided that he liked this part of the country better than anywhere else, so he "homesteaded" some of the land his grandfather had "staked" out in the area still known as the "Middle of the World." Soon afterward, he married Malvina Powers and the Middle of the World was their home until after the birth of their sixth child.

In 1902, Elihu moved his family to Frying Pan Creek, purchasing land from his uncle, William Grizzle. It was here that the last two children were born, Henry being the youngest.

Henry's childhood was like that of most mountain children. He was surrounded by nature and people of strong, moral character. He first attended school at the Old Flint Gap building. His father and two first cousins built this school at no cost to the county. One cousin, Clement, donated the land. The building was constructed entirely of logs. The inside lumber was hand-sawed, tongue-grooved and hand sealed. Mr. Rasnick and his cousins also constructed the first seats from solid wood, yellow poplar to be exact. Henry remembers that school well, and the teachers. Mary Fuller, now Mary Cain, taught him first. Young, smart, good-looking and strong as an ox was Mary. A mountain girl herself, she continued with her education but always returned to teach her "kith and kin." Many a mile she walked to teach her classes and Henry remembers his dad "breaking the snow" along the road to make her walking easier. (Mary is still living with her daughter in Florida. She is broken in

See Rasnick, page 11

ELIHU J. AND MALVINA P. RASNICK, parents of Henry S. Rasnick of Haysi, Virginia.

health, but strong in mind and spirit as she was in the "old days." She is 91 now and would appreciate cards and letters.) Other teachers were Scott Duty, Hoge Tyler Sutherland (later County School Superintendent), John Turner and Troy Sutherland. (Troy is still living in the Tiny area. He is still very alert and knowledgeable.)

Henry remembers how one day the roof of the Flint Gap School caught on fire and the boys had to "snowball" it out. Next day patrons came and made repairs.

After Flint Gap schooling, Henry attended the Old Sulphur Spring School. (This has become a historic place in the county, but help is needed to restore it.) Among his teachers were Grady Rasnick, Phoebe Sutherland, and Mary Fuller.

In 1937, Henry attended the Primitive Baptist Association at the Lick Creek Church and here he met Amanda (Mandy) Estella Edwards. She was staying at the Lawrence Counts home and recalls that Association vividly. She had helped prepare one beef half, one whole mutton, ninety pies (from scratch), and more than one hundred cakes. For a big meeting like this, there had to be a lot of food. After the preaching and during the eating, Henry's mother walked up to Amanda and said, "I've got a good son. I want you to meet him. You'll never regret it."

Mandy, daughter of Andy and Sarah Ann James Edwards, did not regret meeting Henry. The following summer, July 1, 1939, they were married on Nealy Ridge by Preacher Elbert Stevens. Mandy says that her mother "just loved Henry and her daddy would have if he had lived to know him."

The newlyweds moved in with Henry's parents as they were elderly now and looked to their youngest son for help. On February 28, 1940, Henry was drafted into service, World War II and fought in France and Germany, until the war ended. Returning home, he and Mandy lived at McClure, for a short time and then moved back to Tiny, on Jack Branch, to some of the land that his great-grandfather had originally "staked out."

Mr. Rasnick is a man of varied interests and much native knowledge. He deplores the fact that much of this knowledge is being lost and that future generations will know little or nothing of the past which should be so vital to them and their children. Vital for sentimental and historic reasons . . . and maybe someday, vital to our very survival! For instance...how many of us would be able to produce our own "sweeteners" if sugar were not available? There's a few who could make molasses, a few who raise bees, but how many people do you know that could go to the forest and

SULPHUR SPRING SCHOOL, CLASS OF 1918 — Front Row, left to right: Tyl Rasnick, Henry Rasnick, Ester Sutherland, Nannie Rasnick, Lettie Sutherlan Frankie Sutherland; Second Row, left to right: Jonas Jessee, Charlie Rasnick, Rel Rasnick, May Jessee, Stella Sutherland, Violet Rasnick; Third Row, left to right: L Rasnick, Eddie Rasnick, Richard Sutherland, Ester Rasnick, Bessie Rasnick, Por Rasnick; and Mary Fuller, teacher, in back.

get the sugar maple to produce syrup for them? Henry has done this many times and shares his knowledge with us.

First, you find the SUGAR maple, not just any maple. Then after you're sure that you know what kind of tree you need, you find several of them. (There used to be plenty, but we have been quite wasteful with nature.) After you have located enough trees, you take an auger with a 1¾ inch bit and bore a hole two inches back in the tree at an angle. Then, taking an auger with a ¾ inch bit you bore another hole at an upward angle to meet the first. Then assuming you have seasoned out some "Shoemake," reeds or elder limbs, you shape them into a spout and tap one into each of the lower holes you have bored. You should have containers ready to set under each spout (old timers made theirs from yellow poplar) to catch the maple "water" or "sap." As containers fill up, have barrels ready to pour the water in, then cover the barrels with a clean sack to strain the water as it is poured into cast iron kettles. Build your fire under the kettle and let the liquid boil until the syrup is thickened to your personal taste. After removing the syrup, continue to boil the remainder until it becomes sugar. Then cut it into any size or shape desired. The Rasnicks agree that no sugar or syrup on earth has the taste of that produced by the native sugar maple. They admit that it was hard, though wholesome work, and they doubt that few people would "fool" with it today even if they knew how. But the Rasnicks would...they loved the work...the smell of the forest...the sugar-makin' stir-off and the taste of maple syrup on hot, homemade pancakes. "Nothing can beat it," both of them say.

By no means living in the past, the Rasnicks have fond memories. Carrying a "turn of corn" over the ridge on their back...snow hip deep sometimes...the grist mills...water mills... wheat being ground into flour...gardens raised without spraying or dusting...plenty of fresh butter and eggs...neighbors who visited.

Henry is afraid that in making "progress" we're losing much that is essential to real life and meaningful living. Like many of us, he fears we are discarding values we should retain.

The Rasnicks are Christian people. They are now living with their son, Jerry, below Hill Top. Another son, Dean, lives in Clintwood, with his wife, Elizabeth Ann, and daughter, Amanda Carol. Their only daughter, Joyce Nell, lives in Taylor, Mich., with her husband, Andrew Kennedy, and children, Gregory, Debbie and Betty Sue.

Henry and Mandy have a dream. They'd like a small farm, just enough equipment to run it (small stuff, Henry likes to use "muscle power"), their own cows, chickens and maybe a horse. They'd like neighbors to stop by and visit.

Who knows? This dream may come true. The Rasnicks may just decide to go back where it all started...the old homeplace near Flint Gap...just three miles from the "Middle of the World."

Deel family self-sufficient

By Anita Belcher

Jimmy and Clara Deel, affectionately known to their friends and neighbors as "Aunt Clara" and "Uncle Jimmy," are two of the most intelligent and knowledgeable people you can talk to. If their health permitted, they could survive from the good earth without the aid of modern technology, in fact, for many years they did.

A little trip into their past will help us to get better acquainted with the Deel's. Mr. Deel, 91 years of age come April 4th, is the son of Moses and Cansada Woods Deel. Cansada was originally from Scott County, while Moses was a native of Buchanan County. Owning much land around the Deel Fork area, Moses gave each of his six children a farm. When Jimmy married Clara Kendrick, he divided his farm up between his children by a former marriage and bought a farm on Tivis Ridge in the South of the Mountain,

Dickenson County. He and Clara were married April 3, 1944, and moved to their present home in 1947.

Clara is the daughter of John and Sophia Raines Kendrick. Mr. Kendrick came into this area from Pike County, to teach school and while teaching at Prater, he met and fell in love with young Sophia Raines, daughter of Green and Hettie Owens Raines. After their marriage, John and Sophia Kendrick returned to Pike County, Ky., then later into West Virginia, where he continued his teaching career until he moved to Ohio, to retire with his wife.

Meanwhile, Jimmy and Clara had begun their own family, two lovely little daughters, Bonnie and Mary. Mr. Deel also had started developing the farm they had bought. Using a big team of horses, turning plows, disks, harrows, fertilizer-spreader (all horse-drawn), Jimmy slowly but surely produced a beautiful mountain farm. He was greatly blessed with

Mr. and Mrs. Jimmy Deel

the knowledge of tool making and repairing, so his blacksmith shop was a profit not only to him but also to his neighbors. Here slowly, patiently working and shaping the needed tools he spent many hours, making sure that what he made was worthy of the name "Jimmy Deel." Hoes, blades, hinges, staples and bolts were just a few of the items he made. If he happened to get out of nails, he would remark, "Well, I can make some before I could get to the store and back!" It requires strength to farm as Mr. Deel did, run a "Smithy" and have a big

4

molasses "stir-off" every fall, but those are the things he did, plus many more. And speaking of strength, he WAS strong. Today, his fine, old hands are indicative of strength and labor, and his body still reminds one of an aged, sturdy oak, defying the winds of time. And speaking of "winds" reminds one that our old friend is also quite an accurate weather forecaster. Looking into the sky at the windswept, white clouds he'll smile and say, "Marestails is what old timers call clouds like that. We're in for a spell of unsettled weather."

Uncle Jimmy and Aunt Clara are a good match. She's a conversationalist and he is a listener. He has always gone at a good, steady pace, while she "bounces every foot off the ground." In fact, the first time I visited them three years ago, she was in top of one of her apple trees, sawing off the excess limbs!

Weighing in at about 100 pounds, Mrs. Deel's 76 years rest lightly on her face and figure. She is a dynamic lady filled with youthful curiousity that keeps her experimenting with first one thing and then another. Growing up "when a child was expected to work," she learned vegetable gardening at an early age and even then began adding flowers to the landscape. Today, a new flower bulb or flowering plant is a great joy to her, although she admits that working with herbs has become her favorite pursuit. She gained much of her knowledge in this category from her mother who in turn had learned it from Dr. Noah Counts, noted mountain herb doctor.

Clara remembers, "One winter I had whooping cough. There was no preventive medicine. Children just had to suffer and nearly died from all that terrible coughing. I was really sick, missing about two months of school. Mother made a tonic from rattlebead, sarsaparilla, wild cherry bark and burvine. These were boiled together until a tea or tonic was produced and then a cupful would be drunk at intervals. Another time I had "night sweats," probably caused by some basic physical weakness. Mother prepared a tonic made from sage and after drinking this for a while I had no more trouble with this problem." Laughingly, Mrs. Deel adds, "I suppose the bitter taste of the tonic speeded up my recovery."

Walking out the path to Aunt Clara's garden, you find yourself under huge chestnut trees with strawberry plants bordering the walkway. Last week, a riot of color produced by the crocus greeted one at the old fashioned gate, under the apple trees, up the sidewalk, around the old wellbox and out by the garden path. Herbs are just beginning to peep through the ground. Among those growing in her garden are peppermint, spearmint, lemonmint, orange-mint and apple-mint. Also catnip, comfory, sage and horehound can be found amid the primroses and iris.

A strong believer in "natural foods" Aunt Clara is an enthusiast when it comes to "greens." In her garden she raises turnip greens, kale, mustard and spinach, but her greatest enjoyment is picking and preparing the wild greens which still grow so abundantly in this area. These include plantin, purslane, polk (only when the leaves are young and tender), milkweed (when it first comes through the ground), cressy greens, water cress, amaranth and lambsquarter. This herb, lambsquarter, is said to be a rich source of vitamin C and A, also calcium. One of the wild plants that Mrs. Deel prefers is the plain old stinging nettle. Picked while young and cooked like any other green it is supposed to be very good and nutritious. Refering to her nature recipe book, Mrs. Deel shares this recipe; about 2 cups nettles, cooked, (By the way, it would take about a water bucket full to get two cups after cooking.), chop and add 1 small can mushroom soup and one-half cup of light cream. Wonderful over toast.

Mrs. Deel is not suggesting that everyone try her herbs, wild greens or medication. "For one thing not everyone knows what they're picking and you **could eat something that would be harmful**. However, for **herself** she finds that comfory makes a good poultice and crushed watermelon or pumpkin seed simmered in water is good for kidney trouble. These are old mountain remedies handed down for generations but Mrs.

Deel is NOT prescribing them to anyone. However, she DOES prescribe WATER. Just good, plain water and lots of it. She advises a good, sensible diet...stay away from white flour and junk food...leave off all the sugar you can...use honey and molasses instead... eat home-grown food... don't use sprays and "bug" dust, and plant seeds in good, "unpolluted" soil. She home-cans, freezes and dries her food for winter. She recalls how old people used to dry their greens was well as their herbs. She dries her fruits on a dehydrator Uncle Jimmy made for her.

Mrs. Deel, a former teacher, is a very thoughtful, but matter of fact woman. Once when her doctor despaired for her life, she turned to the Lord and nature. Buying a "juicer" she went on a diet of fruit and vegetable juice for several months and today Ms. Deel is a healthy 76.

"All that I have and am comes from the Lord," Mrs. Deel says. "He tells us in His word how to live and what to eat and I believe if we would pay attention to Him, everything would be better. I believe the solution to many of our health problems lies in the good earth at our feet."

I left Uncle Jimmy resting on the bed. Aunt Clara walked to the gate with me. As I got in the car, she called out, "Look, this is good exercise for your back." Catching hold of an apple tree limb above her head, she lifted her feet off the ground and swung back and forth and as I used to do when a child.

The Deel's daughter, Bonnie, and husband, Jack Ratliff, live with their two daughters, Beth and Janet, on a nearby farm. Another daughter, Mary and husband, Jimmy Smith, live at McClure, with daughters Michelle and Susan.

Auty and Maudie Fleming

By Anita Belcher

"To share with you whatever they have is their delight."

"Tell Joe Lee and Lema they should have been here and had supper with us," was one of the parting remarks of Mrs. Auty Fleming (Maudie) as I was leaving their home well after dark, after an enjoyable evening with her and Mr. Fleming. Their greeting to me earlier in the evening had denoted the same kind of hospitality. Mr. Fleming (Auty) was sitting on the porch, wearing what I assumed to be his usual "every day" clothes, but what he didn't know was that I was particularly affected by one simple item that seemed so much a part of him...an old felt hat. My dad must have worn it's twin as long as he was able to be up and about and I smiled in fond remembrance as later Mr. Fleming removed his hat and lay it beside him on the couch. Mrs. Fleming, just as "spry" as a spring robin, was sitting on the porch beside Auty, and as I got out of the car, greeted me with a forthright friendliness which I realized, within a few minutes, was very characteristic of her..." Come on in...did you have any trouble finding the house...you're a little late..."

Yes, I was a "little late". Sometimes I'm very good at that as an unexpected person, place or thing leads me down another path.

MAUDIE AND AUTY FLEMING IN 1934

This certain evening I had stayed on the right path, but a late October rain storm had delayed me. As I drove out the Jerry's Branch Road to the Fleming's home, I didn't hurry. If you'll ride with me for a minute, you'll understand why. The rain had washed all the autumn colors until they were glowing...just as if I were looking at mountains of flowers instead of trees...and the fields were green with their late growth of grass...as green as springtime. The mists were rising, it had been a hot day...and suddenly right in front of me, beside the road, I saw one of the most beautiful beech trees I ever seen anywhere and then another one. God did a special work of art when He made the beech trees and people driving down this road must just thrill at the sight of these with the coming of each new season. So

I just had to see some of these autumn sights, but I was just as eager to see Mr. and Mrs. Fleming. I had never met them, but when we got through with our handshaking and hugging, we felt like old friends. Mr. Fleming had no idea how he was going to surprise me with his first remark which came in the form of a question, "Did you ever hear of Uncle Allen Willis, Uncle Johnny, Uncle Roam? Did you ever hear of Merdie Willis...how about Cain? I believe he lives on Bartlick."

"Did I ever hear of them?" My mind went flying down memory's lane to, when as a little girl, I went to the Old Baptist Church at Bartlick, where my grandfather, Uncle Noah Fuller, sat up with the men on the "men's side" and Uncle Allen sat there by him...a fine looking gentleman, and his pretty little wife, Rena, sat over on the "women's side". How many times I had heard my mother speak of the other men he mentioned. They were all neighbors and, of course, Cain does live on Bartlick, "just over the hill from us."

"How did you know these men," I asked. "They were my uncles, all but Merdie. He was my Grandpa." Well, it's been said before, "It's a small world!"

Did you ever know any of the Bakers?" asked Maudie. On telling her that I did, she informed me that she was a sister to Earl, Grady, and Garfield. In fact, she came from a family of twelve children, eight of whom are still living.

"Tell me about your parents." We, the three of us had been looking through old picture albums and I could have kept looking for days. I am ever impressed with what fine looking pictures the early mountaineers made. I was especially interested in a picture of Melvin Fleming, Auty's father. Dressed in his high-top boots, "riding pants," white shirt and coat and black Stetson hat, along with his clipped mustache, he portrayed a fine looking man. Melvin was the son of

Manual and Betty Fleming whose homeplace was just out the road from where Melvin built. Auty remembers his grandfather was a real farmer and he tenderly remembers his grandmother, Betty, who in her late years became blind, and Auty, as a small boy, would lead her to the table and seat her. "If I had a girl," remarks Mr. Fleming, "her name would be Betty."

His old homeplace holds fond memories for Auty. It was called "the old Melvin Fleming" farm and was one of the prettiest around here anywhere. The house itself was white weatherboarded with big porch posts and white banisters. Outside buildings included double corn-cribs, smoke-houses, spring houses and one big barn. The barn was a huge building with a hall straight down the middle and stalls on both sides. A full-sized barnloft overhead was kept filled with hay and fodder." Auty continued, "Actually, our family owned two farms, both real pretty. One came through my grandmother's family and the other my grandfather's. We worked both farms, raising corn, oats, wheat, cowpeas, cane and anything that could be raised. WE WORKED six days each week...no picture shows...we went to church on Sunday. My daddy and mother raised us right...never a day passed that they didn't talk to us and tell us to stay away from bad company and always live right.

See FLEMING, page 7

Some of the children might have thought they talked too much, but I didn't. They set the right example in front of us and I've never forgotten the advice they gave and how they lived." I couldn't help but think of the verse in the Bible found in Deuteronomy Chapter 6, verse 7 as Mr. Fleming was telling about his parents. But now, back to the farm again! "Dad had some of the best livestock that could be bought or raised. The hogs, three or four raised at a time were of blue ribbon variety. "It took a bushel of corn for them at each feeding time," Mr. Fleming remembers. "The smokehouses stayed full of good meat. How well I remember that country ham and gravy and the sausage! We ground it out and mother would sew it up in white cloth bags, let it freeze hard in the smokehouse and then bring it to the kitchen and slice it at breakfast. The smell of that sausage, homemade bread and coffee could make your feet hit the floor even on a cold morning!

"Dad's mules were probably a part of life back then that I remember best. He had to have the best mules that could be bought. If someone got better ones, he would trade for ones that were even better! He always wanted me to take care of them and keep them in the best shape. They were blue ribbon prize winners. That was the only kind dad would keep. We kept sheep, too, for mutton and wool. Mother made our socks and other clothing from the wool. We raised cattle and kept three or four cows. I still remember those big zinc buckets of milk. Geese, an unusually large variety, were kept for the feather and "down" for pillows and featherbeds. Those featherbeds...nothing will ever feel like them or be as warm. We had all kinds of chickens and we raised turkeys for sale." Mr. and Mrs. Fleming both remember how that after very cold weather set in, that both their families would kill turkeys and ship them in barrels for Thanksgiving and Christmas customers at different localities.

THE OLD HOMEPLACE OF MELVIN FLEMING ON JERRY'S BRANCH. Standing, left to right: Virgil Fleming and Auty Fleming. Seated with dog is Holland Fleming.

The growing up days were filled with hard work, but there had to be some time when the boys got together for fun. Mr. Fleming recalls, "Now, I'll tell you a story. Me and the boys went 'possum huntin' and I climbed a tree to shake the 'possum down. I got on a rotten limb and it broke with me and I hit the ground. The dogs were waiting for that 'possum and they thought I was it...it was after dark...I rolled all over the ground trying to get away, but those dogs nearly tore my clothes off me!" We played awful rough back then. We'd take a bunch of corncobs and divide up into teams...'bout seven on each side. Then we'd start "fighting" with them cobs. Sometimes we'd get hurt. The team that had the most "men" left was considered the winner.

"We got up early every morning to get our day's work done. Mother would get our breakfast and we'd go to the fields...early...then come back in at twelve for dinner. We had a good hour off then for resting and talking things over. Then back to the fields until four o'clock when mother called us for supper. We ate and then went back to work until time to do the evening chores."

Mr. Fleming remembers his father as a logger as well as a farmer. "Daddy and mother were two of the hardest working people I have ever known, but we were always warm and fed...and loved...and I just can't forget how they taught us. They never taught us wrong. I can still remember dad saying, "Don't ever tell a lie, boys, don't ever tell a lie."

During this time, Mrs. Fleming had been busy in the kitchen. I seldom eat anywhere I visit, for that isn't my purpose in being there, but our time had gone so quickly...our fellowship was so good...the food smelled so wonderful and I was so hungry that it just seemed the natural thing to help Mrs. Fleming "take up" the food, put it on the table, have the blessing and eat. FARM FOOD! It can't be beat...fried potatoes, homemade cornbread, fresh creamed corn, turnips and greens, "the last mess of beans" just picked today...

Darkness had fallen and the rain had been beating on the roof as we talked. "Won't you stay all night...well, if it hadn't rained, we'd pick you some lettuce and greens. Won't you come again?"

I promised, that the Lord willin', I would...and I will, for these are two precious people.

Next week — when Auty and Maude got married.

Auty and Maudie Fleming

The Fleming's with grandson, Matthew . . .

By Anita Belcher

"Fifty-two years together and yet it seems as only yesterday when we started out."

When Auty was about 23 years old, a girl named Maudie Baker came into his life. Maudie was born on Rush Creek up above the Cranesnest bridge. She lived here until she was twelve years old, when the family moved to Baker's Ridge. Maudie recalls those early years...years when the children walked through the woods at Omaha to reach the Yates School. They found "near ways" so the distance would be shorter for walking, and she remembers her brothers, Garfield, Hardaway and maybe Earl walking from Rush Creek to Clintwood for further schooling. Sometimes they would ride muleback and put their mules in Columbus Phipps' barn until time to ride home in the evening. Maudie's parents were Ed and Rosa Keels Baker. Both her parents were raised at Rush Creek, but the old homeplace and much of the land is gone now, along with many other old landmarks. Strip mining came into the area "and it doesn't look the same now." Still, there are fond memories, the kind that stabilize a person and makes them keep going, when it would be easier to lie down and quit. She recalls, "Mommy would saddle up the mule, put one child in front of her and one behind her and load up food for the workhands in the fields. She tried to look after the men who were working for them. We raised almost exactly the same crops that Auty's family did...always had plenty to eat."

Mrs. Fleming laughs, "I guess some of my best memories are of us children growing up together. We worked, played, "fought" and did everything together. We shared the good and the bad. Today when we are together, we talk and laugh about those days."

When Mr. and Mrs. Fleming married, they moved to Flemingtown to be near his people. Maudie is very interested in relating how they "started out." She feels that they have been blessed to "come a long way," but she feels that a humble beginning is nothing to be ashamed of.

She recalls, "We started housekeeping in a little two room house. We used flour paste to paper the walls with pages from Sears and Roebuck Catalog. Our furniture was just the necessities. We had a little "step stove," two beds, a table with a bench and four homemade chairs...(we still have those chairs) and also an old trunk". As Mrs. Fleming had been talking, I couldn't help smile for two reasons. We had some similar furniture when I was a little girl and we lived in an old gray, weather-beaten house, probably built by my great-grandfather, George Anderson, before he went as a soldier to the Civil War. And we also papered our walls with unique paper. I think ours was the newspaper dad subscribed for and one of the games my sister and I loved to play at night was "find the word on the wall that I'm looking at". The second reason I smiled was thinking how "times do change"! Today, people are paying fortunes to have gray, weather-beaten homes and newspapers and catalog wallpaper goes everywhere from the fast food restaurants to the nicest home, along with the worm-eaten effect chestnut wood. And Maudie, today, your step-stove and homemade chairs would be considered a real "find"...but then you always considered them that! Mr. Fleming picked up on the story, "We worked hard, kept our debts paid...we were always honest. I walked through the woods behind the house here to get to Clinchco where I worked. I picked out the nearest way and would come out on Big Ridge at the slate dump No. 7 Coal Tipple. It was a 16 mile a day 'round trip...sometimes I'd ride my mule." Mrs. Fleming recalls, "I'd get up at 3:00 o'clock in the morning, get his breakfast, pack his lunch and on the days he rode his mule, I'd go out and hand him up his lunch bucket and coffee." "And you know," Mr. Fleming breaks in, "before I'd get to Clinchco that coffee would be frozen into ice."

For a minute we were silent, each thinking of his own thoughts. Outside the wind is rising...there's a chill in the air..."We'd better fix a fire," the Flemings agree, and soon the warmth spreading through the house causes the rain spattering against the window panes outside to be a friendly melody instead of a chilly intruder. "You know," Mr. Fleming reflects, "I worked at Clinchco during those days for $2.00 a day, "and" Mrs. Fleming breaks in, "the day wasn't ended. I would meet him and we'd go to the fields and work till dark."

Mr. and Mrs. Fleming agree that life has been hard. Maudie has done almost any kind of farm work that one can mention and

Auty has been willing to help her around the house anyway that he could. They have worked together, and working and saving they were able to build a nice, warm, well-furnished home. "I've never been out of work a day in my life," reflects Mr. Fleming. "There was never any reason to be out of work...not if you were able and wanted to work. Besides mining, we had our farming. Our truck farming was one means of making a living...we sold our produce."

Mrs. Fleming worked away from home for several years. She worked for Bill McFall and as custodian at the bank. Then she worked as a practical nurse helping deliver babies. She was called on in all kinds of weather...at all hours of the night. "In the winter we kept chains on the truck so I'd be able to go if they called."

The Flemings had no children of their own, but have raised two boys. One was Auty's brother, Junior, who lives near Abingdon now and visits when his health permits. The other "son", Ronnie, lives in Pikeville, Kentucky and returns home at every opportunity, sharing his life with them as they had shared their's with him. They are a close-knit family.

Yes, the years have been hard..."we couldn't live them over again now," remarks Maudie and Mr. Fleming agrees. Then they look at each other and laugh, "Why, yes, we would live them over again...they've been hard years...but still they were good years...if we had our health now we wouldn't think a thing about it."

Whatever the condition of their health might be, Mr. and Mrs. Fleming have not quit. Wherever you look, you see the planning of quick, alert minds and the touch of

See FLEMING, page 4

★ Fleming

Continued from page 2

determined and loving hands that have served long and well.

How does Auty and Maudie sum this all up? "**Well, life is not easy...hard times come, marriage and life...both of them get rough** at times, but you don't give up...you stick together. We would encourage young people to not give up on their marriages..."

They should know what they're talking about for Auty and Maudie Fleming have been together fifty-two years and yet, "hard times and all" **it seems as only yesterday when they started life together**...and tomorrow is another new day that they look forward to...**together.**

Dickenson First Presbyterian Church Celebrates 50th Anniversary

FIRST MEETING OF PRESBYTERY WHEN CHURCH WAS ORGANIZED IN 1934. NOTE TAGS ON CAR.

By Anita Belcher

Many people throughout several states have been waiting for this article, but time hasn't permitted the writing of it. As in many situations, "better late than never" seems to be the proper thing to say at this point, and with that in mind, I'll proceed.

October 14, 1984 dawned a bright and beautiful day, the kind of weather members of the church had been praying for. Picnic tables had been set up outside and the Harold Powers family had graciously made their lawn and tables available. For you who are not particularly interested in Presbyterians or what they do, you would still be intrigued in some items of interest taking place that day, or in the days past. The church building, itself, is built right beside the main road, Route 80-83 in Haysi. On one side of it is a parking lot filled with mining equipment and cars in varying degrees of infirmity. In front of it is a huge piece of equipment, below that is an old abandoned school bus. For many, many months now, a big hole of water has stayed beside the hardtop on the opposite side of the church. Many times it has overflowed, covering the highway and filling the ditchline in front of the church, making it dangerous for traffic, covering the front of the church and windows with filthy, black dirt and water and causing church goers to have to pick just the "right time and spot" to cross to the church. Above the "waterhole" Harold and Katy Jo Powers have a clean, attractive lot which they allow the church to use for parking.

How did this church happen be here? Well, in 1934, after having organized a Presbyterian work at Sandlick, Tom Mowbray, along with Miss Elizabeth Shoemaker and many great men of God, formed a committee to build a church at Haysi. James (Uncle Jim) and Alice (Aunt Alice) Syphers donated the land and the construction of the building got underway. (I believe that these fine old people, Uncle Jim and Aunt Alice, were the grandparents of Pearl Ramey and Eula Phipps of Haysi and Clintwood, and the great uncle and aunt of C. C. Belcher of Haysi.) Speaking of Uncle Jim, would you allow me a minute to stray from the direct story about the church to a personal recollection of Uncle Jim? Clynard and I were dating. It must have been about 1945-46 and for the lack of transportation, we went for walks. (Sounds funny?) We walked from Haysi up to where the Hilltop is now, and crossed the road and followed a pretty lane down through the woods that came out on the "Devil's Tator Hill". (Appalachian Power Company has a place there now.) Somewhere along the little forested path, we met Uncle Jim. I will never forget that meeting. He was riding a big, white horse, flecked with gray and Uncle Jim himself was dressed in a dark suit, white shirt and a fine black hat. His hair was thick and white and waved around his face and low on his neck. He brought his horse to a stop, removed his hat and sat and chatted with Cly and me. He gave us some quaint but sound advice, waved his hand to us and rode away. We watched him...a fine, erect figure, "riding off into the sunset." We never saw him again, but we've never forgotten him. In the church records, after the recording of his death, are the words, "A good man". When Uncle Jim and Aunt Alice gave the land for the church there was no way of visualizing the traffic that would one day stream by its very door, but even if they had, they gave the land that was most accessible for the people. The church was built and in 1934 was dedicated to the glory and service of God. Now, fifty years later, it has become a place of historical events.

In spite of some unfavorable conditions outside the church building, inside there is a rare sense of serenity, of quiet beauty and good taste. A sense of calm and reverence. Old fashioned lights, (donated by the old Haysi Hardware, I believe, hang from the high ceiling in the sanctuary. Sunlight, stealing through the windows, donated by Mr. and Mrs. Ireland Baker picks up the glow of the old hardwood floors. Grown dark with time and use, and the old fashioned fernstand behind the piano, topped with a lovely Boston fern accentutates the beauty of the deep rosetone carpet. Throughout the building, one finds this sense of God's presence...even in the little things. Perhaps that is due to the fact that down through the years, from behind the pulpit has gone forth the Word of God in truth and power and the present pastor is no exception. Rev. Lindley faithfully preaches the "whole counsel" of God, and he faithfully teaches how that God's Word must be applied to every phase of our life.

Sunday morning, October 14, was a day of rejoicing. As nearly to two hundred people gathered in from various parts of the county and from out of state, it was truly a

See PRESBYTERIAN, page 4

★ Presbyterian

Continued from page 2

great reunion. One is afraid to mention names, for all cannot be mentioned, but several counties in Virginia were represented and several states including Tennessee, North Carolina, Ohio and Georgia. (I can't remember all of them, but how welcome everyone was.) Greetings were read from several ministers who could not attend and from former members in California, Georgia, Tennessee, North Carolina, Michigan, South Carolina, Florida and Virginia. A floral arrangement was sent by the former Miss Bonnie Gilbert of Haysi, now of Florida, and one by Mrs. Ireland (Rachel) Baker, formerly of Haysi, now living in Bristol. Dr. R. T. L. Liston (now in his 90's), former President of King College, sent special greetings. Dr. Liston was very instrumental in establishing the work here and he well remembered the original dedication ceremony. Mrs. T. K. Mowbray, wife of our first pastor, had planned to be with us, but was unable to come at the last moment, but sent greetings. Mrs. P. R. Ball, now of Big Stone Gap, Va., sent her scrapbook of church history but was unable to come...and Mrs. Ireland Baker, who, as anyone might know who knows her, had her seventy-five homemade rolls all ready, but at the last minute, transportation plans didn't work. Mrs. Tinsley Bradley (Edna Wright), was all ready, but had the same problem

as Mrs. Baker. There were many others who could not come, but for the many who did, it was an unforgettable day.

Should we mention the food? One would have thought they had entered the land of "milk and honey" for I have never seen a greater abundance of food or a more beautiful display. That is something that the Baptists and Presbyterians have in common, among other things. Some of the greatest cooks in the world live right here in the mountains and valleys of Dickenson County. If you want to learn how to cook, you don't have to go to some foreign country...just come on "home". And as always, the Lord knew what He was doing, for when he put some of the best cooks here, He also put some of the men here who know fine food when they see it and love that "home cooking". Truly, it was a beautiful and delicious array of food set before us, and we give God the credit and praise.

The afternoon was given over to a program which included officers and members of the church, visiting friends from local churches and out of town. Former pastor's wives were recognized and presented with corsages. These were Mrs. E. H. Anderson and Mrs. John Whitner, as well as our present pastor's wife, Mrs. Lillie Lindley. Former pastors and

charter members were also recognized.

Although this service was held at Haysi, the Big Ridge Church, being a part of Dickenson First, participated in every part of the service for "we are one."

For those interested, just a "word" or more about the church building at Haysi. Completed in 1934, it survived the fire that destroyed Haysi the same year. It was used as a post office and housed the postmaster, Ireland Baker, and his family until the new post office was built with apartments overhead. It has survived two major floods, with water raging through doors and windows, and reaching a height of between five and six feet. Great men and women have passed through its doors and young people have gone out to all parts of the world to serve. They are still coming...and...going.

October 14, 1984 was a beautiful day! The fellowship and the food were wonderful. However, the highlight of the day was the spiritual food served by pastor Lindley as he reminded us in a powerful sermon that we "are surrounded by a great cloud of witnesses" and that we must continue to carry on God's work

Truth is not exciting enough to those who depend on the characters of and lives of their neighbors for all their amusement.

PART OF THE CROWD ATTENDING 50TH ANNIVERSARY
SERVICES OF DICKENSON FIRST PRESBYTERIAN CHURCH.

FORMER PASTOR'S WIFE AND CHARTER MEMBER, MRS. E. H.
ANDERSON. HAROLD POWERS AND ROSS LINDLEY IN BACK-
GROUND.

with the same faithfulness and determination that these men and women of fifty years ago had...for there is the same need and the same God.

Thank you for coming, or for wishing you could come, helping make this a great anniversary.

PRESENT PASTOR OF D.F.C.,
REV. ROSS LINDLEY AND WIFE, LILLIE.

Thanksgiving in "The Hills"

By Anita Belcher

Times change. No matter where you are, as you read this, put on your ''make-believe'' walking shoes, coat, cap and gloves and walk with me over the mountains and through the valleys of Dickenson County. We'll go through the little towns and communities, pause for look at the beautiful county Courthouse and hurry on to cross old rail fences, let down ''draw-bars,'' stop long enough to rub the cows ears at the ''milk gaps'' and we'll stop somewhere between Frying Pan

and Skeetrock for breakfast. We'll choose a house with smoke curling from the chimney and wood stacked on the porch. There'll be a ''chopping block'' outside with an axe firmly imbedded in the top and ''chips'' lying all around. The tinkle of the cowbell will blend with the crowing of a rooster. We'll see corncribs filled with golden grain and the signs of a recent molasses ''stir-off''. And breakfast will be country ham and sausage, gravy and biscuits, home fresh honey and fried apples. Big cups of coffee and glasses of creamy milk.. You

see, in the time that it has taken you to read this, we've gone back forty years...but that's the way ''it used to be.'' Remember?

Remember the school days just before Thanksgiving? We began in October learning poetry to say and memorizing parts for school plays. They, **of course**, always depicted the pilgrims and Indians and the Mayflower, and of course love of the country and Thanksgiving to God was the central theme. Remember the costumes? Made from sheets, construction paper and old clothing that could be found at home...we came up with some pretty authenic looking outfits. Anyway, most of the Indians had real feathers pulled fresh from the old rooster's tail!

Thanksgiving at church was usually celebrated the Sunday before Thanksgiving Thursday, and we heard sermons which directed our thoughts and praise to God for His blessings.

At home, well, each family had their own way of observing the special day of thanks. At our house, Dad got his little family together for Bible reading and prayer and then Mother had a good warm breakfast. Then on to other

★ Hills .....

Continued from page 2

matters. For some, it meant a day of hunting, the boys in the family and their dad's being together while the women got dinner. For others it was a day to gather in the rest of the late crops...check out the apple and potato holes, be sure the late, flat dutch cabbage were well covered...do last minute repairs around the house, barn and outbuildings and replenish the wood supply. Sometimes there would still be those old dark red or green apples hanging on the tree and now was a good time to gather them...and at long last, they were good. **Remember**? Those apple trees had the prettiest bloom on them in the spring and then apples would "set on" but not the bravest boy wanted to show his nerve by eating one. They were hard as rocks, sour, and otherwise, tasteless. But after the first or second frost, or even a good freeze, those apples were great! Remember finding them under the trees, hidden under leaves and straw? Is there any other taste just like that one? And Thanksgiving day might mean gathering in the last of the walnuts and hickory nuts...pawpaws are already gone.

See HILLS, page 4

Persimmons, though, are just right...if the 'possums have left any! Listen to a country boy when he tells you not to eat a persimmon before the frost gets to them...unless you want to be whistling "Dixie" or some other tune for an hour or two!

Thanksgiving week was a good week (so the men said) for doing the winter butchering. I hated those days and stayed in the house as long as I could for I didn't like even the pigs to be killed. Usually on those days it would snow...remember the big tubs of hot water, the men standing around by a hot fire and hominy snow blowing in the icy wind. The meat was good...big hams and shoulders would be carried to the smokehouse and the sausage grinder was set up inside. Pans and pans of sausage fried and put in quart and half-gallon cans to be opened throughout the long winter months ahead assured us of good eating, for the work...hard work during the spring, summer and autumn was now paying off.

Thanksgiving dinner was a sumptuous affair, though perhaps not as elaborate as Christmas. There would be plenty of meat...probably fresh beef, mutton, pork...but for sure there would be chicken. No where in the world that I've ever eaten or heard of can people fix chicken and dumplings like they do here in the mountains of Virginia. Practically any kind of vegetable that could be preserved by canning, or drying would be available. Potatoes, Irish and Sweet...yellow, white and red...pumpkin and squash, apple pies and molasses cake. The kitchen was a busy, happy place...mostly wood stoves to cook on during those days and not much "fast food" from the store, but oh, how good it was when mother and grandmother called out, "dinner's ready!"

Time was taken for the blessing and then everyone ate, talked and laughed...and ate some more. After dinner...remember...there was sittin' around sharing stories, children listened or played games and eventually the women cleaned the kitchen and the men and boys did the outside chores.

A busy and happy time! Has your trip tired you, or do you feel refreshed? Did you know that you could still, in reality, come on home and find some of those good things still going on and maybe some of you will sit down with the children this Thanksgiving and tell the children "how it was back then" and listen to them and their plans for the future. **It's a time of sharing and Thanksgiving wherever you are!**

C. D. and Clara Gilbert

By Anita Belcher

"Pioneering in a certain kind of farming and overflowing with enthusiasm and hospitality...

C. D. Gilbert possesses a keen, intelligent mind. One does not talk with him very long before **that** becomes apparent **and his knowledge is not confined to one or two subjects.** Clara, his wife, is his "right-hand man" and it doesn't take long to see their loyalty to each other. C. C. is one of eleven children born to Henry and Sarah Owens Gilbert, four of whom are still living. These are the oldest son who is C. D., Kenneth, Beulah and Jean, (Mrs. Wilburn Barton). The older Gilberts originally came from Patrick County. From Dickenson County, C. D.'s father, Henry, went to serve in World War I and came back to be a miner and farmer. Here, he and Sarah raised their large family when "times were hard." After school days, C. D. went into C.C.C. Camp and the $22.00 per month which he received was a big help to the family. C. D. had known Clara Cumbo since school days and in 1941 they were married. Clara's family had come from Washington County, for the sake of her grandmother's health. Here, one of the sons, James (Jim), met Alta Baker and they were married. They also raised a large family of sons and daughters. Clara's father, James, was a great Christian man. He was an Elder in the Big Ridge Presbyterian Church and an active leader. In his latter years, he wrote gospel songs and loved to sing them to his friends and neighbors and they loved to listen. Perhaps no word better describes Jim and Alta than "humility." In their last years they moved to Abingdon, but were brought back to their beloved "Big Ridge" when they died. C. D.'s father, Henry, died in 1957 and his mother, Sarah, a fine, upright Christian woman died in 1976 after a life of loving and caring for her.

**C. D. AND CLARA GILBERT
"PIONEERING IN A NEW KIND OF FARMING"**

When C. D. and Clara were married, they moved to Big Rock where he worked in the mines. After about two years, they returned to Dickenson County and soon thereafter, C. D. was called into service, World War II. Joining the Navy, he served in the Pacific Theater and many are the stories he can tell of those times. He made himself one promise while in service, and that was that if he lived to return to the United States, Dickenson County would be his home for the rest of his life.

In the course of our conversation, just as I was getting ready to write about his "plastic" farming, C. D. just happened to mention something that I believe many people would be interested in and very few people know.

When the Corps of Engineers came into the area to begin core drilling for the Flannagan Dam, this dam was to be constructed in one of the roughest, most inaccessible places in the mountains. (My father-in-law and husband used to camp out on the river at the "Firy Camp" where the dam now is, as did many of the mountainmen who could endure the hike.) At any rate, when C. D. learned that the Corps of Engineers had come in and needed men to "hack a road through the wilderness" down to the dam site, he was the first to ask for a job and so far as he knows, the first of the local men to get one. Other men were needed, so Mr. Gilbert rounded up Clayton, Calvert and Clinton Cumbo and Bill Barton. Using handsaws, crosscut saws, picks, axes, and shovels, these men made a road into where they needed to core drill. This drill was the only mechanical piece of equipment used at this point. On

reaching the river, steps had to be made up the opposite side of the mountain at "Low Gap" where the spillway would be built. Mr. Gilbert believes there was two hundred and fifty of these hand dug steps extending from the riverbank to the gap in the mountains. The men hung on with ropes and pulleys. By this time there was need for other equipment to be brought in and here "Uncle" Marion Davis entered the picture. He had two fine black horses and hitching them to his sled, he would leave his home on Big Ridge, travel out to "the Joe Turner Store," on to the Hall Bottom where "the Gobel Branham Store" was located and then followed the old Ritter's railroad track, (now under water) to the dam site. This was an 8-10 hour trip each way, everyday. It's amazing how that even in big, sophisticated ventures of progress that the brawn and brain of the mountaineer has ever been called on and has always responded in a positive way. C. D. believes that he drilled the last core hole at the dam and that he planted the first TVA

pine trees in Scott County.

Always a lover of nature, this love was intensified while C. D. was in the C.C.C. Camp and working for the TVA. Here he learned about caring for the forest, preventing soil erosion, tree pruning and planting and many other aspects of forestry and farming. Though he was now mining for a living, he was farming to eat and feed his family, and the whole time remembering his previous training and continuing to be an avid reader on related subjects. Then an article came out in a paper which a friend, Dexter Church, saw and told him about. It was dealing with the advantages of "plastic" farming and Mr. Church wrote the writer of the article and obtained further information. Then he and C. D. went to work with it. Now C. D. is so enthused with it that he wants to share his knowledge with everyone. "It's so much less work...the harvest is bountiful...the fruit or vegetables or plants so much bigger. I just can't see anyone doing their gardening any other way." Here's the process, and I have seen it in action and know for certain that it works. (If it's done right.) First, you decide on your plot of ground. Let's say you are going to plant a piece of ground 40 by 100 feet. Mr. Gilbert continues, "You plow your ground, adding to it sawdust, (old, preferable) but new can be used. Add lime, more if you use green sawdust to neutralize the acids and fertilizer along with any type barn manure. Plow these all under, then dig a trench all around your plot of ground. Take your plastic and spread over the plot, covering the edges with the dirt removed from trench. Lay weights, (brick, rocks, etc.) every six feet on plastic to hold it secure. Then take a bulb planter and make the holes where you want to plant your seeds. For

strawberries, plants should be two feet apart in the row, three apart in the balk. Corn about the same, only difference is that a hill of beans can be planted between each hill of corn. If ground happens to be wet when you need to plant, remove wet dirt with your bulb planter and have dry soil in

See GILBERTS, page 22

containers to cover the seeds with. After the first year, one does not have to plow this plot again nor fertilize it. The earthworms work it, the plastic keeps it soft and moist, and the root system of the plants carry the necessary gases from the air into the soil."

This is the basic principal of what C. D. and Clara are doing. As he says, "A big book could be written on it, and he wishes he could write it, not for credit, praise or money, but to help others use the knowledge that the Creator has given him."

I, myself have seen the garden of C. D. and Clara. I bought corn from them this summer...they raised 1000 ears of sellable corn on a twenty foot piece of plastic. On a forty by ninety foot plot of

strawberries they harvested 236 gallons. Sometimes one hill of potatoes would yield ten to fifteen pounds. One potato weighed seven pounds. The Gilberts have raised 25 pound cabbages, 35 pound mushmelons, broccoli 16 inches across, turnips over two pounds, as well as any other vegetable you might mention. And yes, Clara, uses plastic around her flowers and they are beautiful. C. D. started out using cardboard and paper, believing it would keep down the weeds and keep moisture in the soil. It worked, but he believes that plastic is better, "because it lasts longer." However, nothing goes to waste on the Gilbert farm. Everything from weeds to corncobs are stacked and mixed in a composite pile and used to enrich

the soil. It was a delight to see the Gilbert's strawberries this summer. The plants grew eighteen inches tall and one berry was 6 and ¾-inches around. (There were others this size.)

Mr. Gilbert does not believe this is the only way to farm...he believes it's the easiest and most productive. However, he will agree that you "can't go at it in a slip-shod manner." It has to be done right and you have to take care of it.

C. D. and Clara did not want this article ended without making mention of their Christianity. Both give all credit to the Lord for everything they have...their mind, their strength, and their every heartbeat. C. D. should know. He has been in the hospital four times this year. He had bypass heart surgery, wears a pacemaker and has had two operations for cancer. Yesterday at church, he "was on the verge of another stroke" but today he had dug up a seedbed and planted his lettuce..."we always

A SMALL PORTION OF C. D. AND CLARA'S SWEET POTATO CROP

have fresh lettuce on Christmas day," he says with a smile. Clara and C. D. plan for tomorrow and for next year...but all "within the Lord's will." Even with his health problems, there is no sense of depression in the air...instead a

feeling of security, well-being and thanksgiving.

I left with some of Clara's specialties from her freezer, some of C. D.'s strawberry plants, but maybe most of all, I left with the knowledge of how much they want

to serve the Lord and help people with all they have, and I left with their "come again...and eat with us next time" ringing in my ears. They meant it, too, for they are overflowing with Christian hospitality and enthusiasm.

Mrs. Mary Cain .... By Anita Belcher

"Ninety-two years old and still blessed with a quick, keen mind and a rare sense of humor..."

So much has been written about Mrs. Mary Cain that it would be a "re-run" to write the same history over again, but her 92nd birthday was a time of joy to her and to her many friends and relatives who gathered at Heritage Hall in Clintwood, on January 1, to help her celebrate. Mrs. Cain, as most readers know, is a great-granddaughter of Fightin' Dick Colley. Her father was Hawk Fuller and her grandfather was Jacob Fuller, who married Margaret, the daughter of Fightin' Dick. However, these are not the facts that have made her so well known and respected in the county. It has been Mrs. Cain herself with her forthright personality, her honesty and integrity, her desire to serve others and her determination to overcome all obstacles in her own life...**to succeed when success seemed impossible**...these are the characteristics that anyone who knows her, admires. Mary Fuller as a little girl, walked long, muddy roads to school, along with neighbor children and her brothers and sisters. After finishing elementary school, she and her brother rode horseback and sometimes walked part way, from Colley to Clintwood, where they

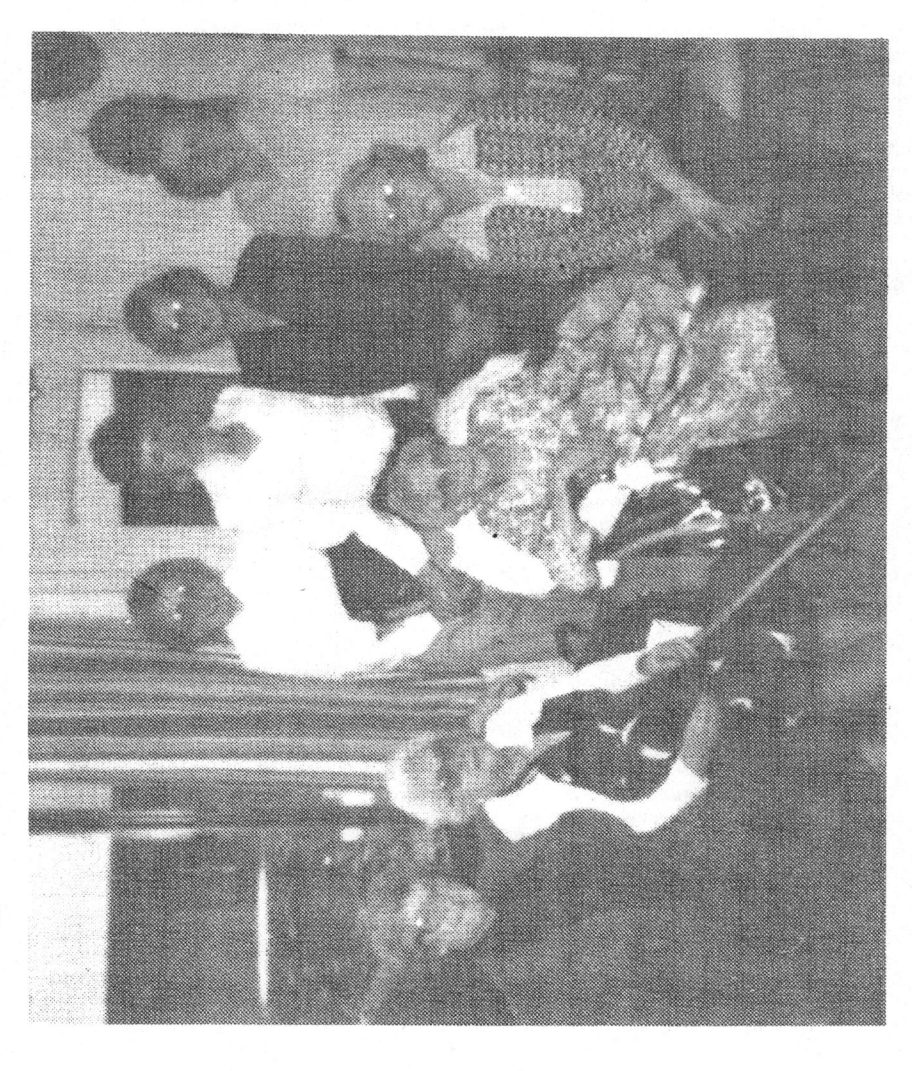

FAMILY PICTURE — (Front Row, left to right): Betty Rasnick, Bertha Sutherland, Mary Cain, Chloe Sutherland. (Back Row, left to right): Merle Fletcher, Carol Breeding, Lenis Thomas, and Lynn Mullins.

23

attended higher classes. (I remember several years ago, Mrs. Cain telling me how they would have to pick a path through the edge of the woods because the road was so muddy.) During these years, she married and had two children, one dying as a baby. She was still continuing her education, and refusing to leave her other little girl, Fairy. She took her along to Radford College. The president of the college remarked to her that it was the first and only time he had ever seen this happen, and that anyone who was trying that hard to care for a child and still get an education deserved the opportunity to succeed. Mrs. Cain didn't wait for opportunities...she looked for them and sometimes, in fact, most of the time, **it was she who knocked on the door of opportunity, not waiting for opportunity to knock.** After many years teaching in the elementary schools, Mrs. Cain, (by now she had married Sarge Cain) went back to college and studied business. When she retired, she was teaching business courses at the Haysi High School. After retirement, Mrs. Cain went back to Colley and settled in a house "down by the creek" not far from the mountaintop where her old homeplace was. Here, she tended her garden, wrote bits of songs and poetry, and cared for the sick in her family. As a girl, Mary had always looked after the sick and elderly. Her parents were very special to her and many a day and night she sat with them doing what she could. She has suffered with, and for, each of her brothers and sisters in their time of need, always doing what she could for them. They are all gone now,

except Bertha, (Mrs. Dewey Sutherland). And Bertha was right there at Heritage Hall to help Mary greet friends and relatives on January 1, and we finally got her to pick a tune on the banjo, though she hadn't touched one for years. "Why that's the way we learned to dance," remarked Carol, daughter of Bertha. "Mother would play the banjo and it just came natural for us kids to flat-foot or whatever. Nobody taught us. Mother just played the banjo and we danced." This was easy to believe, for watching Carol and Merle perform the intricate steps of the old mountain dances as naturally as water flowing down hill...**one knew that it was natural**, for no one could have taught them that well. (Even cousin, Lance Sutherland, sat back and admired them and like me, wished he could "do a few steps".) There were other dancers and age was no barrier. Music was some of the best and anyone who has never been privileged to hear REAL mountain music has really missed a lot in the way of enjoyment. Clayton Belcher, Lonza Mullins, Clay Taylor and Lawrence Colley were there with guitars, banjo and fiddle. Mae Colley picked out a couple of tunes on the banjo and Hallie Taylor and Beulah Lyle sang one or two of the old songs that used to be sung at gatherings. Someone suggested that Herb Yates "line out" Amazing Grace, which he did and the singing was beautiful. Lawrence helped out along with Mae, Myrtle, Beulah, Hallie and others. During all this, Mrs. Cain

was sitting back enjoying every minute of this time spent together with so many of her loved ones.

This woman, Mary Cain, is a remarkable woman. She is very intelligent and her memory is excellent. For 15 years, her health has been bad and most of the time she is in intense pain, but she has an unbreakable spirit. I'll add a personal note about this. When the program "Expanding Horizons" was funded for several counties, Mrs. Cain was one of my key speakers. (I worked as program director.) Mrs. Cain went with me from school to school speaking to groups of children. They adored her and often presented her with flowers or gifts. I, realizing the fragile condition of her body and bones, tried to take care of her, but

one day she caught a ride to Haysi, went to the beauty shop and was walking back up to the intersection at Newberry's where she thought she would meet me. Before I got to the intersection, I was blocked by a long line of cars and someone said there had been an accident. I parked my car and almost ran to the intersection. I had this strange feeling that the "accident" was Mrs. Cain. IT WAS. A car had backed out of the parking lot and knocked her down, and when I got to her she was lying in a little heap in the middle of the road with mud and water splattered all over her. Down on my knees, I went beside her with tears just pouring. "Oh, Mrs. Cain, are you hurt? I can't stand to see you like this..." She

See MRS. MARY CAIN, page 14

★ Mrs. Mary Cain ...... Continued from page 2

caught my hand in her little, cold one and with a twinkle in her eyes, she replied, "Child, I'm alright. Just embarrassed to be lying in the middle of the road like this...get me up..no, I don't need to see a doctor." Of course, she needed to see a doctor and did, and she was hurt, but she insisted on going back to her own home. While she recuperated, she worked on her next speeches.

Soon she was back "on the road again". I took her to Blacksburg, where the leaders of the "Expanding Horizons" programs were to meet. Here, Mrs. Cain met a lady whom she loves to tell about. This lady was just one generation or so from England. She wore pearls at her throat and diamonds on her fingers, and her hair looked like spun silver. We sat at the table with her and she was every inch a lady. Later, Mrs. Cain said to me, "Now what does that lady think of me...Mary Cain from the mountains of Virginia...SHE is such a fine lady." I looked at Mary Cain and thought of the depths of her character, of her keen intellect of her humility and service to others, and I said, in effect, "If she

is the lady she appears to be, **she** looks at you and says, "There is a woman who is every inch a lady!" Mrs. Cain was the star performer at Blacksburg. She was called on to speak and they did an educational T.V. program featuring her and her work with "Expanding Horizons". Many have seen this program and it can still be seen on certain occasions.

After "retiring" from this program, Mrs. Cain went back home again. Once more, she took up her pen to write her friends and bits of prose and poetry. Here she stayed, alone, maintaining her independence as long as possible, too long for those of us who care for her. Now, her home is Heritage Hall at Clintwood, where she is well cared for and loved. In the real sense, though, all of Dickenson County is her home for she has taught children and young people from nearly every area.

Specifically, home is up around Colley where her beloved family lived, worked and played together. Where she and young Sylvia Sutherland (Dye) tried ducking each other in the "baptizing hole" at Christmas, and "Doc Tiv"

Sutherland stood on the bank and bandaged her leg, which she hadn't realized was hurt. Ah, those were the days...and now Mrs. Cain says, "I'm going to write a book...at least a story about my life.

Mary Cain is a Christian. Her well-worn Bible and unshakable faith attests to this...and for this we are thankful."

Happy birthday, Mary Cain! You are a much loved and highly respected lady.

Reflections of . . .
Hetty Swindall Sutherland

By Anita Belcher

"It was just before dusk when we were walking together just back of the Old House...and we came upon them...a sea of blue asters lifting their faces to the evening sky. It was one of the loveliest sights I have ever seen and one I will never forget."

Within her lies the heart of the poet, the artist, the philosopher. These characteristics became apparent as together we studied pictures of her parents, grandparents and great-grandparents, but more specifically apparent as we stood before a painting of the old cabin where she was born and the minutes ticked away unnoticed. It was not that a painting of a mere place or building took pre-eminence over the fine people who had lived there, it was just that the simple landscape with it's cleared fields, wooded knolls, rocks worn bare by the footsteps of time, and a deep hollow sheltering a cold spring surrounded by creek willows...all these, silent yet speaking, told stories as clearly as ever a human tongue could have. One just had to listen...with the heart. And there was the old cemetery where memorial meetings were held, (and still are), the barn, the "big road" that led to Grandpa Swindall's store and house...and there was the Old House, the cabin where Hetty was born..."haunted" some folks said, but be that as it may, it was certainly saturated with memories.

Hetty's grandparents, J. C. (John Calvin or Caly as he was known) and Jane Vanover Swindall came to Dickenson County, Va., from Ashe County, North Carolina. The other set of grandparents, W. D. and Martha Jane G. Austin came from North Carolina, also. In fact, they were neighbors. When John Calvin was a child, he fell through the ice on Elk Creek in North Carolina and was saved from drowning by Matilda Austin. When coming to this section of the country, the Austin's settled in what is now Wise County, but the Swindalls came on into Dickenson. The old Swindall homeplace was located right in the curve of the Pound River opposite the mouth of Camp Creek. Mrs. Sutherland reminisces, "This is a beautiful place...you cross the bridge over the Pound River and the land just spreads out before you...just opens up...benches as if it had been terraced. No, the old cabin isn't there now. It was torn down and the logs used in another building about a mile away. But I remember how it was in those early years when we were children; the cabin itself was built on what must have been a bed of solid rock, for with the passing of years and the treading of many feet, the immediate "lawn" became bare rock in places. The fields were cleared and fences built. The old barn was away from the house, over on the hillside. A path ran from our front door to the "big road". This path and road was traveled many times by us children for it led to Grandpa Swindall's store and on to his house up on the ridge. I'll **always remember the "big road"** for when it was muddy, **it wasn't just mud! It was thick yellow clay.** Bricks could have been made from it, **and it was used to "chink" the cracks between the logs in the cabin.** Across the big road was the school which Grandpa Swindall gave the land for, and also the Little Zion Regular Baptist Church. High on the wooded point above the farm, was the cemetery and the meeting place for special memorial services. Here, as well as in the church building itself, Grandpa Swindall preached the doctrines of the Regular Baptist Church." Mrs. Sutherland paused for a moment, in which time, particular scenes of yester-year passed before her eyes as vividly as if portrayed on a screen. Her face glowed with animation as she exclaimed, "**I wish we could have had a recorder. Just a simple tape recorder, so we could have captured and held the voice of Grandfather Swindall.** I wish I

Hetty Swindall Sutherland

could describe his voice...would it be correct to say that it was **both musical and resonate? It was deep, but never harsh.** If he wanted someone who was not nearby, (there was no telephones, you know) he would step outside and call them...maybe from one hillside to the other. His voice carried whatever the distance, but it was still pleasant and musical.

That was the way he preached, too. Whether inside the church or out on the hillside, you could hear every word he said...even if you were a distance from him, and he always maintained that pleasant,

musical quality with almost perfect enunciation. Grandmother Swindall was a remarkable woman, also. Hetty's own father and mother loved the older Swindalls dearly, and her mother, Ardelia Austin Swindall, (whose own mother died young) loved and looked to Grandmother Jane for advice and comfort. Mrs. Sutherland has heard her mother saying feelingly of Grandmother Swindall, "She was a mother to me." In her obituary, E. J. Sutherland wrote, (in part) She was a consistent member of the Regular Baptist

See SUTHERLAND, page 15

★ Sutherland ......Continued from page 2

Church...she was exemplary and consistent in every way...a virtuous woman whose husband is known in the gates and whose children rise up and call her blessed...(Prov. 31) Truly she was a crown unto her husband, maintaining a hospitable home to which Preacher Swindall could sing out freely in that musically resonant voice of his, "All that'll go home with me are welcome!"

The Austin grandparents were well loved, also, but lived further away...over in Wise. About the time Hetty's parents married, the Swindalls and Austins went into the merchant business together, but again, distance was a problem. Mr. Austin decided to build his own store where he lived and this he did. Grandmother Austin did not live long after Hetty was born, actually Mrs. Sutherland was about five-years-old when her Grandmother Austin died. She well remembers being at her funeral and hearing the song, "Wayfaring Stranger" sung. During several of these years, Grandfather Austin was a traveling salesman. He sold tombstones and books. He traveled throughout the entire area on horseback and Hetty remembers that the first book her family ever bought besides school books was one that her Grandfather Austin sold entitled, "Everyday Wants Book". It was a book of general household information. The first novel she ever read was also sold by her Grandfather Austin. It was "The Trail of The Lonesome Pine."

Perhaps it seems strange to the reader that anyone would take the time to write about people they have never seen and never knew. As someone once said, "Why not write the news...the things that are happening today?" News items ARE **important and tomorrow, they, too, will be history,** and many of them **still important**. They are the stepping stones for the generations to come. But each generation has contributed a stone...a link in a never ending chain, and to forget those who have gone before us is to miss a step on the stone that was laid...or to weaken a link.

In the recent book compiled by E. J. Sutherland years ago and supplemented by Mrs. Sutherland, David Washington Austin makes this observation, "Children, grandchildren and great-grandchildren, remember: "Life is real; life is earnest, but the grave is not it's goal". (Page 18 from **Pioneer Recollections**):

And there is another reason among many others for writing about our older people, and that is...THESE PEOPLE ONCE LIVED. Their blood runs in our veins...because THEY lived...WE live. They loved and laughed, worked and played as we do. They waited for the dawn...for the day to break...and they watched the sunset. There were hardships and much that was ugly and wrong, even as there is today...but **the hardships made them stronger and beauty...and right...somehow outweighed the ugly...the wrong.** We need to know these people and learn from their wisdom and their mistakes.

I think of the years that Mrs. Hetty Sutherland has lived and how she continues to be active in the work that she and her husband begun. It impresses me to see, that even now, the attitude and attributes of those gone before, still strengthen her, and because I live in a world that is seemingly filled with chaos and tragedy, it inspires me to hear Hetty Sutherland say, "You know, I just can't decide **which** was the most beautiful sight I ever saw...the sea of blue asters, a field of purple violets or the apple trees covered with pink and white bloom, sparkling with early morning dew...

JOHN WESLEY & MARY PHIPPS SWINDALL, parents of John Calvin Swindall, and great-grandparents of Hetty Swindall Sutherland.

J. C. & JANE VANOVER SWINDALL. J. C. was the son of John Wesley and Mary Phipps Swindall, grandparents of Hetty Swindall Sutherland.

RESTING FROM HIS WORK — J. C. Swindall had a saying, "Bad fences make roguish cattle." Mr. Swindall was the grandfather of Hetty Swindall Sutherland.

THIS PICTURESQUE CABIN, shown after long years of disuse, was the original homeplace of J. C. and Jane Vanover Swindall, and the birthplace of Hetty Swindall Sutherland.

The Crockett and Sallie Owens Farm

(1900 - 1916)

By Anita A. Belcher

"In the Tom Field there was one of the most beautiful trees I have ever seen...a huge "sarvice" tree covered in the early spring with snow white bloom and later with large red berries. It was just right for climbing, too."

So the memories run like a steady, refreshing stream through the mind of Fern Owens Ratliff. Memories that helped to shape her life, and in turn were used to shape the lives of others as she took her place in the county as wife, mother, teacher and grandmother.

She relates, "Our farm was divided into many fields which were all named. I recall the names. There was the Far Field, the Wheat Field, the Flat, the Sim Field, the Steep Field and the Orchard. Also, there was the Little Side Field, the Point, the Middle Field, the Little Orchard and the Tom Field. There were three vegetable gardens which were usually called the Potato Patch, the Garden and the Big Garden. Between the Wheat Field and the Tom Field, was a persimmon tree, which produced a good crop of fruit each year. In the Little Field was an enormous walnut tree, which covered the ground with bushels of walnuts every fall. Near the spring, which was in the orchard, was a medium sized mulberry tree. It was just right for climbing. (One needs to climb mulberry trees so as to shake the berries off.) In the Tom Field, was one of the most beautiful trees I have ever seen. It was a service or "sarvice" tree, and it, too, was just made for climbing. In the spring, it was covered with beautiful, white bloom and later with large, red berries. There was a peach tree in the Tom Field. It was known as the fall peach and didn't ripen until late summer. This tree produced bushels of peaches every year. In those days, we didn't have glass jars to can in, so the only way we could keep these peaches was drying them on a dry kiln, which we did.

Many of the peaches were also given to neighbors. A few chinquapin bushes grew around the edges of the field, but bore only a few nuts. There was also a chestnut orchard, but it produced poor crops. There were a great number of apple trees, (later Fern recalled that there was a hundred trees, apple, or more.) There would be an apple tree or two in nearly every field. These trees also bore well. Some varieties of apples were leather coat, greenskin, annet, horseapple, sheepnose, Jim Ramey, Jonathan Winters, June Mountain Boomers, sugar loaf, and the winesaps. Also, there were two sweet apple trees, one yellow fruit, the other red. Little crab apple trees grew in several different places, but they were used only in the making of jelly and preserves. We had a few trees which had been bought from the nurseries, such as the York, Striped Bens, yellow transparent and Early Harvest. There was only one pear tree and it did not bear fruit. There were no grapes or cherries. A few plums grew in out-of-the-way places and there was a large beautiful wild cherry tree where we milked the cows. We were always told that the wild cherry was poison, but I wonder...

At the lower side of the Rye Field, there was a very high cliff, known as the Dog Cliff. At some time or another, a dog had fallen over it and was killed. A little nook at the corner of the Little Orchard was called the Thicket. At the top of the Thicket was a high point. This point was known as the Floyd Hill because from here we could see the Floyd Viers house. Later, my dad purchased this house and lived in it the rest of his life. Near the Chestnut Orchard, was knoll known as Buzzard Hill. When baby lambs died, they would be hung high on this knoll so the dogs

2ND GENERATION — Dulcy Owens Sutherland (now deceased) and grandson of Kenny Turner. Dulcy was the daughter of Crockett and Sallie Owens, and a sister to Fern O. Ratliff.

could not reach them and become "sheep-killing" dogs. A sheep-killing dog would not be tolerated. (To get a vivid picture of this truth, I believe that one needs only to read "The Little Shepherd of Kingdom Come" by John Fox, Jr.) I believe buzzards visited the hill where the lambs were hung, thus the name "Buzzard Hill".

There were two good springs near the house. One provided our water supply, the other had a big box built around it. This was used to keep the milk and butter cool and safe. The water from this spring was piped into a big tub for the horses to drink. As a little girl, I often wondered how that water could go up their long necks.

The house on the farm was a modern farmhouse for that day, and would stand the tests of today's standards, had it been kept in repair. It consisted of six large rooms and three large porches. One was a large front porch with banisters around it, except where two sets of steps were. The other two porches were L-shaped and also had banisters. The entire house was painted white. It had two big fireplaces which were built for burning wood (not coal). Our entire fuel supply was cut and hauled in from the forest near the

See FARM, Page 5

32

★ Farm

• • • • • • • • • • • • • • • • • • Continued from Page 2

house. Oh, yes! Our house had 11 windows and seven outside doors. It was covered with shingles, which lasted well over 50 years.

Our lawn (yard) was small, as was the case with many farm homes. It was enclosed with a picket fence. There were pussy-willows in the front yard and in the spring when the catkins began to bloom, the aroma was unequaled. The two flowers I remember are the hybiscus and day-lilies. An Althea bush grew by the front gate.

Near the house, was a large barn...big enough to house four horses and seven cows. It had a big loft. There was also the crib, smokehouse, pigpens and a smaller barn. We owned many cattle, sheep and hogs. Chickens and turkeys were allowed to run all over the farm. Finding a turkey's nest covered up with a big pile of leaves is one of the most exciting things I can remember...and being chased by a big turkey gobbler! Our farm was more than a mile from the county road...then we had to cross the river or a creek before we were on the road. The hill to the

farm was not steep, but it was a long, weary walk each evening after school.

"Would you like to go back to the farm on the mountain?" I asked. "no, the children have offered to take me, but I want to remember it the way it was...the big, white house...the cleared fields...the apple trees." I understood. I knew what she meant.

Next Week
Growing Up on a Mountain Farm

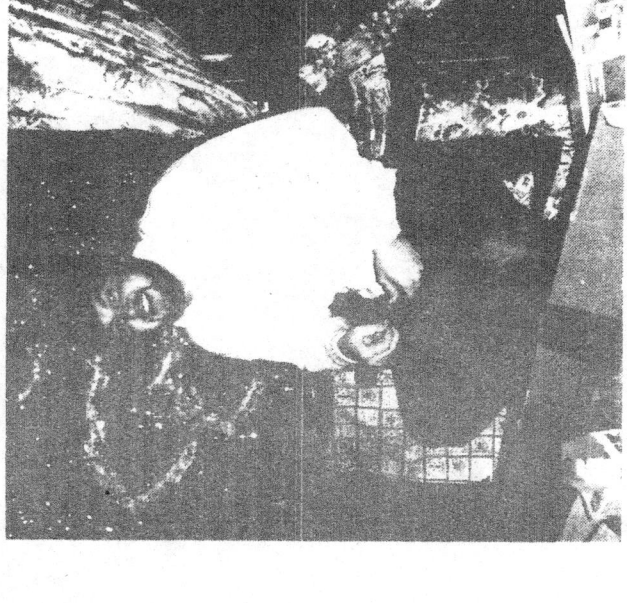

4TH GENERATION — Freddy Lee Sutherland, son of K. R., great-grandson of Uncle Crockett and Aunt Sallie Owens. He was killed in a mining accident last year.

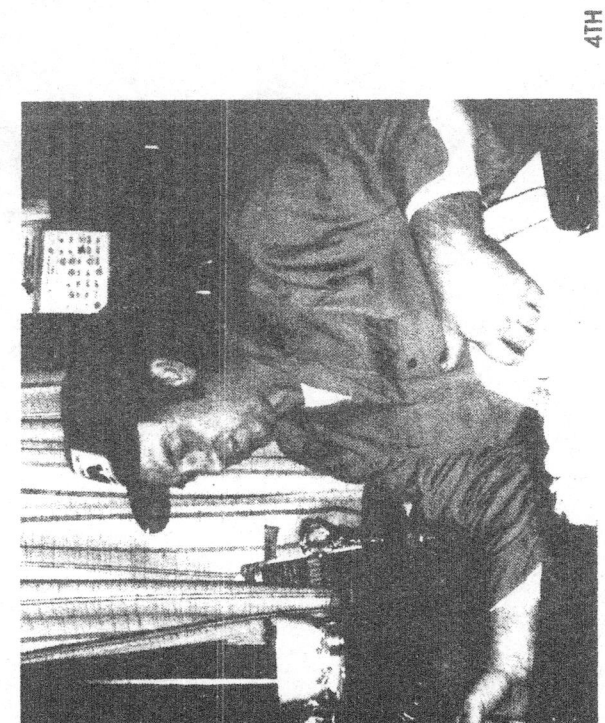

3RD GENERATION — K. R. Sutherland, son of Dulcy and Kermit Sutherland. Grandson of Uncle Crockett and Aunt Sallie.

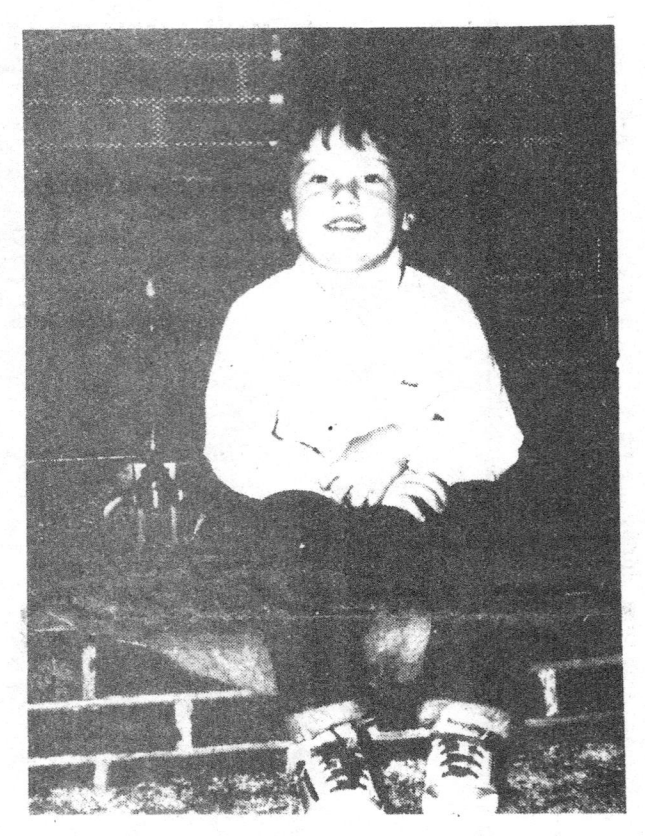

5TH GENERATION — Jonathan Kermit Sutherland, **son of** Freddy Sutherland, great-great-grandson of Uncle Crockett and Aunt Sallie Owens.

Especially for children

BY ANITA BELCHER

"I don't have anything to do...I'm bored..."

Several weeks ago in looking through some boxes and papers, I came upon a letter. That's not unusual in that I've saved an unbelievable number of letters, but this one caught my attention because it was written by me about twenty years ago. This is how it started; "Dear Hughie, I'm sorry we had such an unpleasant day yesterday and I'm sorry for where I was wrong, **BUT**, it really upsets me when I hear you talk about being bored." Many of you will know that "Hughie" in that letter was our oldest son, Hugh, and far from being bored today, he will appreciate me sharing some of the contents of that letter with other children and their parents...so...to boys and girls everywhere and to interested parents and grandparents, here is something especially...for the children.

When I was a little girl, I don't believe I was ever bored. Life was too interesting and it was just so good to be alive and **really** living! Well, what did a little girl or boy do when there wasn't any TVs, radios, VCRs, movies, video games or electronic toys? What would **you** do right now if all these things were taken away from you? The answer to that question depends a lot on where you live, but the same principles would apply anywhere. Let me tell you what you would do...**you'd learn to entertain yourselves, you'd learn to appreciate life and you and your parents would spend more time working and playing together and there would be time for grandparents.** What did I do that made life so wonderful and every day exciting? Well, I lived in the mountains and all around me was the forest and little patches of farmland cleared off on the hillsides and there were trees and mountain streams and a river that slept it's way along to the ocean until a storm came and then that river flooded, and roared like an angry lion. And there were the windstorms that swept through the trees along the mountain tops and down the hollows. The thunder would roll and lightning flash and we would look and listen and see and hear the beauty of it and know that God was at work. What does all this mean to you...fifty years later? It means...**use your eyes and ears. They weren't given to you for decoration...but to use.** If you can be blessed to stand on a piece of ground not any bigger than a man's handkerchief, there are exciting things to discover right where you stand..and have you ever known the joy of planting a

SIX CHILDREN who will enjoy this story are Anne Morecraft, Emily Rogers, Jenny Rogers, John Calvin Morecraft, Jon-Issac Rogers, and Joey Morecraft of Atlanta, Georgia.

★ Children

Continued from Page 2

"fished" with a bent stickpin!

And I had a horse. Besides "Blackie" my cat, this horse was one of my favorite friends. His name was "Zero" and we traveled many happy miles together. He had a bridle...but no saddle. At night I tied him to a bush in the kitchen yard and each morning I untied him and we rode over our own special trails until tired out, and then we rode home and both of us rested and ate lunch. You can well imagine that when old "Zero" died, I was heart-broken and cried and cried. What you can't imagine is that...Old Zero, my horse was nothing more or less than a big, long stickweed. His bridle was a twine string and his feet and mine were the same! I wonder though...was any horse ever loved more?

Whatever your age, don't insult God by being bored. Life is too precious. Right, Children?

seed? Have you ever **really** looked at the sky and watched the different shapes and colors? For some reason, when you lie flat on your back and look at the sky and watch the clouds it seems you can dream and plan wonderful things. Try it! Besides all that, **I had my parents. Do you have parents...or somebody who loves you?** My dad walked with me...he taught me the trees in the woods..what side did the moss grow on...the different kinds of bark and leaves...he took us ice skating and swimming. He told us stories and recited poetry. And there was mother. I was allowed to get little pieces of cloth and sew together out of her quilting box, and mix-up dough in the kitchen and have my own little garden and mother took us fishing. At night we had Bible reading and prayer and on Sundays we were in church **together**. It wasn't perfect...but it was...good. And children, do you have a favorite place to play? I had a lot of "favorite" places! One was by a little stream that rushed and crept over the rocks in the hollow close by our home. I played here and made small dams and let my paper dolls swim, strung up laurel blossoms on long grass blades and

See CHILDREN, Page 3

Delta Sutherland Arrington

"Like the stream that flows past her home, she is quiet, unhurried, and pleasant to be around."

BY ANITA BELCHER

Not too many years ago, there was an old homeplace on Frying Pan Creek that was owned and probably built by James and Nancy Counts Sutherland. One of their daughter's, Nancy Maryland (Little Granny), married William Floyd Sutherland, and he, being a carpenter, probably built a home almost directly in front of the older home which was owned by his father-in-law. William and Nancy were the parents of Delta S. Arrington and this was the home where she was born. At the time of Mrs. Arrington's birth, the Colley Post Office was housed in the store owned by William Floyd and Nancy. This store was close by the house and when Mr. Sutherland was busy with other duties, his wife cared for the store and post office.

The Sutherland home was always open to neighbors, and travelers also found "bed and board" here.

The traveling salesmen, or "Drummers" as they were known then, finished and started another leg of their trip when they reached the Sutherland home . . . come morning, they would travel on to the next country store. Mrs. Arrington loves the memories of her father's water mill. Here, on corn-grinding day, the neighbors came from off the mountains and ridges, riding horseback, with their sacks of corn secured behind them. Sometimes the men brought the corn to mill, but just as much of the time it was the women. It was an opportunity to visit while the grinding was being done and "catch up on the news," Here, too, Mrs. Arrington's mother, Nancy, worked just the same as in

THE PARENTS of Delta S. Arrington, Mrs. Nancy M. Sutherland and William Floyd Sutherland.

MRS. DELTA S. ARRINGTON at her home on Frying Pan.

the store or home or field or garden. The hard work and heavy lifting were no problem . . . it was all a part of the day's work.

It's funny how certain little memories stay with us over the years. For Mrs. Arrington, the memory of her mother operating the water mill on corn grinding day and the cheerful, hard-working women leaving with their two sacks of cornmeal (tied together) across the horse's back behind them, is a precious memory. There are other memories of her mother . . . "She was a lover of flowers; she grew them in her yard and certain kinds of them in her garden — there were the lilacs, snowballs, lillies, and poppies, and she loved her vegetable garden." From the garden came the great meals she cooked, and "she was such a great cook as well as a great

provider for the winter months." Food was canned, dried and pickled . . . nuts were gathered and stored. These were the days of the great chestnut trees and Mrs. Arrington well remembers going to the woods and bringing back chestnuts to roast or boil, and hickory nuts, as well as walnuts, were a part of the autumn harvest.

Sheep raising was another important part of Mrs. Arrington's growing-up days. From the sheep came many of the basic needs of the early Dickensonians. For the Sutherland family, they meant good, warm clothing. Mrs. Arrington remembers the dresses her grandmother made from the wool; the long skirts, small waists and long sleeves. She remembers that her grandmother loved pretty colors in her clothing and that she

See ARRINGTON, Page 7

wore white aprons. She remembers, as a little girl, going in and out of her grandmother's house, but perhaps the best memory of all is summed up in three simple words, "I loved her". The sheep, too, made memories that have lasted, for down through the years has come the unforgettable music . . . the tinkle, tinkle of the sheep bells as the flocks wandered home at night.

School for Mrs. Arrington began at Sulphur Springs when she was six-years-old. Among her teachers were Corbet Senter, John Rasnick, Leonard Sutherland, Harlen Counts, Ira Yates, and Izora Sutherland. She also remembers the three months of "free school" for several years with E. J. and Troy Sutherland, Parkis Fuller, and Mary Fuller Cain, teaching. After finishing school at Sulphur Springs, Delta went to Clintwood and took the "Big Seventh" taught by Arthur Countiss. Here, she received her teaching certificate and came back to teach one year at Lick Fork (Bucu), where she boarded at the Spurge Penland home.

While visiting her sister at Little Paw-Paw, she met her future husband, Floyd Arrington, as he was returning from a squirrel hunting trip. Within a year, the two were married by Preacher Bill Sutherland at the Mouth of Priest Fork with both sides of the family attending the wedding. Delta remembers that she wore a light blue, ankle length dress to be married in.

Housekeeping for the young couple began not far from where they were married. Their first home (after one year with Mr. Arrington's parents, Johnny and Cansada Owens Arrington), was at the old John Kiser place, a log

Arrington . . . .

Continued From Page 2

house at the Mouth of Priest Fork. Mr. Arrington was a farmer and a "timber" man. He began logging for Ritter Lumber Co. and later, he used his team to haul the logs from the woods. When trucks began to be used for the hauling of logs, Mr. Arrington was among the first of the log truckers. Eventually, he would go into the coal hauling business. The last five-years of his life before he became too sick to work, was spent as a school bus driver. Mr. Arrington died August 23, 1972.

The Arrington's were the parents of three children: Brady, died at age five; Merle, married Marion Hubbard; and Johnny William, married Alma Marie O'Quinn. Johnny and his wife live near to where the William Floyd homeplace was, and are good to visit with his mother. Merle and Mr. Hubbard live with Mrs. Arrington in the home Floyd built for them (he and Delta), after the death of Mrs. Arrington's mother. Mrs. Arrington also raised two stepchildren, Lonnie and Thelma. Lonnie, who is now deceased, had one son, and Thelma has four children, three sons and one daughter.

Mrs. Arrington became a member of the Sulphur Springs Primitive Baptist Church in 1945. She was baptized in the waters of Frying Pan Creek by Elder Gorman B. Sutherland. She has been a faithful church member over the years, hardly ever missing a church service at regular meeting time. Over the years, and even now, as much as she can, she cooks for the church dinners and the after-church visitors, just as her mother and grandmother did. These two ladies left wonderful examples for Delta to follow and she has endeavored to do just this and has tried to leave the same example for her children and grandchildren.

Charlie Breeding

By Anita Belcher

"Charlie shares most stories and history of the Davenport area with us..."

Higher standards of living and better education have always been the goals of the early settlers of this area. This is easier to understand when week after week one interviews those people who have lived here for generations and whose parents, grandparents and great-grandparents have lived here and been a part of the struggle for progress.

Schools were an important part of the overall picture which our forefathers visualized and these schools were dotted over all Southwest Virginia, in the mountains and up the hollows. In appearance, they ranged from tiny hunter's cabins built of logs on Lick Creek to the impressive "college" at Sandlick, and on to the Mission Boarding School at Council.

School for Charlie Breeding began at the old Hurricane School and as he remembers it, "This was a four-room, two-story building, two rooms downstairs and two overhead. This building burned and was later replaced with a one-room building, which stood until recent years."

Mr. Breeding smiled as he continued his recollections..."Before the school building was rebuilt, there was a church house right up the road here that was used for a school. A one-legged man by the name of Tom Grimsley was the teacher. He had two sons, Jack and Spark. The boys had a pony and when we needed fuel for the old Burnside stove, the boys would hitch their pony to a sled and bring it, loaded with coal, straight up the aisle of the building, unload it at the stove, turn the pony around and take the pony and sled back out." There was another recollection..."This same building was used for holding court once a month. This was when Clyde Dennis was judge. He would come to Davenport and hear the cases. It seems that times used to be worse than they are now, when it came to the mean things going on. There seemed to be so much killing. It seems there were three or four murder cases every month in Buchanan County."

After finishing elementary school at Hurricane, Charlie moved on to the Council High School. He is one of the few people I have talked to who remembers the "Buchanan Mission School of Council." This school opened January 16, 1911 with two teachers, Mrs. J. W. Reams and a Miss Yates. The Mission Board began looking for some specially qualified person to assume charge of the school and upon hearing of the fine work that Professor Henderson and his wife, Helen, were doing in church related schools and colleges in Franklin, Va., the job at Council was offered to them. They accepted and Charlie Breeding had the privilege of knowing them, and I believe, being taught by Professor Henderson.

(This last paragraph was taken, in part, from E. J. Sutherland's "Some Sandy Basin Characters"). Many readers will recall that Mrs. Henderson was responsible for getting a road through the Honaker-Council area and this road carries her name, "Helen Henderson Highway." She deserved and won that honor, and Mr. Breeding recalls the family with much respect. Not only so, but he also feels that the old Mission School (Council High) should not go to ruin. As a

See BREEDING, Page 3

EFFIE AND GEORGE BREEDING, parents of Charlie Breeding.

carpenter and a man who worked for the Buchanan County School Board 42 years, he believes that some of the best work, solid and lasting, went into the building of the old school. He recalls that, "The stone was hand-quarried by a crew of Italians who knew about stonework and he feels, not only a personal sense of loss to see the building deteriorate, but he feels that a part of the heritage of the area and Buchanan County is being lost. Charlie graduated from this school in the spring of 1938.

Working for the School Board in Buchanan County came naturally to Mr. Breeding. His dad, George, started working for them around 1935. These were the years when a carpenter supplied his own tools and transportation, and was paid 25 cents an hour. The average workday was 10 hours. Mr. George Breeding was not only a good carpenter, he was a much beloved man in his community and the different localities were he worked.

Of the 80 some schools scattered at one time throughout Buchanan County, Charlie believes his dad built at least one-third of them. If there were time and space, it would be more than interesting to know the names of many of these schools and how they came by them.

Next week, we will go into Charlie's own work as a carpenter

FIVE GENERATIONS OF BREEDINGS. Left to right, Charlie, his daughter, Joyce Mitchell, granddaughter, Tenita Snead, Charlie's father, George (now deceased), and Tenita's daughter, Casey. Tenita is the baby pictured in last week's paper.

Charlie Breeding .... Continued from Page 2

for the county school system and share with the readers some of his present carpenter work. There are many things that the Breeding's are interested in, and while I was sitting at their kitchen table talking and listening, the subject of apples and applebutter came up. Mrs. Breeding had just finished a batch of "oven applebutter" and she said I could share this recipe with the readers of the Times.

This is Charlie's favorite applebutter recipe — 8 cups cooked apples, 5½ cups sugar, ⅓ cup vinegar (less if desired), ⅓ cup candy cinnamon drops, a few drops of oil of cinnamon (to taste). Mix ingredients with apples, except for cinnamon drops and let cook in slow oven for approximately 2 hours. Stir occasionally. Add cinnamon drops when finished cooking. The longer apples cook in the oven the thicker the applebutter will be, so everyone should flavor and cook to their own taste, and thickness desired.

Webb and Fannie Cantrell

"They're a part of our county and a part of our history...."

By Anita L. Belcher

This story is like some of our mountain streams in that it doesn't follow a given course, but instead follows it's own sense of direction until it at last reaches it's destination. Mr. Cantrell, (Webb) Fannie and I started off on "course", but we hadn't any more than begun until we became interested in looking at old pictures and talking about the things they reminded us of. I'll share some of those stories with you readers, but first a little background history on the Cantrells.

To most of us living in the Haysi area, Fannie is "Fannie Rose", for that's the name we knew her by in our growing up days. Fannie's parent's were John and Linda Thomas Barton. The Thomas family came from South Carolina, probably following the timbering industry. The Bartons were already here and Linda met and married one of the boys, John. Two of John's brothers were 'Lige, who died fairly young and Floyd who lived until a few years ago. Floyd, who became known as "Uncle Floyd" was almost ninety-five years of age when he died and was a sort of "landmark" for all of us. . .one we hated to lose. John and Linda Barton had a family of twelve children, all who lived to marry and have families of their own. For the sake of folks who may want to see if they're "a-kin" to any of the family, Fannie has given me their names and who they married. Minnie, the oldest, married a Fleming, Mae (m) Charlie Turner, Flora (m) Rufus Turner then married Clarence Willis, Emma (m) ? Sykes, Bill (m) Edith Baker, Ellen (m) Basil Edwards, Fannie (m) Clinard Rose, after his death, she married Birk Ratliff. They were married several years and after his death Fannie married Webb Cantrell.

Lizzie (m) Joe Rose, Virgie (m) Ottie Willis, Earl (m) Versie Woods, Stella (m) Leslie Woods, Maggie (m) Carson Woods. Fannie and Webb live in Haysi where Fannie has lived many years, though Webb is from the Pound (Bold Camp) area of Virginia. Webb is the son of Levi and Sarah Cantrell (more about them next week) and they lived close by the Levi Cantrell cemetery, in fact I believe Mr. Cantrell gave the land for the cemetery. The following is a short sketch of a vivid recollection Webb has of those early days at home and the September Association Meeting at the cemetery. "There would be horses hitched everywhere, just like today you'll see cars parked. . .well, then it was horses. All the neighbors came to the Association meetin' of course and then some from a pretty far piece off. Back then they held the Association for three days, Friday, Saturday and Sunday. If the weather turned bad, they called the meetin' off but if it started raining while the meetin' was going on, everyone just went to someone's house for a visit. Uncle Bill Boggs on Boggs' Creek slept over a hundred people during one Primitive Baptist Association. . .don't know how they managed to sleep. . .probably set up and talked most of the time, or some would sleep awhile and then let others have their bed. There was a lot of good fellowship. . .a lot of good food, too. People done a lot of cookin' at meetin' time. . .it took a lot of cooking for that many people. Hogs would be killed and a whole lot of chickens lost their lives! Mother prepared big meals, everything was from her garden or the fields"

As we talked about Uncle Bill Boggs on Boggs' Creek, Mr. Cantrell made a comment in regard to naming places, something that many of us grew up with. "Every place had a name back then, like Lewis Gap where Lewis Stanley accidently shot himself while hunting." (This place, I believe, was on the head of Duck Branch on Bold Camp.) Another place or two, (and we'll have more next week) was the Barn Hollow and the Coal Bank Hollow. . .Icy Curve. I have always been interested in names that are given to places, so I added a few I was familiar with. . .The Greasy Bend, The John Hall Hollow, Lonesome Branch, Dark Hollow and Wildcat. The Cantrells and I also talked of how every field was named and also the gardens.

Webb and Fannie Cantrell — Haysi, Virginia

Another interesting topic conversation between the Cantrells and myself was crime. . .the crimes of earlier years as compared to today. Liquor was one of the major factors contributing to crime and the making and selling of moonshine was a commonplace thing. We agreed that there was more crimes committed even here in our area back in the "good old days" than most people would dream of, but we also agreed that there are two major differences. Lifestyle. . .back in those days there were practically no drugs, homosexuals, TV's, or abortions and there was a great sense of family and personal shame when a kin person went wrong. Today, we are overrun by the first four and there seems to be very little of the last one. . .shame. This last paragraph is just exactly as the Cantrells and I discussed it, and young people would be profited if they would take the time and listen to some of the stories in "real life" that some of our older citizens such as Fannie and Webb can tell.

There was one more story that Mr. Cantrell told me that was of great interest. "Uncle John Cantrell, brother of Pa, fought in the Civil War. I believe he was captured by the Northern forces. During the fighting he was shot and his life was probably saved by a big silver watch he carried in his pocket. The bullet struck the watch and ricocheted off." It was Uncle John that loved dogs and had "rather hunt than eat". Next week we'll hear more stories than Fannie and Webb have to tell and I'm looking forward to it, for these people and the stories they tell are an important part of our American history.

Una Katherine Mullins

By Anita Belcher

"I've always tried to be as honest as the wind that blows or the birds that fly...."

Some people are just simply refreshing to be around and Aunt Una Mullins is one of those people. I met her this past week for the first time and wished I had known her all my life. She has an alertness that belies age and a combination of characteristics that command respect. As she says, (to one of her

MIGHT AS WELL BE HAPPY

Why be mad? or Why be sad?
When it's just as easy to be happy
and glad.

good friends) "you can't 'out-sharp' me" and I'll agree that Aunt Una would be hard to "out-sharp" or "out-wit" as some might say. Her "peppy" remarks are well seasoned with salt and she deserves a listening ear and a receptive heart.

Born Una Katherine Mullins, March 10, 1898, she is the daughter of Lilburn and Nancy Jane Fuller Mullins. Nancy Jane was the daughter of Jonas and Rhoda (Fuller) Fuller, thus two sets of Fullers enter the picture. These included the well-known Uncle Emory and Aunt Jane Fuller and their son, Beverly, as well as the Haysi merchant, R. H. Fuller, Alta Fuller Arrington and Pearl Fuller Davis. Lilburn and Nancy Jane had

a large family. Besides Una Katherine there were John David, Jonah Clarence, James Harvey, William Brady and George Tilden. Sisters were Nervie Jane, Tiny Minerva, Isabelle, Ruthie Emeline, Minnie Delphia, Pricy Jane and Nannie Jane. Nannie Jane's name may have been Nannie Ann.

I did not ask Aunt Una for a story for one simple reason. Nearly everything she said WAS a story. Even in the list of names I've mentioned in the preceding paragraph there are stories that would fill several pages...stories about how the children got their names. Were the different Jane's named after one person (their mother) or perhaps the older "Aunt Jane's" on both sides of the family? Was George Tilden named after the old man Tilden Cochran on Bartlick? Maybe so. Aunt Una remembers her parents mentioning him. One thing she knows for certain. . .three of her little sisters died of diphtheria, two of them on the same day and were buried in the same casket. They were probably about six and eight years old. The other one was age eleven.

Una went to school on Prater Creek and was taught by some of the first teachers in the area. John Raines, Zack Raines, Madison Viers (from over on Warfork) Charlie Perkins, (a one-legged man) Mae Owens from Sandlick, Sindy Cantrell and Alex Ramey. Fred Raines was her teacher when she was a teenager and he encouraged her to become a teacher or a nurse. Una did some teaching. Once when the regular teacher was sick, Una substituted for her. There was a girl (a grown-up girl) who wouldn't study but just sat in her seat making faces at Una. Una ignored her the first day, but when she continued it the next day, she decided that "enough was enough". She got a big beech limb and "just about wore that girl out". Needless to say, there were no more ugly faces. Una became a nurse also in a special kind of way. "Old man Lum Clevenger and his wife, Katherine didn't have a family to care for them. My sister and I stayed there until they both died. I fixed them their last bite to eat, combed their hair and washed their feet. Aunt Katherine died first.

UNA KATHERINE MULLINS with neighbor, Bill Raines. This picture was made at Una's brother's home in the early 1900's.

. .I wouldn't leave Uncle Lum by himself." Aunt Una would not leave her parents, either. "I could have married, but then there wouldn't have been anyone to care for mother and dad. I couldn't go and leave them. I believe people ought to read in the Bible what it says about caring for your family. I learned to read the Bible and pray when I was sixteen years old. I believe in the Bible. . .I'm a Christian, though I can't get to church anymore. I don't believe in lying. . .I've always tried to be truthful and just as honest as the wind that blows or the birds that fly."

Aunt Una has several pieces of interesting furniture. Some of it is being kept by family members but a couple of interesting pieces I say was an old, well-kept "talking machine" and a "clothes safe". I first thought the safe was a "pie-safe", but I was wrong. This is a tall piece of furniture, with doors at both top and bottom. Instead of glass in the doors, there are pieces of dark tin which are nailed neatly to the wood. Then a small nail has been used to make a design around the sides of, and in the center of each piece of tin. I believe flowers are featured on this particular one. It's a fine looking old piece of handwork and I find myself once again admiring our mountaineer ancestors for endeavoring to bring what beauty they could into their lives as well as that which was practical. Aunt Una explained about the clothes safe. "They would hang their clothes out on the line and let the wind blow them dry. While they were still fresh and smelling good, they'd bring them in, fold them before they could wrinkle and stack them in the clothes safe. The little holes in the front panels kept them from getting musty. In the pie safe, the holes let the air in, but kept even a little gnat from getting to the pies."

Aunt Una is a dear person. She can be "snappy" if you don't mind your "P's and Q's" but she has a twinkle in her eyes and little smiles chase each other around the corners of her mouth. Next week, if she feels like having me visit we're going to have a story about her old homeplace which she'd like to see one more time. . .and her special friends, Nettie Moore and Faye Wampler are going to try to help her out with that. Maybe I can, too. . .

Eura Blankenship Fuller

By Anita A. Belcher

"Eura is our walking almanac."

Eura is the daughter of George and Sarah Deel Blankenship of Prater (Greenbrier Creek), and one of 13 brothers and sisters. Three of these children died in infancy. Those who lived to adulthood were: Delphia (m) Jim Harve Stuart, Hulda (m) Henry Fuller, Eura (m) Ebb Fuller, Lettie (m) Rufus O'Quinn, Bertha (m) Floyd Mitchell, Stella (m) Walter Kelly, Virginia (m) Ed Bailey, Nicky (m) Margie Blankenship, Delmon (m) Prudie O'Quinn, Toy (m) Bonnie Owens.

Eura, as most people who were born in the mountains in the early 1900's, can recall a good, but very hard way of living. For the girls in the family work was not just house cleaning and cooking, but much of the outside work was their responsibility also. Helping to care for the horses, the field work and building rail fences were only a few of the outside tasks which the girls and women shared in. The home of Eura's parents burned when Delmon was a baby and for many years the large family lived in two rooms. Everytime one of our older people tell me of situations like this, I am amazed anew for in today's society, we seem to think we need about 10 rooms to raise two children, while "back then" 10 children were raised in two rooms.

"And what did you children do for fun when your work was finished," I asked. "We played games, ball (straight town) was one of our favorites and we played blindfold, tag and Jack-in-the-corner. Our big barn was one of the best places to play. It was warm and dry. Daddy put us up a big swing that several of us children could swing on at once. We spent many happy hours there. Once a lot of us could have gotten killed or hurt bad...Ebb's sister, Carrie, was hurt and carried a big scar to her grave. We were all playing and swinging on a big barn joist and it pulled loose. We all ran, but Carrie was caught against a manger and a big spike nail split her leg wide open. No, they didn't take her to the doctor...we didn't have doctors then. They just did the best they could for her at home and it finally healed. Some of our best fun times were spent riding horses. Daddy didn't care and we'd go to the fields and get them and ride up and down the creeks. If daddy had cared for us riding them, just his "no" would have been enough. We wouldn't have thought about disobeying him." I asked Eura about her school days. "I went till I was almost 19-years-old, till I got married. School was for seven months then. The teacher I best remember was Mary (Marrs). She stayed with us a few nights, but boarded at Uncle Floyd Deel's."

Uncle Floyd has another place in Eura's memory. When she was getting ready to marry Ebb Fuller, she wanted a wedding dress. Uncle John Clevinger had a store and along with other cloth there was a piece of white material...just what Eura needed. She hoed corn for Uncle Floyd for 50 cents per day and worked out enough to buy her wedding dress material and then she made her dress. It was long, gathered at the waist and had a high neckline. She wore her hair braided. She was married at her home by George Fuller. She and Ebb started housekeeping with one table, a step stove, one bed, two quilts, a straw mattress and two straw pillows.

Eura Blankenship Fuller

just an example, that the moon is at a certain phase. Thus there is no superstition involved in this, it is simply facts dealing with the weather.) For those who are interested, this is "Eura's Almanac" in part.

"Plant your above ground crops on the light of the moon. At this time the signs would be in the head, neck, breast, arms, heart. However, keep in mind that many times crops that are planted in the heart, while they grow well, will not bear sound produce. According to Eura, "It will likely rot on the stalk." The only thing one should plant during the sign of the bowels is flowers. "They will bloom their heart out," says Eura, but if you plant any other crop at this time, all you will get will be bloom." The dark of the moon is when you plant your underground crops...potatoes, onions, carrots, beets, turnips, etc. If

See FULLER, Page 13

'The straw had a good smell," Eura laughingly remembers, "but it stuck through the pillows."

Eura's parents and many of the older people planted their crops and did many of their other chores by "the signs." They went by the light of the moon, the dark of the moon, or to make it easier, the system of planting according to different parts of the human body. (Keep in mind that when the "signs" are in the feet,

★ Fuller . . . . Continued from Page 9

you plant these crops on the light of the moon, "then you'll have to keep "kivering" them up to keep the sun from baking them," warns Mrs. Fuller. When it comes to harvesting your crops, be sure that you dig your potatoes and onions on the dark of the moon. Otherwise, if you so much as nick them, they will start rotting by the next day...and one other thing, don't make your pickles or kraut when the signs are in the bowels. They will turn yellow, rot and stink."

Eura has a lot of other information pertaining to the weather and how it affects our lives and it would be interesting and informative to spend a day with her. Many of us call her when we want some "scientific facts" about our planting. She is our "walking almanac". Aunt Eura and I agree that God is the one who blesses our planting and harvesting and without Him nothing would produce, no matter when it was planted and we believe that the information she has shared with us is simply "weather facts which He has ordained." Eura, is herself a gardener and a lover of flowers. Her mother, but most especially her daddy, instilled in her a love for beauty. She recalls, "When you topped the hill above our house, you could see the flowers, just shinin'. Big beds of marigolds, pinks and hollyhocks and old-fashioned roses."

Aunt Eura has more good advice, other than about planting. She has been a faithful church member, Old Regular Baptist, for over 40 years and her desire is that "everyone should go to church, especially young people for whom she has a deep concern. Visit with Eura if you can and listen to what she has to say. You will come away with much to think about and with more knowledge than you had before.

(After finishing this article I realized that I had left off an important part of Eura's story. Not only did she come from a family of 13 children, but she and Ebb were parents of 13 children. They are: Clyde and Claude, both deceased, Donald, Sarah, Herby, Foster, Thomas Monroe, Perry, Jerry, Dewey "Buck", Betty, Susie, and Roxie. Also of interest to old and young alike is the fact that Eura got her driver's license at age 80.)

"Hardy Mullins — friend to all"

"One of the quiet people that the world would be richer for knowing..."

By Anita A. Belcher

I've read that "some of the best musicians in the world will never be heard by the general public for they live a quiet life, off the "beaten path" and their family and friends are, for the most part, their audience." I believe that statement is true and I believe the world is a poorer place for having never heard them. In the same way, I am firmly convinced that some of the finest people who have ever lived or ever will live, fit into that same category. The world will never know them and be the poorer for it, but those whose lives they touch will be the richer for it in many ways.

Hardy Mullins of Caney Ridge is one of those quiet, unpretentious people that I wish our world could know... I met him for the first time one afternoon last week, and it took a little less than a minute for us to become "old friends", but then, it isn't hard to become friends with someone whose eyes twinkle with laughter under bushy, black brows and a shock of white hair, and whose face is continually breaking into smiles. We talked about our families and who was "akin" to whom. Mr. Mullins, who was born at Baden in 1904, is the son of Andrew and Alifair Mullins. Mrs. Mullins, came from the Brush Creek section of the county and Mr. Mullins from George's Fork. Baden was the name of the post office, and "old man Cam Colley" was one of the first postmasters that Hardy Mullins remembers. There were eight brothers and sisters in the Andrew and Alifair Mullins family; Hardy, Delmon, Palmer, Logan, Letcher, Ethel, (deceased) Hibbert, (deceased) and Nora (deceased). Nora was born during one of the bad flu epidemics and both she and her mother, (Mrs. Alifair Mullins), died at the time of her birth. Mr. Mullins (Hardy) remembers his growing up years as well as, and probably better, than the events of last week. "Dad made a living for his family by farming and bee keeping. He had a hundred or more stands of bees and worked with them as a business. When he needed to go in among them he always rolled his shirt sleeves up as high as they would go and never wore a hat. You have to understand bees, though, to be able to do this. Dad was not afraid of them. He seldom got stung but when he did the stings didn't hurt him unless one got him around his finger nails. When he needed help with them, he always called on me. One thing dad would do was when the bees got ready to swarm, he would spray them down with water so they couldn't fly.. you know, at certain times bees will leave their hives." Yes, I did know that and now I had a question that was prompted by our discussion. "Did you ever beat on a dishpan with a spoon to capture a swarm of bees or to bring your own back?" Mr. Mullins laughed. "We beat on a bulltongue plow with a hammer. It was louder."

We talked about the price of honey back in those days. "Dad sold it for 12 1/2 cents per pound. . .in fact, a lot of things sold for 12 1/2 cents. Eggs were 12 1/2 cents a dozen, cloth was 12 1/2 cents a yard." "Why", his daughter Joyce and I wanted to know, was there a half cent added on? "So that two pounds, or dozen or whatever it was would be an even quarter," Mr. Mullins answered.

A couple of other interesting things in regard to this discussion. "Lynn honey was the best honey you could get, and that cloth that sold for 12 1/2 cents was "outten". We all had a good laugh about the "outten" and decided that it was really probably pronounced "outting", but most of us mountaineers don't "waste" good breath on our "ings".

Many people who read this will remember the "outten" cloth. It was like flannel, usually white and was used for many purposes, but especially in making baby gowns.

There is one special story in connection with Hardy's growing up days that he wants the public to share with him so that parents can see the wisdom that his father used on one particular occasion. "It was time for the first day of school," Mr. Mullins recalls, "and I didn't want to go. I gave the teacher a hard time and when I came home that evening

HARDY MULLINS

★ Mullins

Continued from Page 6

HARDY MULLINS and his wife, the late Cynthia Mullins. Picture was made in summer of 1985.

I announced that I wasn't going back. Daddy could have told a little fellow like me what was what but all he said the next morning was, 'Hardy get your work clothes on. We've got a big rock bar that has to be cleaned up.' "

"We started piling rocks when the other children left for school, took off enough time to eat a bite of dinner and went right back to piling rocks. When the other children came home that evening I could hear them laughing and talking and when they got their chores done, they were busy playing and having a good time. Daddy and I went right on piling rocks. By bedtime I was so tired I could hardly walk. Next morning, daddy said since I wasn't going to school that we'd better get back to piling rocks." Hardy replied, "daddy, I reckon I'm going to school today!"

It's been many years now since Hardy and his dad worked out that situation, but Mr. Mullins has never forgotten the wisdom his daddy used nor the lesson he learned. By the way, for any of you who have never heard the expression "rock bar", it simply means a piece of land that is covered up with rocks.

Hardy Mullins first met his wife when he was only about six

See MULLINS, Page 7

years old. Over the years he saw her on two or three more occasions but it was when he was a young man working for Ritter's Lumber Company that he knew she was the girl he wanted to marry. It was at that time he decided "that the fishing looked good over on the Cranesnest"; so he took his fishing poles and went. When his fishing trip ended, he had caught what he really went fishing for. . .a wife, Cynthia Mullins. "She bought her wedding dress at John Nicewonder's store and we set up housekeeping at McClure."

Hardy worked for Ritter's over the years and he was the man who turned the steam off during a tragic accident which took the lives of three men, Bobby Scott, Lawson Ramsey and Mont (Slim) Richardson. Hardy's main job was baling flooring and he can show you one of his fingers that was re-shaped by this work.

After a few years, Mr. Mullins and his family moved to Norland on the Pound River (Mouth of Camp Creek). Here he became a strawberry farmer and raised some of the best to be found in the area. His brother, who also raised strawberries in the Wise area, wanted to know what his secret was and Hardy told him he had discovered a spray that helped a lot. In answer to what it was, Hardy replied, "Elbow grease and sweat!" Hardy sold his strawberries for $1.00 per gallon, or an 8 pound lard bucket. The only time he ever got "put-out" with the strawberry pickers was when a courtin' couple came to pick and "did more kissin' than they did pickin' " and stepped all over his biggest berries!

Over the years Mr. and Mrs. Mullins became the parents of 11 children; Tennie, (m) Ocie Meade, Hercel (m) Pat—, Delores (m) Larkin Carty, Cloey, Delores' twin (deceased), Jean (m) Lee Conley, Billy (m) Myrtle Vest, Thelma (m) Richard Woodward, Joyce (m) Thurl Mullins, Marlene (m) John McFall, Johnny, Jequeta (m) John Brisky.

When the children grew up Mr. and Mrs. Mullins moved to Ohio and while there, Hardy went into farming in a serious way. He loves the Ohio farmland and says he could raise the "biggest onions, rhubarb and salad peas there that you've ever seen."

Hardy and Cynthia were a happy couple and celebrated their 60th wedding anniversary shortly before her death in May of 1986. This story would not be complete without paying tribute to Mrs. Mullins. "She was a wonderful mother and wife. . .she was a home-maker. She loved to do everything, cook. . .can. . .work inside, work outside. . .she loved people. She worked like a man but lived like a lady. . . The thing that perhaps I remember best about her was her ability to care for us when we were sick," Joyce recalls. She could lay her hand against my forehead and I would feel better." And again this from Joyce "I remember the feeling of security that mother and daddy gave us. When the Pound river was flooding and everyone was scared, I could go to bed and not worry. Daddy and mother would take care of us."

That feeling of security comes from a higher power than just people can instill in children. The parents had their trust in God and when it's that way, children can feel and know it. Hardy and Cynthia were both Christians and Mr. Mullins will tell you now "that he can't remember not being a Christian. His advice to young people today, "go to church. . .stop running around and spreeing. . .love the Lord."

If you don't know Mr. Mullins, go by and get acquainted. . .if you do know him, you know what I mean when I say, "your life will be the richer for having a friend like him."

Fred Columbus Powers

"A determined scholar — A dedicated teacher. . ."

By Anita Belcher

Fred Powers is a well-known figure in Dickenson County, and like so many fine people, he should be better known than what he is. Fred is the son of Samuel Jahile Tilden Powers and Elizabeth C. Sutherland Powers. The "C" that Elizabeth used in her name did not stand for anything but was put there by Elizabeth herself to keep from being mixed up with others by the same name. Fred's grandparents on his father's side were Charles and Nancy Powers and on his mother's side were Newton and Elizabeth (Dyer) Sutherland. The Powers family lived on Priest Fork and the log home they lived in is still standing on the Arville Sykes property. There were twelve children born to Tilden and Elizabeth, ten who lived, two dying in infancy. Cousins living nearby were constantly in the Powers home and added to the fun of growing up. "The days were never long enough," remembers Mr. Powers, "and farming was from daylight 'til dark. My favorite part of farm life were the animals and I was riding the horses by the time I was five years old." Food was plentiful in those years for the hard working farmer, but, as Fred has written in story form for his children, "Clothing was our biggest problem. We sold a calf or some sheep occasionally. We dug ginseng, mayapple, wild ginger, and other herbs for a little money. We sold some wool that was not needed for yarn. Dad made our shoes until we could work out the money for our own. The first pair of dress shoes I ever had I worked them out at forty cents a day and paid five dollars for them. Mother knitted all our socks until we were old enough to go courting. Sometimes mother would swap work with Aunt Hannah Duty and get her to make me a pair of pants."

Fred speaks and writes of his mother and father with deep respect and love. It was his mother who gave him the exciting news that he would be attending school. "I'll

FRED POWERS during his Abner's Gap school-teaching days.

never forget that day," Fred recalls. "Mother and I were digging potatoes. . .I was about six years old. . .we sat down on a rock to rest and mother said, "Fred, tomorrow you'll be going to school." That was the happiest day of my life."

Mr. Powers was a determined learner. His older sister taught him to write, how to make his letters. After that he just "seemed to pick up learning" and was soon helping this same sister do her arithmetic. The evening his mother told him that he could go to school and the days following can be appreciated more if written in Fred's exact words. "I hardly slept that night. I knew my older brother and sisters had gone to school but no one had ever mentioned me going. I stayed awake for hours wondering what school would be like I could just see a teacher with a big bundle of

See POWERS, Page 11

switches in the corner waiting for someone to violate a rule. . . .and what could I do without a book? What was in store for me. I was a bit frightened but happy to take a chance. Next morning I was up at daylight ready to face whatever the day would be like. Bessie and I left bright and early but by the time we walked the two miles over the hill it was almost time for books (as it was called then). Everything went well that day. I was seated with Guy Sutherland whom I knew and he had a book I could probably borrow. The teacher took our names and I got down to work. I learned to read the first page in the Primer. This was the way it read — "This is Will.

How do you do, Will? This is May. How do you do, May?" The teacher was a pretty young girl. At time for recess she counted "1" pick up paper, "2" put away all books, "3" recess. Guess what! There were windows on three sides of the room. Some of the boys and girls jumped out of the windows and then the rest of us did it at will."

Fred finished the first grade in the first few months of school that year and the next year he learned to read better, spell more words and mastered his multiplication table. The third year the one-room school which Fred was attending was divided by a wall into a two-room school and Charlie Compton taught "the little room". Charlie and a brother, Clarence, and he and Fred were "seat-mates", and good friends. Again Mr. Powers' own words. "We did everything together. We could even whisper so long as it was about our work. By the end of that year we could do addition, subtraction, multiplication and long division." Fred was at the head of his class that year and helped to teach his classmates long division. "That was the best school year of my life. . .a lot of work and a lot of play and I was promoted to the 4th grade in the 'big room' ." Kilby Fuller was his teacher the next year and he got the first report card he can remember getting. The following term, Mary Fuller (Cain) was his teacher and Mr. Powers speaks highly of her. "Everybody really liked her. She worked with us inside and played with us outside. She was the second teacher, (Charlie was the first), to give me special attention (due to my bad eyesight). She allowed me to do my math on the board, some of it. I learned a lot of English that year and finished the

fifth grade with a pretty good basic education." The sixth grade came with Fred Stiltner as the teacher. Fred recalls, "Only a few weeks had passed when he (Mr. Stiltner) told us that with hard work we could finish both the sixth and seventh by the end of the year. That's when we really got down to business. In math we started on page 66 of an advanced arithmetic book which had about 700 pages. We were to put on paper every problem we came to then. If we failed to solve one we carried it over until one of us worked it. If anyone failed to work a problem, it became everybody's problem until it was solved. We never asked the teacher or anyone else for help. By the end of the term not one was left to be solved. We did much of this work at home, sometimes spending nights together working. Sometimes we'd hear the chickens crowing before we went to bed. This gave us our time at school for other subjects. I have never regretted all this work and I have never had any trouble in high school or college with math or arithmetic."

Mr. Powers and I talked for a long time about many things but there was so much to be said about schools and learning that I decided to devote this one article mostly to that subject. Mr. Powers gave me two problems for the readers of the TIMES to read and solve. Here they are: Take a cylinder glass that is 4 inches in diameter and 8 inches tall. Fill it half full of water and drop a marble which is 2 inches in diameter into the glass of water. How much will this raise the water level?" OK! Do you have that one worked? Here's another one: "Take one room 10 foot square and 8 foot high. What would be the distance from one corner of the floor to the opposite corner of the ceiling?" Mr. Powers got six days out of class while in college for working one of these. It presented no "problem" to him as he had worked it back in early school days.

Fred Columbus Powers

PART 11
"A man determined to succeed"

Fred Powers is undoubtedly one of the most interesting people one can talk with. The fifth of 12 children, he remembers how it was to grow up behind a "hoe and a plow." As I write this I am visiting in the city of Atlanta, Georgia, and thinking of the difference of life here as compared to life in the mountains and thinking too, of "now and then." "Our farm was rocky and hilly," recalls Mr. Powers, "and it took a lot of hard work to raise food to eat (for the family) and to feed the cattle, horses, hogs and sheep. In the fields we raised mostly corn and oats. In the gardens were the usual garden stuff and we had one large bottom that we always planted in cane. From that cane we usually made about 100 gallons of molasses. These were always on our table. For winter food we holed up potatoes, turnips, cabbage and apples. We pickled corn, mustard and mixed pickles. We dried beans, apples, pumpkin and cushaw and we gathered lots of walnuts, hickory nuts and chestnuts."

Mr. Powers' early life with his parents, brothers, sisters, grandparents, aunts, uncles and cousins would fill a book. Some of his experiences were funny — some were sad. He recalls the death of his favorite gray horse which for months left him sleepless, and within a short time his dear Grandmother Sutherland died. For a small boy, both of these events were heartbreaking. Again, Mr. Powers shares some memories with us.

"Not long after Grandmother's death, Grandpa Sutherland became blind. It fell my lot to spend a lot of time with him, leading him around and doing chores for him. I loved him, but these were long, hard, lonesome days for a little boy who was hardly six years old." But then, there were the good times too. "We "broke" every animal on the farm, riding every cow, bull, horse, and once a big hog. Sometimes when the older folks were gone to church, us children would play church and have pretend weddings. Nothing would please me better than to get started up to Uncle John's or Uncle Floyd's. We would play games such as fox and dog, base, pleased-or-displeased, hully-gul, and ball. When darkness drove us indoors, we played inside games. Sometimes we would sing religious songs and maybe a love song or two. When we were at Uncle John's this could go on until far in the night without interruption because the old folks were part of the players. This was the best part of our lives and the days were always too short."

Sometimes a young fellow could get into trouble before he had time to explain what the true facts were. Mr. Powers can laugh about one such case now, though at the time it was not funny. "It was during the war (WWI). . .some of the neighbor boys had gone to the Army and occasionally we would get a newspaper and hear of the fighting that was going on. "Playing War" became one of the favorite games for the older kids. They would use laurel buds for bullets and divide up on sides. One day Bess and I decided we'd play war and use small rocks in the place of laurel buds. We each had a pile of rocks and then we "declared war". It didn't last long. I got hit in the face and started crying. In a minute Dad appeared with a switch and gave me and Bess both a "few cuts" with it without waiting for explanations."

FRED POWERS at the Hamilton Edwards homeplace about 1930.

An important part of Mr. Powers' history is his preschool days, those formative years of his life. "During my preschool years," he recalls, "I did an awful lot of work even though I was small. I went to the fields as soon as I was able to cut weeds with a hoe. On wash days I helped with the washing. I carried buckets of water from the spring and it was my job to rise early every morning and feed all the livestock."

When Fred was about 15 years old his Dad sold his timber. As soon as he was paid he bought Fred his first blue serge suit for the price of $20.00 "and with this purchase," laughs Mr. Powers, "I was happy as a lark."

About this time Fred's father bought a farm from Uncle Dick Sutherland. The land here was not so hilly and was more fertile. Mr.

Powers comments, "We got this farm, a big team of mules, a wagon, a mowing machine, and a lot of other farm tools. I worked hard here after school, Saturdays and during the summer for about two years. By that time I was ready for high school."

In 1925, Fred entered Junior High School, at the Sandlick School. "During these years I would get out of the bed, put on my clothes, drink a couple glasses of milk and be off to school. I ran the first two miles and walked at a long pace the other four miles. It was six miles each way and although I missed a few days, I was never late. Rain, cold, or snow never stopped us. "I have added these last paragraphs in the hope that as parents, young children and teenagers read them they will see and respect the way that our older

people were brought up, how they were disciplined and the responsibilities they had as a part of the family. I hope some young person will read this and say, "If Fred Powers could do all that work from the age of six and walk all those many miles to get an education, well, then, I'm going to strive with every ability that God gives me to do the same." And keep in mind, these things were nothing compared to the fact that from the time of his birth Fred Powers had, and still has, a problem with his eyesight that would cause most people to "give up and quit." Not Mr. Powers. This simply presented a challenge to him - a challenge which he accepted and was a better person for it. There is a challenge for each of us. Mr. Powers should inspire us to accept it — to never give up.

Mrs. Brownlow (Garnett) Mullins

SIM & JANE STANLEY BALL, grandparents of Mrs. Garnett Mullins.

By Anita A. Belcher

"She represents true hospitality"

Mrs. Garnett Mullins of Caney Ridge would like to write a book some day. Not about herself, but about others whom she has known throughout the years. One of these people would be her Grandmother, Jane Stanley Ball, at whose home Garnett was born and with whom she lived the first several years of her life. Mrs. Mullins would like to share a few of the memories about her Grandmother. "Grandmother was one of the sweetest people who ever lived. Grandpa died at a rather young age and Grandmother was left with all the responsibilities of the home and farm. Everything from wood-cutting to plowing was up to her. I have seen her many times roll in the big backlog for the fireplace and roll it in place by herself. I've seen her plow, a big apron covering her dress and her arms spread like the wings of a bird as she "man-handled" the big bull-tongue plow." Added to this was the job of carrying the mail from Fremont to Omaha, a trip that was made on horseback summer and winter. Garnett lived with, and came to love and respect her Grandmother Jane and Grandfather Sim, very much. In fact, to this day, she thinks back on Mrs. Ball as "Mother". While staying here she attended the Yates School until she was in the second grade and then went to live with her mother and step-father, Mary and George Puckett. Her new home was at Greasy Creek, Ky., where her step-father worked in the mines. Garnett remembers the closing down of the mines at Greasy Creek when the owner died, and also the closing down of the mining camp, the boarded-up windows. . .the people leaving family by family.

While living at Greasy Creek, Garnett's mother received a telegram stating that her father, (Sim Ball) had died. The Puckett family flagged the train at Marbone, rode into Elkhorn and spent the night there at the hotel. Garnett still remembers the colored man who carried in their suitcase. Next morning they caught the train at Elkhorn and rode to Fremont where they were met by Larkin Stanley, who drove a taxi. The road was such that he was able to take them all the way to the Ball home. This was the year of 1925.

Returning to Kentucky, Mr. Puckett moved the family "just over the hill from Greasy Creek to Wolf Pit". Here Garnett completed the fifth grade. Another move was made to Hellier, Ky., where she attended the Edgewater School, and it was here that she saw two large homes that she has never forgotten because of their size and names. One was "Noah's Ark" and the other "The Titanic".

It was here, too, that she became acquainted with "Mama-a-dore", the big colored lady "who made such good biscuits".

Still other moves were made by the Pucketts, as Mr. Puckett moved from one mining location to another. Finally one move took them to Matewan, W. Va., where Mr. Puckett worked in the Red Jacket Mines. This was to be Garnett's last year of school. . .the year was 1928.

Garnett has never forgotten certain things about Matewan. . .the Red Jacket Company Store, the drawing of scrip, the scrip cards, the miners coming in to do their trading. She remembers the school she attended, the cows in the lots, a certain place where she and a little friend took an iron skillet and built a little rock fireplace and made their own cottage cheese. She remembers

quite well the home where two beautiful peacocks strutted in the lawn and she believes they were owned by the brother of W. M. Ritter.

In 1987, she returned to Matewan for a visit. Garnett can tell you how it was. "My old school has been remodeled into the W & E Chevrolet Sales showroom. . .the old Red Jacket Company Store was being remodeled into the Red Jacket Market. This was where we went to draw scrip, buy groceries and get our mail. I got some pictures before it was all remodeled. I want to go back once more and try to find just where Mrs. Asberry's house was located and I want to find the place where the old spring was that we carried our water from".

When she was about 12 years old, Garnett came back to Dickenson County to stay with her Kenady Grandparents, Win and Healtha. Her Grandmother Kenady was a well-known mid-wife and Garnett would work for the new mother until she was able to be up and

See MULLINS, Page 12

59

★ Mullins .... Continued from Page 2

Mrs. Garnett Mullins

around again.

In 1933, Garnett married Brownlow Mullins. I asked her how they met and she laughingly replied, "I had been tying oats all day and Brownlow came to see Daddy. He sat on the porch and talked a long time...I wished he would go home so I could get cleaned up and rest, but he just kept on staying and talking. After that he kept coming back and after about a year, we got married." "And where did you get married,?" I asked. Again she gave a laughing reply. "Out here in the hay field...Uncle Wash Mullins was the preacher and he was tying oats that day. His wife was picking dried peas off the vines to keep for seed. We went and asked him to marry us and he did." Garnett wore a pretty wedding dress. Her Aunt Addie Powers, (Scottie's wife,) had a Mrs. Lutz at Coeburn to make it for her. Mrs. Lutz charged fifty cents and the material cost ten cents per yard—the thread was five cents per spool. The dress was print, pink apple blossoms sprinkled over the white background. Her hair was worn in the "going" style of the day, a "shingle bob".

After marriage, Garnett and Brownlow bought a house from Cas and (Darl) Orlena Kenady Stanley. They lived there until 1940 when they moved to their present home. Mr. Mullins worked as a truck driver, hauling anything that needed to be moved. His last job was with Ira Cabe on Bartlick, working as a loaderman. In 1982, he suffered a stroke and was paralyzed on his left side for 22 months before his death in 1984. Garnett faithfully cared for him in spite of periods of bad health, which she herself suffered. Brownlow died a Christian and Garnett is also a Christian and a member of the Rachel Chapel Freewill Baptist Church.

She and Brownlow were married almost 52 years. There are four children in their family; Kenneth Ray, Thurl, Douglas, and Judy. There are seven grandchildren and 2 great-grandchildren.

Garnett did not tell me a lot about herself. She didn't have to. It didn't take long for me to realize that here is a woman who tries to live a good life before the Lord and her family and who prays faithfully for her family and her friends. She is a person who cares and who shares.

She is the kind of mother and neighbor and friend whose worth perhaps will not be measured until she is gone. It so often happens that way.

The first time I visited Garnett we shared homemade biscuits and we dug flowers...the next time we went visiting. The last time it was a terribly hot day and we sat on the porch just talking and sharing and enjoying cold water from the well in the yard. You'll never go to Garnett Mullins' home that she doesn't want to give you something...but the best thing she gives is her true hospitality and friendship. I know.

Mollie Counts Viers

Part 1

By Anita A. Belcher

Aunt Mollie (Mary Ann) Counts Viers is the last living child of Uncle Noah and Catherine Compton Counts. Born February 8, 1900, Aunt Mollie was one of 12 children. Others were: Ezra (m) Bertha Rose, Martha (m) Bunyon Counts, Jesse (m) ??? Silcox, Rachel (m) Levi Hall, Maggie (m) first time John Hall, second time Arthur Anderson, Pricy (m) Cleat Hay, Jonas and Henry died as young boys, Caudle remained unmarried, Fletcher (m) Edra Counts, Mollie (m) Taylor Viers, and one child died at birth.

Uncle Noah and Catherine lived on Lick Creek in a house given to them by his father, Preacher Lige Counts. It was here that Molly learned the importance of herbs, for Uncle Noah was the well known herb doctor of these parts. Aunt Mollie recalls, "I had to miss school during the last part of August and the first of September because that was the time of year that herbs had to be dug." This digging of herbs was not a hobby or a pastime, as it might well be considered today, but rather a "life and death" matter. People far and near relied on "Doctor Noah" and even today his name and his remedies are respected and referred to. Not too long ago, I was talking with a young man about one of the children in his family who was being troubled with a kidney infection and I remember him saying, "Mommy told me if I would go find a certain plant that Uncle Noah Counts used, she'd bet anything that infection would clear up." He continued, "I believe it, too, because my younger sister used to have this

Mollie Counts Viers

same kind of trouble and mommy always used the herbs that Uncle Noah recommended and she'd get better. Trouble is, the place where we used to dig it is gone and I don't know where to find it anymore."

Aunt Mollie remembers many of the herbs and what they were used for and if her eyesight and health would permit, "she could find the same herbs again and know how to use them." Uncle Noah had an herb book with illustrations of each herb and what their use was. Aunt Mollie recalls, too, that her father used the herbs both fresh and dried. They were made into teas or dried, ground

up and made into pills. As Aunt Mollie talked about the medicine that her father made, I remembered visiting her sister, Maggie, not long before her death and I recall a remark she made, "The trouble with medicine nowadays, is that all the good is burned out of the medicine before you take it."

Aunt Mollie has so many interesting memories, some of which I will share with you readers. "Once when I was a small girl, daddy and mother took me to visit Uncle Jake and Aunt Sally Blair...you know he was a good part Indian. When we got to the house, Uncle Jake asked

Continued from Page 3

us if we'd like some honey. Daddy said yes and Uncle Jake told us to get a bowl and spoon and come and sit down in the yard. We did and Uncle Jake just took the honey from the hive right there and we ate all we wanted. Daddy asked me if I'd like to see where Uncle Jake slept. He

See VIERS, Page 4.

took me in the house and in front of the fire was a big log hollowed out with blankets in it. Aunt Salley said the Indian blood in Uncle Jake made him like to sleep like that."

Strange as that may seem to all of us now, the forest used to provide many of our forefather's necessities. In all the people I have talked to, I had never had anyone tell me about making barrels out of tree trunks. Yet, that's the way it used to be done by many people. "They would cut a tree, and measure the size of the barrel they wanted, then chisel out the inside until they got the depth they needed." Trees used for this purpose were usually poplar, if Aunt Mollie recalls correctly. Pickles were made and preserved in these barrels and smaller ones were made for other purposes. Wooden wash tubs and buckets were commonplace, some having come by the way of the old country store packed with pickles, herring fish and other food stuff.

As we talked about products of the forest, those of us sitting in Gladys' living room recalled the days of "sarvice" berry picking and all of us remember the good times we had "sapping." We agreed that young adults of today and their children are missing out on one of the best times and one of the most unique and refreshing tastes in life by not becoming acquainted with birth sap. It's getting that time of year, so when the sap rises, take an axe, bucket and spoon and go sapping. Don't cut the tree or take the bark off all the way around...just take off a section of bark on one side of the tree, take your spoon and scrape out the white, inner bark, fill your bucket with this, bring it home, add some sugar (not much), cover with water and let set for a few hours and you'll have a drink that can't be bought. Aunt Mollie told us of the many items that could be made from the birch bark and how that it was quite usual to make a birch bucket when berry picking. Today, we would pay a high price for one of those as well as the white oak baskets that were considered a necessity in those days.

Aunt Mollie spoke of attending school around a "brush fire" while men of the community finished building the school house. She recalled three of her first teachers as being Frank and Avon Sykes and Patton Edwards. She remembers Mary Fuller Cain. She remembers the days when 25 pounds of brown sugar was $1.00 and flannel was five cents per yard. This lady is a delight to visit and talk with and she has much knowledge and wisdom.

Many people think that when you talk with one of our older people, "you've talked with them all." After all, didn't they all do the same thing and have the same kind of life and experiences? The answer is no! Some of the same basic principles are necessarily alike, but as for the people, each have their own unique characteristics and, like fingerprints and tracks along a mountain trail, they each have their own story to tell.

Molly (Mary Ann) Counts

MOLLY COUNTS VIERS and husband, Taylor. Picture was made in 1916.

"A Beautiful Lady"
By Anita A. Belcher

Molly Counts met Taylor Viers while going to school at Turner on Backbone Ridge. At first he was one of the students, then he was "too big" to attend school, so he came as a visitor. Molly had been "talking" some to another boy or two, and Taylor had been a little interested in another girl. However, he soon began coming to Molly's house, and it was apparent to everyone that he was serious about the pretty Counts girl. The teacher at Turner School was boarding at Taylor's home, and Taylor found a way of getting messages to Molly. He would write letters to her and put them in the teacher's dinner bucket. The teacher would put them inside Molly's school book. She would read them and send a return answer the same way. After about three months of serious dating the two were married at the home of her parents. Uncle Walk Counts performed the ceremony, and when I asked Aunt Molly if Uncle Walk was a preacher she said, "I reckon...he preached his own funeral"! Molly remembers that she wore a pretty white dress for her wedding with a big collar and probably button-up shoes. Her sister, Pricy, made her dress. Taylor wore a nice suit. "He might have bought his suit," Aunt Molly reminisces, "but his mommy might have made it for him. She could make anything...pants, shirts, jackets. She made all her own clothes and made for other people, too." Aunt Molly and Taylor were married Jan. 13th, 1916, a little less than a month before her sixteenth birthday.

The young couple went to housekeeping in the home of Taylor's parents. His mother was not well and Molly took over many of the household chores. The chores in that day and time were hard for a seasoned mountain woman, much less a young girl just starting out in life, but Molly- had been well trained. "I grew up in a big family," she recalls, "and I knew what it was to work. It didn't bother me." These were the days when nothing came easy. "Taylor's mother had only three quart cans when we got married," she remembers. "We used syrup buckets for canning, stone jars or crocks for preserving apple-butter and the homemade wooden barrels for storing molasses. We dried much of our foodstuff for winter, almost any vegetable, or fruit, and even tomatoes." Molly had watched and helped with the cooking at home before she married, and now this experience was to

be valuable as a young wife helping to look after her in-laws. "Mother used to make the best dumplings," she told me. "Of course she made them on chicken, but also berries and fruit. You know, peaches used to be as easy to raise as apples." Apple dumplings was one of Molly's favorite dishes, and she shared her recipe with me at the same time, saying she could make them just "as good as ever if I had some dough stirred up and ready to use". Here's the recipe. "Have enough boiling water in a kettle to cover 12 dumplings. Roll dough to a medium thickness and about the size of a fried pie crust. Fill with uncooked, unsweetened apple slices and pull the dough together, twisting the top shut. Drop gently into the boiling water and let cook until done (time depends on the type of apple used). Lift out into a bowl, sweeten to taste and serve with desired topping." One of Granny Viers' recipes (Taylor's mother) that Aunt Molly loves to talk about is her light bread. She couldn't tell me just how she made it, because she knew how to make it and didn't measure. "She made it for the family and for sick folks...they would send for her to make it. For years she had a big "baker", what we today call a dutch oven. She would bake her bread in this baker, setting it on top of hot coals and covering it the same way. Many times we ate a supper of

Granny's hot bread with fresh milk and butter."

Aunt Louisa Viers, wife of Charlie, who was Taylor's uncle, holds a fond place in Aunt Molly's mem-
See MOLLY, Page 5

★ Molly

Continued from Page 4

ory. She taught the young bride many things, including the use of the "block and paddle" for washing clothes. Over the years the older woman and young Molly became good friends.

For the next seventeen years, Molly and Taylor would be living at the home of his parents, Andy Jack and Lindy Owens Viers. During this time they became parents of eleven children; Gladys (m) Ernie Turner, Whetsel (m) LaVern Ramsey, Maggie (m) Emory Edwards, Bonsel (m) Ruth Viers, Jessie (m) Diane Roberts, Kelsie (m) John Poe, Fred (m Betty Kirby, Gene was unmarried, Asie (m) Thelma Fuller, Sue (m) Woody Barker, and Luther (L. C.) (m) Darlene Vercamp. Aunt

Molly at the present has 28 grandchildren, 38 great-grandchildren and five great-great-grandchildren. She and Taylor were married 64 years before his death in October of 1980. Over the past eighty-some years Aunt Molly has experienced much in life, and I have barely touched on a story, and a part of history that will never be relived...times are different now and only a few are left to tell about "how it used to be". I hope that some of the grandchildren will visit with this fine lady and write down many of her memories, and keep them for the generations to come.

When you look at the picture of

Mollie Viers with her husband, Taylor (made when she was hardly sixteen-years-old), you're going to say, "Wasn't she beautiful?" But...if you visit her today, you'll find yourself saying, "Isn't she *STILL* beautiful?" And the answer is "Yes, she is."

Mrs. Rachel Matney Baker

By Anita Belcher

Many people in Dickenson County, particularly in the area around Haysi, remember Rachel Baker as the wife and co-worker of Ireland Baker who was the postmaster in Haysi for many years. In Clintwood, the Bakers were well known by many people, for this was Mr. Baker's home and some of his relatives still live here. Most people, though, who knew the Bakers, learned to respect and love them for the standards they set and for the honest, dependable lives they lived.

For the first ten years of my life, I hardly knew them for we lived at Sandlick and got our mail at the Birchleaf Post Office, but the few times I was in the Haysi Post Office stand out in my memory.

Mr. Baker had a drugstore in the front section of his building where he sold ice cream and fountain drinks. Everything about the building was clean and attractive and I remember once or twice getting to set at one of the pretty tables and eat ice cream. I watched the people come and go, getting their mail, money orders and packages. Mr. Baker was always there, steady, calm, quiet and helpful. I would see Mrs. Baker busy at work but never too busy to extend a cheerful, friendly greeting.

Mrs. Rachel Baker was not a native Dickensonian. She was born between the towns of Grundy and Raven, the oldest child of John W. and Lydia Deskins Matney. Mr. Matney was a farmer, a cattle raiser, a postmaster and a teacher. He was one of the first three men in Buchanan County to make what was then required to teach school, "The first grade certificate". He and the other gentleman had to travel to Dorton, Ky., to accomplish this and Mrs. Baker wonders yet how they traveled. I met Mr. Matney a few times before his death and I came to the conclusion that "here was a real gentleman of the old school", and every time Mrs. Baker tells me anything about him, I realize more than ever that my conclusion was right.

Just this evening while I was visiting in her home and we were talking of past days, Mrs. Baker related something that her father told his sons upon hearing about the death of a neighbor. They were working in the field when they heard the news and Mr. Matney said, "We'll finish hoeing our rows out, boys, and go see what we can do to help. We don't work when one of our neighbors is dead."

Mrs. Lydia Matney lived by the same creed. No one who ever knew her could forget her. The Lord's

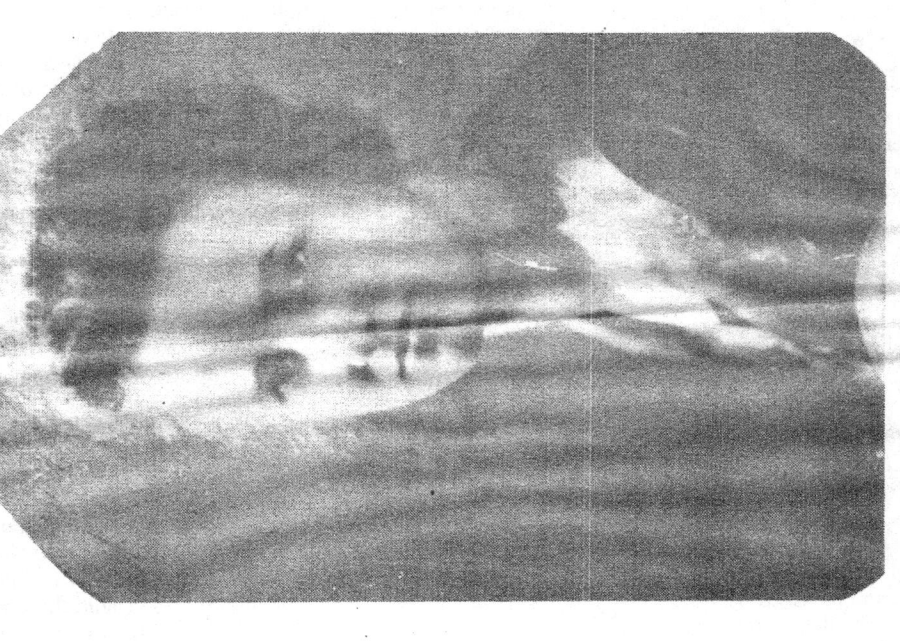

Rachel Matney (Mrs. Ireland Baker) 1917-18.
Mrs. Baker now lives at 124 Keith Road, Bristol, Tennessee 37620. She would enjoy hearing from friends.

hand seemed to be upon her in a special way for she was a much talented woman. She was a teacher of the women who lived in her community and came to her home. She taught by word and example.

"Times were different," Mrs. Baker recalls with a chuckle. "Everybody got together in those days for whatever was going on. . .corn hoeings, corn shuckings, quilting. . .whole families would come. The mother would be carryin' a baby with another child holding to her skirttail. Even the dogs came! Mother would cook big meals. When workhands came they started early. By eleven o'clock, mother would have a big dinner ready." Lydia Matney became known for her kind deeds and loving concerns. One day, some men were sitting on a porch and one of them said to one of the others, "Wonder who died?" Another one of them replied that he hadn't heard of any one being sick or any death and he asked why the first one thought that anyone had died. "Well," the questioner answered, "I saw Lydia Matney walking up the road with a chicken under her arm and a bucket in her hand. I know something's happened." When there was a need, Lydia Matney was there, still her own family was always loved and cared for.

Rachel Matney lived in the days of one room schools and the old McGuffy reader. She was already advanced in basic education before she went to school. "We got to school by walking or riding the 'old jenny' who was so ugly that we children wished we could tie her in the woods and walk to school," Mrs. Baker laughingly relates. From the one-room school Rachel went to the high school at Grundy, boarding through the week. After finishing her education in Grundy she attended Normal School at Radford which was later to become Radford State Teacher's College. Here she received her certificate to teach and

See BAKER, Page 5

★ **Baker**

Continued from Page 4

going back into the Raven area she taught the two-room Layne School.

The Matney family was at this time living at what we now know as Oakwood, the post office then being Hanger. The White Oak Lumber Company had moved into the area and with them came a young man who was working as a log scaler and office worker. Ireland Baker had served his country in WWI overseas and after several months in the hospital was home again. It wasn't too long before Cupid was at work and in April of 1922, Rachel Matney and Ireland Baker were married. They lived in the Garden Creek area for awhile and then moved to Pickens, S.C., where he continued his work with the White Oak Lumber Co. Coming back to Grundy, Mr. Baker worked in the bank and then they came to Haysi where he had a drug store and later, the post office.

There are many, many experiences and much history that Mrs. Baker has known about and lived through, particularly in Dickenson County.

This afternoon we looked through old ledgers and voiced amazement at the low mail order fees of years ago. We looked at petitions signed by residents who wanted to be sure that Mr. Baker stayed on as postmaster and, as Mrs. Baker says, "It brings tears to the eyes to see those signatures of old friends so many years gone."

The Bakers lived through the big fire that destroyed Haysi and for awhile the post office was in the Presbyterian Church. They were there in the '57 flood and Mrs. Baker was showing me a newspaper article that was written at the time, in fact, several articles. Perhaps before very long we can get some of that information together for the readers of the C.T., but now I want to share a special story with you all.

I have many special memories of Mrs. Baker. I promised her that I wouldn't write anything that would embarrass her and I won't because I know she doesn't want a lot of attention focused on her or a lot of praise. I know that everything she does is out of a heart full of love for the Lord and her fellowman. Still, I have to say that she has set a Godly and Christian example for many a child, young person and grown woman.

One of my most lasting memories was the spring when I was about thirteen years old. It was Easter and I dreaded to go to church. I knew everyone would have on new clothes. . .slippers, hats, coats and some would even wear flowers. I didn't have new clothes so I thought the best thing I could do would be to get there early and sit far over in the corner of the pew. Then no one would see me.

That's what I did, and sure enough it was just like I had thought. Everyone was all dressed up in their Easter clothes and I just wanted to go through the floor and not come out again until everyone had gone.

Then Mrs. Baker came in. She was wearing the same suit that she had worn several times before. Her slippers were not new and she was not wearing flowers. She was carrying flowers, though. A vase of jonquils which she had picked from her hillside, and her face was aglow with smiles and love. When I saw her I felt I had been given a new lease on life or something like that. I thought, "If Mrs. Baker can come without new clothes, it must not be too bad, and I wasn't ashamed anymore."

Margie (Hayes) Lawson

April 26, 1989

By Anita A. Belcher

"I do not live here by necessity, but by choice. I love the peace and quiet, the beauty of the sky, moon, horizons...the green fields, hills, mountains and stars. As I sit in the porch swing, writing, the shadows begin to fall and I listen to the sounds...an airplane in the Eastern sky, a dog barking across a ravine two miles away, sheep bleating for their lambs, a hornet flying in pursuit of a fly for his supper, crickets chirping, calves calling for their mother and my cat purring in contentment as he sits by my side. Everything is fresh and clean, the air is nice and cool because we had a good thundershower this evening. The gardens will revive and the corn and meadows got a good soaking...it is getting cooler now and so dark I can hardly see to write, so I will stop for now."

The paragraph you have just finished reading was beautifully written by Margie Lawson in the late summer of 1977 and now nearly 12 years later she still writes and her feelings remain the same.

Margie Lawson lives on a farm of more than 100 acres atop Brushy Ridge. Her driveway leads through a wooded area and opens into a lane bordered on either side by fields, fences, barns and a farm pond. At the end of the drive is Margie's home. You enter her yard (not a lawn, she says) by opening an old-time garden gate and walking up

MARGIE [HAYES] LAWSON

stone steps. On the right are her beds of early spring flowers, on the left are her mother's roses and peonies, red, pink and white. Above her flowers is her garden, already planted, with spinach and lettuce about ready to eat. To the side and above her garden are her fruit trees. Stuck around in various places and in a very orderly fashion are herbs, other old-time flowers, winter on-

ions, a grape arbor, berry vines and other delightful growing things. Once inside her home you realize that there is another side to Margie Lawson. This lady is an artist outside her home, it shows in her landscaping. Inside it projects itself in her sewing, quilting and painting. Margie Lawson is a unique lady. She is forthright, outspoken and practical. She is enthusiastic, tough, a fighter, a worker. Having lived through many rough times, she does not know the meaning of "give up" or "quit." She is a lady, (don't let her "farming garb" fool you), a lady with an indomitable spirit. This is part one of Mrs. Lawson's story in her own words.

"I was born September 1, 1916 in a log cabin in Dickenson County, Virginia, the eighth of nine children. My family had moved from Wise County about 1905 from land belonging to my father, James William Hayes, Sr. Our log cabin was built of large poplar logs hued to a thickness of 8", and notched at the corners. It was 30-feet long and 18-feet wide with two windows and two doors, and a staircase leading to the attic, a large A-shaped bedroom and storage space. On the northeast side was a log beam too, which was the kitchen and dining room and storage space. The cookstove was what they called a step stove, but it gave us fine cooked foods and warmth. Of course, wood was the fuel and was the only fuel available. In the main room, was a large fireplace made of sandstone hewn out of sandstone on the place. The chimney was daubed with mud (there was no cement), as was the cracks in the log frame of the house.

Now this land was black and loamy, very rich and productive, but could hardly see the soil for the rock; rocks everywhere, some too big to move, some small cliffs, and thousands of smaller ones which were piled so there would be room to plant corn, and other crops and most of all, apple trees, peas, plums, and other fruit trees. We had wonderful apples every year, which were kept by burying in holes or in socks under the beds. My mother once remarked that the devil owed her a debt and paid her in rocks. The land was steep, and the planting and cultivating was done by hand.

I can remember the log barn over near the gardens, which didn't have so many rocks on it. The barn also had one big divided stall and a lean-to on the northeast side. I remember playing around it when I was a small girl, and there were always copperheads around. Don't know why we didn't get bitten, except the Lord took care of us. Once mother said, I was a baby crawling around on the floor in the house, and was peeping under the dresser. When she investigated, she found a coiled copperhead. Guess it

knew I wouldn't hurt it, so it didn't hurt me.

Now how did they make a living in such a place? Well, they raised a lot of corn on the rich land, as they cleared the beautiful timber and burned it to make the steep fields. They put some of that corn in a jar and sold it as "moonshine." Though we had prohibition of making and selling "moonshine," almost everyone did, and it was made at nights, so no one would be out hunting and see the snake, called moonshine. My dad made fine whiskey. They all said he had made a copper still, with copper cap and "worm" (condenser). He had regular customers of the doctors, bankers, and big "shots" in Dante, our nearest town, being built as a coal mining town. I can remember that I wasn't supposed to talk to anyone about what daddy was doing. But in those days, children didn't talk. We were seen and not heard, most of the time, we weren't even seen when friends and relatives came to visit. By day we were out playing in the rocks and snakes, by night we were in bed.

We were a husky bunch of children, five girls and four boys in all, and as I write this we are all still living. Elsie will be 77 on August 16. Fairy, the youngest, is 56. We were blessed to be healthy, and we believe the rugged way we were raised up made us strong.

Elsie was 16 when I was born, and she says she was mad at me because that was the first time she had to make biscuits for breakfast and they were hard as rocks. There was no doctor at any of our births, except Fairy's. Mother was 42 and a doctor was present then. The rest of us had midwives for doctors. Mine

was Mrs. Sabra Ann Kilgore from Lick Creek.

Life must have been very hard on this steep land and as the family grew, more land was cleared, and in 1907, some of our land which extended to Open Fork Creek and the main highway at that time, was swapped to Clinchfield Coal Company for 22 acres on this ridge, called the Moore Tract which was not so steep, but very poor soil. It seemed a family called Moore had lived there and had worn out the land."

Because Mrs. Lawson represents many of the qualities of yesteryear's Dickensonian, and because she retains many of the qualities that today's generation needs to survive, I will share her stories in at least one more column of the CT, maybe two more. If you don't know this lady, make her acquaintance and I believe you will find her to be a true friend — one worth knowing.

Margie (Hayes) Lawson

PART II
By Anita Belcher

"I have always wanted to write the story of my life and call it, 'The Live and Times of Margie Hayes Lawson.' Someday I hope to get started on it and write as it comes to memory down through the years. Perhaps someday someone will read it and understand my joys and sorrows, my fears and triumphs, challenges and adversities, my ultimate victories, my losses."

These are the words of Mrs. Lawson, penned in early fall of 1977. Margie Lawson would be the first to say that she lays no claim to fame, but instead a claim to victory over constant hardship and trial that few of the present day generation would understand. (Many older Dickensonians would).

She writes, "On the Moore tract of land we worked very hard to build good soil. With two horses and some cows we had manure from the barns which was hauled in sleds and put in small piles on the fields after they had been plowed and harrowed and "laid off." The manure would be carried in buckets and put in hills three feet apart for the corn to be planted on. On this tract of land, dad, the boys and Uncle Jim Hayes, Jr., built a four-room, boxed house of boards from a sawmill. The chimney rocks were hewn from sandstone and daubed with mud. The arch rocks were five feet long and 16 to 18" wide, all in one piece. It took a lot of picking with small picks to make those rocks smooth. Our fuel was wood, huge logs, cut down, snaked into the wood-yard with horses, sawed with the crosscut saw, and split with wedges. My job as I grew up was to carry in wood, enough every night to fill the wood corner. I can remember carrying one stick at a time, falling in the snow, getting up and trying again. Everyone in our family had a chore.

MARGIE [HAYES] LAWSON

My mother was always interested in education. She went to the third grade and excelled in spelling and definition. She and her sister, Elizabeth, alternated in the weeks they attended school. One had to stay home and do the cooking for the working men. Mother sometimes got Lizzie to let her go a day or so in her week. Mother was very interested in sending us to school. We packed lard buckets of biscuits and jam, and went off to school, the older ones carrying the lunch buckets and leading the smaller ones. When the snow was very deep, Dad took the smaller children on the horse and "broke" road in the deep snow for the rest. We went to the Cherry Knob School about two miles away, a two-room school, but one room had been abandoned because it was not needed since a school had been built at Cold Spring three miles away. The extra room was used to play in during the winter. We sat where we pleased because when a class was called, we sat on a recitation bench in front of the teacher's desk. We had a small library of books we could look at any time. There was no whispering or running over the floor and eating was intolerable. A switch would be used on anyone caught disobeying. Time flew by fast. At age 13, I was in the 7th grade, excelling in reading, spelling and English, but falling back in arithmetic. It was now time for me to enter high school and Clintwood was 28 miles away. I had no transportation, so I walked the four miles from my home to the high school in Russell County. I was shy and felt so out of place among so many strangers, about 400 children in all. Somehow (I cannot remember how) I got started, bought my books second-hand and was on my way (I hoped) to becoming a nurse. It was hard, but I would not quit...I was learning and mother encouraged me to go on. Sometimes, when I think back, I wonder why I wanted to go on...I had only a couple of print dresses. As time went on, I grew more confident, but I cried when I was voted, "the most beautiful girl in the freshman class." I graduated from Dante Central High School in May of 1934. I wasn't the smartest student there, but neither was I the dumbest. I changed my mind about being a nurse and decided to go to college and become a teacher.

During the years that Margie was getting a high school education, her family was left without the protection and care of a man in the family. Her father decided to return to his old home in Wise County and her brothers had grown up and left to make a life of their own. That left Mrs. Hayes and five girls to fend for themselves. Mrs. Lawson writes, "Since we had the little farm, we raised everything we could eat and sell. We kept two cows and about 30 hens. Mother peddled our eggs, butter, milk, vegetables and fruit in Dante. Every year we had a couple of calves to sell for $10 to $15. Every Saturday and Tuesday we would trudge the four miles into Dante and sell our produce. After dad left, mother called a family council meeting and set down rigid rules for us girls to follow. When we went anywhere and if any boys wanted to see us, they must come to our home. Elsie, my older sister, was 30 years of age then and had an eye like an eagle, but we obeyed the rules. Well, I thank God for my mother and her good advice and discipline. I've heard her say, "When your good name is gone, you're gone too! My mother guided us through the trials and hardships of early life. I still see her leading the way to the cornfields and us girls following behind like chicks. By hard work and cooperation we went through the great depression without welfare or food stamps. The work and outdoor life made us strong and husky. We girls went to the woods, cut down trees, sawed them into stove-wood lengths, and the old horse pulled the sled home. We tried to get enough wood in the fall to last all winter. Later, we bought a grate and bought coal for $2.00 a ton and we didn't have to use so much wood."

It was now time for Margie Hayes to enter college. How was a country girl without any ways or means going to manage this?

To be continued.

Margie (Hayes) Lawson

MARGIE LAWSON IN COLLEGE
By
Anita A. Belcher

I am writing this third article about Margie Lawson for two main reasons. One is so that people who experienced the same hardships and difficulties as they struggled to get a college education can read this and say, "Oh, yes, that's the way it was back then. . .it was very hard."

The other reason is, that hopefully, some young people will read this and realize that the difficulties that once stood between them and an education have now, for the most part, been removed.

A young person of today who really wants to amount to something in life and who really desires to get a good education has very little to hinder him. Even paying for a college degree has today become relatively easy when compared to how it was not so many years ago. Transportation and communication do not have to be considered by today's high school graduate for most have their own car (or access to one) and to be without a phone in one's room is almost unthinkable.

None of this was true in the generation of Margie (Hayes) Lawson. This is her story (in part) in her own words.

"We, (Pauline Dishman) and I reached Radford at 11 p.m. We traveled by train. Some representative girls from the college met us and were there to show us around the college dorm. Some boys from the college brought our bags to the college in a truck. The next morning we got up and went outside early. We went down the front porch to get a view of our situation. We had never been away from Dante and were like lost sheep.

Pauline began speaking to the other students as they came by. . .she was very talkative. . .I was very shy. Pauline spoke to one girl who seemed very snobby and prissy. "How are you?" Pauline asked. "Are you homesick. . .I'm awfully homesick." The "snobby" girl replied that she was not homesick, that she was going to enjoy herself. This only served to make us more homesick. . .we were 150 miles from home and it might as well have been around the world.

We struggled to keep from crying and Pauline wanted to go home, but I talked her out of it. My mother was no "quitter", and I knew she wouldn't allow me to be either. I couldn't go home, not now. We finally got registered and settled into the routine.

We applied for work in the dining room to help pay our board. The second quarter starting January 1935, we were given the job of "waiting tables" at $45.00 per quarter. We had to get up at 5 a.m., serve sixteen people breakfast, clear the tables, carry the dishes back to the kitchen, and then set the tables again for lunch. We had to get to our rooms, dress and get to class by 8 o'clock. At noon, we came to the

★ Lawson

Continued from Page 2

analysis which most of the students feared. Each student was called into the office of the Dean of Women for private consultation.

Margie remembers that she was not afraid because by now, she had become very confident and had made very good marks.

Mrs. C_, who was doing the evaluation, was a well-dressed, full-figured lady who loved to wear fashionable clothes. Her favorite dress, being one of white.

Mrs. Lawson recalls that this lady wore her hair in waves close to her head with "never a hair out of place". She gave Margie excellent marks on everything remarking that she would make a fine teacher, "but", she said, "you need some nice clothing." This was a remark that cut deep into the heart of Margie Hayes, for no one knew better than she that she needed pretty clothing, but she had done more than well just to stay in college.

"I had three or four old dresses which I tried to keep clean and one pair of black, suede pumps".

Mrs. Lawson is glad to share this story because she wants young people to realize that everything doesn't come easy and that many things in life are going to hurt, but one can't afford to be "a quitter".

Margie continued to work hard in the dining room and studied hard so as to be able to graduate. She recalls, "Graduation came before I knew it. I had actually finished two years of college and had earned a Normal Professional Certificate. I was proud to walk across that stage and receive that certificate. I had worked hard for it."

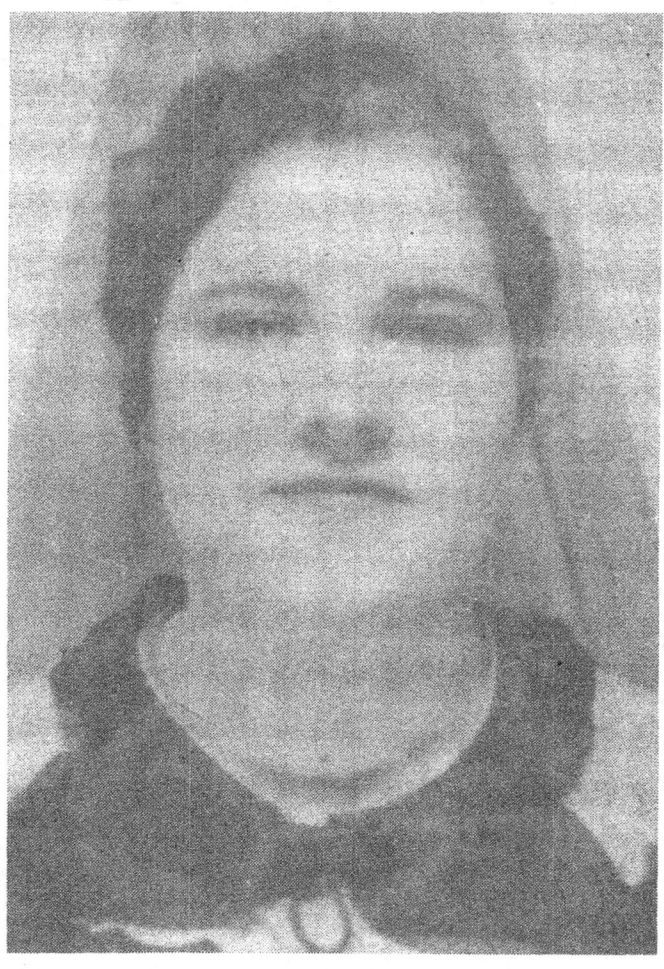

**Margie Hayes — 1936
Radford College Days**

kitchen and grabbed a bite to eat, served lunch, cleared the tables and set them again for dinner. We rushed back and forth to the kitchen carrying food, dishes, etc. An average of four to six hours a day was spent in the kitchen and dining room and five to six hours a day in class. After all this, I was too tired to study.

I just wanted to sleep, but I couldn't.

Sometimes, when I think back, I wonder how I ever made it. I didn't have the money to buy a lot of the text books, so I had to take notes on the lectures, and before exams, would cram and try to memorize the notes.

During the next year, Margie would take her "practice teaching", be assigned to "playground duty", and then came the final evaluation

See LAWSON, Page 3

College did not change Margie Hayes when it came to working. After graduation she came back to the mountain farm on Brushy Ridge and did the plowing, hoeing, woodcutting, berry picking and canning for the winter. Corn was raised and it was Margie's job to take it to the mill for grinding.

In the meantime, she had applied for a teaching position out of the county since she had a brother and sister already teaching in the Dickenson County school system and they would not hire another person from the same family.

One day the letter she had been waiting for came, and Margie had her first teaching position at Rowe Mountain in Buchanan County, and that begins another whole story.

If you want to share more "mountain stories" with Margie Lawson, go see her at her farm. She still lives not too far from where her life began, in the Brushy Ridge section of Dickenson County.

Standing in certain places in her fields, one can see far beyond the blue mountains that encircle her home. No doubt, but that many times as a young girl, Margie stood and looked and dreamed of days when she could leave Brushy Ridge and go beyond those mountains. Her days at Radford took her into another world, but it was not her world.

One day a visitor from the city remarked, "I don't see why you live here (Brushy Ridge) like a hermit!" Mrs. Lawson replied, "I live here by choice, not by necessity. I love the sky, moon, stars. . .the fields, hills and mountains."

Mrs. Lawson will always love those things, and if by necessity she ever has to leave them, her heart will never forget.

Margie (Fuller) Mullins

By Anita Belcher

"A fine Christian friend."

Margie Fuller is the daughter of Richard M. and Rosabelle Compton Fuller. For those of you who are interested in tracing family trees and looking up kinfolk, there is a whole network of names in this article that will be interesting and informative. Rosabelle was the daughter of Shadrach and Arminda Owens Compton of the Prater area. Her brothers and sisters were Erbert, Lee, Arthur, Floyd, Burl, Flora, Barbara and Emma. With the help of Maude (her sister), Margie remembers who the girls in the family married.

Flora married Charles Selfe, Barbara married Frank Owens and Emma married Jake Owens. Richard, "Uncle Dick," as he was known by the neighbors, was the son of Jacob and Margaret Colley Fuller. Margaret was the daughter of Richard (Fightin' Dick) and Crissie Counts Colley. Brothers and sisters to Richard M. Fuller were Jim, Noah, Hawk, Didama, Crissa, Mary "Polly" Anne, Martha Lurinda and Margaret Jane.

Marjorie (Margie) grew up on Bartlick Creek, one of eight children. Brothers and sisters were: Jim (m) Aurora Mullins, Flora (m) Arville Mullins, Maude (m) Jim Mullins, Maxie (m) Pridemore Mullins, and Margie married Dee Mullins. (The Mullins family was from the Skeetrock community and were of the generation of Doc and Sally Reed Mullins and Jack and Tilda Sykes Mullins.) Dewey and Fred married sisters, Goldia and Vada Counts, and Dora married Cleve Wallace of Elkhorn. Out of all these children, their husbands and wives, Margie, Maude, Flora, Fred and Vada are still living.

Growing up on Bartlick 80 years ago was a bit different from what it is today. At that time, it was an area of giant timber, productive farmland, and a creek that never runs dry. There was plenty of good hunting and the rich coal beneath the surface had not been touched except for small private "coal banks."

Margie's father was a farmer, merchant, miller, and logger. Such was the lifestyle in those days for those who would survive and prosper. Potatoes, beans and corn were the main crops with other garden produce filling in. Fruit was raised in the family orchard with apples being holed up for winter the same as potatoes. Bean stringings were common and were enjoyed by all ages. Uncle Dick had a grist mill across the creek just above where the Vada Fuller home now is and here was the big mill pond where the children swam on hot summer days. "Maude could swim like a duck," recalls Margie, "but I would sink to the bottom." "Maude always had to pull me out."

Maude and Margie were good friends as well as sisters. Much of their time was spent together and one of Margie's favorite memories is of their playhouse built along the cliffs that formed the bank above the mill. Here they gathered their "treasures," things built from rock and whatever else they could find. Here the wild flowers grew in sweet profusion and here Margie and Maude treated their little friends to candy from a big barrel in their dad's store. "After mother died," recalls Margie, "her sister, Aunt Flora, made Maude and me little coats with big pockets. We would fill those pockets with candy and give to our friends at the playhouse." And who were these friends? They were the children of George and Mint Burchett, (Inis, Draxie and Turner), there were the Riley Lee children from Camp Branch (Bertie and Nannie). Nannie is Mrs. John Hill. There were other neighbor children from up and down the creek.

MARGIE (MRS. DEE MULLINS) with young neighbor, Garrick Tackett, at Halloween. Garrick is the son of Gary and Alene Owens Tackett.

Christmas holds special memories for Margie. Her dad would gather sacks of goodies from his store and carry them down the creek as far as the old Mitchell Senter home and give them out to the children. He and Margie's mother would see that their children's stocking were hung by the fireplace and after everyone had gone to bed, her dad would hang a stocking for her mother and fill it. Margie remembers how much her dad and mother cared for each other and it is a good memory. She also remembers how well her mother cared for her family and how she cared for other people. "Mother was always cooking for visitors, especially for the church people — table loads of food."

Mrs. Richard Fuller died when Margie was only seven-years-old, leaving seven children at home. Dora was married and the care of the family fell to Flora, "who," recalls Margie, "did a wonderful job."

Margie has the Fuller sense of humor. She recalls hearing the old people say that when the first whip-porwill called in the evening that if you laid down and rolled over three times and made a wish, it would come true. Margie tried this by wishing the old cow would come home so she wouldn't have to hunt it. She laughs and says, "It worked, at least something did."

Another recollection which is not pleasant is that of their big two-story home burning down. "Flora stood outside waiting and asked dad if he had saved her organ. He replied, no, but he would get her another one."

What did teenagers do in those days? "Well, we went to pie suppers, played ball in the school bottom, just got together and had fun. One of the most interesting things was going to lower Bartlick and riding the train to Elkhorn City, Kentucky. The tickets cost 15 or 20 cents." Two of Margie's friends

See MULLINS, Page 4

were Bertha and Anne Fuller, along with their brothers and sisters. These two families were first cousins and their friendship lasted a life-time.

Margie was about 18-years-old when she married Dee Mullins. For the first few years of their married

76

life, they lived at Splashdam where three of their children were born. They then bought a mountain farm on Big Ridge and here their daughter, Barbara, was born. Margie became a Christian at a tent revival in Haysi and was baptized into the Presbyterian Church not far from where she now lives. Dee became a Christian not long afterward and was undoubtedly one of the finest men to be found anywhere. Perhaps the word "faithful" would best sum up his life, for he was faithful in all areas of his life, especially to his family, neighbors, church and Lord.

Margie and Dee had four children. Claude first married Dolly Powers and they had the following children: Rita, Linda, Michael, Danny and Sherri. He is now married to Maxine ??? of Cincinnati, Ohio, where they live. Janice married Joe Smith and they are the parents of three children, Gloria, Debbie and Patty. They live at Hurricane, West Virginia. Carol married Carl Baker of Clintwood and they live at Tazewell, Virginia. They have two children, Ronald and Carla. Carol is a nurse at Humana Hospital at Richlands. Barbara was first married to Clyde Varney of Grundy. They are the parents of three children, Michele, Chris and Karne. She is now married to Pet Schlick and they are the parents of twin daughters, Denise and Patrice. Margie is the proud great-grandmother of 15 children and so the Fuller-Mullins generation continues.

Margie Mullins is a fine woman to know. I have known her all my life and love her dearly. So does everyone who knows her. She too has been, and still is, a faithful friend and servant of the Lord. She and Dee were charter members of the Big Ridge Presbyterian Church where Dee served as deacon until his death and where Margie still attends when her health permits. Margie loves her neighbors and her church brothers and sisters. Her home has always been open to all and many, many times has she fed friends and ministers of the church. I think the word "love" best sums up Margie, for she is filled with love.

"What message would you leave for your children of future generations and other young people," I asked Margie. Very quickly she answered, "Stay in school...become a Christian and stay in church." Margie Fuller Mullins is a wise woman and it is to be hoped that the present and future generation heed her advice.

BILL CHILDRESS

September 6, 1989

By Anita A. Belcher

"Sharing stories of generations now gone. Stories that make us think whether we laugh or cry."

Bill C. Childress of the Breaks, is a well-known figure to friends and neighbors. This started out to be his story, but he had so many recollections about his parents and grandparents that it wouldn't be right not to share them with others who love these stories.

Bill is the son of Samuel and Maxie Colley Childress. Samuel was the son of Westley and Delilah Branham Childress. Bill gives the following information: "Grandpa Westley was from Louisa, Kentucky, and Grandma Delilah was from Virgie, Kentucky. After they married they made their home in the Elkhorn community (then Praise) and here their son, Samuel, was born. Grandpa was a team driver for the Yellow Poplar Lumber Company. He drove a team of oxen, hauling timber in the Fall Branch section of Bartlick. He also operated a ferry boat across the river at Bartlick just above the big splashdam. The water was deep here at the junction of the Russell Fork and the Pound Rivers, and made deeper by the water backing up from the dam."

Bill does not remember seeing the ferry boat nor the oxen. They were before his time, but he remembers the stories of them. Progress was being made by the time Bill's father, Samuel, was old enough to apply for a job. Bill recalls, "Dad grew up working in the coal mines at Elkhorn, Bartlick and Splashdam, but he was a team driver, too, like his father had been, yet there was a difference." Mr. Westley Childress had driven a team of oxen, his son had a team of mules. Westley had hauled timber for Ritter's, Samuel "hauled transportation" for the building of the railroad through the Breaks into Elkhorn. Anyone who can remember anything about the road from Elkhorn to Bartlick back in the "old days" will appreciate Bill's story about his dad.

"Hauling transportation for the railroad," says Bill, "was hauling supplies." "Dad had a team of mules and he used them to haul wagonloads of steel and other heavy supplies. The road from Elkhorn to Bartlick was sometimes almost impassable. The bottom of the wagon would drag and there were times when one or more of the mules "would get down" in the deep ruts and dad would have to cut the harness so they could get back on their feet." And so it was that a father and son had a part in the early progress of the county.

Bill has fond memories of his mother's parents, also. She was the daughter of Napoleon Bonaparte Colley and Matilda Edwards Colley. Matilda was the sister of Uncle Dean Edwards of Sandlick, and thus, another thread of relationship and kinfolk is realized. Bill loves to

talk about his Grandpa Colley. "Everyone knew him as Uncle Poad....that was the name he went by," Bill recalls. Bill remembers him as one of the early school teachers and recollects that he was always interested in education. His interest in this direction would greatly influence his children and more than one of them became well-known teachers in the area. Two daughters, Crissie and Lockie, taught in both Dickenson and Buchanan Counties and Josh Colley (a son) was a man respected and loved throughout the two counties. His influence was responsible for more than one mountain boy going beyond "the seventh grade" and even getting a college education, which in those days was not an easy thing to do. Josh himself, after a time, left the mountains of Southwest Virginia to become a professor and Dean of Men at Elon College in North Carolina. An interesting sideline here

Bill Childress of Breaks, Va.

which has nothing to do with education is that Josh Colley entered a "name the drink" contest when Royal Crown Cola was getting established as a soft drink and Josh's name "Royal Crown" was the one that was chosen. Bill laughs over some funny stories about his Grandpa Pode such as when he "painted himself" in on the barn roof and when he sawed off an apple tree limb that he was sitting on. Bill laughs as he recalls, "Grandpa had the straightest aim with a rock of anyone I ever knew...he could kill a cow with a rock."

But perhaps what he remembers best about his grandparents is their hospitality. "They didn't run a boarding house," he reminisces, "but it was as if they did." Everyone passing through, the drummers, land agents, travelers of all sorts stopped at Grandpa's and Grandmother Colley's. Neighbors would come to visit and at churchtime it was unbelievable how many people Grandmother would feed. It was also unbelievable how good her food was and the many different kinds she cooked and set with the same depth of feeling that most of us remember these same kind of stories with. Everyone has their memories, but for those of us who grew up when times were hard...even "good times" were hard...it seems that we have very special memories...the kind that aren't being made anymore. That's why I took the space this week to share some of Bill's memories with you, knowing that they would stir up a few of your favorite stories...maybe some you had almost forgotten to share with someone.

Bill and Elsie Childress are very wonderful people to be around. We'll have another visit with them next week and maybe you'll be surprised as I was to find out what very talented people they are.

Anita Belcher's Mountain Echoes

Cynthia Willis Lyall (Mullins)
"Mrs. Lottie Lyall shares memories of her mother-in-law and of Tom Bottom as it used to be..."

As I visited and talked with Mrs. Lottie Lyall last week, the name of her mother-in-law was frequently mentioned. Sometimes I would ask the question and Mrs. Lyall would reply, "I wish 'Aunt Cynthia' was still alive...there would be so many things she could tell you."

Sometimes Emma Jean, Mrs. Lyall's daughter, would voice the same feeling and would speak of "Granny Cynthia" with so much respect and affection that it made me want to know more about the person of which they spoke. I found myself wondering how a simple, mountain woman could, after all these years, still retain a place in the heart and memory of her family just as if she were still living.

I asked Mrs. Lyall if she would share some memories with me and she was glad to do so. This is not an attempt to write a family history of Aunt Cynthia, if I were doing that I would talk with other family members also, however, this is simply a tribute from a daughter-in-law in honor of a mother-in-law of whom she cannot speak highly enough, and of other memories of Tom Bottom when Aunt Cynthia lived there.

Cynthia Willis Lyall (Mullins) was born in the Fall Branch section of Tom Bottom. She was the daughter of Meredith and Ibby Mullins Willis . Meredith was a prosperous mountain farmer who owned a large farm in Fall Branch, which sprawled on over to adjoining land on Camp Branch, now known as Breaks Park Road.

The only way out of Tom Bottom during those years, besides the railroad (either walking the tracks or riding the train), was to walk the path over the Meredith Willis farm or ride a horse, which many people did.

Wagons were used on this road for hauling supplies or whatever else they were needed for. When wagons got on the main road leading to Elkhorn, Kentucky, driver's hoped and prayed they would not meet another wagon along the "high nar-

Cynthia and Patton Lyall

rows" for there was no place to pass, and it was a sheer drop to the river on the lower side.

The road over the Meredith Willis farm was also a favorite place for groups of young people to ride, and many enjoyable hours were spent in this manner. Lottie Lyall recalls with a smile how she and the other girls bought material and then made their own riding skirts.

Cynthia Willis would have been a young girl when Hamilton Lyall and his son, Patton, came into the Bartlick-Tom Bottom area of the county.

Logging was a big business for several lumber companies during those days, and parts of Dickenson County was unsurpassed for its forests of virgin oak and poplar. Hamilton Lyall was a logger, and he followed the logging industry from North Carolina to Virginia. While working in Tom Bottom at Skegg's Hole, he caught pneumonia and died.

His son, Patton, Married Cynthia Willis, and they built a home in Tom Bottom, just a few miles away from the farm where she grew up.

She and Patton were the parents of three children, Mike, Aaron and Meredith. After Patton's death, Cynthia married Alex Mullins, and

three children were born to them also; Rosa, Dolly and Vol.

Cynthia was a faithful wife and good mother. Lottie recalls what a hard worker she was, always planting and caring for a big garden, and then canning and preserving enough foodstuffs for her own family and any others who were in need.

She knew her field and garden herbs and how to use them for whatever they needed to be used for. No one ever left her home without being fed a good meal.

She was a very intelligent, possessing much "down to earth" common sense, and was able to give good advice when it was needed. She wanted to see her own children, and the other children of the community, educated and gave the land needed for a one-room school.

Some fine men and women taught at this little school, among them Brian Burchett and Hampton Osborne. These men were highly respected and loved by the people of the community. A young lady by the name of Velva Davis boarded with Aunt Cynthia and taught at the Tom Bottom School and, she too, was dearly loved. She later became the wife of Andy Mullins of Haysi. There

were others who taught at the school at Tom Bottom, but these were the ones Mrs. Lyall remembered at the moment.

Cynthia Lyall Mullins was a Christian woman, joining the church at an early age. It thrilled me to learn that it was she who gave the Reverend T. K. Mowbray some land beside her home to erect a big tent in which to teach Bible School because she wanted the children of the community to learn about God and the Bible.

Reverend Mowbray had a little grey car in which he traveled all over the county, roads permitting, and although the road to Tom Bottom was rough, he cared enough for the people who were there to travel it.

Going along to help teach, were: Miss Asilee Holland, who later
See ECHOES
Page 2, B-Section

★ ECHOES ..... Continued from Page 1, B-Section

married Reverend Mowbray, Miss Elizabeth Shoemaker, E. H. Anderson and his wife, Anne.

A little four-year-old girl went on this trip, which she thought was wonderful and, to this day, remembers the big trees surrounding the area and the sound of the Russell Fork River making its way into the Breaks Canyon. That little girl was me. Today, Mrs. Lottie Lyall showed me exactly where the tent set those many years ago.

Everyone that was connected with that group has died now, except Mrs. T. K. Mowbray and myself. I am told that Mrs. Mowbray is feeble now and almost blind. Perhaps someone is still living who attended that Bible School and remembers the fine adults that helped bring it about.

I think all of us can understand why Lottie Lyall can say of Aunt Cynthia, "Everyone who knew her loved her." Wouldn't it be good if all of us could leave that testimony...

When I arrived at Mrs. Lyall's this morning, the weather was pleasant but brisk.

"Anita," Mrs. Lyall said, "would you like to walk up the road and let me show you where all these places are? You can understand better what you are writing about if you see for yourself."

I was delighted with the idea and anxiously waited for Lottie to get a jacket and a pair of walking shoes.

As we walked along, she pointed out the places...the cemetery where Mike and the other family members were buried, the place where Uncle Tom Mullins had his house and little store, Aunt Cynthia's home, the old school site, and the place where the tent set. She showed me where the railroad houses were, where one well was drilled and where a wonderful spring of water used to be. She pointed out where the home of Charlie Patton Mullins and where the Hampton Osborne house were located. We kept walking out the road, up Fall Branch and past Buckeye Hollow.

"Aren't you getting cold?" I asked, for the air was definitely chilly.

"Not at all," Mrs. Lyall answered, "it just smells so fresh and clean out here...I love it!"

We walked up a steep grade.

"Shouldn't we go back...I'm afraid you'll get to tired," I said.

Without any shortness of breath Mrs. Lyall replied, "No, let's go a little further. I used to walk this road with Uncle Roam's wife. There was a big beech tree up there by the road and I'd like to see if it is still there."

We found the tree, and I picked up a pocket full of big beechnuts. We went onward to the top of the first hill, and Mrs. Lyle pointed out where the old farm used to be and the road that leads to the Meredith Willis cemetery.

Coming back, she pointed out the river peeking thru the trees at Skegg's Hole and called my attention to the clearness of the water flowing down the Fall Branch river.

Always, she spoke with enthusiasm. It made me think of how happy she must have been when she, Mike and their two children walked the railroad down to the Garden Hole, pulled off their shoes, waded the river, and walked onward to the Flat Woods to enjoy a home cooked picnic!

By the time we reached home, Lottie and I had walked about a mile, up and down hill and she was ready for another mile if we had the time, but time was running out...

I'm sure we all thank Lottie Lyall for sharing her memories of Aunt Cynthia Lyall Mullins, "who was loved by everyone that knew her," and I thank Lottie for sharing her own time and memories with me.

Remembering life on the old Eli Davis farm above Haysi...

Fayetta Davis Campbell is now a resident of Belpre, Ohio, but most of her "growing up" memories are rooted in Dickenson County. The daughter of Israel W. and Ella Roberts Davis, Fayetta was orphaned at an early age and she and her brother, James, lived with different sets of relatives until they came to live permanently with their Uncle Eli and Aunt Elizabeth (Lizzie) Davis on Big Ridge. Fayetta recalls, "We were staying at the home of our Uncle Andy and Aunt Ida Davis when father was killed in an automobile accident near Jenkins, Kentucky. In the meanwhile, he had written to Uncle Eli and Aunt Lizzie to ask them to take his children and raise them." Mail was slow in those days and his letter did not reach the Davis couple until after his funeral. Fayetta continues, "When Uncle Eli and Aunt Lizzie received the letter, Aunt Lizzie and her daughter, Ellen Davis Owens, went to Draftin, Kentucky to get James and me. Aunt Ida told me that Aunt Lizzie was my new mama, so from then on I called her Mom Davis, but Uncle Eli was always "Uncle Eli." From that time on, our home was with Mom Davis and Uncle Eli until we were grown."

Fayetta has good memories of her father... "He was a veterinarian and a farm boss over 200 horses and mules in the coal mines of Jenkins, Kentucky. My folks tell me that when daddy was alive, nothing was too good for his "little girl." He made sure that I got black patent leather Roman sandals instead of white ones because he knew I loved the black ones. He told the ladies I stayed with to buy pretty dresses for me because I hated overalls or pants back then. I am told that he had one of the most lovable personalities that you could know, and that my brother, James, was just like him.

My Uncle Eli and Aunt Lizzie (Mom) had a big six-room house

Fayetta Davis Campbell and husband, Grey, in their square-dancing clothes.

out on the ridge, so there was plenty of room for us, and that became our home, and they became our parents. As I recall, Uncle Eli owned about 75 acres of farmland. We raised nearly everything we ate, buying only staple stuff from the store. He and his daughter, Ellen, owned a store in Haysi at the end of the lower bridge. It was an expensive hand-hewn stone building. Some of the stone masons stayed with us while they were working, and Mom and I had to cook

for them and pack their lunches. Friday after school, I had to start house cleaning. I started upstairs and sometimes got carried away looking at pictures or reading a book. Mom would call up to me, "Are you asleep or something?" That would start me moving again. It took all day Saturday to clean downstairs,

See ECHOES, Page 4

★ Echoes

Continued from Page 2

but after I finished and the other chores were done, James and I would get dressed and head for town.

From the time I was big enough to reach the stove, I had to get up very early and cook a complete breakfast. I cooked on a coal and wood stove, so I had to build a fire, make biscuits from scratch, fry meat, apples, and eggs. Also, I made gravy every morning. Uncle Eli had to have a big breakfast to start the day off right.

In the summer time, I loved to work in the garden. Well, I *had* to work in the garden. Sometimes, Mom's grandchildren, Earl, Kermit, and Junior would come in to help, and I can remember they would do my hoeing for me, so I could go in the house and make applebutter pies. They ate them faster than I could make them. When I worked in the garden, Mom could always tell my row because it would be clean. The row James hoed just looked "sick." James and I had to dig potatoes and carry them upstairs in a bushel basket, which was really more than we could handle. Trying to get them up those stairs, step by step, was very hard for two little kids. One of us would push and the other pull, and sometimes we would get so tickled that we would grow weak from laughter. James and I would have to roam all over the farm looking for the cows. While I was looking, I would sing every song I knew at the top of my voice. I got pretty good at yodeling. I knew every Gene Autry and Roy Rogers song by heart and loved to sing them. When we found the cows, we had to milk them all and take care of all the other farm animals, except the horses. Uncle Eli did that.

In the wintertime, Mom would cook a big dinner, then after school, chores must be done: milking, feeding the animals, getting in the coal, wood, and water. Then we had supper which was always milk and bread. Mom would fix Uncle Eli a big bowl, herself and her mother a medium sized bowl, and James and I would fix ourselves a glass of either sweet or buttermilk with bread. Sometimes, we would eat a big onion too. We all ate around the fireplace, as that was the only heat in the house. Lots of time after supper, the four of us played rook together and had so much fun.

RUTH EDWARDS RAKES, a lovely lady to know . . .

Would you like to live in another world for a while... a world of rushing mountain streams, grapevine swings, and laurel thickets where children climbed, ran, hid, and built playhouses? If any of these things stir your memories or your desire to learn more, then you will want to take an hour or two and visit with Ruth Rakes of Clintwood. As she talks and shares her growing-up days with you, you can close your eyes and believe you're right there in the middle of it all.

Ruth was born Sept. 5, 1907 at Dog Branch, above Sandlick. She is the daughter of Charlie Bruce and Vadna Louise Sutherland Edwards. Because of the many people who are related to both sides of the family, we will give the names of the grandparents, brothers and sisters. Vadna was the daughter of Richard D. (Uncle Dick) and Unicy Powers Sutherland. Mr. and Mrs. Sutherland lived on Frying Pan Creek and were the parents of eleven children who were as follows: Elizabeth (m) Basil Sutherland, Vadna (m) Charlie B. Edwards, Garmon (m) Estelle Tiller, Clinton (m) Myrtle Hay, Stuart (m) Hattie Hamilton, Walker (m) Roma Powers, Eura (m) John Fuller, Verna (m) Garfield Bowman, Chester (unmarried), Dixie (m) Mae Anderson, Bonnie (m) Ray Wright. The Sutherlands also raised a granddaughter, Mollie. All these children are deceased now, with the exception of Verna who, at the age of 94, makes her home between two daughters, one in Ohio and the other in Florida. Her health is fair, Mrs. Rakes believes.

Charlie Bruce, the father of Mrs. Ruth Rakes, was the son of Noah C. and Margaret Counts Edwards. They lived in the Twin Branch section of Dickenson County. Other children in the Noah Edwards family were as follows: Polly Ann (m) Jim (Uncle Jim) Colley, Hamilton (m) Iowa Colley, Walker (m) Barbara Sutherland, Richard (m) Lillie Mae Mullins, Pearl (m)

RUTH RAKES of Clintwood, Va.

McKinley Deel. Pearl is the only one of this family still living, and she makes her home with a daughter in Abingdon. Richard died when he was about 30 with typhoid fever, and his wife died in 1920 with the flu. Many, many families lost several family members back in those days with sicknesses that today are easily controlled.

Ruth Rakes has been blessed with a wonderful memory, and there are many things that happened when she was as young as three or four years of age that stand out vividly in her mind. Her first memories of a home was when the family moved to Twin Branch (Lower Twin) and their house was the old Twin Branch log school house. She loved it there and loved the sur-

rounding area. Fork Ridge, where Uncle Jim and Aunt Polly lived, was a beautiful place, and Ruth would like very much to visit there again and recall the old days. Some of her best memories are of those times spent with her cousins. These were Uncle Jim, Uncle Hamilton, and Walker's children (until Walker moved away). There were other children to play with who were not cousins, but whom Ruth remembers with a great deal of fondness. The Hesque Hall family was made up of the parents and twelve children, and these two families of children were best of friends. Ruth remembers Elvina, Belva, Rosie, Flora, Tolby, Gilbert, Grady, and Dempsey, and she laughs as she recalls a funny little rhyme the boys made up to tease her. It went something like this, "Virginia Ruth with her head full of knowledge, got her education at the Twin Branch Cottage (college)!" She remembers that later on the boys died with measles and another one was drowned in the nearby river. She isn't sure where any of the family is now but would like to hear from them. All these children played together in ways that today's children can only read stories about. These were the days when our mountain streams ran full and clear, and Ruth and her friends spent many a summer day playing in the Lower Twin.

See ECHOES,
Page 2, B-Section

When the river was big, the brown chokes would come up the branch and the children could catch them. There were thousands of the white silica stone (that the surrounding mountains are famous for) in the branch, and Ruth collected these to play with and to border her flowers with. Together, the children dammed up a hole of water which they called their swimming pool and here they swam, splashed, and played many a hot summer day away. The laurel thickets seemed made to order for children, and in among the twisted old laurels, the children ran, hid, and scurried in and out like so many little rabbits. Playhouses, the likes of what could never be manufactured, were built and decorated with bits of everything from the forest and stream. Moss cushioned the chairs, rocks were the tables, and acorns made good cups and saucers. Sticks made good dolls for the "families," and sometimes paperdolls were cut from the mail order catalogues. These dolls were at the beck and call of the busy little housekeepers and had many adventures if they could have just talked to them. Perhaps, in their doll way, they most enjoyed swimming in the stream and lying on a big, flat rock to dry in the sun, and perhaps they were the most scared when a big gust of wind picked them up and carried them up and away, and excited little girls had to run and rescue them! What a pity it is that today most of our children are denied this kind of fun, excitement, and imagination.

Grapevine swings were a natural past-time for children in those days, and many there were that hung from the great old trees, before the lumbering companies cut them. Ruth recalls the wonderful times they had on these swings, but also recalls one incident that almost ended in tragedy. One of her older sisters had discovered an unusually good grapevine high on the hillside overlooking a deep hollow. She told Ruth to watch what a good swing she had, and grabbing hold of it, she swung far out and up in the air over the hollow. Ruth watched in horror, for she knew that if her sister's hands slipped or if the vine should break, that at such height, she would be killed. When the swing came back within reach, Ruth grabbed it and held on, refusing to let her sister swing again. Feeling upset at a younger sister telling her what to do, the older girl snatched the vine and swung it out into space, when suddenly, with a loud crack, the vine snapped and fell into the hollow and down on the rocks below. The two girls just stood and looked at each other, realizing what could have happened. Needless to say, the older sister was thankful to Ruth for having saved her life.

Ruth Rakes is a lovely person to be around. There is a soft quietness about her that is relaxing and soothing. Her mother, who died when Ruth was only twelve, had a great deal of influence on her, such influence in fact, that even though she has been dead 70 years, Ruth can say, "As long as breath warms my body, I will never forget my mother and the things she taught me." Such is the influence of a mother...

Continued next week.

RUTH'S FAMILY: C. B. Edwards, his wife, Vadna S. Edwards, Edna, Ruth and Emma. This picture was made about 1912.

Ruth Edwards Rakes
Part II
She is like a soft, summer day...

"Smothering, hot days were made bearable by the dark coolness of laurel thickets," recalls Ruth Rakes with a laugh, but one year when she was about five-years-old, there was a big change in her life and in how she was to spend her days.

The new school term was starting, and Ruth with her hair in neat braids, her feet in slippers, and a pretty dress made by her mother, was traveling down the road with the rest of the children to start "filling her head with knowledge" like the little Hall boys had so teasingly sung about. The first school Ruth attended was a log building on the old Dick Mullins farm. (Uncle Dick was married to Cynthia Stone at that time, Kedrick, their son, was just a young man. Later, Kedrick married one of the school teachers who came there by name of Tilda Fuller, and Tilda still lives at the old home). To reach the school, the children had to turn from the main path, which was a wagon road, and go down a long lane between two rail fences. They carried their lunches with them, such lunches as only country children can remember. Of course, there were buckets of milk and bread, but there was

**RUTH AND BERTIE RAKES
50TH WEDDING ANNIVERSARY**

also ears of boiled corn, ripe, red tomatoes (with a little salt wrapped up in paper), ham and biscuits, and jam and biscuits. "Mommy made everything we ate, and she made the best blackberry and raspberry jam you ever tasted," Ruth recalls. A little added luxury that Ruth sometimes had for lunch was oatmeal carried to school in little jars.

The school was typical for a mountain school of that day...logs outside and split-log benches inside. Sometime later, the benches were replaced with seats that had desks and each desk had an inkwell. Whether or not the inkwells were used for the intended purpose can be discussed by anyone who sat at one of them, but Ruth remembers one thing they were used for. The boys sitting behind the girls would take the long braids of hair worn by the girls and slyly slip the end of one of them under the inkwell and secure it there. When the girls would start to get up, they would be jerked back down to their seat, literally by "the hair of her head"! All this sounds just like a story-book which in reality it is, and one would think that Ruth must have had a wonderful first day at school. Not so. "It was awful," says Ruth. "I don't know what was wrong, but I cried and cried.

See ECHOES, Page 8

I made my 'will', giving my aunt, Pearl, my pencil and my sister, Edna, my book. That was all I had, and I wanted somebody to have them since I wasn't going back to school anymore!" "When I got home, I told my mother all about it, and she didn't say too much, but the next morning, she got me up and started getting me ready for school." "What are you doing," I asked her. "Getting you ready for school," she answered. "Why, you're going to love it there today. You'll learn a lot and make so many friends, and have such good times..." Ruth recalls that her mother laughed so much about the whole thing and made it all sound so good, that she didn't even think about not going back. She just went and was glad she did. Ruth remembers several of her teachers, but the one that stands out in her mind was her beloved "Miss Lillian" who, at that time, was Miss Lillian Artrip. Later, she married Terry Mullins of Clintwood. Ruth remembers Miss Lillian as being kind, gentle, and always pleasant. One day she called her to her desk, and Ruth recalls being scared and wondering if she was going to get punished for something. Instead, Miss Lillian put her arms around the little girl and told her that she loved her and that "she was a pure, little lady." Even now, Mrs. Rakes says that "there is a place in her heart for this teacher that nothing can take away."

After finishing elementary school, Ruth went to work at any honest job she could find. Most of these jobs consisted of staying with families who needed help with housework or children, and many times she was called on when new babies were born, and the mothers needed someone to stay with them for a while. However, one job out of the ordinary was during the time she carried the mail from Tivis to Lower Bartlick. The postmaster at Tivis was Cleve Willis, who, along with his wife, also owned a small country store. The postmaster at Bartlick was Ed Coyle who had a deep concern for this young girl carrying the mail in all kinds of weather...sometimes snow, sometimes ice, and at least one big hail storm. Regardless of weather, the mail "must go through" and Ruth carried it by horseback three days a week.

Ruth's father made a living for the family during those early years mainly by farming. On one particular day in March (about the 6th), he was clearing new ground, and Ruth's mother sent her older daughter, Edna, and her niece, Pearl, to the field with his cap and some water. Ruth, a little "tag-a-long" four-year-old, followed them. Mr. Edwards did not realize the children were coming and they did not know he was felling a tree, until it was almost too late. He tried to grab the three children out of danger, and succeeded with the older two, but Ruth, too little to understand danger, ran from him into the path of the falling tree. It caught her, knocking her to the ground, but as the good Lord would have it, the main weight of the tree fell across a fallen log, thus saving her life. She was hurt, but not seriously, but her father almost collapsed from fright before he reached home with her. Her mother, in bed with a two day old baby (Vada), was not told of the accident that night, and Ruth was kept out of her sight.

Mr. Edwards was a good farmer, "It seemed he could do anything he felt needed to be done," recalls Mrs. Rakes. Besides the regular garden and cornfields, there were fields of hay and oats that must be cut, cradled, and harvested by hand. Strawberries were quite a novelty at that time, and Mr. Edwards raised some of the first in the area. Mrs. Rakes thinks back to those days and speaks of how productive the land was. "It seemed that everything you planted came up and bore so well. The land was so productive...beans hung from the vines in big clusters or pods, and it didn't take anytime to pick a bushel of them. Also, it seemed that the seasons were different then...better for growing food stuff."

Most of us have heard about the terrible flu epidemic of the 1920's, but most of us were blessed to not know about it first hand. The Edwards family, like many others were not so fortunate. First, Grandmother Margaret (sister to Dr. Noah Counts) became very ill. They brought her down the hill from her house to stay with Charlie Bruce and Vadna. Two days later, Vadna took the flu and then the children. Grandmother Edwards who was a tender and loving person, and a mid-wife, got out of bed to try waiting on the rest of the family. "I can see her yet," recalls Ruth, "trying to cook for us." "She would have to sit down, bending her head into her hands...I remember she had her black bonnet on, and try to regain the strength to get back up and cook. She couldn't do it, and on Feb. 23rd, she died. She was in the same room with Mommy, and the relatives gathered around so Mommy wouldn't know what was happening. But Mommy, though she was only semi-conscious, seemed to know. Two days later, Mommy died. She had tried to prepare me, by telling me she didn't think she was going to live, but I couldn't accept it. I couldn't look ahead to life without her...it just wouldn't be right. Besides, there was a little nine-month-old baby. What would happen to him without Mommy?" But Mrs. Vadna Edwards died on February 25, 1920. "She was burning with fever," Ruth recalls, but just before she died, we heard her singing a hymn in a beautiful clear voice!

Bertie and Ruth (Edwards) Rakes
Part III

It is seldom that I write three articles about any one person, but Ruth Rakes is a local "historian" whose information should be preserved, as should all the information that our older generation shares, or is willing to share with us. Ruth loves to talk of past days, and that is exactly what we need to retain for future generations.

Ruth's growing-up days and teenage years were spent at Twin Branches and it was there that she met Bertie Rakes. She had known him quite a while, just as a casual acquaintance, for he was often in that area visiting with his brother, John Henry Rakes, and his sister, Rosa Ann Willis. Suddenly one day, she realized that he was pretty special in her thinking and about the same time, he asked her for a date. He told her later that he'd had "his eye" on her and so it was on June 19, 1924 (six months after their first date), they were married. They were married at the home of her father and then went to Bertie's home for their wedding dinner. Ruth remembers that she wore a long, pink dress, with a hat and white slippers on her wedding day, and Bertie wore a suit and tie with dress slippers. Preacher Steve McCowan performed their wedding ceremony.

Ruth and Bertie first lived in a little house on the "Jim Point" at Twin Branches. Their first furniture consisted of a bed that Mr. Rakes had bought, a solid oak dresser that Ruth had ordered for $8.98 and a step-stove loaned to them by Bertie's father until they could get one. He also made them a kitchen table and a cupboard for her dishes. Later,

BERTIE AND RUTH RAKES and five daughters. Left to right: Loraine, Anita, Gaynell, Mildred and Irene.

he made them a large dining room table. There is an interesting story about Ruth's dishes and silverware. Before she was married, she got up a "Lee dish order" and as premiums and bonus premiums, she purchased her own dishes, her silverware, cooking utensils, and some "extras" including a nice water bucket and dipper. Ruth and Bertie had their first daughter, Irene, while living in their first home. Doctor T.C. Sutherland traveled from Haysi to Twin Branches to deliver the baby, making the trip as he always did, by horseback. Shortly after Irene was born, the family moved to what was known as "the little log house in the hol-

low," living there only a short time until they moved into a nice home built by Bertie's brother, Sol. Here, their first little boy, Herbert, was born and died two months later. Happier days came when the second daughter, Mildred, was born, and then the third daughter, Gaynell. By this time, the Rakes' had bought property on Mullins Ridge and moved there to oversee the building of their new home. The fourth daughter, Anita, was born there, and then Loraine. The last child born to Ruth and Bertie was another little boy, who "was the darling of their heart"...his sisters dearly loved him, but he only lived six short months. There was a bad outbreak of scarlet fever, and it claimed the life of little James. Mrs. Rakes, in her gentle way said, "I already have quite a little family waiting for me in Heaven."

90

During these years, Bertie worked in the mines, as a carpenter for the county school system, and of course as a farmer. "We both did everything we could to make an honest living for our family," Mrs. Rakes recalls, "We both worked very hard. I did all our sewing and canning, and for five years, ran a small grocery store." Bertie died June 22, 1978, just after their fifty-fourth wedding anniversary.

Bertie Rakes had an interesting family history which can barely be mentioned here, because there is so much and it is so interesting that there needs to be more space devoted to it.

He was the son of F.C. "Lum" and Sarah Jane (Sally) Mullins Rakes. The parents of F.C. came into Dickenson County from Patrick County by covered wagon and many were the stories that Grandpa Lum could tell about that trip. He and his sister, Lucinda, played many games inside the wagon on rainy days and outside at other times. His father, Aaron, settled his family on Rakes' Ridge (hence the name of that particular re-

See ECHOES, Page 4

 **★ ECHOES** .. Continued from Page 2

gion) and made their home there. Aaron Rakes was a Primitive Baptist minister, preaching along with Preacher Bill Sutherland. Other children in the F.C. Rakes family besides Bertie (who married Ruth) were Lucinda, Rosa Ann (m) Cleve Willis, John Henry (m) Rebecca Willis, George Washington (engaged to be married, but died at age 21 with the flu), S.D. (Sol) (m) Vergie Sykes, Beldon Scott (m) Vergie Mullins, Alex Thomas (m) Lou Vernie Colley, Columbus Paris (unmarried), David Ross (m) Vonnie Branham, and Ernest Stewart (m) Genoa Colley. Nannie Jane died in infancy.

Ruth also came from a large family. Sisters and brothers were Edna (m) George Branham (after his death, she married Graden Stanley), Emma (m) Luther Stanley, Vada (m) Claude Younce, Richard (m) Roma Cochran, and a little boy, Willie Arvid, who died at 18 months. Ruth's father re-married Judy Viers, after his first wife died and their children were Trinkle (m) Dorothy Owens, Mary (m) Delmar Gentry, Maggie (m) Leon Coleman, Walker (m) Ollie Mae Coleman,

Letcher (m) Sid Coleman, Willard (m) Cathy Mullins, Avery (m) Claudette Coleman, Arbutus (m) Leon Belcher. Out of this big family, the following children are still living, Ruth, Emma, Richard, Mary, Maggie, Arbutus, Walker, Willard, and Avery. Aunt Judy is also still living, but in very ill health.

Ruth and Bertie were the parents of Irene (m) Vance Counts, Mildred (m) Bill Mullins, Gaynell (m) Avery McCoy, Anita (m) Bruce Adkins, and Loraine (m) Gerald Triplett. There are now 12 grandchildren and 14 great-grandchildren, and one more on the way!

In closing, Ruth would like to say, "If you have a good mother, give her roses while she lives...she won't know it when she's dead," and she also adds that "we should think on the fact

This is a story of a dream, of hard work, disappointment and success. A story of mingled joy and sorrow...

It is seldom that I write about anyone as young as Carvel and Connie Edwards in my *Mountain Echo* stories, but sometimes when a person or a couple has been blessed of the Lord to accomplish something that is very unusual, then their story should be shared. First, a little background...

Carvel grew up in the Prater Creek area of the county. He is the only child of Trinkle and Dorothy Owens Edwards and the grandson of Bertie and Bertha Owens, Charlie Bruce and Judy Viers Edwards. He attended Prater Elementary School and graduated from Haysi High School in 1964. After receiving his Industrial Certificate from VPI, he taught in Giles County for a year, then returned to Dickenson County to work as a teacher in the school system here. At the present time, he is the drafting instructor at the Dickenson County Vocational School and is the VICA advisor. Carvel is dedicated to his work, not only because of the opportunity to use and teach others his skills, but perhaps even more so because of "the chance of a lifetime" to influence young people and guide them in the right direction. To him, this is what teaching is all about.

Connie grew up in Bristol and Grundy, the daughter of James and Patsy (Lambert) Singleton. She attended elementary school in Bristol and graduated from Grundy High School. While attending Bristol Business College, she met Carvel and after a whirlwind courtship of two months, they were married. They both admit it was truly love at first sight, and after 22 years together, it's still love for each other...a deeper more mature love. Connie had majored in business administration, and

Carvel and Connie Edwards
"Connie's Creations"

her father presented her with a gift of a typewriter when she graduated from business college.

Shortly after the birth of her first baby, she sold the typewriter and bought a sewing machine, and this was the beginning of what was to become "Connie's Creations." At first, she did only the family sewing, anything and everything they needed in the way of clothing. Carvel recalls she made his suits as well as many other items. Gradually, she began sewing for other people, relatives, and friends. As word of her abilities as a seamstress grew, she developed a business in her home without really thinking of it as that. She was "just sewing." When arts and crafts began to be featured as a part of *Pioneer*

Days, Connie decided to display some of her work, and everyone who saw it was deeply impressed. Once again, word got around. Connie and Carvel credit Gary and Janet Ratliff at the Breaks Interstate Gift Shop as giving them their first opportunity to enter the business world. "It was that $500 order that gave me confidence," Connie recalls. People coming into the Park saw Connie's work in the gift shop, and soon she was contacted by buyers from Ohio, and her business took another step forward. Carvel and Connie decided this was the time to get serious about her work, and they began traveling to resort areas, gift shops, and trade marts. They rented space in the large trade mart in Nashville and from there, they went to Washington, D.C. In Pigeon Forge, while looking through a gift shop, Connie realized that her work was as good as, and in some cases, better than what she was looking at. So why not set her goals even higher? Getting the name of one of the big trade companies, Connie came home, packaged up a sample of her work, and mailed it to the company's main representative. That was a BIG break! Today, you can find "Connie's Creations" in forty states, in many of the highest quality gift shops and resort areas. She has a contract with a nationally known chain of stores, and she no longer goes to trade marts or buyer's conventions.

This end of the business is all handled by sales representatives of the company she works with. Last year, she sold in excess of $65,000, this year she has already passed the $35,000 mark in sales and can't keep up with the orders.

Has this all been easy, and is the Edwards family getting rich? The answer to both questions is "no." It has been an uphill climb all the way, physically, emotionally, and financially. "It takes a lot of money," Carvel will tell you, "money that we didn't personally have." You've got to have capital, money to buy equipment, materials, and money to make contacts and pay employees. Even when you begin to see some profit, you have to put it back into the business for at least three to five years. "It takes work," adds Connie, "hard work." "Many days I have stayed at work for 16 hours, non-stop."

Both Carvel and Connie have high praise for their employees. "They are the greatest, without them I would have no business...I could not succeed. I expect almost perfection, and that's the kind of work they turn out. We furnish high quality material to work with...they do the superior work. We try to make sure that every little detail has that personal touch, just as

if it were being made exclusively for the person who purchases it...We like to feel that our work represents the talents and abilities of our mountain people," Connie says.

In the midst of the ups and downs in the business world, a great sorrow came into the life of the Edwards family...a heart-rending sorrow. Their son, Craig, nearly sixteen was killed in an automobile accident in November 1986. "It seemed as if we couldn't go on...life became almost impossible. The easiest thing to do was to give up and drown in our grief. Perhaps God used the business to make us keep going, for there were deadlines to meet... orders to fill. That year and it's work seems like a blur, but somehow we kept going. Perhaps, too, we had the knowledge that we were continuing something that Craig had an intense interest in, and it helped to know that he would be so excited with every sale we made, every order we received, every little success."

Connie does not look on her

See ECHOES, Page 5

★ Echoes

Continued from Page 4

business just as a "money maker." "It's an opportunity for me to expand in the use of my talents...to learn more about people and places...to use skills that God has given me...but also it is an opportunity to see that others have a job that is more than just a job. They become creative, they take pride in their workmanship...they have an excitement and joy over a job well done and the knowledge that they are a part of it."

Carvel and Connie have two other sons, Chris and Carvey. Chris is married and working for Sandavic (soon to be in their engineering department). Carvey is a junior at Haysi High School, loves football, and plans to be a football coach. Both boys have been a real comfort to their

parents in their sorrow and an inspiration to them in their business.

Future plans? Connie will continue with her business...Carvel with his teaching and his plans to develop a recreational facility in the county. Both want to have time with their sons and other young people. Their advice to young people... "develop your life mentally, physically, and spiritually." Connie adds, "without God there is no success, no matter how successful you may seem to be. Without Him, it would be meaningless...empty."

Connie and Carvel pursued a dream. It took hard work, prayer, and determination. That's how "Connie's Creations" came about.

Anita Belcher's Mountain Echoes

Willie Burns Arrington Hay
A lady who is loved by all who know her...

Willie Arrington Hay is the daughter of Floyd and Lucretia (Aunt Crissie) Yates Arrington. Aunt Crissie was the daughter of Jeremiah and Polly Ann Deel Yates. To give me an example of the close family ties involved here, Willie remarked, "You know I'm a first cousin to Uncle Noah Yates." Floyd was the son of Brice Madison and Polly Stinson Arrington.

Willie was born on Nealy Ridge where the family owned a big farm. She was the seventh of twelve children, two of whom died at birth. The Arrington's had thought their seventh child would surely be a boy since the others were girls, and so they had the name "Willie Burns" picked out. When another little girl was born, she still got the name chosen for a boy, and over the years, Willie has learned to love her name "for it was the name my parents saw fit to give me" she says.

Floyd Arrington, Willie's father, worked as a logger, carpenter, and farmer. At least half of the 125-acre farm was tended and the produce sold for a cash income. Ten bushels of potatoes were planted each year, and patches of raspberries and strawberries cultivated, while fields of blackberries grew wild and were there "just for the pickin." Other farm and garden produce was raised for home and market. Mr. Arrington always kept four orchards in which he had every kind of fruit tree that would grow in this area. Apples, peaches, pears, and plums were among the greatest fruit bearers. Peach trees did not live as long as the others, and Mr. Arrington worked out a good rotation system so that he always had new trees coming on. "We had so many apples," Willie recalls, "That we didn't know what to do with them. We had a one-horse dray that we hauled our produce in to sell at Clinchco, but even then we had apples left over. People could come and pick them up for 25 or 50 cents a bushel.

An interesting note here is that Willie remembers the name of the company from which her father bought his fruit trees. "It was Lassiter... and Mr. Lassiter himself came around selling the trees. Daddy would always buy several, and Mr. Lassiter would usually give him five or six free ones." It was not a hard matter to sell the fruit or produce of any kind in those days, because the mines were starting up at Clinchco, the railroad was being built, and there was a great demand for foodstuff.

Willie remembers her growing-up days very well. With nine sisters and a family of cousins living close by, there was always something to do, although play time was scarce, indeed. "We all worked from the time we were very young," Willie states matter-of-factly. "We were in the corn field to carry water or thin corn before we were big enough to hoe it. Besides the field work, there was the yard and the garden, the cooking, sewing, and the farm animals to be looked after. Remember, we had no boys in the family. Mommy had to spend so much time sewing for us. Sometimes she would sew until midnight...later, sister, Polly, helped with this. Polly could sew anything. She could just look at a person and know what would suit them, and she could just sit down and make it. Had she lived in this day and time, she would have been a designer. We girls started young in the kitchen, too. I was making corn bread for the family by the time I was eight years old and doing other basic things in the line of cooking. Very often I would make corn bread for supper for our big family. We would eat a big country dinner at lunch time and then at supper, eat milk and bread. Milk and bread, as anybody raised in the country knows, was not only a staple item, it was a favorite dish...a meal within itself. It still is, and I wouldn't care to bet that anyone reading this up in Michigan or down in Florida or anywhere in between, if they ever lived in Southwest Virginia, will this very evening, if possible, stir up a pan of corn bread, enjoy one piece with butter, (while it's hot) and "crumble" another generous piece into a bowl, add the milk, and then sit down to enjoy about fifteen minutes of good eatin'! Nothing is better except maybe onions and lettuce cut up with hot bacon grease! When Willie and I got to talking about milk and bread, the conversation just naturally turned to cow-hunting, or to put it the way we said it, "huntin' the cows." There was a certain art to this, and I really feel sorry for children who never got to, and never will get to, hunt cows. First you had to figure out the direction the cow or cows

94

probably took. You had to know their favorite grazing place and where was the most likely place for that particular feed to be growing. Then you had to be careful and watch for snakes; because, since you had to work in the field till nearly dark, there wasn't much daylight to guide you, especially once you got in the woods. Fence rows were a bad place for snakes, and sometimes we would get briers in our feet, and sometimes we would "stump" the end of our big toe off on a rock or old stub of some kind, for of course we were barefoot. The real test came when it was milking time, and although a few of them would start ambling home about that time, most of them would find a thicket and stand there, stockstill, not moving because a movement would make their bell ring ever so slightly. They were especially bad about this at calving time. "Well," you might ask, "where was the fun...why was this so important?" Ask Willie and a lot of cow-hunters of past years. Or ask me. I'll tell you of the forest, the cool wind blowing through the trees, the flowers and ferns, of learning to watch for danger, of learning to put cool, damp earth on nettle stings, of the challenge to find the cow and then find my way home, of mountain streams with creek lettuce, and of the late evening bird songs and the early call of the whippoorwill.

Willie and I talked about all this and laughed and wished

See ECHOES, Page 3

★ Echoes ...... Continued from Page 2

that children of today had some of these opportunities.

The neighbor children that Willie played with (cousins) were Uncle Hop and Aunt Cal Counts' children. "We had to make our own playthings, (I had one doll in my life) and we had to

or chicken was the main meat. We hunted eggs at Easter that were dyed with dried leaves, nut hulls, or onion peelings. We were taught the Christian meaning of these holidays, because, though Mommy and Daddy were not members of a church at that time, they believed in the Bible and w ere careful to teach us. On the Fourth of July, we had a good time. From some store, we got firecrackers, and we had a big picnic dinner out in the yard, with mush melons and watermelons. We could get ice cream from Joel Mullins' store. He went to the Fremont train station and got it, and kept it packed in dry ice. Joel was married to sister, Carrie.

The Floyd Arringtons were one of our big mountain families. The only boy died at birth and one little girl. There were ten other children, all girls. Eva died at birth. Carrie (deceased) married Joel Mullins, then Tilden Counts. Polly (deceased) married Frank Mullins. Maxie (deceased) married Lawrence Counts. Stella (deceased) married Corbett Dell, then Earl Baker. Maude married Cecil Hay. Willie married Willard Hay. Beulah married Glen Harlow, then Dewey Lyall. Margaret married Henderson Mullins, then Edgar Hillman. Charles died at birth. Bonnie married O. J. Dickerson. Norma married Wendell Buchanan.

figure out our own games. Mostly we liked playing in the woods and among the trees. Holidays were special days for us back then. We celebrated them all. For Thanksgiving, Christmas, and Easter, there was always a big dinner. Turkey

Willie has strong, tender memories of her mother. "She was an upright, religious woman. I never heard a bad word pass her lips, not even a little one. She had so much sympathy for the down and out, the poor. She always told us that the Bible taught us to care for them. She didn't join the church until 1928, but she was always a godly woman, setting a wonderful example before her children. Her creed was, 'Never say a harsh word against anyone. If you can't say something good, don't say anything.'" That was the way Willie was raised, and that is the way she has tried to live.

We'll share more with you next week.

Anita Belcher's Mountain Echoes

Willie Arrington Hay

Her ready smile and cheerful disposition are two good reasons why people love her...

Willie was still going to high school when she met Willard Hay. Back in those days, some of the fine old families had closely supervised dances in their homes as a means of young people getting together, enjoying themselves, getting acquainted, and getting a break from the hard week's work. Of course, some of the dances weren't that closely supervised, but as Willie said, "Mother was a deeply religious woman, and Dad was always some kind of county officer, so everyone knew how to act." Willard was one of the fiddle players that weekend, and Willie recalls that it was "love at very first sight for both of us." She laughs as she recalls, "There was only one time when I decided to break up with Willard. We had a date, and he broke it to take his mother to church. I told my mother I was calling it quits with him, and she wanted to know why. When I told her, she said, "Well, you can quit him for something else if you want to, but not for that." There were no more problems, and after about a year of steady dating, the young couple was married on March 3, 1927. Their wedding ceremony was performed at Fuller Gap in the home of "Uncle" Johnny Fuller by John Edwards, who was probably a Justice of the Peace. Mr. Edwards had became ill and couldn't make the trip to Nealy Ridge, so the young couple walked and met him at Fuller Gap. Willie well remembers her wedding day and what both she and Willard wore. "My dress was navy blue georgette (flapper style), trimmed with blue satin. I wore black, patent high heels

Willie Arrington Hay

and real silk hose. That was the only kind of hose you could buy then, as the synthetic materials had not yet come on the market. I also wore the string of pearls that Willard bought me as a wedding gift. Willard wore a beautiful grey suit with a white shirt and tie and black slippers." After the wedding, there was an "infare," a time of visiting, music, and eating, in honor of the newly married couple, and then it was time to settle down to the serious business of housekeeping. Home for Willie and Willard was a small house he had built not far from his parents, (Ambrose and Elizabeth Counts Hay) on Backbone Ridge. Household goods were limited but comfortable. "We ordered two

beds from Speigel and we had a stove, table, two benches, three chairs, and a trunk," Willie recalls.

As we were talking about these things, a heavy rainstorm swept across the ridge...torrents of rain with wind. It made us both recall the bad "windstorms" of years ago. That was what we called them because we had no reason to be exposed to the term

See ECHOES, Page 3

★ Echoes •••••••Continued from Page 2

"hurricane." Now though, both Willie and I wondered if our old "windstorms" weren't the aftermath of a hurricane, and Willie recalled one particular instance... "It was a hot evening...Willard was doing up the outside work or had gone to work. The sky started clouding up, and I thought I had better run outside to the woodpile and pick up my apron full of chips to start a fire with before it rained. We had two small children then, and I left them in the house because it would only take a minute to get the chips. I had started back in the house when the storm struck. The wind blew me against the garden paling fence...I fought against it and finally made it almost to the house. I had to struggle all the way and was blown against the side of the house. I was worried about my babies and wondered if I was going to make it back to them. Later, we found that the wind had blown the roof from our barn."

Willard was a miner and walked from Backbone Ridge down to Mill Creek and then on to Steinman where he worked. For about the first 18 years, he worked as a brakeman on the motor and the last 18 or so years, he worked as a motorman. Both jobs were very hard...with one he did a lot of running to throw switches, in the other, he did a lot of bent-over sitting, and at age 55, he retired due to health problems.

Willie and Willard had a good life together. "We got along good...we loved each other, and we were a close family," Willie recalls. Willard played baseball, and I would fix a picnic dinner, and the children and I would go with him to the games he played. Willard loved his children so much. It was hard for him to see any fault in them, and he wanted the best he could get for them. When they married, he loved their husbands and wives the same way. Willard died the 19th of May, 1985, professing "a good hope in Christ." He and Willie had been married 57 years. They were the parents of five children: Theta (m) John Artrip, Janice (m) Bill Patton, Kerry (Fon) (m) Sula Fields, Mack (m) Lorena Bartley, Terry (m) Johnny Gortney. There are twelve grandchildren and six great-grandchildren.

Close by the Hay home is the Hay Cemetery, and it is so beautifully kept that I couldn't help noticing it. I asked Willie about one or two of the headstones I could see from the road, and she told me that they were probably the stones of Luther and Kerry Hay, brothers of Willard. Since we are nearing Memorial Day, I will share their story with you, as Willie told it to me. "It was during WWI and Kerry (just a young man) volunteered to go into service. He and Luther were always very close, so as soon as Luther turned 18, he volunteered so he could be with Kerry.

On the way to France, aboard ship, Luther became ill with the dreaded flu that was raging in those years, and he died before reaching France. His body was returned home about a month later. Kerry was badly wounded in battle, 'shot to pieces' Willie recalls, and the doctors said he would never live. He did survive, came home, married Carra Arrington, built the house that Oak Hay later lived in, (where Bonnie now lives) and he and Carra had two little daughters. One little girl died at birth, the other at age nine. Kerry died as a result of his wounds when he was about 24 years old. As we go to the cemeteries this Memorial Day, our hearts should once again be filled with gratitude and respect for the ones who gave their all for us, as well as for the others who lie sleeping there.

I asked Willie how she felt now, as she looked back over the years. She answered without hesitation, "I feel good...life has been and still is wonderful. The Lord has been so good to me...I just can't praise or worship him enough. I don't know why he has been so good to me...I don't deserve it, but He has been so good. He has let me see all my children grow up and have good lives...I've been blessed to see the grandchildren grow up and not have problems with drugs or drinking...now I'm getting to see the great-grandchildren grow up...God is so good to me." And what are you looking forward to, I asked? Again without hesitation, she answered, "To whatever the good Lord has in store for me."

And your advice to young people of today... "Well, my advice is not so much to young people as to their parents for the parents are the ones who are responsible. Young people should have responsibility... they should have to work. They have too much money that they don't work for...they are turned loose too much. Young people are usually what their parents make them..."

Willie Hay is a lovely person to have for a friend. She is ever ready to break into a smile or laughter, and when you combine that with her love for the Lord, it isn't any wonder that the years have been kind to her and she just seems to "get better instead of older."

Willie & Willard Hay with 10 of their 12 Grandchildren

Anita Belcher's Mountain Echoes

Will Richard Mullins and his wife, Pearl, live on Backbone Ridge, above Haysi. Will is the son of Clintwood and Nannie Dutton Mullins, whose people originally came from Kentucky. Clintwood Mullins was know as "Little Clint" and was the son of Will Mullins, who owned a sixty-five acre farm at the head of Big Lick on top of the Cumberland Mountains. This was near Raven Rock and was known by many people as the "Meadows" because of the spreading beauty of the farm. Here, Mr. and Mrs. Mullins raised a family of seven children, including Clint, the father of Will R., of Backbone Ridge. Grandpa Will Mullins did not get to see his children as grown-up men and women, because of his death when Clint was only twelve. Will R. recalls the story as he has been told. "There was a forest fire broke out in the mountain around where Grandpa Will's land and home was. He and other mountain men fought to control it, and Will breathed the smoke from the thick laurel and ivy thickets, where the fire was burning. He was overcome by the smoke but was diagnosed as having brain fever, as a result of the ivy fumes he had breathed in. After his death, Grandma couldn't take care of the large farm, so she sold it for $100 and traded that out in staple groceries at a small country store. She later married Charlie Reed, had three more children, and lived her last days at Clintwood."

Will and Pearl (Salyers) Mullins

Will R. (of Backbone) was born at Clintwood, then the family moved to Potter's Flat in Kentucky, later they moved to East Elkhorn. From there, they moved back into the Clintwood area "into the hollow above Bill Bise straight-a-way, where it seemed like we were continually clearing up another new ground," recalls Mr. Mullins, "for that was the way Dad made a living for his family. He didn't follow mining or timbering...farming was his way of living. All of us nine children pitched in and helped. We had to... that was the way of life back then."

The story that led me to visit with Mr. and Mrs. Mullins and write about them was one that Will told my husband, Clynard, one day when they were standing around the Whistle Stop just "yarning" together about this, that, and the other, and the topic of huckleberry picking came up. This was Will's interesting recollection. "When we lived at Potter's Flats, I would go huckleberry picking up on the Cumberlands. I didn't take a bucket or basket, but instead, made my own. I would climb a young poplar tree, and about seven or eight feet up from the ground, I would "ring" it, then slit the bark down the side, "ring" it again close to the bottom, then "hull" the bark right off the tree. Then I'd cut me a small hickory sapling, strip off the bark and "sew" up the side of the poplar piece of bark I'd cut with the hickory bark, then fasten up the end, put some leaves in the bottom, and I was ready to start picking up berries. When I'd finish, I'd put my big container over my shoulder and take off to Elkhorn where I sold the berries to the engineers and other men connected with the railroad."

Mr. Mullins can tell some pretty scarey snake stories, too. Once when he was huckleberry picking, he started to reach in a bush for a handful of berries, and just in time, he saw a huge golden rattlesnake stretched out across the bushes about midway up...not on the ground. He also remembers a certain place in the Cumberlands where the berries grew the biggest, but was known for its dens of rattlesnakes. "Why, you could walk close to that place and hear the singing....that was one place nobody went berry pickin'."

Right after Will and Pearl were married, about a year or so, Will had a painful experience of being bit by a rattler. He had been working in the hay field at his home on Backbone Ridge, it was mid-afternoon or a little later, and Pearl decided she could help for a while at whatever she was needed for. She worked for a while, but becoming tired (she was expecting their first child), she told Will that she was going to sit with her mother on the porch and visit with her while he finished up the work in the field. She walked down the path to her mother's, and after a bit, she noticed that the sky was growing black and threatening a storm. Glancing out at the field, she saw that there was a wagon load of hay that would be ruined by the rain. Calling to Will, who had busied himself at other chores, she called his attention to the dark clouds and the hay waiting to be hauled to the barn. Will hurried down the same path Pearl had walked down a short time before, and he felt something "snag" his ankle. It felt like a piece of sharp tin, and thinking something of that sort was lying by the path, he hurried on. He noticed the pain was pretty severe, and glancing down at his ankle, (he had his work breeches rolled to the knees and was barefooted) he saw the blood and decided he had better see what had caused the "cut." Going back down the path, he discovered the big, black rattler lying by the path.

He called to a neighbor. They saddled up their horses and started to the doctor. On the way, they met his father-in-law, Rudolph Salyers, driving one of the few trucks there was in the area at that time, and Mr. Salyers took him on to the doctor. "The doctor didn't know much to do...he put iodine on the bite and bandaged it up. When I got home, I took my knife and split the bandage off, for my leg was swelling so bad it was coming out over the top of the bandage." Will suffered a lot from the bite, but it also knocked him out of doing his farm work and working his regular job which was carrying the mail from Martha Gap Post Office to the Delano Flag Station, by horseback. For nine weeks, he went on crutches, and when he went back to work, he still had to use them. His mother-in-law would hold them for him while he mounted his horse, then reach them up to him.

Will and Pearl spoke of the necessity of his work. "Fourteen dollars a month may not sound like much, but it was a whole lot back then and would buy more than fourteen dollars will buy today."

Pearl and I talked a long time, but most of our discussion was about her mother, who was so sick during her last years, and I couldn't help but think as we talked of the difference in how aged and sick parents are cared for and with what tender devotion Mrs. Salyers was given by both Pearl and Will.

Pearl also called back an almost forgotten memory for me when she spoke of knowing that "Dog Days were here because the dog day bushes were in bloom." When I was small, these beautiful bushes were a basic shrub at our house for they didn't require any care, and could survive the worst winters. We had the pale lavender, the white, and the deep rose, and during summer months, they were a source of joy to me not only because of their beauty, but because of the many hummingbirds that continually flitted from one bloom to the next. As I grew older, people began referring to these bushes by their proper name "Rose of Sharon," and the old name had just about slipped my memory, as well as that period of time we refer to as "Dog Days." Thanks to Pearl for not only recalling those two memories, but countless other ones surrounding those wonderful summer days when many of us were children.

Next week, we'll share other stories from Will and Pearl... stories of horseback riding, (both of them were experts), stories of blacksmithing, ginsenging, and lots of other recollections of bygone days. I know each of you will be looking forward to reading these, just as I'm looking forward to another visit with these two fine people.

Will and Pearl Salyers Mullins

August 1, 1990

Two good people you should get to know...

Pearl Salyers Mullins is a mountain lady...quite, gentle, and thoughtful. She never pushes herself to the front, but is always helpful, generous, and sharing, and always has a sweet smile. She is the daughter of Rodolph and Mazie Lyall Salyers and was born and raised in this area. Rodolph came from Kentucky; and Mazie from Road Branch, the daughter of John and Alice Lyall. Pearl is one of five children: Hester, who died about age, two; Trimble, who died in 1980; Trinkle, who lives in Charleston, SC; and Donna, who now lives at Road Branch, having retired from Dan River Mills in Danville. Pearl recollects her growing-up days, and many of her thoughts center around her parents: "Mommy and Daddy first lived in Davenport (He carried the mail from Haysi to Davenport by horseback for about four years. That must have been in the early 30's. Anyway, it was when people said times were so hard...). Then we moved to Haysi, back in behind the old Stamp Fuller house (where the funeral home is now) and daddy was town police in Haysi for several years. He also had a sawmill in the bottom, just above the old Mary Woods place, but his main work was logging. Daddy always picked the hardest work and never missed a day...it didn't matter what the weather was, he worked just the same in rain, snow or heat. At first, he did his logging with horses, but later he bought a truck and hired a driver, for over all the years he worked, he never learned to drive. Eventually, daddy and mommy bought this farm on Backbone Ridge, and here they farmed, raising such awful big fields of various crops. They had about everything a family needed to live, raising their own cattle, meat and horses."

Pearl herself was an expert horseback rider. Mr. Mullins will tell you that "no horse ever bluffed Pearl." Pearl recalls "Daddy had a beautiful horse, one of the best I've ever seen, and I would ride him, saddled or bareback and take some of the sharp curves at such speeds that I'd think I wasn't going to stay on, but I did." Will was also a horseback rider...the kind you see on TV. Get him to tell you some of his stories, such as leaping into the saddle from behind the horse or the one he had so much pleasure riding and never taking down the drawbars. "We just went over the top of them," laughs Will. Pearl loves to recall how she would ride her horse down a shortcut trail that came out just about where the Texaco station is now, leading another horse for Will to ride back from work. "The road was steep, but it was much shorter for Will to come home in the evening. Our big, German Shepherd dog would follow me and lie and wait for Will to come."

Will left Dickenson County in 1953 and went to Maryland where he took a job at the Aberdeen Proving Grounds as a boiler fireman. This is a government plant where tanks, guns and other army supplies are tested. It is also the home of "Little David," one of the largest guns in the country. When they fire it, " says Will, "all the residents in the area are asked to raise their windows and still some are

Will and Pearl Mullins just "takin' it easy."

broken. That gun is so large, I can stoop over and crawl thru the muzzle." Here also one can see one of the biggest German guns ever captured. Pearl and the children wen to Maryland in 1958, the childre

Continued from Page 7

have to fix up his shops on Backbone Ridge and enjoy the mountains from afar! I will always remember one of the first things Will said to me when we first started talking... I loved what he said, and I loved the way he said it, "Miss Belcher, I've waded every river and clumb every mountain in the Cumberlands!" It does me good to hear some of our old words still used.

Pearl and Will are Christian people and will tell you that their Christianity means everything to them. Both of them wish that people everywhere were in church and especially that young people were being taught in church. It was a joy to share their Christian beliefs with them...in fact the whole time I spent with them was a joy.

The last of the Mullins-Puckett stir-offs?

We hope not, for this is a tradition as old as the first mountain settlement...

There is a feeling among the Mullins-Puckett families that the stir-off beginning on Monday of this past week and ending with the grand finale on Saturday may be the last, but many of us who were onlookers and last-minute participants hope not. And we each have our own reasons, but there is a whole lot more that goes into a stiff-off than the skimming of the cane juice as it boils in the tub and the filling of the jars when the process is completed. That Sunday morning breakfast that some of us enjoyed with fresh molasses poured over hot buttermilk biscuits was the result of much hard labor, sweat, and love. Let's talk about it for a few minutes, keeping in mind that the same process goes on anywhere that old-time molasses are made (I just happened to get in on the one held by the Mullins-Puckett families).

Now for a lesson in cane raising and molasses making - you experts check me out and see if I've passed the test. First, the location of the cane patch - just any place won't do. The right soil combination along with good drainage is a must. Prayers go up for the ideal amount of rain and sunshine, and if those prayers are answered, another one goes up at harvest time that there will be no windstorms to lay the cane flat or twist it up. After the location of the field is decided upon, then comes the plowing, now done with a tiller or tractor, and when the ground is ready, the planting is done. Each hill of cane has approximately eight grains of seed planted in it, or as Mr. Hie Mullins says, "a pinch between the forefinger and thumb, which will be about eight seeds." Cane hills are planted sixteen inches apart to allow for tilling. The first hoeing is done when the young cane is very small, and

since it appears as small blades of grass, the work is quite tedious. After the first cultivation, the crop must be fertilized with 5-10-10, and then after three weeks, hoed again. After a summer's growth, heads begin to appear on the cane along with green fodder. At first, they are green, gradually turning to a bronze-red. When heads reach a certain shade of red, the cane is ripe and ready for stripping. Stripping cane is very close the same as "foddering" and the old-timers bundled up their cane fodder for roughage for livestock. Next the heads are cut off with the use of a sharp knife and are allowed to fall on the ground. Once again, the old-timers never wasting anything, gathered up the heads and used them to supplement their chicken feed during the winter. The best of the cane seed was, and still is, saved for next year's crop, and Mr. Hie Mullins says, "you've got to be mighty careful about cane seed for it is easy to mold. I dry mine in a screened box so that the air can circulate through it." After the removal of the cane heads, the stalks now stand bare, awaiting the final step. Workers with sharp, short-handled hoes go through the rows, cutting it off close to the ground and carrying it to the cane mill. Here, a whole new process begins as cane stalks are

fed to the cane press and the juice runs into a big, screened-over tub. When the tub is full, the juice is emptied into large containers, allowed to set overnight, and the next morning, poured into the big molasses pan to boil. Both the cane press and the molasses pan are the work of the Mullins-Puckett family and

comprise a whole story within themselves, and everyone should know the art and the genius that went into their making. I was impressed with it all, but when I realized that Hie had to go to a certain place to get a certain kind of clay to chink the furnace with, I was doubly impressed. Not only so, but I was impressed again, when I realized that his seemingly easy-going Mullins man, who never seems to let anything ruffle him, and who doesn't even seem to be concerned with all that's going on, suddenly with hawk-eyed alertness seemed to almost jump from his chair with the words, "that won't do a-tall. I can see some fire under the sides of the tub," and he immediately begins to fill in the open spots. Nothing escapes his attention that has to do with his work.

From the time juice is poured into the tub until it is taken off, it must be skimmed, then stirred. Skimming takes off the green froth and stirring keeps it from scorching...however, do not scrape the bottom of the pan as your stir, or the molasses will stick (some kind person had to tell me that)! It's a beautiful sight to see those golden molasses boiling in the pan, and on a crisp, Fall day, the heat from the glowing embers and the fragrance of the burning wood...the wood smoke sifting between workers and filling the air create an atmosphere and memories that linger long after most material things are gone.

After about six hours of boiling, the finished product is about ready for sampling. The skimmers are laid aside, and four strong men pick up two steel bars, long enough to clear the furnace, put them through two steel loops on each side of the pan, and lift the boiling mass off of the furnace onto two poles lying on the ground. Here the foam is dipped off into cups held by eager folks who have been waiting for just this minute.

Some have pieces of cane stalk to dip out their foam with, others turn it up and slowly sip, while still others have poured it over popcorn and are enjoying a taste that can't be bought. Once more the molasses are strained (for the fourth time) and poured into hot jars and sealed. Now we can

See ECHOES, Page 10

 # ★ ECHOES Continued from Page 7

buy a quart for $5.

Now, there you have the story of the molasses stir-off from the plowing of the ground to the sealing of the jar and the Sunday morning breakfast of hot buttermilk biscuits and molasses. What did I leave out? Oh, I didn't tell you how a crowd of friends gathered, probably close to one hundred... I didn't mention Kenny Mullins' story of the stir-off where the dog chased the cat, which jumped in the molasses pan and back out again, and when people were sympathizing with the farmer for that tub of molasses being ruined, he said, "it's alright, I only lose what was on the cat!" I cannot remember all the other stories that were told around the furnace while we skimmed and stirred...I cannot even remember, though I asked him twice, how many yellow-jackets Carl Puckett said were allowed to the gallon of molasses! I cannot describe the feeling that all of us felt when we listened to the music of guitars, banjos, french harp and accordion, and sometimes joined in with voices singing the old familiar songs. It was good to see young people coming and bringing their babies, young people "courtin'" and sharing the same cane stalk. People of all ages were there from many walks of life.

People who came brought a favorite old-time dish to share. Soon the tables were loaded, and we needed more tables. I cannot begin to name the food, but anything you might have found on your great-granny's table was probably there. I can tell you of one highlight, among others, that was both educational and tasty. Grandson, Phillip, went to the cornfield and brought out a big bag of semi-hard corn. Hie brought out his handmade corn gritter and several of us got to try our hand at gritting corn. When there was enough meal, Ella Fay and I went to her house and made a big iron skillet of gritted cornbread. Talk about something good! We took it back down to the stir-off along with some butter, and that stuff was gone like the cat that jumped in the molasses.

Well, what more can I say that would help persuade all of you who read this to believe in the necessity of carrying on one of the oldest mountain traditions - the molasses stir-off? Can I tell you of the joy of seeing children and young people see how food is produced instead of just going to the store to buy it? Can I tell you how wonderful it is to see them talking to and sharing with the older people, watching them, helping them, learning from them? Do we realize that times like these are not just fun times, but fun times plus education in many ways? Can I tell you how much it means to young adults to watch and participate in something that is their heritage, and what a joy it is to see the older folks renewing old friendships and re-living old memories?

No, let's not let this be the last stir-off for the Mullins-Puckett family, but let's join in to help out with the work so that Hie can just boss and Phillip won't be worked to death! No kidding! If you know anyone who is trying hard to maintain our old customs, give them a helping hand where its really needed. And when it comes to the stir-off (any families' stir-off), let's do what we can to keep them going for "they are a tradition as old as our first mountain settlement."

James Sifers South
Part I

Jimmy South shares some history of the South-Sifers-Belcher family with us, plus some interesting stories.

James Sifers South, "Jimmy" as all his friends know him, was born November 11, 1919, in the living quarters over his father's store "right in the middle of Haysi." His father was Zack South, and Jimmy is sharing some of the South-Sifers history with us before we get underway with his own story. Mr. Zack South was an interesting person and very much a part of the history of Haysi. He came here from Sparta. N.C., probably riding horseback, for he was a lover of horses and always kept one or more. Zack's father was John South of Sparta, and little is known of him except that he was a very "colorful" character and is buried in Lexington, Ky. His mother was Nancy Osborne South, who came into this area with the rest of her children, lived here (in or near Dickenson County) for a while before moving to West Va., where she died and is buried. There were eight children in the South family, including Zack, four boys and four girls. Three of the boys found work in the mines around Coeburn, and two of them, Preston and John, (who was a Baptist minister) were killed while mining. Tom went to Pittsburg, then to Florida, finally coming back to Virginia where he lived at Keen Mtn. until his death. The girls married and settled in different sections of the country. Zack went to work in what was probably a company store owned by a man by the name of Alderson. It was here that he met Belvia Lockwood Sifers who was staying with her Aunt Winnie at Coeburn. Winnie was probably running a boarding house or store or some such business in that area for she was quite a business woman for that day and

time. In these days, she would probably head up some corporation for she had a business head about her, and among other things, she was a very stylish dresser. Many folks can still remember seeing her dressed in silky dresses, heels, a black lace shawl and black gloves. She was probably the last person in the county to own a black servant girl. After this girl died, Winnie kept a hired woman until Winnie herself died. It was "Miss Winnie" that owned the hotel in

James Sifers (Jimmy) South

Haysi which was quite a prestigious affair for a small western-type town with board sidewalks and a single street of hard packed clay, mud or dust, depending on the weather. Belvia Lockwood Sifers (Jim's mother) was the daughter of James Colley Sifers and Alice Belcher Sifers. Alice was the daughter of William Lewis Belcher and Mary Epling Belcher. William Lewis was from Kentucky and Mary from the Breaks. They had several children, one being Aunt Mellie Mullins of Georges Fork, who lived to be about a hundred years of age. One son was Riley, who was the father of John and Marion of Haysi, as well as several other children. Jim South can well remember his grandmother, Alice, but he can also dimly remember his great-grandparents, William Lewis and Mary. On the Sifers side of the family, Jim loves the memories he has of his grandfather,

See ECHOES
Page 2, B-Section

Jim: "Grandpa was a wonderful man...I was never afraid when I was with him... I always felt secure. He was a big man, well-made, and had such strong hands, but it wasn't just his size. It was a certain "something" that gave one a sense of security. He was a calm, pleasant man, highly respected and at ease in town or on the farm. He had wonderful stories to tell me such as remembering the sky being dark with carrier pigeons and hunting coons with the light of a pine torch. Once he told me of having to wade into the river at Haysi to rescue his dog from the "biggest coon he ever saw"...he went into the river barefoot or with homemade moccasins on. Jim's grandpa, James Colley Sifers, was the son of Josephine Colley Sifers and Jonathan Sifers. Josephine was the daughter of James (Jim) and Emma Ferrel Colley. James was the oldest son of Richard (Fightin' Dick) and Crissie Counts Colley. James was also the young man who was shot and left for dead by John Harden, but thankfully the Lord saw fit for him to live and be the forefather of many, many outstanding citizens. Jim can also remember his great-grandmother, Josephine Sifers, who was a tall lady who I best remember seeing when she came to visit Aunt Winnie. He also remembers his Aunt Martha Sifers Puckett (married to Johnny Puckett) who was also tall, slightly stooped, white haired and generally wore a white apron. She was a serious minded person, but was humorous enough to own a parrot that sat on his stand in the corner of the room calling, "Polly wants a cracker!" (What little boy wouldn't have noticed that and remembered it all his life?) Aunt Nan Sifers Belcher is well remembered by both, Jim and his wife, Rita. "Aunt Nan was an excellent cook, (no doubt she inherited that from her father, Lewis, who loved to cook) and she was also filled with a great sense of humor. Nobody loved a good joke better than Aunt Nan." Nan was married to Riley Belcher. These relatives are very important to Jim because many of his boyhood days were spent with these aunts, uncles, and their children. "John Belcher's home was a second home to me," Jim recalls, "and I loved to go to my Uncle Marion's farm up on the mountain. I guess that's where I got interested in raising chickens."

Zack and Belvia South lived for awhile at Coeburn or Bondtown, straight across from the old Kilgore Grocery. From there, they moved to Dwale, (Nichols Gap) to a farm. They stayed there for awhile, and then moved to Haysi where Zack went into the store business with living apartments over the store. It was here that Jimmy (James Sifers South) was born and named for his grandfather, James Sifers, who in turn had been named for his Grandfather Colley. Jim remembers Haysi and the surrounding area well back in those days, for this is where he grew up and attended school until his junior year of high school. He remembers the layout of the town and was quite familiar with all the buildings and their proprietors. In the middle of town, the buildings were positioned somewhat like this: first the Haysi Bank, (that was its first name) then the hotel, barber shop, feed store, and Zack's general store, which later also housed a mining office. Jim recalls being very much at home as he came and went through the back door of his Aunt Winnie's hotel, and he also recalls the bullet hole in the wall of the barber shop, the result of a shoot-out where one man was killed and another one escaped by "the skin of his teeth." (These gunfights were not uncommon in the streets of Haysi, for it was a time when many considered their gun to be the law and the way to settle spur-of-the-moment disagreements or long standing disputes.) Jim remembers, too, the street running through the cen-

JIM SOUTH'S DAD, Zack South, with his horse and buggy.

ter of town. He played marbles there or in the vacant lots nearby. Hoop-rolling was a big thing in those days. To see how long you could keep a metal hoop rolling in the direction you were guiding it or to bring it back on course without losing control of it was a great challenge. Jim loved to take his through the mudholes in the street and come through the winner.

NAN (NANCY) OSBORNE SOUTH — Jim's grandmother on the South side of the family.

JAMES COLLEY SIFERS "UNCLE JIM" — Jim South's grandfather on his mother's side of the family.

A tragedy that he prefers not to talk about was the day a little friend, a Sloane boy, rolling his hoop fell under the wheels of a big lumber truck on the old R. H. Fuller bridge and was killed.

Swimming was a big pastime. The rivers and creeks were clean in those days, so clean that Jim's dad had an ice house where he did a profitable business throughout the summer. Big blocks of ice were cut or sawed from the river, packed in straw, and sold during the hot days of the coming season. Jim and his friends swam anywhere they desired, but a favorite place was a big hole of water behind Doc Tiv Sutherland's house on Prater Creek. This was "the swimming hole," and many a summer day was spent there enjoying the de-

See ECHOES
Page 3, B-Section

lights that the best modern swimming pools could not afford. Imagine if you can...here's a hole of water, fed by numerous mountain streams, converging in Prater Creek and caught in a natural basin. On the one side is the sandy, rocky shore, and on the other a steep shoreline where moss-covered cliffs shed their continuing supply of cold, trickling water. The hole is protected by a forest of pine, beech, oak, and maple, some whose limbs stretch far out over the creek. Somebody finds a good place to dive or jump from and others find rocks that are hiding places for water snakes or "crawdads." Everyone has his favorite spot on the bank to sit and sun awhile for though the hole is a mixture of sunlight and shadows, the water is cold and there's a need to come out and rest a bit and bask in the sun. Even the warm sand added to the day's delight, for there's many interesting things to be found on a sand bank. Of course, these were the days when bathing trunks were unheard of and an unnecessary item of clothing, so Jim and his friends did what was natural...they shucked their clothes, dropped them wherever they fell, and jumped in! It was on such a day that Jim's mother heard about the swimming hole, and fearing for her son's safety, walked up the road to the place where the boys were swimming, and then and there, she commanded Jimmy to "get out." He didn't come out, where upon Mrs. South began pelting the swimming hole with small rocks! At that, little boys came out in a hurry, including Jim. Mrs. South had broken her a switch, and before Jim could get his clothes on, she had switched him good! Jim loves to tell this and counts the memory dear, one for sure that he will never forget.

Jimmy South's mother was one of the people that had great influence on his life. Her loving, sharing attitude, along with her firm discipline, did much to shape his future. In fact, it was from here that he inherited his love of fishing and from her he learned many of the basics of the port. Next week, Jim has other stories to share with us...how he traded Clynard Belcher (his cousin) out of a fish, how he earned spare money, how his folks faced the depression years, and of course, a few fish tales. Stay tuned in!

Anita Belcher's
Mountain Echoes

JAMES SIFERS SOUTH
Part II

Jim shares some more stories and some Haysi history...

It is impossible to record seventy years of life in two or three short articles, especially a life that has been, and still is, as full as Jimmy South's. Growing up in Haysi offered a rare opportunity that perhaps Jimmy has realized more in later years than he did at the time. Haysi was a pioneer town, and Jim's folks were a part if its birth and development. I would like to share with you a couple of paragraphs from E. J. Sutherland's *Pioneer Recollections*. These are quotes from James Colley Sifers, (Jim's grandfather) as he was interviewed by Mr. Sutherland some several years ago. "The name Haysi originated by Charles M. Hayter. About 1904 or 1906, he and my brother-in-law, Otis L. Sifers, were running a store as partners at my father's old homeplace. They were trying to get a post office established there, and the Post Office Department had called upon them for a name for the new post office. After thinking it over, Hayter suggested that the first syllables of each partner's name be used, making "Hay" and "Si" to become "Haysi." It was agreed upon, and C. L. Sifers became the first postmaster. I have heard another version to the effect that someone called to a man named "Si" with these words, "Hey, Si," and the name came from that expression. That story is purely imaginary."

Further on in his account, Mr. Sifers gives more information pertaining to the town and those involved in its growth. "About 1914, Albert Ellis put a stock of goods in the old Paris Charles store, but he sold out in about six months to Burb Mullins who built a substantial store house. This building is still used as a store house by Zack South, and is the oldest now standing in Haysi...the first owner of the land around Haysi was Frank or (Andrew) Habern who had made a survey for 5000 acres. When he died, his son-in-law, Bill Jessee, was appointed administrator of his estate, and as such, sold this tract to James Colley, my grandfather. My mother inherited from him all the land around Haysi. Her sister, Martha Powers, inherited land on Prater where Mart Owens later lived. My mother gave me the land on the east side of the Russell Fork and McClure Rivers, which includes most of Haysi..." (Let me say here that some of the richest reading about early settlers in Dickenson County can be found in *Pioneer Recollections* which can be purchased from Mrs. Hetty Sutherland of Clintwood).

So it was in this setting that Jimmy South was born and grew up in a mixture of fun and responsibility. Some of the responsibility is seen in the fact that it was his job to run down the stairs every morning quite early to get the first class mail to Toy Davis, the mail carrier. (Zack now had the post office). This mail had to be delivered to the train at an exact time and that, along with the fact that passengers came twice each day from Tom Bottom, Bartlick, Elkhorn, and points beyond caused somewhat of a flurry for those who cared for their needs at the post office, general store, hotel, and other business places, for the train schedules had to be met. There were other responsibilities...mules, cows, hogs, and chickens to care for the feed. The fun side of this was that Jim liked it, especially working with the chickens and many times there was his Grandfather Sifers to work and share with. There was a big garden to tend, and Jim did his part. The fun side was that his mother worked with him, and when the work was finished, the two of them went fishing right beside the garden. This was located where the Ireland Baker bridge now is and the large sycamore tree still stands where Jim and his mother sat under while they fished.

Something else Jim likes to remember about those days are the two wonderful ladies (at the time, young women) who worked for his mother. One was Eura Edwards, daughter of Uncle Dave Edwards, and the other

111

was Vivian Edwards, daughter of Hamilton Edwards. These ladies were so good to Jimmy that he remembers them almost as "second mothers." Vivian later married S. D. "Sim" Powers who became one of Jim's big fishing buddies.

Jim always felt that he should make his own way in life as much as possible. He raised his own chickens partly because he wanted to make his own spending money, but also because he was interested in that type of work. Another way to earn his own money was by digging mayapple root and selling it and picking berries for sale. Many times, Jimmy walked from Haysi to Grassy (Breaks) to well-known blackberry patches, and this was a long, hot walk for a youngster, especially a youngster who was getting hungry. "I will never forget Uncle Noad Owens and his wife, how they welcomed me in and fed me, a hot, tired little boy. That was some of the best food I ever ate, and they were the kindest old people," Jim recalls.

It's a well-known fact that every country boy needs a dog, and every dog needs a master.

Jimmy became the owner of his favorite dog in an unusual manner. Here's the story... "When a Holyfield family came to Haysi, they brought along their German Shepherd dog, Bill. Mr. Holyfield was the resident engineer for the state highway department and didn't have a lot of time to spend with a dog, so Bill took up with Jimmy. Everywhere Jimmy went, Bill went along. The two felt like they belonged to each other and when the South family moved to the farm at Dwale, Bill went along too. Mr. Holyfield gave him to Jim and Grandfather Sifers consented, though at first

See ECHOES
Page 2, B-Section

★ ECHOES ●●●●●●●●●●●●●●

doubtfully. Bill finally proved his worth by being a real snake-killer, and that brings us to our next story!

When Jim was about thirteen, he and his friend, Corbett Hamilton, decided to have a "fair." Jim doesn't recall all the details, but he well remembers the featured attractions. He caught a big rat by the tail that was escaping from the feed store to safety underneath the boardwalk and caged him for display, and then he and old Bill went snake hunting. Together they caught a substantial number and displayed them in a barrel. However, the most exciting event, and one worth the nickel admission fee, was when Jim held up his arm, and carefully guided a water snake into and down his shirt sleeve, on down into his breeches leg, finally to make its exit under Jim's foot under the watchful eye of old Bill. One other thing Jim does remember about this was that Corbett said he "couldn't sleep a wink that night for dreaming about snakes!" Well, those were the days when a boy had to shoulder his share of the responsibility but managed to find time to have a little fun along the way. Maybe some of you, like me, wonder whatever became of old Bill, the German Shepherd. I called Jimmy back and asked him. "Oh, he lived a long and happy, useful life. He just quietly died of old age."

Another recollection that Jim told me about over the phone was the sawmill that set exactly where the Presbyterian Church is now located at Haysi. "That sawmill fascinated me," he recalls. "Dad Cumbo was the sawyer and I always thought of him as being like the captain of a steamboat. I still remember how they would feed the furnace big slabs of wood and how the smoke and steam would boil out and how the sparks would fly, sometimes coming down to burn holes in the hats of the crew. When that happened, I got out of the way." Jimmy paused in his reminiscing to pay tribute to his Aunt Mary Woods. "Many people didn't understand her, but I did. She and my mother were sisters. Complete opposites in their lifestyle, (Mother was an "indoor person and Aunt Mary loved outside work) but I loved them both. Aunt Mary was always my friend, and I could trust her to listen to me and try to advise me right. I could count on her to back me in any way she could in any of my efforts. She was a woman with many admirable qualities and I hold her memory dear..."

The depression of 1929 did to the South family what it did to many, many American business men. Zack was running his own store in Haysi, he had the post office, and a mining business. He was the first president of the old Haysi Bank and was the man who first brought running water and electricity to Haysi, but the Depression didn't play favorites. Mr. South moved his family to one of the large white houses that stood on the hillside directly above the old Chevrolet garage. These houses were also located just back from the hollow where the Haysi pop factory was located and below the reservoir from which Haysi got its water. They were living there when Haysi was destroyed by fire, and

Jim can recall that event quite well. "One thing that stands out in my mind was people trying to save their belongings and merchandise...how they kept carrying things out of line of the fire and having to move them again and being fearful that they would be stolen when they went to get another load..."

In 1937, the South's moved to Dwale to Mr. Sifer's farm, and shortly thereafter, Jim changed from Haysi High School to Clintwood, D.M.H.S., so as to cut down on walking distance. He says this was the best move he ever made, not because of the schools, but because it was due to this change that he met "the girl of his dreams," Rita Jo Artrip. It was at a pie supper at Flemingtown Elementary School, the first pie supper Jim had ever attended, and Rita was there with a pie. Jim didn't get to buy it and neither did he get to walk the cakewalk with her. She "was already committed." However, Jim was persistent, and Rita admits she had her eye on him too. So, in 1939, they started dating. Jim finished high school, went to Johnson City Business School, had several good jobs, but decided that working at the Glen L. Martin Plant where B-26 bombers were manufactured offered the most security at the time. While there, he went into the army, serving most of his time in Hawaii. Just before he went to service, he and Rita were married in Whitesburg, Ky. by a Presbyterian minister. They had a quite ceremony. Jim had to leave soon for basic training, and Rita joined Jim at Camp Adair, Oregon. When the war was over, Jim and Rita made their home at Skeetrock, not far from the old homes where they had been raised. That's the way it is with us mountain people...our roots grow deep and we like to stay where we were planted....

Next week, we will include some fishing stories which we left out this time in order to give some of the history of Haysi. Some of you are asking if I'm going to write anything about Rita and the answer is "yes." Week after next, I'm going to write about Rita and her family. Next week, Jim, Rita, and their family, plus a few fish tales.

January 23, 1991

Rita and Jimmy South

Jimmy's Family in 1959 — Elva, Eula, Mrs. Belvia South, Jimmy, and Junior.

Anita Belcher's Mountain Echoes

Rita Jo Artrip South

Rita shares some history of the Artrip, Childress, Wright, Stone, and Reed generations, and a few stories of her own...

Living in a big world that is often filled with confusion and chaos, we sometimes feel the need of a friend who seems to be filled with an inner peace and calm... a friend who has wise counsel and understanding which they are willing to share with us. Rita South is such person, but let's start at the beginning and share some of her memories. "I was born at Skeetrock, VA, April 9, 1922, the daughter of William James and Lydia Childress Artrip. My father's relatives were from Russell County. My grandfather, Jasper Artrip (Bas), came from there when he was a boy, one of five children brought to the South of the Mountain by a widowed lady, Mary (Pop) Breeding Artrip. Mary's husband, John Artrip, was killed in the Civil War fighting for the South. There were two sons in the family, Jim and Bas, and it is from them that the Artrips in this area originated. During this time, there was a gentleman by the name of "Big" Jim Farmer living at Tivis, and he took it upon himself to help out a lady by the name of (Aunt) Polly Ann Rowe, whose husband had also

Rita Jo (Artrip) South in her Pikeville College days.

115

★ ECHOES ...••• Continued from Page 2

married to the well-known dentist, Dr. W. G. Burkes, and Eura was the sister who was a second mother to the family. (These three sisters have all died within the past 3 years.)

"After daddy's first wife died, he married my mother and six children were born to their union: Mary, Tona, myself (Rita), Bill, John, and Betty. All of us are still living with the exception of Mary Ann, who died in 1931 at the age of 20."

Rita shares some of the events of those tragic days with us... "Mary Ann had always seemed more frail or easier to tire than she should. The doctor couldn't find anything wrong, but even so, he suggested that her tonsils be removed. During this surgery, she almost bled to death. After recovering from the operation, she continued with her schooling, graduated from high school, and went to Radford College for one year. She came home and taught one school term at Ramey Flats and part of one term at Skeetrock before becoming ill. Daddy took her by train to Baltimore, MD, where my two older brothers, Al and Floyd, lived, hoping to get help from the doctors there. There was no help

for her. She had a rare blood disease and died three months after reaching Baltimore, never seeing her home again." Any of us who have ever lived through the loss of a young family member can appreciate the sorrow this family must have gone through at this time, but it was years later when Rita learned that emotions don't always show. She and her mother were talking about death and about Mary, and Rita recalling all the sorrow and heartache her family went through, also recalled how her mother had kept on going and asked "how were you able to do it?" Her reply was "at times like that, someone has to be strong, and I knew it had to be me."

Rita went to school at Skeetrock through the 7th grade. Her three teachers during those years were Orville Branham, Claude Sutherland, and Joel Phipps. Each of these teachers were related to her, and each of them was an excellent teacher. The Skeetrock school had three rooms, one having just been added the year before Rita started first grade. A high school was taught there with Mr. Charlie Stradley from Lee County teaching. He boarded at the Ar-

trip home, for in those days there was but little means of transportation.

Rita says, "I remember the high school students had a good basketball team and played against other high schools in the county. I recall that Clyde Sutherland was an outstanding player. (Mr. Sutherland passed away this past week). Before that time, children who went to school had to board in Clintwood, my older brothers and sisters boarded there." The next bit of Rita's recollections will seem strange to many young people who in this day and time simply walk out the front door to catch a warm school bus, but to those of us who walked in the heat of late August and September, the icy winds and snows of December and January and the mud of February and March, we understand quite well what she is talking about. There was need for transportation for school children and Mr. Artrip (Rita's dad) understood that need and did something about it.

Rita related the story... "Daddy had the first school bus in our area. It was a ton truck which daddy had a bus body built on and seats constructed along the sides. There were cellophane windows along the sides also. After school buses were purchased in the county, Dad bought the first one in our area. I rode that bus for the four years I went to DMHS, 1934-1938. The bus started from our house before daylight and got back after dark during the winter months. It had two other runs to make and many times we got stuck in the mud. We had chains but no heaters. Dad built a garage to house the new bus and hired a driver who always stayed at our house. The first bus cost about $1,000, and Dad, not having the money, borrowed it from Uncle John Ratliff. When he paid it back, he caught a horse, put my two young brothers, John and Bill, on the horse's back, pinned the $1,000 in greenbacks inside one of their shirts and started them off on a trip several miles through the woods to Uncle John's house. I recall how proud they were to be carrying that much money and yet how scared they were, knowing the potential dangers!"

been killed in the Civil War. She was receiving a pension check from the government, and the nearest post office was at Lebanon, VA. Mr. Farmer rode with her to Lebanon to get her check and since they could not make the trip in one day, they made friends with the widow Artrip and spent the night with her. Later, Mrs. Artrip married "Big" Jim and came to the Tivis area with him where she lived the rest of her life. She is buried in the Kedrick Mullins Cemetery. The Farmers of this area are their descendants."

Rita continues, "My grandmother on my daddy's side was Elizabeth (Betts) Stone, daughter of Lewis and Pernetta Reed Stone. They came here from Raleigh County, W. VA, and they and the Reeds both lived in the Blowing Rock - Skeetrock section of the county. One of the Reeds (Henry) had a large family of 12 girls and one boy. My daddy knew all of them and who they married. Most people in our area today are related to the Reeds. Dad talked to us often about his folks and instilled in us a knowledge and respect for them.

As I mentioned at the first, my mother was Lydia Childress Artrip, the oldest daughter of John Wesley and Vicey Salyer Childress. Grandfather Childress bought and moved to the Adam Childress place from Elkhorn Creek, KY in 1900 when my mother was 12-years-old. They were very devout members of the Primitive Baptist Church, and Grandma was a "shouting" Baptist. I remember it used to embarrass us children when Grandma got up to shout! I've heard my grandfather say that he was present at the Mt. Olive Church when it split over a matter of doctrine, predestination I think. They had met on several occasions and debated the question but could not reach an agreement. More than one family was divided, some staying with the Primitive and others going with the newly formed Regulars. Both churches met once a month, and the association met once a year. My grandparents, and later my parents, were all members of the Primitive Baptist Church, and my Grandmother Artrip also joined this denomination. She rode horseback from Skeetrock to Sandlick for many years. Since traveling was hard in those days, the preachers would often stay in a home over the weekend. (Rita and I discussed the fact that with a name such as "John Wesley" there had to be some Methodist blood in the family, and she remembered that in the earlier days some of the family had been "old time Methodists.")

"My father was first married to Mary Ann Wright, and they had five children: Eura, Al, Floyd, Rose, and Stella. They are all deceased now except Floyd, who lives in Washington, D. C., and is a very alert 90-years-old as of this February 27th." (Stella was

See ECHOES, Page 3

THE ARTRIP FAMILY — The children, grandchildren, great-grandchildren, and some of the in-laws of W. J. and Lydia Childress Artrip.

Front row, left to right: Kim Artrip, Debra Mullins, Beth McClanahan, Rob McClanahan, Pat Artrip, Greg South, Ronald Dale Mullins, Bill Artrip III. Second row, left to right: Al Artrip, Eura Artrip, Betty Artrip, Tona Artrip. Back row, left to right: Stella Artrip, Rose Artrip, Rebecca Mullins, W. J. (Bill) Artrip, Floyd Artrip, Rita Artrip, John Bill Mullins, Dr. Burkes, Phyllis Artrip, Gerry Burkes, Denver Damron, John Artrip. Picture made about 1963.

Rita continues, "After graduating from DMHS a few days before my 16th birthday, I enrolled in Pikeville College and after two years there, I earned my teacher's degree and came back home to teach. Daddy thought there was only one career for a girl and that was teaching. He had been a teacher as had five of his daughters and two older sons. I started teaching when I was eighteen and continued my own education by attending college at East Tennessee State and Clinch Valley. Those years of teaching were among some of the most rewarding in my life...the many lives I've touched and the many that have touched me...the friendships that were made and still remain, years after some of the "book-learning" has been forgotten...the thought that perhaps that even in some small way I have helped to make a better world as reflected in the lives of my students... these are the things that count with me."

Rita spoke of the advice her Dad gave her before she started teaching. "You can't make great scholars out of all your students," he said, "but try to make good citizens of them all." He also strongly insisted that she spend one night with each of her students, for only in this way could a teacher come to understand a child as an individual and know the whys and wherefores of their attitude. Rita and I agreed that he was right and both of us and many other teachers during that time visited in the home of all our pupils. Mr. Artrip also instilled in his children the desire to make something out of themselves and to contribute something worthwhile to their fellowman, and each of the Artrip children have succeeded in doing just that.

As you have read Rita's story, I'm sure you have understood why my description of her at the beginning of this article is so correct. From her father, she inherited a sympathetic concern for people and from her mother a calm strength. As a Christian, she has constantly sought for God's wisdom, and these characteristics are evident in her everyday life. She would be the first to tell you that she isn't perfect, but she's a good friend to have in today's world.

Mrs. Fronia Fuller of Bartlick.

In 1916-17, the Yellow Poplar Logging Company came into the mountains of Kentucky, for here were stands of poplar of enormous size. Men came from different parts of the country to work at the various logging jobs, and among them came young Bud Fuller of Bartlick. It was Fronia's job to take care of a young nephew who her parents were raising, and as the men came from work and stopped by the store to buy something or just to talk, they would take time to talk to a little boy. Bud in particular liked the little fellow, and before long it was obvious that he also had a special liking for Fronia. About this time, Mr. Dotson sold his store out to the Yellow Poplar Company, and Bud and Fronia decided to get married.

"Do you remember what you were married in?", I asked, not really thinking that after so many years she would remember, but she did. "Oh yes," was her quick reply. "I wore white organdy with slippers to match, and Bud wore a suit with a white shirt. I was married at home by Preacher George Coleman." Fronia and Bud Fuller were married March 18, 1918, seventy-three years ago, and she remembers every detail.

The Fullers lived on Johns Creek until 1930, when they moved to Bartlick "up the hollow at the old Jim Fuller place." They lived there for several years, then moved to the Jacob and Margaret Fuller place where they lived until Bud's death in 1947.

"What was Bartlick like when you moved there?", I asked. "Well, there was lots of big timber, and the creek ran full all the time. It was never low. Uncle Dick Fuller had the gristmill where the creek runs to go up to the old Waites Stanley place, and when traveling you had to ford the creek at the lowest point. A few people had foot logs, although there were not many families living there at the time. There was Uncle Dick (Richard) Fuller, Uncle Noah and Aunt Belle, Will and Polly Scarberry, Uncle Jeff Presley,

See ECHOES, Page 5

Allen Willis and Aunt Rena, and on down the creek was Uncle Bennie and Aunt Mary Edwards, and then there was Mitchell Senter and his wife. Uncle Noah had a sawmill over in the bottom, and he had a general store also. Men made their living by mining, timbering, and farming. Families kept what livestock they needed."

Life was rough on Bartlick Creek in those days, rough in every sense of the word. The roads were just wagon roads, and sometimes even wagons couldn't make it. After reaching "Carbeech Gap" (where the Willard Stanley home now is) it was both tortuous and dangerous to try to make it on into the Breaks during the winter or rainy seasons. (Ask Madgie Owens to tell you how Bill (her husband) remembered the brakes on a wagon failing and what happened or ask Bill Childress to tell you about how his dad hauled railroad steel up Camp Branch and over Carbeech Gap). Those are the days Mrs. Fuller remembers also. The nearest school for the children to attend was a little one-room, log building down below the old Bennie Edwards place (where Vesta Cochran now lives) and the nearest church was on Grassy Creek. Mrs. Fuller remembers when Preacher Mowbray with the Presbyterian Church came to the community, taught Sunday School, and held a revival in the old school bottom. Later, Uncle Noah Fuller gave land for a school to be built there, and he also gave land for the Regular Baptists to build their church on, just up the creek a short distance.

By this time, the extensive timbering was taking its toll. There was now "washouts" and flash floods, one of these taking out the Baptist Church house. (Later another would sweep through the community taking the lives of a father and two sons on down the way). Mrs. Fronia Fuller has lived through the two eras of Bartlick, the one when the mountains were undisturbed by the ax or the timber saw, when the only land cleared was just enough for farming and grazing, when the creek ran full and clear and there was no better drinking water anywhere. She remembers when there was wildlife throughout the whole area, and the only highwalls were those that had existed since the creation. She is living in the other era now, and progress has changed Bartlick Creek. Mrs. Fuller will tell you that while some aspects of life are much better, there's some things she wishes hadn't changed.

Bud and Fronia Fuller had a large family, most of whom are still living: Noah Ransom (Buster) lives in Florida with his wife, Helen; Jim married Eileen Charles (deceased): Hazel married Clarence Thomas; Junior Bud married Vera ? (both deceased); Ann married Henry ?; Kemp (unmarried); Fred married Glema Duggins; George lives in Michigan; Raymond lives in Georgia; Roy married Julia Conway and lives by his mother on Bartlick. One child died in infancy. Mrs. Fuller has about thirty grandchildren, several great-grandchildren, and several great-great-grandchildren. Out of this family, five of the sons served their country. Fred was in the Navy, George was in the Army, Junior Bud served in the Army in Germany, WWII, and died as a result of his wounds in later years, and Kemp was killed in Korea. Roy was also in the Army.

Mrs. Fuller has seen much sorrow in her life. Besides the loss of two sons, she has had to face the death of several of her grandchildren. Just this past summer, she lost a grandson who was as "dear to her as her own child." Through it all, she has maintained a calm and quiet spirit. She is a Christian woman and looks to the Lord for strength. All of her children and her neighbors will tell you that she is a good person who "would not say a harm word about anybody and who would help you if she could." That is a mighty good reputation to have.

Mrs. Fronia (Bud) Fuller

A woman who has faced life calmly and quietly.

In a world where the desire of many people is to see, hear, know and tell everything that's going on, Mrs. Fronia Fuller of Bartlick presents an amazing contrast. From the time I was a very small girl and visiting my grandparents on Bartlick, I can never remember "Aunt Fronia" expressing any interest in anyone's wrong doings or sharing in any type of gossip. Even if there was no other reason to recognize her in the "Echoes" article, that is reason enough.

Mrs. Fuller was born at Johns Creek, Ky., August 14, 189?. She isn't quite sure of the year, and I didn't ask her to look up any records, but she has passed the "mid-nineties" mark. Her parents were Ruben and Mary (Mantz?) Coleman, both of Johns Creek. Mr. Coleman died while Fronia was still a baby so that the only father she knew was her mother's second husband, Ransom Dotson. "My own father couldn't have been better to me," Mrs. Fuller recalls," and I loved him very much."

"What was life like, growing up in the mountains of Kentucky ninety years ago?", I asked. I know it must have been rough. Her answer was direct and to the point: "Back in those days even the easiest living was rough, but our family had it better than lots of others. Dad had a general store there on Johns Creek where he sold everything the early settlers needed. It was a large store with shelves that held everything from canned goods to bolts of cloth. There was sugar, flour, tobacco, and many other staple items. Dried peaches were packaged and sold from boxes or barrels, and vinegar and lamp oil were hauled in and kept in barrels also. Outside the store in a separate building "almost as long as my trailer" was the herb house. It was here that dad housed, separated and sold the many different herbs that were brought in. Back in those days, people dug a lot of roots, besides the leaves and bark that were used and sold for medicine."

I asked Mrs. Fuller about the size of Johns Creek. When Dad went to buy goods for the store, he traveled down Johns Creek about three miles, turned right handed and went about four miles until he reached a mountain which was about two miles across. Then he traveled along Peters Creek until he reached a river, which, if it was low, he forded. If it was high, he left his wagon and horses and went across on the ferry, bought his goods and ferried back across to his wagon."

Anita Belcher's
Mountain Echoes

Joe Lee Baker

A man who tries to help his fellowman on a personal level and through the printed pages...

God has given to each of us the very precious gift of memory. Sometimes we forget about an appointment we are supposed to keep today, but those things that happened twenty or forty or fifty years ago seem to be indelibly impressed on our mind. Especially if we start talking about them. So it was when Joe Lee was sharing some memories of his growing-up days, of times spent with his Pa and Ma Baker, of court days and boarding house meals, of Ma Baker hurrying around to prepare the early morning breakfast of bacon, sausage, tenderloin, gravy, jams, jellies, applebutter, all served homestyle with pitchers of milk and pots of coffee. Joe's mom, Parkie, was there

helping out his grandmother Ma Baker, is a part of his early memories. Court days also provided some extra spending money for enterprising young businessmen.

Joe had a shoeshine box, and for men who walked out of muddy "hollers" or along miles of dusty roads, this provided a real service. Some of the men felt that they only needed a "brush off" which cost them one cent, a good shine was five cents for slippers or shoes, whereas boots were shined for ten cents. One thing that Joe remembers with a good feeling was that Haskell Arrington always paid him more than the price of the shine. Some of the other men who Joe remembers coming to the boarding house were Lundy Wright, Uncle Floyd Arrington, Albert Stone, Poley Willis, Uncle Ezra Sutherland from

Skeetrock. There were many, many others. There were other ways that a young man back in those days could earn money if he was of a mind to, and Joe having been taught that every man should work for a living, started out early to make his own way in the world. Besides his shoeshining business and berry pickin', there was always the lure of the woodlands where a hard day's work could provide thirty pounds of green mayapple root. Perhaps some of the most interesting work he did was driving some older businessmen around to their various jobs or on business trips. You recall that Joe learned to drive while just a boy. He remembers the first driver's permit he had, costing either twenty-five or fifty cents, and when he started driving for Dr. Phipps, twenty-five cents was his day's earning. Dr. Phipps made house calls anywhere from Clintwood to Bondtown, Caney Ridge or Skeetrock, and his charge was $2. Joe also drove for Cowan Smith and Cuba Sutherland, but perhaps the most interesting of his driving was done for "Big Dan" Crabtree. "Big Dan" had an old truck, and he bought up just about anything that anyone had for sale... herbs of every kind, furs and hides, scrap metal, chickens and eggs. Chicken coops were carried on the back of the truck, and "Big Dan" made it a point to be home by dark so he could look after the chickens. His buying routes took him all over the county, and by the time evening came, he was well-loaded and ready for the selling end of the business. "Big Dan" was a congenial man, and Joe loves to recall the times spent with him and how at lunch time they would stop at some country store and always "Big Dan" would say, "Buy what you want... everything you can eat."

Joe went into service in 1945, training at Camp Blanding, FLA. He was on his way to the Pacific Theater when he was transferred from the Infantry to anti-aircraft training. After returning from service, he went into the trucking business for awhile, and then in 1950, he became the Town Police for Clintwood. In 1951, he was appointed as an ABC Investigator for the state where he continued working until 1961. His work as an ABC officer was not "a nine-to-five job" behind the desk. Although he had the same authority as the State Police, he worked mainly with the Alcohol Beverage Control Board, which

meant that he spent a lot of time tramping through the woods, over the mountains, and up the hollows. Many nights were spent in the woods for observance and surveillance, and Joe will tell you that his work was both exciting and dangerous. Isolated spots where "time and progress" had passed the people by were the worse for moonshining and shootings. Family feuds erupted over the moonshining business, one man shot his father "dead center" of his bow-tie, and "squealing" on each other was a common practice for self-protection. There were "foot" races; Joe caught one man hiding in an old coal bank, after a long chase, and once, instinctively glancing up, he came eye-to-eye with a man standing above him with his gun aimed at him. There was a mail fraud case which Joe and Elva Rose were assigned to solve, and they brought their prisoners to justice. Visit Joe one of these days and swap some yarns...

Like many of us, without even knowing it, our careers start very early in life. Joe's career as a newspaper man actually started when he was about 11-years-old, and the name of the newspaper was **The Dickenson Forum**. It was owned by Henry Taylor, W.C.D. Rush and Cuba Sutherland (Mr. Rush was the

See ECHOES, Page 5

Mayor of Clintwood during several of these years). Joe's job was to do anything that needed doing. He swept floors, cleaned up the printing messes, distributed the hand-type, fed the hand presses, just about anything that a willing-to-work youngster could do. At first, he was paid 25¢ a week, and finally fifty cents for a week's work. Within a few years, "Mayno" Sutherland (Herbert Maynard) took over the paper, changing its name to **The Dickensonian**, and Joe, who by now was fifteen-years-old continued working at the paper for $15 a week. This was a good salary in those days, enough for Joe to do his courting and buy a car with. That first car was a beauty.. "can see it right now," Joe relates. "It was a '31 Chevrolet Coach, dark maroon, 18-19 inch wheels, with two extras, one on each side of the car. I paid $154.60 for it," Joe recalls.

Joe's responsibility at the newspaper was increasing. Now, he was operating the linotype, distributing the hand-type back into the cases, making up the pages with type molded from hot lead, carrying on the work even then as a veteran printer, and all the while added more and more knowledge and experience to what was to become a life's work. After his time spent in service, he returned to work at **The Coalfield Progress, Richlands Press, Powell Valley News**, and the **Pikeville Daily News**. The next ten or 11 years was spent at police work, including his time as ABC Investigator and then he went to Eastern Virginia where he worked as a linotype operator and printer for the **Northern Neck News**. After 3 1/2 years, he and Lema moved to Richmond where he worked for the Lewis Printing Co., and had "the best boss a man could ever have." Joe had a good job there, but Lema was getting homesick for Dickenson County. There were other newspapers with good job offers, but the mountains of home were calling, so with the help of his brother, Robert, Joe bought all the equipment that he needed to start a county paper, loaded it in a U-haul, and left Richmond in 15 inches of snow.

The late Remire Sutherland was interested in seeing a county newspaper printed and was a great encouragement to Joe. So in a little building owned by his aunt, Grace Short, the first issue of **The Cumberland Times** was printed June 9, 1966. Fitz Beverly helped out with his little press, as Joe's messed up at the last minute. 1,000 copies were printed.

Joe has much to look back on and be thankful for. He is now equipped with the only offset newspaper printing press in the county (the only one ever in the county) and one of three in all of Southwest Virginia in the weekly field. He has the most modern presses, computers, cameras, and dark room equipment. He has a fax machine and copier. All of this plus much more enables him to print almost anything that needs printing in black and white or color. At this time, 6,000 papers are being printed and distributed per week, and it's my opinion that **The Cumberland Times** is one of the most widely read county papers in the country.

Joe Lee gives much credit to his wife, Lema, and to his family members who have worked with him so diligently over the years and not for one minute does he forget to give credit to what he considers to be one of the best working staffs a newspaper could have. However, he never forgets that those who support his efforts are the final answer to the success of all his hard work and all the team work that goes into publishing the **Times**. "Those who advertise and those who buy... without them the paper couldn't be published, and I thank each and everyone." Joe emphasizes with deep sincerity and gratitude.

Anita Belcher's
Mountain Echoes

Dessie H. (Mrs. George) Hill
"A lady who accepts the joys and sorrows of life with a gentle spirit and a deep faith..."

Mrs. Dessie Hill of Big Ridge (above Haysi) is a much loved mother, grandmother, friend and.neighbor. She is the daughter of Floyd and Maggie (Mary Magdalene) Puckett Hill and her ancestry on both sides of her family is so interesting that we will document some of it for those of you who might find it useful. Maggie Puckett Hill was the. daughter of J. W. (Uncle Johnny) and Martha Syphers Puckett. J. W. was the son of David and Mary Jane Gibson Puckett. He was born in Floyd County, Kentucky on March 12th, 1865 (the year the war between the states ended.) His father and mother moved from Kentucky to the Davis Ridge Section of Dickenson County where they raised a family of several children including J. W., Drewery, Buck, Pea, Liz, Belle and Tiny. (There may have been others. These are the ones Dessie remembered on short notice.) David Puckett was born June 8th, 1842 and died February 4th, 1894. His wife, Mary Jane, was born September 12th, 1843 and died January 20th, 1902. They are both buried

DESSIE HILL — today.

in the Davis Cemetery on Davis Ridge. Dessie recalls, "my mother, Maggie, used to spend the night with her grandparents, David and Jane. They were fine people and very kind to Mommy. Their home was still standing during my growing up days and Will and Emma McCowan used to live there, but it has long since been torn down." Maggie's mother, Martha Syphers Puckett, was a very special person in Dessie's life so I am going to write a feature story on her next week especially for Dessie and for Clynard and for dozens and dozens of grandchildren who hold her memory dear. (If any of you have a special story or picture of her you'd like me to print, call me before Monday, August 12th.)

Dessie's parents, Floyd and Maggie had a very romantic courtship and marriage. Dessie laughs and says, "He stole her!" In other words they eloped. Dessie tells the story... "Mommy hid her clothes in the chimney corner outside the house. In the middle of the night, daddy, (Floyd) came riding up on his horse, helped Maggie into the saddle and the two of them rode off together. They rode till they reached Maggie's uncle's home, (Jim Syphers) and the next morning they went on into Clintwood where they were married. Their first home was a small one-room house at Splashdam and Dessie recalls her mother telling her how that when she wanted to come home to visit her parents, Floyd would swim the river with her as there was no bridges. Dessie believes her own birthplace to have been in the old log house on the J. W. and Martha Puckett farm above Haysi. Shortly thereafter her parents moved to Big Ridge where Maggie's grandfather, J. W. Puckett owned a great deal of property. Growing up as the oldest of all children, Dessie had many responsibilities, "but life was good" she says with her gentle smile. As we might imagine, caring for the younger children was one of the tasks assigned to her, but a task she thoroughly enjoyed. She recalls, "the babies were healthy despite the lack of modern day medicines and doctors. We had no disposable diapers and baby food consisted of food from the table as soon as the babies were old enough to digest it. Until then they were breast fed and there was never any problem with bottles or formula. Playtime for Dessie came when the dishes were washed

and the babies asleep and her playmates were the Allen Music and Bert McCowan children. School was at Davis Ridge which was first a one-room, then later a two-room building. Dessie remembers some of her teachers, but there was one in particular whom she remembers because

he had fallen in love with her and there were plans for marriage when suddenly a young man by the name of George Hill entered the picture and so far as Dessie was concerned, there wasn't another man in the world. History repeats itself, and Dessie and George made their wedding plans...another elopement!

Even now Dessie recalls the story with tenderness and the memory will never grow old..."I went to school as usual that morning after carefully arrang-

See ECHOES, Page 4

ing my hair in the stylish "puff" fashion. I wore my new blue mitti dress which had a pleated skirt' and the collar and cuffs were trimmed with white braid. Mother came in while I was getting ready and said, "I hear you are going to marry George Hill." I answered her by saying, "Now, where did you hear that?" She didn't say anything more to me...just turned and walked out of the room. I think she knew...I went on to school and about 10:00, Delbert Davis came in from outside and said someone wanted to see me. I knew who it was for that was the message I had been waiting for. George was there waiting for me and we walked together to Uncle Watson Davis' house where the preacher, Tyra MacFadden was waiting. The wedding ceremony took place immediately and we rode double on George's horse to the home of Mary and Ayers Good, sister and brother-in-law of George." The young couple started housekeeping at Splashdam where George was working at laying track in the mines. They lived there for a year, then moved to Big Ridge to George's homeplace below the Mt. Olive Church. They lived there until 1938 when they built the home where Dessie now lives and where they raised their family. The Hills had a family of six children..Eugene who died at age 7, Clifford (M) Fay Ratliff, Juan (wife deceased), Ruth (M) James C. Yates, Dolly June (M) Ray Fink, Maggie (Unmarried.) Dessie's brothers and sisters are as follows; Thelma (deceased), Tony (deceased), Ernest, Mac, Phillip, Winnie, Constance, Landeras (deceased), Herbert and Eliza (Stillborn.) George was the son of Jerome and Tilda Anderson Hill. Tilda was the daughter of George and Mary Anderson whom I hope to do a story on in the near future.

Dessie Hill looks back over her life with a feeling of peace and contentment. Of her childhood and growing up days, she can say with deep conviction, "they were good." There are wonderful memories of her parents and grandparents. Two women who had a lasting influence on Dessie's life was her mother and Grandmother Puckett. "They were wonderful women," she recalls. "Grandma continually gave of herself and my mother was just simply a wonderful mother...she had such a sweet personality and was never ill with us children...I never saw her get mad...she was very patient and loving. After her death, people would sometimes ask my dad why he didn't remarry, and he would reply with

tears in his eyes, "because there will never be another Maggie." Dessie feels the same way about her husband, George, who died in 1973. Whereas for some people the newness and joy of marriage fades away and for some it dies completely, for Dessie and George Hill that walk that started for them when they left the old Davis schoolhouse hand in hand so many years ago, never ended. They continued hand in hand for 51 years. Their romance never ended, it simply matured and ripened.

Today, Dessie lives on at the homeplace. She isn't as well as she used to be, but she still has a loving heart and a kind and encouraging word for friend and family. Like her mother and her grandmother, she gives of herself and as her daughter Ruth,

says, "Mommy is, and always has been a wonderful mother. If there were more people like her in the world there wouldn't be so many lonely and homeless little children."

Dessie is a Christian who endeavors to live each day according to God's word. From the Lord she receives her peace and contentment, and the sweet personality that she so admired in her mother, and those of you who know her best know that she is willing to share her love, her faith and her friendship. Stop by and see Dessie. You will come away feeling good.

DESSIE HILL a few years ago.

GEORGE HILL in the early 70's.

WOODROW W. RASNICK

"Today we walk with Woodrow through the rooms of his old home, out over the lawn, down through the sugar maple orchard and back to the sugar camp..."

Three or four years ago, Cly and I were hiking through the mountains up in the "Middle of the World" section of the county when we came upon a site of an old homeplace. Apple trees, seedlings from older trees of years past, was our first bit of evidence and then we saw the old outbuildings. One was a small structure, built of logs with a low door opening and a tiny window on one side. The other, also built of logs, was a somewhat larger building. Of course, I was intrigued because old homeplaces have a way of tugging at my heart and I was determined to find out who had lived there. Finally someone told me to ask Clynard's good friend, Woodrow Rasnick, for they were sure he would know, so one evening after a long day's hike, we stopped by Woodrow's, got a good cold drink of water and I described the old homesite to him. Even as I spoke, his face began to light up with a smile and he answered my question readily. "That was my old homeplace," he said. "I grew up

WOODROW in front of his home on Counts Ridge.

there." Here's the story as Woodrow told me... 'That is the site of the home where I was born. It was a part of the original tract of land belonging to great-grandfather, Jonas. By this time the 2,000 acres (or more) had been divided into 300 and 400 acre tracts and given to the different children. My grandfather, Elijah, inherited the land at the head of the left hand fork of Lick Creek which stretched between Breeding Branch on Frying Pan to Laurel Branch on Lick Creek, then down from the Middle of the World and back to Flint Gap. The spring of water which we used was the origin of the left hand fork of the creek and it

was here that great-grandfather, Jonas, build one of his hunting cabins. It was also here that the Selton post office was established and my father, Joseph, was the postmaster for several years. Later my sister, Lou, and lastly my sister, Ester, kept the office. It was a commonplace thing in those days for people to say, "I'm going to Selton today." The old Rasnick homeplace is well worth describing and again Woodrow gives the details... "The 'Big House' or main house was built from hewn logs, hewed by grandfather Elijah and Uncle Jim Rasnick. A brick furnace was built above the house by a spring and here

See Echoes, Page 4

Continued from Page 2

the bricks were made for building the chimneys. The chimney of the main house was hewn sandstone up to the shoulder, then on to the top was brick. The chimney in the dining room was all brick. This chimney was back of a huge fireplace where two or more 'goose-necks' were placed to hold the hanging iron pots for cooking. The big house consisted of one room down stairs and a porch where a set of stairs led to a big bedroom overhead. A closet was under the stairway. Two good-sized windows were in the upstairs bedroom." (Mentioning windows caused Woodrow to recall a story. He leaned forward in his chair and with a laugh described the following incident.) When I was a boy, we had a dog who was a real snake hunter. He'd fight and kill any snake he could find. Well, you know this part of the county has always been bad for snakes, especially copperheads and rattlesnakes. One day my dad looked out the door and saw a big yellow rattler crawling across the yard. He hollered to us boys and told us to fasten the dog up in the upstairs room or else he was libal to try to kill that snake and get bit. We did as he told us and dad got his gun and shot the snake. The old dog had gone to the window to look out and when he heard that gun go off he leaped through the window, bringing frame and all with him! No, he wasn't hurt!" Now, back to our story...Woodrow continued, "The upstairs was used for sleeping and it was a cozy, warm place, but it was also used for storing food and nuts for winter. There was barrels of dried fruit, peaches and apples, and what a wonderful perfume they gave the room! Bags of dried apples hung across the back wall and dried beans hung from the rafters overhead. Bags of hickory nuts and butternuts hung from the beams and of course we stored black walnuts, too. Later another bedroom was built and there was the dog-trot, or "breezeway" as it was later called. Downstairs in the living room the fireplace was so large that it took two men to carry in the backlog. Smaller logs lay in the front and provided us with a good warming fire. In the middle of the room was a big center table where the oil lamp set that I like to read by. Later this lamp was replaced by the more modern, Aladdin lamp which was prettier and gave better light. Also, mother kept a scarf or centerpiece on this table, one that she made and crocheted the edging for. Our mother was an expert seamstress and could do any kind of fine needlework and taught all the girls to do the same. This was the place where the family Bible lay and each night after the day's work and play was finished, mother read to us from it. Mother also had a New Testament which was written in verse form and she loved to read it because of the musical arrangement of the words.

Mother and Dad were both Christians, belonging to the Sulphur Spring Baptist Church. Speaking of music, we had a big Addler organ in one corner of the room. All the girls could play but sister Nannie was especially good, also Vi and Reba. We would gather round the organ at night and sing religious songs and ballads. Other furniture in our living room was two big beds in the back of the room, a big bureau and two large trunks. Straightback, bark-bottomed chairs completed our furnishings. We had good windows with pretty curtains mother made. Also on the walls hung the heavy framed pictures of our Rasnick grandparents, one of cousin Robert and one of our two brothers who were in W.W. I, Charlie and Grady, and oh, yes, something else comes to my mind...in the doorway, overhead on a big shelf adjoining a joice was where mother kept her maple sugar stored... "Did you have your own sugar trees?" I asked "Oh yes, the sugar orchard was just a short way from the house and covered one whole hillside. I figure grandfather must have cleared everything else off and just left the maples. Some of them were 3-4 feet through. The sap was gathered in early spring, late January and February. The weather had to be cold enough to freeze at night but warm enough in the day for the sap to run. After it got a milky appearance, it was too far advanced to use. We tapped as many as 75 trees and it was the responsibility of the younger children to carry the sap to the sugar camp. The orchard was so rocky it was hard to walk in it at any time but especially in the early spring when the rocks were snow-covered and slick. I well remember how the sap would slosh out over the sides of the buckets and soak our breeches legs! The sugar camp was a log building with a long shed which covered the furnace. At the back of the furnace set two large hogsheds (barrels) which we filled with sap. In the front of the furnace was a 50 gallon cast iron kettle which contained more sap for filling the large pan (similar to a molasses pan) that set over the furnace. Sometimes ice would freeze over the sap and we got to scrape it off and eat ice-like sugar candy. The sap was boiled down over the furnace until it reached the maple syrup stage. Mother would can some of it and some of it was taken to the house where she poured it into a big copper double boiler and stirred it with a seasoned popular paddle until it reached the right consistency for sugar. Then she poured some of it into crocks which were small at the bottom and large at the top so the sugar would come out easier.

Rev. Charlie J. Sluss Remembers...

"A gentleman of 92 with a keen memory, a love for the Lord and a rare sense of humor..."

When I first met Mr. Charles J. Sluss at his home a few evenings ago, I thought I was meeting a gentleman on whom the responsibilities of life had fallen heavily, so heavily in fact that at the age of 92 he certainly would not have retained much of a sense of humor, and even if he had, he probably wouldn't feel like sharing much of it. I was right on the first count...I WAS indeed meeting a gentleman, one of the old school, but on the second count I was wrong. With twinkles in his eyes and "laugh lines" firmly etched around his lips, I was soon to find that Mr. Sluss did, and does have a great sense of humor and when he told me of his Grandfather Dock's "toll" corn pretty nearly breaking the floor through and about the big catfish that got caught in the Millwheel...well, we all realized that he could bring out OUR sense of humor! More about those things later...right now time out for a little history.

on Route 607 and two miles from John Flannagan Boat Dock. He is the son of Elijah Preston and Aurora Mullins Sluss. Aurora was the daughter of Dock and Sallie Reed Mullins of this county and Elijah was the son of Noah and Dellie (?) Sluss of Scott County. Noah was a school teacher and a Church of the Brethren minister and though Mr. Sluss is not certain just why his grandparents came here from Scott County, he does know that his grandfather Noah taught school here and that he held church services in various homes as there was no church house available. Though he is not certain about this, Mr. Sluss wonders if perhaps his grandfather was the founder of the Brethren Church in this vicinity. However that may be, he does know that the Lord used him greatly in preaching the Word and in laying a strong spiritual foundation for the church that would be established. Rev. Noah Sluss and his wife lived in this area for some time, then moved to Martin County, Kentucky on Wolf Creek, then returned to Skeetrock. During this time, he continued his teaching and

REV. CHARLES J. SLUSS, 92-years-old, retired Church of the Brethren Minister.

preaching. During the same period of time, Grandfather Dock Mullins and his wife, Sallie, had a log home on Pound River and a watermill which provided the means of a cash income. Mr. Charlie Sluss explained it this way, "Grandfather Mullins ground meal for the people of the community. When they brought a bushel of corn, Grandpa took a gallon of it for his part, the "toll" it was called. He kept his toll corn in barrels in the upstairs of the house and from an upstairs "hopper" he would run his corn down to the mill rocks where it was ground into meal for family use. Corn that was not ground into meal was fed to the livestock and in turn the livestock were sold for cash providing the family with the necessary income." Here Mr. Sluss paused for a good chuckle... "I've offen heard Grandmother say, "Dock if you don't stop storing that corn overhead, you're going to break the floor through. I can hear it a-poppin' and a-crackin'!" "And what was the price of livestock 85 years ago?" I wondered aloud. Mr. Sluss' answer, "A good milk-cow would bring fifteen dollars, but a calf could sell for fifty cents. There were so many hogs running wild that a brood sow with a litter of pigs wouldn't sell and if the pigs couldn't be given away, they were offen killed. A good horse could be bought for seventy-five dollars." "Will you describe your Grandparent's home for me," I asked. So Mr. Sluss went back in time to tell me of a two room, two story log house built on the banks of the Pound River where a family was born and raised. A simple house with the necessities of life...upstairs were the beds and barrels of toll corn, downstairs were beds and homemade chairs and a fireplace, probably four foot in length. Rods hung over this fireplace for the cooking kettles and much of the baking was done on the hot coals which would soon become grey, cold ashes. Cornbread in the big cast iron baker was offen the order of the day and right at this point Mrs. Norma Mullins, Mrs. Cline Sluss and myself had a right down-to-earth discussion on why we don't do some of that today. We couldn't come up with any good reason for we know the cast iron skillets and bakers are around, some of us still have

See Echoes, Page 5

fireplaces, many of us can still get home ground meal...so...why don't we do it? Mrs. Sluss is going to check it out with her Home Extension Club, and I told her I'd be first in line to buy some of that good cornbread, which I am told the likes of can't be re-produced any other way. To continue now with Mr. Sluss's story as he pictured for me the small boxed-in kitchen on the porch with it's little step stove, homemade table and chairs and the cupboard that held the few family dishes. Around the walls hung many of the cooking utensils, but perhaps one of the most unique utensil I have yet heard about was a pumpkin or cushaw hollowed out and used for a spoonholder! I asked about the clothing which the family wore... "All of it was homemade," Mr. Sluss replied. They grew some flax and Granny had her spinning wheel. Of course they had sheep, and the wool was the basis for most clothing needs." Again those of the listening had our memories. My own Grandmother Fuller had a flock of sheep and I have seen her shear them and she too, had her big spinning wheel. Once she made me a little pair of socks and dyed them black with walnut hulls. Mrs. Norma Mullins and Mrs. Cline Sluss also had their memories and I was fascinated by their recollections of the socks that were knitted and dyed for the family, but they, along with Mr. Sluss remember in particular the socks which some of the ministers wore. Each of the three added their own descriptions... "The socks were basically grey, but the top had a red circle around it, then just below a blue, then a white, then red or blue whichever the lady of the house desired." At the moment, none of them could remember how the grey or blue colors were obtained but the red was derived from the berries of the "shoe-make" (Sumac) tree. That was something I had never heard of before and Mrs. Sluss remembers exactly how it was done and I told her I'd have to get her "recipe."

Folks had brought food and we'd had a good time of worship and fellowship and everyone started home. Dad and Uncle General warned everyone for not too many to get on the bridge at once because the cables might snap, but people just went on talking and laughing and didn't seem to hear what they were being told. Suddenly a cable snapped and the bridge just flopped to one side. People fell in the river and on the rock bed shoreline. There was no drowning but had injuries, the worse being to James O Mullins (Orvie). When I went home, I called Mrs. Orpha (James O. Mullins) or rather, she called me about something else and I asked her for more details on the story. "We had a small child at the time," she recalled, "and when my husband saw that the bridge was falling, he held her in his arms in such a way as to protect her from the fall. She wasn't hurt but most of his ribs were broken as well as his shoulder. The suffering he went through that summer was awful...he never really recovered." Kenny Mullins of the Cumberland Mountain Trail Riders recalls of that time, "I remember crying because of how my dad was hurt and I remember when finally they took off the adhesive tape how raw his flesh was and how he suffered." The child that Mr. Mullins was holding was Shirley M. Lowery,

Dr. Senter's nurse. Mrs. Orpha Mullins recalls one other incident, "You know this all happened during the second WW, 1945, I believe. I had saved my shoe stamps and bought me a pretty pair of dress slippers to wear to church. When the bridge fell, I hung on to the cable as long as I could, but finally had to drop to the rock bed below. Yes, I was hurt, bruised and cut and skinned. I still bear the scars, but one of the things that I can laugh about now is that my pretty shoe heels were broken, at least one of them!"

I asked Mr. Sluss about his marriage. What a beautiful marriage it was, and to hear him and his children speak of their home, their family, their mother and father, and to hear him speak of his wife does something to one's heart. "We never had a quarrel," he recalls "and if there was a disagreement of any kind we just got quiet and waited till we could talk about it in the right way." "Mr. Sluss," I said, "I've heard it said that if two people agree on everything that one of them don't add much to the marriage...that the marriage isn't exciting or interesting. Do you believe that to be true?" He leaned forward in his chair and on his face and in his eyes was the look of truth and love. His answer, "on the authority of "God's word, I can tell you that our marriage was wonderful and that we never quarreled. You

know, when you have Christ in your home, you have love and peace. My marriage lasted 68 years, until Bessie's death, and it was a wonderful marriage." "Mr. Sluss, as you look back over life, what is the main thought that comes to your mind and what is the thought that you would leave for other people?" "Well, I've lived through the bad times (so called) and the good. But the bad times were the ones that I call good in that people loved each other. When a man was in trouble, he could depend on his neighbors to help him, and in turn when he was back on his feet, he helped them. People loved to be with each other and would travel a day's distance to spend the night with a friend or relative. You could feel the love. Today we think we are too busy, but they were busy then, too, under much harder conditions. Today we need more real love. My biggest regret in life is that I didn't come to know the Lord sooner. If only sinner people knew the joy and peace they are missing out on they would come to the Lord."

Before my daughter, Beckie, and little granddaughter left, Rev. Charlie Sluss led us in prayer. I will never forget this old soldier of God kneeling before his chair, thanking God for his many blessings, thanking him for life itself and praising God that He had seen fit up to the present time to not number us "among the pale nations of the dead" but thanking him for the fact that when death comes, we need have no fear if we are in Christ. I am so glad that my little granddaughter, Mercy, could be there and that Uncle Charlie's prayer included her.

Note: I got so interested in writing Mr. Sluss's story that I forgot to mention his fine family. There were five children, Cline, Norma, Afton (deceased), Irene and Trula. I hope that each of you have enjoyed these stories your dad has shared with us as much as I have.

We'll have to continue this next week. Just one more story for Jimmy South. Mr. Charlie Sluss told it with a deep-down chuckle... "One day Grandfather Dock's water wheel quit running. He always kept everything in good condition so he was puzzled as to what could be wrong. When he checked it out, what did he find, but a large catfish caught in the wheel, thus jamming it up!" Naturally we all laughed at this one and perhaps it was me who said Jimmy South needed to construct him a waterwheel to help out with his fishing!

One more little note, but a very important one...when I asked Mr. Sluss if he was a retired minister, he said, "Well, yes, I guess you could say that." His daughter, Norma, answered me in the truest sense that I could be answered... "Dad has retired from preaching," she said, "but not from serving the Lord." Personally, I believe that is the greatest thing a child of any age can say about a parent, and may God grant to each of us the ability to leave our children such a heritage!

Anita Belcher's
Mountain Echoes

Rev. Charlie J. Sluss

"A man who believes that true peace, love, joy and happiness comes through knowing and serving God..."

This is the last of the articles on Rev. Charlie Sluss and for me it's like coming to the end of a good book. I always wish good books could last right on and on and as it is with so many of the fine people I visit, I wish I had more time to record the history and personal memories that Uncle Charlie has lived through and made. For the sake of readers who have missed the first of these articles, I will give a brief account of Mr. Sluss' family tree. Charlie J. Sluss is the son of Elijah and Auroa Mullins Sluss. He was one of six children; Saronia, Zidona, General G. W., Cleophas, Charlie and Hattie. All these children with the exception of Charlie are deceased now. Zidona died as a young mother after walking to church in cold weather which caused the measles to "go in" on her. (This is an old expression which we mountain people still use). Her three months old baby soon died from the whooping cough. Four of these children had very unusual names and most people probably didn't realize that General Sluss' name was General George Washington. Many of the older generation named their children for famous men and women of history and from the Bible. We have shared stories of Uncle Charlie's life through boyhood and teenage years up until the time he met Bessie Willis. Bessie lived on the mountain from above Lower Bartlick which I have described in one or two other stories and she was the daughter of Tom and Elvira Hill Willis. She and Charlie met when they were sixteen-years-old at church and continued dating for the next four years. They were married June 3, 1920 and set up housekeeping at a place near Mt. Olive Church. Mr. Sluss remembers that Bessie wore her "Sunday best" for the wedding and he wore a suit which the Rakes boys had tailored for him. There were 10 of the Rakes men, including Alex, Sol and Bertie and it seems that all of them at one time was more or less involved in the tailoring business. The cost of the suit was $20.00 - $25.00. Along with dress slippers, socks, shirt and a bow-tie we can well imagine that Mr. **Sluss made a handsome groom**

135

Echoes

Continued from Page 4

for a pretty bride! After the wedding, Mrs. Rome Willis served a big country wedding dinner and the young couple were ready to start life together in their own little home! Mr. Sluss continued with his farming for the remainder of that year and the next year he started working at the Splashdam mines which was then commencing work. Charlie's job was hauling the coal out of the mines with a pony team. He can tell you many stories about those days which maybe later we can write about, but one thing I will mention is how he recalled the road around the side of the hill to the mines being dug out with picks and shovels. When their oldest baby, Cline, was six-years-old, the little Sluss family moved to Mullins Ridge where they have lived ever since (Mrs. Sluss died in 1988 but Mr. Sluss still lives on at the homeplace).

There are so many true stories that Mr. Sluss can share with us...sometimes a whole story is just tied up in a few remarks. I was telling him about Clynard and I going huckleberry picking in Grayson County and instantly it brought to his mind a vivid picture of scenes long ago passed. "Have you picked berries in the Cumberlands·lately...is it all growed up now? I remember

See Echoes, Page 9

when the autumn fires burned out the underbrush and the huckleberry bushes would come up new every year, about knee high. We could stand in a swag or at the bottom of the mountain and look up and the whole side of the mountain was blue with berries. No, we didn't have much trouble with snakes at those places where the fires had burned. I remember how dad would "bark" a chestnut tree, cut it off all the way 'round in one big piece, make a bottom out of another piece and fasten the sides with twine or hickory and carry it home on his shoulders. Did you ever hear of "Jenny-strings?" Well, that's the inside sap of a chestnut tree pulled off in strings. It has a real sweet taste...." I asked him about the weather now as compared to then. He just shook his head and smiled. "Yes, there's a difference. Back when I was a boy and even years later, Spring came in March. Early garden stuff was planted, even some early corn. We started going barefoot in April...wintertimes were hard. It would start snowing in November, 'round about Thanksgiving and the snow never was off the ground till March when things began to warm up. The Spring floods came...ice two inches thick or more would begin to break up. It could be heard a mile away. Our parents warned us to stay away from the river because not only was the flood waters dangerous, but that the rolling, mad water would fling pieces of ice out that would kill anybody. I've seen sheets of ice as big as a wall..."

"Mr. Sluss, I'm sure you remember the terrible day when the swinging bridge fell over the Pound River. Would you tell me about it?" "Well, we'd held church that day at my parent's home...they were up in years and not too well so we would sometimes meet at their home.

September 30, 1992

THE CUMBERLAND TIMES

REV. CHARLIE J. SLUSS and his wife, Bessie.

Getting To Know Phyllis Bush H. Colley

By ANITA A. BELCHER

I never really knew Phyllis Colley until I visited her home to talk with her and Lamar about the Colley family and about the community of Tivis. I did know that she was friendly in her quiet way and I knew that she was an exceptionally hard worker, but that was about the extent of my acquaintance with her, except that I did know she was a blue ribbon winner at the county fair in the canning category. Because of her expertise in canning and old time applebutter making I wanted to make sure she was planning to participate in the fair this year. During the course of our conversation I realized that I was talking with a very talented lady, a lady who taught a class on "Appreciation of God's Beautiful Creation", or perhaps one on "Sheer Determination is How You Get the Job Done"!

To those of you who might wonder who Phyllis Colley is, let me introduce you to her. She is Lamar Colley's wife, she lives on Tivis Ridge and she oversees, as well as doing, much of the work on the old Tivis Colley farm where she and Lamar live. On this farm you will probably find about what you would expect on a mountain farm, but the Colley's specialize in beef cattle which is a vocation in and of itself, and Phyllis specializes in other categories as well. This farming life is not new to her nor is she a stranger to hard work. Phyllis was born in Scott County on a farm between Nicklesville and Dungannon. One of nine children, (one of whom died at birth) she and her sisters and brothers were expected to work...playtime was that wonderful time when the "work was caught up" for a little while and the most enjoyable times were those times when the children piled in the back of the pick-up truck and went to church with their parents. "All week long we looked forward to that,"

Phyllis recalls. The farm where the Bush family lived encompassed two hundred acres (more or less) and depicts an era in which the survival of families and communities depended on farming. It also pictures for us a time in which families worked together, the very young and the very old, from "sun-up to sun-down" to make the land produce and to harvest and preserve the crops. I enjoyed Phyllis's recollections so much that I am sharing them with each of you as nearly in her own words as possible...She recalls, "It was hard working there on the farm. Daddy was a brakeman on the Clinchfield Railroad for 10-12 years and we children were trained to work along side of mother wherever we were needed. Of course there was a bonus in Dad working for the railroad, in that, sometimes we children got to ride the train down to Miller's Yard where we got off and walked the rest of the way to Grandfather and Grandmother Bush's house. It was exciting to ride through those dark tunnels! When dad wasn't working his job on the railroad he was working on the farm. We raised everything there that we needed except for the staple items such as sugar and coffee. We had huge fields of corn, wheat and tobacco as well as big gardens and pasture land. Our land for the most part would have been easily worked with a tractor but few people in those days had one. Most of us used mule teams. There was one piece of machinery in the community which the owner used to help everyone...it was a threshing machine. At harvest time the thresher was used from farm to farm on a regular schedule. I remember Mommy keeping account of the days till our wheat would be harvested for the women made quite an occasion out of the threshing season. It was really exciting. Some of the women would cook for two or three days and the men looked forward to those big meals. Dad took some of our wheat to mill to be ground into flour. I remember the old Mill, it was known as Bush's rolling mill and was pretty with a big stream of water flowing constantly out of the mountain to keep the mill wheel turning. The flour was really good...it was whole wheat and Dad brought home the bran for Mommy to cook for cereal. It was very good and of course, a real health food."

Not only did the Bush family farm in the usual way but the father in the family had another vocation, that of raising horses for sale. Phyllis relates, "He usually kept between 12 and 15 good horses. Tennessee Walkers were his preference. We had a big barn, about 15 stalls for the horses and a silo where part of the feed for the animals was stored. Yes, I had my own horse and rode until I was married and left home." It was at this point in the conversation that Phyllis modestly admitted that she was selected as "Calendar Girl" for

Scott County the year she was 16 and her picture was taken standing beside one of her dad's horses. Ironically, the work that Mr. Bush liked so much was the cause of his death. Walking up behind his favorite mare, Bird, one day he startled her by giving her a friendly swat. She kicked him in the chest and he never fully recovered from the injuries, though he lived for five or six years. After his death, Mrs. Bush sold the big farm, for as Phyllis says, "She needed the money to keep seven children in school. Just as hard work was not a stranger to the Bush family, neither was sorrow. Besides the death of the father, a sister died a few years ago and a 19 year old brother was killed in Vietnam.

After the birth of her second child, about the time of her first marriage ended, Phyllis decided to enter the field of nursing. She finished the course as an LPN and took a job at Wise Hospital and it was there she met Lamar. After their marriage, Phyllis found herself "back on the farm" working, overseeing, cooking, canning, caring for people in need and enjoying the beauty around her.

For everybody who is interested in the County Fair that's coming up this next paragraph is very important. Phyllis entered beautiful canned goods in last year's fair and received several blue ribbons. However, she along with many other folks didn't get to enter some important items because of the garden field crops had not matured. What every one needs to do is let someone on the fair committee know what the best time is for farm products. I imagine Mr. Jack Childress (Clintwood) would be a good person to contact. Mrs. Colley entered her canned beans, beets, some beautiful pickles and I think some apple butter. She and I and everyone who is connected with the fair urge all Dickensons to begin planning now to participate in the fair for we have "winners" all over the

Phyllis Colley and her son Billy.

county in nearly every category.

Phyllis Colley is a good friend to have. She is interesting and she is very talented. She will tell you that farming is the "dirtiest and hardest work" there is, but in almost the same breath she will tell you that it's the most rewarding. "You feel closer to God", she comments, "then there is the beauty that surrounds you. There is the wildlife and the song of the birds, there is a feeling at night that you have accomplished something, there is the joy of working and watching things grow."

Thanks Lamar and Phyllis for an interesting and informative visit and of course for the good apple butter, the kind my mom used to make! Next week, through the kindness of Richard and Roma Edwards we are going to visit Tivis again, and give a little time and space to some old timers that the Edward's will tell us about. I'm looking forward to it and I know our readers are also!

Life Hasn't Been Easy But We've Been Happy

March 17, 1993

By ANITA A. BELCHER

Richard Edwards is the son of Charlie Bruce and Vadna Sutherland Edwards and is one of six children, the others being Edna (m) George Branham (1) Alfred Hall (2) Grade Stanley (3), Ruth (m) Bertie Rakes, Emma (m) Luther Stanley, Vada (m) Claude Younce and the baby, Arvid who died at age 18 months. Richard's childhood was drastically influenced by the terrible flu outbreak of 1918-20 and though he was young he recalls with sorrow how many families were brought to grief during those years. He recalls, "Our whole family was down at one time. Grandmother Margaret Counts had come to see us and she got sick...then mother. One of them died one day and one the next. I remember how Uncle John Ratliff would carry loads of wood and put it on the porch for us and Ersel Edwards came and did the cooking." The grim reaper entered many other homes nearby. Tolby Ratliff was married to Rosie Sluss and both caught the flu. Upon being told of her death, Mr. Ratliff simply asked them to wait for her burial so they could be buried at the same time. Eight hours later he died. Three days later, Rosie's father, Uncle Tommy Sluss fell victim to the same disease. Right down the road, Lillie Mae Edwards died. It was a terrible February, a terrible two years. Added to the other sorrows the baby son in the Edwards family died. During these awful days Doctor T.C. Sutherland went beyond the line of duty caring for the sick and dying. Riding horseback he went from family to family up hollows and out ridges. Once he remarked, "If I see smoking coming from the chimney, I go in, but if there's no smoke, I ride on."

When Richard was born the Edwards family was living on the Lower Twin Branch, where the recreation park now is. His father worked the land, worked at timbering jobs and some in the mines although as Richard says, "mining as a job was hardly in existence until after WWI." Richard loves his memories of the river before the dam and lake became a reality. "I've traveled up and down that river many a day bare-footed," he reminisces, "and I've caught a lot of fish using a stick pin for a hook. Of course a lot of them got away because a stick pin has no barbs, but it was a great sport and I've actually caught messes of fish that way." However, life was not made up of just fishing and enjoying the river he loved so well...there was work to do even for a young boy. "I suspect I was only 13-14 years old when I began plowing for the neighbors," he recollects, "and then there was also the grain crops to cut, the stalks to plow under, fodder to be cut, oats to be tied. Fitzhugh Colley taught me a unique way to tie oats and no one else could keep up with us. I remember one day tying 10, 12 acres of oats."

School was taught at the school house "out on the point." First teachers were Tolby Colley, Draxie Fleming (Strouth) Auty and Luther Ratliff. "In those days we really had to learn," Richard observed. "The teachers were strict, discipline with a switch or "limb" was a certainty, students didn't get by with anything. We asked permission to be excused to go us the outhouse, laid a book in the door till we got back...first recess was the time for getting drinks and using the toilet but lunch time was play time where we really got involved with our games of ball, ante-over and marbles. Our school lunch, we called it dinner, was usually a lard bucket filled with milk and bread or sometimes biscuits and meat."

During his growing up years, Richard was good friends with the Cochran boys who lived on Upper Twin Branch. He learned to love their parents and even now speaks with deep affection for Larkin and Minnie Belle Cochran. "They were wonderful people," Richard recalls "so friendly and made me feel so welcome. The atmosphere of the home was great and Mrs. Cochran was a wonderful cook." At this point Mrs. Edwards joined the conversation..."My mother always did a lot of gardening and us children started to work as soon as we were big enough to hold a hoe in our hand. Mother sold her garden and farm products...rode horseback to the mining camp at Clinchco and across the mountain to Edgewater, Ky. These were all day trips. She sold chickens and went into the mountains and picked huckleberries to sell...she was such a hard worker and got so much done. One of the things I remember about my dad is seeing him hitch his team to the wagon and leave for the warehouse at Haysi where he would buy our staple items...barrels of flour (eight 25 pound bags of flour was considered 'a barrel' Richard informed us), cloth bags of meal, wooden tubs of lard, sugar, rice, beans, coffee beans, soda and baking powder." So over the years Richard Edwards and Roma Cochran had known each other and on Nov. 14th, 1933, in a simple ceremony performed at Clintwood by Lee Stanley they were united in marriage. "Those were the days," observes Richard, "when you had to ask a girls father permission to marry her. I sent my dad to ask for me and Mr. Cochran consented, then I paid a man $2 who worked for Ritter's Lumber Company and who owned an A-Model Ford to take me and Roma to Clintwood. It was an all day trip and when we returned my sister, Emma with the help of other relatives and neighbors, had prepared our wedding dinner. They had cooked for two days and it was a feast with all the fixings."

Both Richard and Roma wanted me to tell how they started house keeping with the bare necessities... "we had so little and yet were so happy," Roma says in her quiet way and Richard adds, "I left the house whistling and singing every morning and came home that way in the evening." And what was it that made them so happy...a bedstead and feather tick...a table with boxes for chairs...a stepstove and an alarm clock bought used for $1? Perhaps it was the $1 a day wages for 10 hours work, which in the winter time started before daylight and ended after dark. Come to think of it, maybe those ARE some of the reasons Mr. and Mrs. Edwards were so happy. Today they look back on those hard years as some of the best in their life. The coming of the babies, completed their happiness. There are seven of the children, Rita, Harold, Shirley, Sue, Cline, Kay and Scottie. Today the Edwards family maintains a close relationship even though many miles separate some of them. This is not surprising considering their relationship when the children were

See Echoes Page 13

Continued From Page 12

small. The birth of each child was looked forward to, both parents worked with and for their children, and in spite of hard times they had good times together, and I believe "together" was the key to the closeness they still enjoy. Mrs. Edwards is glad that in those days there were very few jobs outside the home for women for her goal in life was to be a homemaker and mother and there was no temptation to go any further away from home than these two occupations took her. "I was a particular mother," she says with her quiet laugh, "I watched over my children like a mother hen." Life was not easy for Richard either, for jobs were scarce and usually there were many miles to travel usually on foot. Ritter Lumber Company began paying higher wages than they had at first...Richard laughs as he recalls how it was at the beginning... "When a new man came looking for work he would ask the old hands how much the job paid. "Well," we'd say, "three-sixty day". That's pretty good wages," they'd answer. "Then we'd tell them how it really was...three meals a day and sixty cents in cash! Later they paid us $2.28 a day but it was still a rough go. A pair of low top shoes, "cutters" they called them, cost $7 a pair and the high top ones that we really needed cost $11. Mining was the next job that Richard worked at, working a little in West Virginia, then going to Clinchco in 1936 and staying there until they worked out in 1954. He then went to Splashdam where he retired in 1969. In 1936 Richard bought his first car, a Chevrolet with a rumble seat, from Hadley Arrington at Riverside Motors."

I was about to forget to mention Richard's other brothers and sisters. After the death of his mother his father married Judy Viers from Sandlick and they had the following children: Trinkle, Walker, Letcher, Willard, Avery, Mary, Maggie and Arbutus.

Richard and Roma Edwards have had a good life and their love has grown over the years. Having THINGS was not important they both stress, it was just being together and facing the future and living each day side by side. Their's has been a faithful, constant and true love... "we have stood by each other over the years." Sixty years to be exact this Nov. 14th! Other important

anniversaries this year...a 45 year Union pin, 50 years living in the same home and 45 years membership in the Tivis Chapel. Richard and Roma join in telling me about their love of the Lord and their church. "We were baptized the same day by Bruce Mullins and Alex Rakes...the Lord has been with us over the years...He has been good to us and we are thankful."

Richard and Roma Edwards on their 50th anniversary.

A Walk Through The Past With Mrs. Bertha (Larkin) Turner

By ANITA A. BELCHER

April is the month that gives birth to so much beauty in God's creation that we can hardly take it all in, and 91 years ago today she was the birth month of a beautiful baby girl who has never lost that beauty despite raising a large family and laboring faithfully day in and day out to help provide for them. Happy birthday, Aunt Bertha!

Bertha Barton Turner of Backbone Ridge was born April 15, 1902. (Her son, Fred, reminded me that that was the day the Titanic was sunk, Bertha was then ten years old). She is the daughter of William Floyd and Sindusty Fuller Barton. Uncle Floyd, as all his friends knew him, was originally from Patrick County and several years ago his sister, Alafair related certain details of the trip into this area...she was 10 or 12 years old at the time... "We had to ford the New River as part of a wagon train group. It was rough and dangerous. The wagon master told us to circle our wagons while he explained to us what we were facing. He informed us that it was a very dangerous undertaking and probably some of us wouldn't make it across. He asked some of the women to make some hoe cakes before we started over, which they did. Like he said, the trip was rough, but we all made it over safely." (For those of you interested in family trees, Fred interjected the thought that the first of the Bartons migrated from Portugal, or so he had been told. It would be a good family project to work on!) Mrs. Turner's mother, Sindusty, was the daughter of John and Minty Edwards Fuller and Mrs. Fuller was the daughter of Lewis and Hettie Ann Edwards.

Bertha was born on Mill Creek where her parents lived for several years. Uncle Floyd worked as a farmer, a logger and a railroad tie hewer, in fact he was well known for his expertise with the broad axe, the tool he used for hewing the eight foot long ties.

"What was it like growing up 91 years ago?" I asked Mrs. Turner. "It was very hard," was her quick response, "a pretty hard job...all us children had to work from the time we were big enough to help with any job there was that we could do". When Bertha was about 12 years old the family moved to Backbone Ridge on a 70 acre tract of land, a good part of which was tended. Corn and potatoes were the main field crops with large gardens providing year round food for the family of eight children, Granville, Della, Arville, Bertha, Henry, Hettie, Gracie, and Alta. All these children lived to adulthood and raised families and all are deceased now with the exception of Hettie and

Bertha. Mrs. Turner recalls her mother as being a good mother and wife, "a hardworking woman doing all the work that a mountain wife and mother saw needful to do both inside and outside the home, as well as bearing her children and caring for them." After the death of Mrs. Barton, Mr. Barton married Nervie Harrison and they, too, had a large family. The following children were born to them: Stanford, Cecil, Otis, Stacy, Mary, Ellen, William Toy, and Harold. There were 19 children in these two families, three dying as infants.

"Back to your growing up days, Aunt Bertha, you have talked about you children having many responsibilities...how about funtimes? I'm sure you all had time for playing together when your work was done?" "Oh, yes," she answered. "We played all the outside games such as ball and hoopie-hide, sometimes what started out to be fun didn't always end that way. Once mother had made me a new dress and I was wearing it going up to my aunt's house to get some eggs. Some of my cousins tossed me over into a nearby pigpen and my new dress was ruined.

Not just muddy...those pigs nearly tore it off me. It's a wonder they didn't hurt me, but it was my new dress that worried me. New dresses were hard to come by in those days! Another time we were playing hoopie-hide (hide and seek) and as I turned the corner to hide behind the smoke house I caught just above my eye on an old nail that was sticking out. It bled something awful and I ran into the house and told my aunt that now I would be blind and couldn't see my mother again. She told me not to worry, I could see her out of my other eye! I got alright, it didn't hurt my eye at all. I still have my scar, though!"

There was fun for the adults and teen-agers, also. One of the characteristics that I have always observed and admired about the mountaineer is his ability to find pleasure in doing his work, to enjoy the everyday and small things in life and many times to turn work into a game so that it was more enjoyable and accomplished sooner. Also, by doing so he involved the whole family as well as the neighbors. So it was at Aunt Bertha's home...there was the bean stringings, the corn shuckings, the various small prizes and when all the produce was strung or shucked, the real fun began! That was when the furniture was carried out of the front room and the dancing started! With Uncle Jim Colley playing the fiddle and Morgan Turner the banjo, (there were others, these were the two Aunt Bertha remembered right at once) the dancing would continue until the early hours of the morning! That's

Bertha and Larkin Turner several years ago.

another characteristic I admire about our mountain people...it seems on the one hand they never got too tired to do good toward their neighbors in time of need and on the other hand they never seemed to get too tired to have a good time! Imagine splitting rails, hauling logs or working from "sun-up til sun-down" in the fields and then dancing the night away!

Of course another interesting part of the "frolics" was the courtin' that went on, for courtin' there has always been and there will always be, no matter what name you call it, and bean stringin's and corn shuckin's was a mighty good place to look the prospects over and maybe single out that certain person that always made your heart flutter a little faster everytime you saw him or her. "Aunt Bertha", I asked, "did you do any

courtin' during those times?" Her quick response was, "no, I didn't", and then with twinkles in her eyes and a smile breaking out all over her face, she added, "well, not much!" Well, beyond the shadow of a doubt Aunt Bertha could have had about any young fellow she set her heart on because not only was she a girl with high moral standards but she was also a beautiful young lady...she still is!

Next week we'll find out more about "the life and times" of this very precious lady, and once again, happy birthday, Aunt Bertha. May the Lord bless you with the joy that only He can give and with health and with the ability to continue to love and enjoy your family and friends!

More Of The Past With Mrs. Bertha Turner

By ANITA A. BELCHER

Visiting with Aunt Bertha is good therapy...in other words, just plain relaxing! After a busy day of doing a "hundred and one" necessary things and needing to do a hundred and one more I found myself sitting at Aunt Bertha's kitchen table enjoying her practical observations on our present day life style and her memories of how life used to be. Aunt Bertha has a quick, alert mind and can give a well thought out opinion on almost any subject and her reminiscences of past years are interesting and educational. How would you like to open up a history book that was written 91 years ago and suddenly have the characters come alive? In a sense that is what happens when we talked with folks who lived then and are living now to tell us how it was...

"My first school year was at Tenso with Simpson Dyer as a teacher," Mrs. Tuner recalls. "He was rough on us but I learned well. I remember having to stand at the blackboard with my friend, Flora Willis. Both of us had to stand for so long a time with our nose in a ring. I remember she got real tickled while standing there. I don't remember what we were being punished for...talking, I guess. After we moved here on the ridge I attended Turner School and Uncle John Turner was my teacher. I went to the fourth grade but I learned a lot, especially in spelling. Up until recently I could spell almost any word and I think I could out-spell most of my children. Once the advanced students in school were having a spelling bee and they thought they could beat us young primaries real fast, in fact they were laughing at us, but that soon changed. I outspelled them all and was the winner of the match!

"Did you celebrate Christmas when you were a child?" I asked. "Oh, yes, the best we could do with what little we had. There was no Christmas trees until after my children was born, but before I married, Uncle Sam Viers dressed up as Santa and brought us children about five little pieces of candy. Later we had a tree and now I wouldn't do without one." (Mrs. Turner's son, Carroll reminded us that the top cut from a spruce pine made a beautiful tree.)

"What about 'sarvice' (service) hunting and sapping?" I asked. "Were they a part of your life?" "Oh, yes. We would bring home buckets of services, I believe they get ripe sometime in June and we did a lot of sapping, too. There's nothing that tastes like the sap of the birch tree. (We all three, Carroll, his mother and I, agreed that the mixture of sugar and water that sets overnight in a bucket of birch sap has a unique flavor that can't be reproduced by any other method and it certainly can't be bought.) I recalled taking a spoon with me into the woods and scrapping the sap from the birch bark whereas Carroll remembered using an oldtime canlid." "What about herbs?" I asked. "Did they play an important part in your life?" "Yes, yellow-root and gin-seng were both plentiful and were used as home remedies and were also dug for sale. Yellow root brought about five cents a pound and gin-sing about 10 cents. The best medicine for diarrhea was the dollar vine. Diarrhea killed a lot of children, you know. One of mine was bad off, look like he'd die with this sickness and I made tea from the dollar vine and it cured him. Another of my children suffered from asthma, sometimes almost smothered to death. I used fried onions on his chest. It was the best I could do and it helped." Before anybody doubts that these remedies really worked, let me remind you of the NBC medical report one night last week, in which they informed us that the root of the Mayapple has been found to be effective in the treatment of cancer, and might even, in some cases, replace chemotherapy! Along this same line of though, Aunt Bertha recalled the terrible fly epidemic of 1917-18 when "there was a new grave being dug every day."

I must not leave the subject of sickness without mentioning the "Faith doctor" and those who were gifted in the art of "blowing the fire" out of a burn. I was well acquainted with both these methods from hearing my mother talk, and without a doubt she knew that Aunt Pricy Fuller at Bartlick could blow the fire from a burn. Aunt Bertha shared with me how that faith doctors would come to the homes and sometimes the patient carried to the faith doctor for prayer. When rightly done, faith was never put in the man but in the God he prayed to, the God of our Bible. Aunt Bertha recalls that her husband carried one of their children on his back many miles to the home of Uncle Lige Kennedy to be prayed for. She also recalls that Uncle Lige lived "in a big log house with a puncheon floored porch". Along this same line of thought I asked Aunt Bertha about childbirth in those days and what medication could a woman have to help relieve her pain. "There was nothing we could take to help, except maybe a little brandy. The doctor or mid-wife was there to help with the delivery but we had to bear our pain. No, we would have never thought of abortion when we found we were going to have a baby...that is a terrible thing. Once I lost a baby when I was three months pregnant and they let me see him. Every little part was perfect."

Aunt Bertha Turner at grandson's wedding in 1981

Aunt Bertha, Carroll and I talked about many other things that she was the real authority on...making hominy and the good taste after it has been washed and washed and washed (lye is used in the making of it) and how that the manufactured kind just can't compare in taste...the making of lye soap, Aunt Bertha could make some right now "if she just had the right ingredients," those being meat skins, old lard and lye. "You used an iron boiler, added water to your ingredients and kept stirring with a wooden paddle until the liquids thickened. Then you let it cool, took a knife and cut it out in cakes. It's the best soap you can use and leaves the clothes smelling so good...I'd like to have some now".

Speaking of soap makes me think of one of the first things Aunt Bertha told me while we were talking to-

gether. "You know," she said, "the winters were a lot rougher back in those years, the weather colder. Well, we had to do our washing outside and we'd get terribly cold, especially our feet. We would take a board (an old chestnut) and heat it over our wash furnace and then stand on it while we worked. That was the only way we could keep warm..."

This was to have been my last article on Aunt Bertha but as I read over the notes I had jotted down, I realized that bits and pieces of our conversation held so much of our history, so much of our roots that it would have been like closing a book before it was finished not to have written it. Thanks, Aunt Bertha for a quiet, relaxing evening and for filling in some pages of the past we would have lost had you not shared with us!

Continued next week.

145

More Of The Past With Mrs. Bertha Turner

By ANITA A. BELCHER

Up until a few years ago just about everybody in Southwest Virginia knew just about everybody else for miles around. Neighbors helped neighbors out in time of need, time was taken out to visit and fellowship was an important part of most everyone's life. Neighbor's children worked and played and fought together...they walked to school together and then it seemed almost overnight they weren't children anymore...they were young men and women, ready even at a young age to take on the responsibility of marriage and raising a family. So it was with Aunt Bertha, who was then young Bertha Barton. Over the years she had known all her neighbors, among them being the family of Sparrel J. (Jefferson) and Rachel Canady Turner. The Turners whose ancestry was Irish came into this area from Greenbrier County, W.Va. Land was plentiful here and it is believed that Mr. Turner's father, Jimmy R. Turner, who was a veteran of The War Between The States (Civil War) settled here and homesteaded close to one thousand acres of land. Sparrel and Rachel probably built their home on some of this acreage. There were eight children in the family, Jim, Rufus, John, Lee, Deliah, Jane, Cecila and Larkin, (all deceased now) but it was Larkin that Bertha began to take special notice of. Though she was only 15 years of age she knew she was in love, and although she felt like "Larkin was the only boy in the world", truth to tell there were other young fellows who were mighty interested in Bertha, one who swore to love her till his dying day. Bertha sent him on his way, telling him that he was a "good boy whom she respected, but 'I don't love you,'" she told him. She and Larkin dated for about a year before they were married at her parent's home, April 21, 1917. Yes, she remembers what she wore on that important occasion... "a gold-strip silk blouse and blue skirt. Mommy made my skirt, my blouse was ready-made. The materials for my skirt and my blouse were bought at Cowan Jackson's store at Sandlick. I believe Larkin wore a suit...our marriage ceremony was performed by Uncle John Edwards of Sandlick...Mommy fixed a big wedding dinner, just about everything to eat you can think of."

The young couple started housekeeping in a one room house just below Larkin's parent's home. They were very happy, too happy it seemed for a war to intervene, but that's what happened. Three months after they were married, Larkin was called into service (WWI) received his training, was sent to Germany and remained there for almost two years. While he was gone, Bertha gave birth to their first child, so we can imagine the happy reunion when he returned. Jobs were scarce in those years and like so many men, Larkin found a livelihood in logging, sawmilling, farming and some mining. During those years he and Bertha built a home close by his parents, later they built where Bertha now lives. Mrs. Turner now recalls that life was hard, there were difficulties to face, but she and Mr. Turner were determined to overcome the hard times and raise a good family. Fifteen children would have been a part of their family but Mrs. Turner lost six babies before or at birth. Nine children are still living with families of their own. They are Flornia, Gaynell, Leonard, Guy, James Fred, Robert, Betty, Carrol, Jeff and Barbara. (One adopted child) Mr. and Mrs. Turner (Larkin and Bertha) were married for 46 years before his death in 1963.

Aunt Bertha was always, in spite of hard times, a happy person. She tells of one lady, a clerk in Alex Arrington's Department Store who would tell her that she'd rather see her come into the store than anyone because "she was always smiling". She has always been a busy lady, providing for her family, going where there was a need among the neighbors, even in the days when neighbors lived miles away and she had to walk.

Over the years she has made all her children quilts and most importantly has showered them all, including 26 grandchildren, 42 great-grandchildren, and 11 great-great-grandchilren with a soft gentle love that none of them will ever forget. Neither will her neighbors forget and even those who simply know her as a friend. My own father, (E.H. Anderson) who taught at Turner School highly respected the Turner family as did my husband during the time he stopped by selling insurance. In fact, both these men spoke highly of the folks living on Backbone Ridge.

Out of everything that will bring us joy about Aunt Bertha is the fact that she is a Christian. Her trust is in the Lord. She was baptized into the Regular Baptist Church in September of 1932 by Elder Dave Church at the Mouth of Road Branch in the McClure River. "I could take you to the very spot," she says with a smile. She also remembers that she is now the oldest living member of the Turner Regular Baptist Church.

Visiting with Aunt Bertha is like finding a quiet pool of water in an otherwise rough stream. She is gentle and kind...when she smiles her whole face smiles. Her eyes which have looked upon death and sorrow, still have the ability to twinkle...Thanks, Aunt Bertha, for the two evenings I spent with you, and may the good Lord continue to bless you!

Bertha and Larkin Turner with their first child Flornia, on his return from service in Germany WWI.

Frances Anderson Shares Her Memories Of Sandlick Area

It was Memorial Day, this year, and several of us were gathered at the George Anderson cemetery at Sandlick.

The cemetery is located on the mountain above the old Starling Anderson homeplace, on property owned by the Andersons over the generations. The path that we once used is hardly ever traveled anymore. Instead a four-wheel drive road has been provided, circling around the hillside through an old field and meandering by big rock piles, which were fashioned many years ago by faithful, sturdy hands.

Mrs. Frances Anderson, widow of Starling, sat looking at the scene before her and said in her own simple words, "Youngans, I can't believe it's like this now. See these old fields, they are grown up. And look how tall the trees are! They're right in the fields. It didn't used to be this way. Starl kept it all so clean."

Most of us remembered what she was talking about. Uncle Hiarm Anderson (father of Starl and several other children) kept the fields I mentioned clean and tended. The old path, I mentioned, led through an orchard of several trees (apple and pear) and there were fences that separated the crops from the grazing farm animals.

At the top of the hill, just below the cemetery was a fine old barn and later Starl built a smaller one. Rock piles, not thrown together haphazardly, but structured carefully like a work of art, dotted the fields. It was a sight often seen in those days, rarely seen anymore, so most of us understood when Frances said,"It didn't used to be this way."

Frances Edwards Anderson was born in 1910 on Rakes Ridge, Prater side. She is the daughter of Benjamin J. and Mary Madgelene Sutherland Edwards. Her mother was the daughter of Jim and Almeda Sutherland of Frying Pan Creek. Frances does not remember her grandfather, but her grandmother is one of her dearest memories.

She reminisces, "We loved Grandmother so much. When we were living in the old Smith Reece house on Prater, Grandmother would come to see us. And we would run to meet her calling out, there comes my grandma, and we would grab her and hug her. Grandma would make over us, hugging us and bringing us small gifts sometimes. She dressed in long dresses and skirts that were very pretty. Her shoes were the button-up kind

MOUNTAIN ECHOES

WITH ANITA A. BELCHER

that she had to use a button hook with. She usually wore a white apron when she came to see us, or when she went visiting other places, even when she went to church.

"Some of my mother's family were Grimsley, Keny, Dewey, Elizabeth, Rachel, Tilda, Winnie and Nancy. I may have left some out, but I remember particularly my Uncle Dewey. He was a real good dancer, he danced the old timey dances. He was a good singer, too and I believe he played several musical instruments. But it's his dancing that I remember most, for he was so good at it. He married Bert Fuller, sister of Mary Cain (Fuller), you know."

Uncle Bennie was the son of Benjamin F. and Sindusty Edwards.

Again Frances reminisces, "Grandmother Sindusty, whose name was often shortened to "Duck" was sick for many years before her death. I remember she wore the old timey night caps."

Childhood days hold special memories for Frances. She loved to work with her mother and would ask her to "please give me something to do". Brothers and sisters played together.

She recalls, "We had good ways to have fun though we didn't have much to play with like children do today. We had to make most everything, we played with. We built play houses, using moss and whatever else we could

Starling and Frances Edwards Anderson shortly after their wedding. She is wearing her wedding dress.

find for our furniture. I remember my first doll that had hair with curls and eyes that opened and closed. It had pretty clothes and I think we had a little doll furniture. I know I'd have to hang my doll up high where the smaller children couldn't get it.

"We celebrated Christmas. We had a small tree with decorations, which were pretty, but not as pretty as they are today. I remember the candles how pretty they were. We hung our socks over the mantle and I tried to stay awake to watch Santa come down

See ANITA, Page 9-B

Continued From Page 1-B

the chimney, which of course we were never able to do. Though my cousins and I all tried. We didn't get many gifts, but all of us got something. Usually for us girls, it was a doll and some candy. The boys would get a capbuster and sometimes a wagon.

"It seems like to me," Frances continued, "that winters back then were colder. Anyway they were cold. Big icicles would freeze and the creek would freeze over so hard that we children could skate on it. Sometimes we would try skating on the thin ice and end up getting wet and cold. Mother would make us snow cream and at Christmastime she fixed a special dinner and would always bake a big cake."

Starling and Frances Anderson about 1980.

"Did your mother like flowers," I asked. "Oh, yes," Frances replied. "She loved flowers and grew them all around the yard. She loved the old time hollyhocks and especially roses. She grew lots of roses, and the ones that bloomed in May were so beauti-

Bennie and Mary Edwards family. Top row: Vesta, Frances, Elizabeth, Alta and Gladys. Front row: Earl, Bennie, Mary and Ernest.

ful. You know, her mother had loved flowers, too."

And so the generations come and go. Memories that are tender bring tears and laughter, especially it seems, when family and friends share them together. But memories are more than

just tears and laughter. They help provide a foundation to build on. And we thank Frances, who is living in

Michigan now with her children, for these memories. Her story will continue next week.

Frances Anderson Recalls Her Past With Sweetness, Humility

July 27, 1994

Truly our lives "are swifter than a weaver's shuttle," each day blending into the next, until suddenly we realize that we have lived a lifetime. That in itself seems strange, but stranger still is the fact that those details of our lives which are now past history seem clearer to us in many instances than this morning's news. And memories of those past days, sweet or bittersweet whichever they be, have a stabilizing effect on our present day life.

So it is with Frances Edwards Anderson who recalls past days of joy and disappointment with a certain sweetness and humility that tugs at one's heart.

"I started to school at Prater on Brushes Spur in a one room building," she relates. "It was a rough place to get into and I remember children could be disciplined in those days with a switch or paddle. One of our teachers would 'nettle' our legs with a switch if we whispered with the promise of more if we didn't stop, in other words, a 'real switching'. Uncle Rene Owens was one of my teachers who was very good but very strict."

"While we were going to school we still had to work hard at home," she said. "I remember the coal banks that dad would open up to dig out the winter's coal. When he got the coal out, us children would have to carry it to the house. We raised most of our food, too. We always had three big meals each day cooked on an old time step-stove that used wood. Grandmother Sutherland had one of those stoves and later my mother got one.

"I remember mother's big kettles of soup beans, green beans and 'roast ners' (corn) and I loved her cornbread. She would bake little cakes of cornbread and call them 'little hobbies.' Her biscuits were wonderful. She would mix them in a big dough pan, then pinch off big pieces and bake them into delicious biscuits. Some of our food we didn't have to plant or care for. There were nuts and berries and one of our favorites was the old time plantain (greens), which grew everywhere.

"Breakfast at our house was always a big meal. Mommy hardly ever failed to have bacon, eggs, gravy and biscuits," she said.

Uncle Bennie and Aunt Mary moved to Bartlick when Frances was about 10 years old. There was no vehicle to move in, such as a car or truck, "so we had to move everything by wagon," Frances recalls. "Mommy and daddy had some pretty old time furniture and daddy had to hire Howard Deel, Uncle Floyd's son, to use his mule and wagon to take us to our new home. We spent the night with Aunt Ida and Uncle Howard and Aunt Ida fed us corn flakes. We ate them without sugar or milk, just plain corn flakes. Aunt Ida let us take a box with us the next morning when we got in the wagon, and we'd set there on top of the furniture eating corn flakes. I loved to hear them crunch, and ever now and then I'd holler, 'Floyd, would you like some corn flakes?' "

The Edwards family moved into a log house at Bartlick, which Frances believes was built by Ernest Willis. "It was a good house, nice and warm," she recalls.

Frances remembers the neighbors

on Bartlick and remembers going to the Uncle Noah Fuller store and buying candy there.

Two memories that Frances recalls with sorrow is the death of her little sister, Lena, and the time her dad developed appendicitis.

She recalls, "Dad worked a lot of the time with timber and logging. He would come home in the winter time, wet and half frozen. One night he came home in bad pain and it was appendicitis. Dr. Sutherland came from Clintwood and operated on him on our kitchen table. They wouldn't let me go in, but I could hear him hollering. They couldn't put him to sleep, you know. A neighbor had to hold him on the table. I tried to slip in, but the neighbor told me to leave. I thought my daddy was dying."

Frances met Starling Anderson at the Primitive Baptist Church at Sandlick. Starl was the son of Hiram and Arnetta Gilbert Anderson who were early settlers in the Sandlick community. Hiram was the son of George Anderson, who was a teacher and Civil War veteran and Arnetta was the sister of Perry Gilbert, well known teacher.

Frances recalls her meeting Starl with laughter.

"I was at church and felt someone tapping me on the shoulder. I turned around and it was Starl. He asked me if he could walk a little way home with me. 'Well, you can walk down to 'the Sugar Bottom' with me, but no further,' I said. Well, he walked down to the old Tom Colley place, and the next time a little farther. We just kept on walking together until we began to like each other real good and one day he walked all the way home with me. (And they kept walking together down life's road 'til death parted them.)

"Before long we decided to get married. We were married at my home and Uncle Rene Singleton was the preacher. I wore a blue crepe dress with a big white collar and matching slippers. My hair was short and wavy. Starl wore dress pants and a white shirt. Mother fixed a big wedding dinner and many of our friends and relatives were there.

"We started housekeeping at Sandlick where the Francis Owens home is now. Those first years were pretty rough. We lost our first three babies, but were blessed to have four more who lived."

Bulah Ann Owens, Peggy Carol Wise, Mary Ruth Hurt and Dennis Anderson along with 11 grandchildren and several great-grandchildren all live in Michigan where Francis and Starl became professing Christians many years ago. They joined the Presbyterian Church at Sandlick and were baptized by the Rev. Tk. Mowbray. Frances has been a faithful Christian wife, mother and grandmother over the years.

Starl was of an "easy going" nature but worked hard to provide for his family. He kept the old farm tended, fenced and cared for. He was of the "old school" who knew how to use a mowing scythe and all the older type tools, which was all there was at that time. His paths were clean, his fences strong, his rock piles neat and his gates, which never sagged, were fool proof against inquisitive animals, but

opened easily for the traveler who needed to cross through his fields. Shortly before his death, Starl began writing some beautiful Christian songs, which carry a heart felt message.

Frances closed our visit with these words: "The Lord has been with me over the years. The message I want to give my children and grandchildren and leave for them is, I want you to live a Christian life, go to church, serve the Lord and be good to one another."

Frances with her four children Beulah (Anderson) Owens, Peggy (Anderson) Wise, Mary (Anderson) Hurt, Frances Anderson and Dennis Anderson.

Hiram and Arnetta Anderson's family. Back row: Ezra, Hiram, Arthur and Arnetta. Front row: Starling, Edgar and Edna. Virgie, Carra, Ruby and Pearl were born later. Edna, the little girl sitting on Mrs. Anderson's lap, married Lee Byers who was pictured in the "Old Pop Factory" edition of The Star. She died a few days ago at the age of 82 and was buried in the George Anderson Cemetery at Sandlick.

Colley, Pressley, Fuller

If you are interested in the continuing Pressley family tree (as I have found you to be), you might need to go back to last week's Star to make connections with this week's information. Last week we mentioned the children of Jefferson and Margaret Hicks Pressley. Because there are (were) nine of them, it would be impossible to trace each one, but we'll instead take the one son, James H. Pressley and follow his descendents down to the present day.

James H. Pressley was married the first time to Kate Charles and the second time to Florence Mullins. Children of James and Florence Mullins Pressley were Myrtle P. (Sneed), Melster (Colley) and Jessie (Belcher). James died at the early age of 26 years, being born in 1887 and dying in 1914.

Florence Mullins Pressley married the second time to Bruce Senter and they were the parents of two children, Gene and Jack Hale Senter. Jack was born in 1928 and died in 1983. Florence, who was born in 1888 and died in 1937, was the daughter of Johnny and Sallie Powers Mullins. John Preston Mullins was the father of Johnny Mullins and was married to Sarah "Sap" Colley, daughter of Richard and Crissie Colley. Johnny (husband of Sallie) was born in 1859 and died in 1934, and Sallie was born in 1864, dying in 1925.

Up to this point, we've been looking at statistics which are of vital importance, but there is more here than just that. Many outsiders who try to write about our mountain people many times hardly scratch the surface. Many times our older people are pictured as underprivileged, unintelligent people. That couldn't be more wrong.

True, our mountain people lived through rough times with very little of

Families Are All Connected

the comforts of life. But this very fact was one of the elements that formed their strong characters and brought out the creativity that they were and still are known for.

I would like to share with you a poem written by Sallie Powers Mullins

Baptism of Uncle Noah N.C. Fuller at Bartlick.

(1864-1925) on the 27th of October, 1921 at Bartlick. Her granddaughter,

Myrtle P. Sneed writes: "I was at her house that night, I stayed down there so much and did her writing and reading for her. That night she had a (dream or) vision and the next morning I wrote it down for her just as she told it to me and "Johnny Paw."

"These sad days are passing by and the autumn leaves come down

All the flowers are withered away and I am still upon the ground.

The lonely winds come sweeping by so softly from the west

When all my children are gone from home they think it is for the best.

I wander all about the yard where their foot steps have trod

I think they would be happy if they would meet their only God.

See ANITA, Page 11-B

Anita

Continued From Page 1-B

I wander all about the place where
my children all did roam
I were away from home.
At times I think it would be best if
I were away from home.
Now here I lay upon my bed with
troubles on my mind
I could not sleep a single moment
until after the train went down.
I heard the echo of the whistle
come rumbling down the line
It filled my heart with grief and I
begin to cry.
I rose up in the morning with that
burden on me strong
I hope it will flee from me like dew
drops on the corn!
The bright sun's pushing up its
modest face while I am happy and gay
With Jesus in the foreign land
where I do hope to stay!"
Today we often talk about how
smart children are. But we need at the
same time, to remember that by the
grace of God much of this "smart-
ness" talent and ability came down
through the generations that have gone
before. And we need to give them
credit for it, and tell our children and
grandchildren how blessed they are to
have the forefathers they had. Many a
young person today is an artist whose
grandparents carved and quilted.
Many a young medical student or
doctor today can trace his abilities
back to grandparents who were experts in the field of home remedies
and herbs. Check it out and you might
be pleasantly surprised.

Now, back to the Pressley family
following the line of James H. and
Florence and choosing their daughter, Jessie's line. Jessie Pressley married Park Belcher, son of James David
and Nancy Hill Belcher. (Here we
have two new family names to enter
the picture and we'll have some of
their pictures later.) Jessie and Park
were the parents of Joann (m) Arthur
Stilner, Charles, Don, James, Jerry,
Florence, Linda and Patsy. Most of
these children are still living and have
children and grandchildren, but space
does not permit naming them all. I
followed Jessie and daughter, Joann's
line because it was from Joann I received the information I'm using.
Even so, I am not going into Joann's
grandchildren, for the reason mentioned above. However, she and
Arthur are the parents of Chester Bill,
Jessie Delphia and Sally Jo.

I want to mention, too, that I knew
Jessie and Park Belcher and they were
two fine people. I did not know Myrtle
Pressley Sneed, but she is highly
spoken of by Joann. Meister Pressley
Colley, mother of Selma Colley
Owens, was one of the finest women
one could know. She seemed to be a
friend to everyone and loved children
and young people. She was one of the
great supporters of school athletics
often riding on the bus with the teams.
Perhaps there will be one or two
more articles on "connecting" families such as the Hills and Belchers and
there are some very interesting old
pictures. The picture today is that of
Noah C. Fuller, son of Margaret Colley Pressley Fuller and Jacob Fuller.
Noah gave the land for the church
building and the baptism is taking
place just above the church in Bartlick creek, which used to run full and
clean the major portion of the year.

MOUNTAIN ECHOES

WITH ANITA A. BELCHER

Colley, Pressley, Fuller

As do most of the original settlers in Dickenson County, we find the Pressley family's roots intertwining with those of the Richard (Fightin' Dick) Colley family. I want to thank Joann Stiltner of the Breaks for this information and I pass it on to you just as it has been passed down to her, either by word or written records. Both Joann and I would be glad if anyone has any additional information or if there is any corrections that need to be made. Just let us know. Now for some interesting history.

Richard Colley, husband of Christine (Crissie) Counts died while visiting his son, Joshua, on Grassy Creek and is buried in the Mullins graveyard there. (This cemetery is now bordered by the Willow Brook Golf Course) Richard married Crissie about 1814. She was a member of the Sandlick Baptist Church. She was buried (in what was then known as the Colley graveyard) at Sandlick just opposite the mouth of Lick Creek.

Children of Richard and Crissie were 1. James Colley (m) Emma Ferrill, daughter of W.M. and Jane Jackson Ferrill of Finney in Russell County. 2. Mary "Pop" Anne Colley (m) David Widener Deel, son of Benjamin and Polly S. Deel. 3. John Colley (m) Annie Davis, daughter of Jefferson and ? Davis. 4. Matilda Colley (m) Charles Anderson, son of Charles Anderson of Elkhorn City, Pike County, Ky. 5. Joshua Colley (m) Didema Mullins, daughter of James (Dr. Jim) and Polly Mullins. 6. Sarah Colley (m) John Preston Mullins, son of Dr. James and Polly

Mullins. 7. Margaret "Pud" Jane Colley (m) first time, Ephriam Pressley, son of James and Biddy Hatfield Pressley. Ephriam Pressley died during a typhoid fever epidemic in the year of 1848 and Margaret married Jacob Fuller, son of Thomas and Annie Gobble Fuller.

In the year of 1858, Margaret and Jacob moved to Bartlick Creek where they lived until her death, raising a large family. Jacob was born in Washington County and he and his wife, Margaret, are buried (on what used to be a part of their large farm) on Bartlick Creek. (This plot of ground became a community cemetery with other graves surrounding those of Jacob and Margaret.) It was also graced by a huge oak tree whose limbs extended far out over the cemetery and I was told by one old timer that when the tree was just a sapling that Jacob Fuller pulled it over and pruned the limbs. This tree died a few years ago, probably roots destroyed by the many graves dug there.

Also of interest is that either Jacob or Margaret, maybe both, requested that a shelter be built over their graves. So for years a little lattice-work building protected their graves from the weather. I watched them slowly decay and finally fall to the ground and I wonder if they were ever rebuilt. These last observations were my own (Anita).

Children of Margaret and Ephrian Pressley were 1. Jefferson Jesse Pressley 2. Joshua Dickenson Pressley.

Jefferson Pressley, born in

Buchanan County, married the first time Margaret Hicks Jennings, daughter of Jess and Elizabeth Hughes Hicks. They lived in Buchanan and Dickenson counties in the year of 1904. Jefferson was married the second time to Jane O'quinn, daughter of Major Roddy and Elizabeth Conaway O'quinn. They had one son who died at an early age. Children of Jefferson and Margaret Hicks Pressley were 1. Jesses Ephrian Pressley 2. Didema Pressley 3. Joshua Pressley 4. Biddy J. Pressley 5. Rena Elizabeth Pressley 6. James H. Pressley 7. Ida Francis Pressley 8. Margaret Pressley 9. George Pressley.

Now the Colley-Pressley-Fuller connection. Margaret Jane Colley Pressley Fuller was the daughter of Richard and Crissie Counts Colley, the wife first of Ephrian Pressley and the second time, wife of Jacob Fuller. Her children by Ephrian Pressley were Joshua and Jefferson Pressley.

Margaret and Jacob were the parents of 1. Christin Fuller (m) Mack Owens, son of James and Pricey

Traced In County Connection

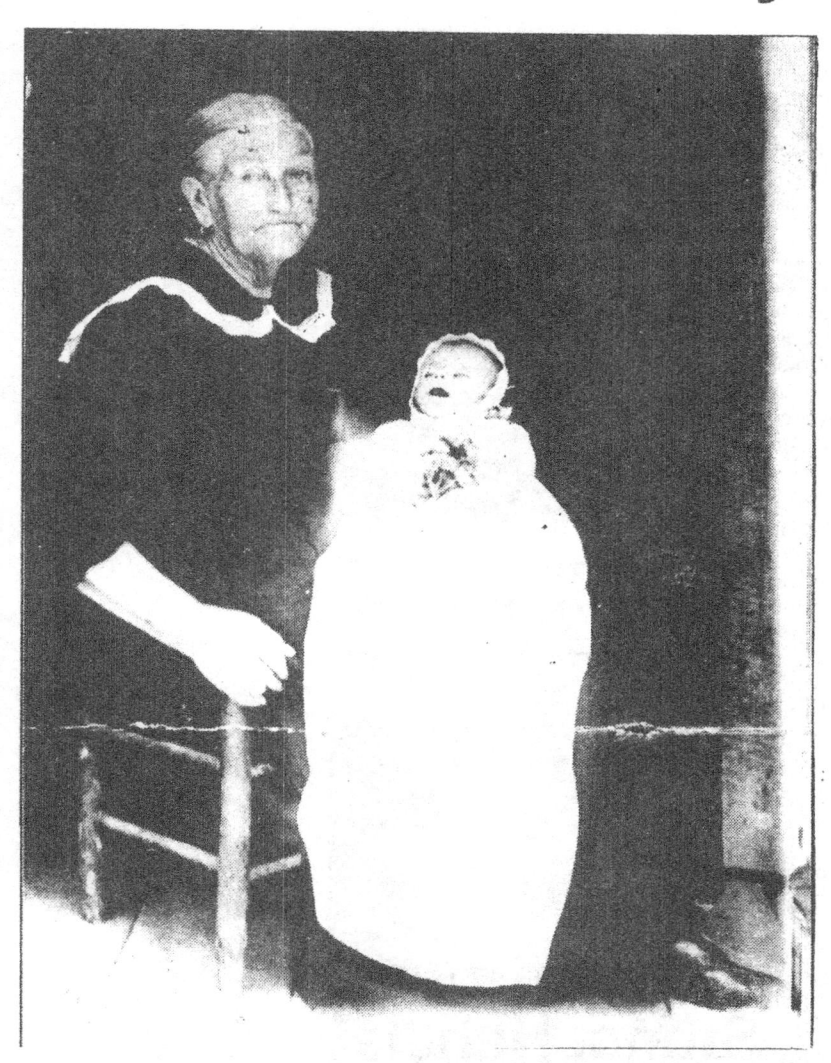

Ramey Owens 2. Henry Hawkins Fuller (m) Elizabeth Kiser, daughter of John and Sylvia Burchete Kiser 3. Mary Polly Anne Fuller (m) Jack Counts Sutherland 4. James H. Fuller (Uncle Jim) married Christiana ? 5. Didema Fuller (m) Manuel Owens, son of James and Pricey Deel Owens. 6. Martha Fuller (m) G. Wash Mullins, brother to Enoch Mullins 7. Almeda Fuller (died young?) 8. William Walter Fuller 9. Margaret Jane Fuller (m) George Owens 10. Richard Morgan Fuller (m) first time, Rosa Belle Compton, second time, Pricey Rose 11. Noah C. Fuller (m) Belle Stanley, daughter of Waitzel and Mary Mullins Stanley.

This will be continued next week. I think most of you will look on this information as I do, not just dry statistics, but as vital, living history.

Many of us in reading through this have found our relatives and realize had it not been for them, we wouldn't be here.

That's a good enough reason to be interested in them, isn't it.

Pictured are Mrs. Jefferson Jessee (Margaret) Pressley holding baby. Does any relative know who the baby might be?

Early Life Of Harold Powers Family Explored

When I was writing the articles on Mr. and Mrs. William Arrington of Haysi, I asked Harold Powers, son-in-law of the Arringtons, if I could also do a story on his parents, George C. and Pinkie Hall Powers. He agreed, and we thank him for the following information.

George C. (Cowan) Powers was born in 1896, the son of Charles and Annie Goff Powers. He was one of three children, his sisters being Roma P. Colley and Lena P. Worsham (second marriage Mullins). Charles W. Powers' picture hangs in the courthouse at Clintwood as he was one of the county's treasurers.

"I believe," Harold said, "that Grandfather Powers was the only man in the county to hold three county offices. He was treasurer, clerk and sheriff. I could be wrong about his being the only man to hold three offices. If so, please correct me."

Harold continues, "Grandfather Charles and Annie lived on Bartlick at what later became known as the Mitchell Senter place. Charles made his living as many of the early settlers did, by farming and logging.

"After entering the political arena and serving in the county for several years, he decided to make a big move, one that would take him to Chellias, Wash., where he went into the redwood logging business. He probably traveled there by horseback and train.

"When he got settled in Washington, he sent for his family. Annie ran a boarding house in Chellias and Roma and Lena helped out. The move to Washington cost Charles his life, for while there he was killed by a falling redwood tree. (Another source recalls that it was supposed to have been a sawmill accident. Maybe someone knows for sure.)"

(Just an interesting note here. You recall I mentioned that while sitting in the airport waiting for our flight to leave, we did some visiting with other waiting passengers. Well, there was a young sailor sitting in the seat near us,

See ANITA, Page 10-B

Pictured is George C. Powers as a young man.

Gilmer Hall, brother of Pinkie Powers, killed in 1932. This is a typical miner sometime in the mid 1920s.

Anita

Continued From Page 1-B

and in our conversation he mentioned that he was from Washington, not far from Chellias. It seemed so odd to have never heard of the place in my life, then within a matter of days to hear of it while in Haysi, then again on my way to Spain.)

To continue with the Powers story, Harold says, "After Grandfather was killed, Grandmother Annie brought her little family back to Bartlick to her homeplace. Dad was about seven years old then. Sometime later, Grandmother Annie married Mitchell F. Senter from the community of Dwale. Mitchell was a teacher, a Justice of the Peace, and a member of the Board of Supervisors.

"He also discovered that it was profitable to be in the 'moss business' and for a number of years he bought up moss that local folks gathered from the woodlands and sold it (shipped by train) to nursery (floral) companies."

(Note — this kind of business was a big thing for both the local people and the florists during these years. I understand the city of Galax was so named because of the leathery, waxy Galax plant that once grew in abundance there and was gathered for the same reason as the moss was gathered here.)

Harold remembers Mitchell very well and recalls that he was a very patient man, especially with children, and was "so good to grandmother." To quote Harold, "Mitchell was a good man."

Going back a generation or so, the father of Charles W. Powers was George Washington Powers whose wife was Martha Colley, granddaugh-ter of "Fighting Dick" Colley. His grandson, George, father of Harold, grew up on Bartlick, and in 1918 he (George C.) volunteered for service in World War I. He was on his way to Germany to join in the fighting when the war ended.

While in service he became a first class cook and he never lost the "knack." His family recalls that he was a first class cook at home and many times the children would come home from the movies to one of his special meals.

After he returned home from service he went immediately into the mines at Splashdam. Harold loves to tell the story of his dad's A-Model Ford, and what a family project it was to keep it in running shape.

Every night (in cold weather) the Ford had to be drained of every drop of water. Every morning before he went to work it had to be refilled. This meant getting up at 4 a.m. each morning, walking about a fourth of a mile from the house to where the car was parked, and refilling it with water carried from the house. Then George Powers would crank his A-Model up and take off around the ridge to Splashdam, where he worked in the mines for between 40 and 42 years.

During some of this time he was making all of 1.87-1/2 cents per shift. During Depression days there were sometimes only two shifts of work per week. His payday, his daughter Juanita recalls, would pay for one pair of shoes for one child in the family, salt, sugar and flour.

Meal was home ground by Dave Adkins. Everything else was raised on the farm, "and plenty of it," recalls Harold. "I plowed up every field around that old home place (the Betty Hall home). Sometimes I'd get so tired and hot that I'd just have to set down and cool off for a while. Those were hard days but they were good."

There is more to write about George Powers, but our space has run out. Next week we'll write of his marriage to Pinkie Hall and the exciting time when he took his family up to where the Hall cemetery is now to watch the circus go by! It was fun, especially since he carried along a watermelon and a cantaloupe to eat while they watched the parade! We'll share more next issue!

Powers Family Story Concludes

This is the last of a two part article about George and Pinkie Hall Powers.

George and Pinkie Hall were married in 1918 shortly after George returned home from service. There is an interesting story connected with their meeting and courtship, but none of us could recall the details. (I believe it is in the article I did on Mrs. Powers several years ago, probably in 1987-88.)

Anyway, the gist of the story is that Mr. Powers was driving with a friend below his home on Bartlick and went into the coal camp which was located on the banks of the river at the old splashdam. This is where the Russell Fork River and Pound River converge. At one time this was a thriving community, complete with homes, school, church, railroad station, company store (commissary) and boarding house.

At the time of our story, Aunt Betty Hall and her daughter, Pinkie, ran the boarding house. When George and his friend came riding by, somehow he and Pinkie met and after a short courtship were married. Their wedding took place at Davis Ridge and the ceremony was performed by Preacher Steve McCowan.

George and Pinkie started housekeeping in a little red school house across the river at Bartlick, and this was where their oldest son, Harold, was born. (In the flood of 1957 the school house, in fact everything that remained of the coal camp, was swept away, as was much of Haysi and all of Splashdam. That is, everything but the memories were destroyed.)

From Bartlick, the young couple moved to Steinman where Pinkie and her mother once again ran a big boarding house, feeding and housing miners who lived too far away to stay at home and travel (by foot) to work. George worked there in the mines at that time.

MOUNTAIN ECHOES

WITH ANITA A. BELCHER

George and Pinkie Powers in the late 1950s.

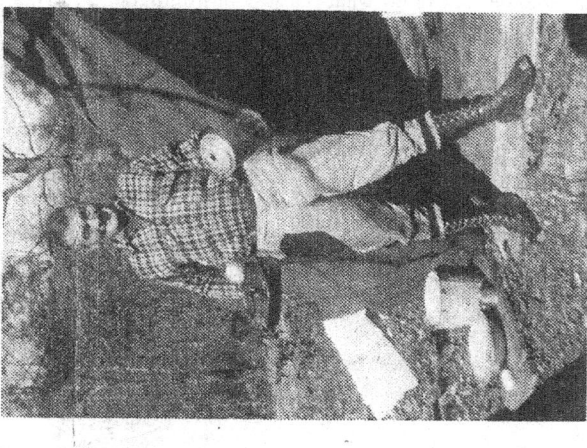

George Powers on a hunting trip in Bath County.

From Steinman the little family moved to the "Aunt Betty Hall" place on Big Ridge, actually Pinkie's old home. There their daughter, Angetta, was born, and also their daughter, Juanita. In those years, there was a constant searching for work which is another story in and of itself. Suffice it to say that conditions in the mines were far from satisfactory, from both the wage and safety standpoint, so often a man would find himself looking for a place that might prove a little better.

So it was with George Powers. Once again they made a move, this time to Wheelright, Ky., where their daughter, Norma, was born. Working conditions in the mines there were extremely dangerous, and before too long the family moved back to the Betty Hall place.

It was here that Harold recalls the A-Model Ford that his dad had, and the constant responsibility to keep the water drained from the car on winter nights and filled up again in the morning about four o'clock. It was also here that Harold did his hardest manual labor, "plowing every field around that old place."

It was here, too, that Mr. Powers shared a special occasion with his children. Harold recalls (along with Juanita), "The circus had come to Clinchco and of course we children would have loved to go, but we couldn't. On the day they left the area, Dad said he was going to take us and we asked him 'how?' since they were leaving. 'I'll show you,' he said.

"He took a watermelon and cantaloupe and told us to come along. We went out to the point where the Hall Cemetery now is and sat down along the road and watched. After a while along came the circus with all their animals and performers. When they saw us, the elephant handlers put on little acts for us. Yes, it was exciting."

When Harold was 12–13 years old, his family moved to Haysi, into "The Fork Bottom." He believes that G.C. and Bill were born there, though perhaps G.C. was born at the Hall homeplace. George continued working in the mines and Pinkie took over a restaurant in town, later becoming manager of the Haysi High School cafeteria. (I might add here that Pinkie was renowned for her cooking, at home, in the church, school, and community.)

Katy remembers her mother-in-law as a "wonderful person who just seemed to adopt me as her own. She was a marvelous housekeeper and a good mother," and Juanita adds that "she was everything a mother should be."

Life was not easy for George and Pinkie Powers, but they took everything in stride and faced everything together. Pinkie had become a Christian early in life (about age 27) and

See ANITA, Page 4-B

161

Anita

Continued From Page 1-B

joined the Presbyterian Church where she was a faithful member until her death. Nothing hindered her from serving the Lord, her family and fellow man.

She was a strong woman with a faith that matched her determination to do that which was laid before her to do. For many years she had spoken to George about becoming a Christian, but for some reason he always "put it off."

"One morning," Harold relates, "Dad came in from work, it was about seven o'clock, and just simply said, 'Call 'Lihu. I want to join the church.'" So in 1957 George became a Christian and joined the Presbyterian church. ('Lihu was Rev. E.H. Anderson, pastor of the church and good friend of Mr. Powers.)

In 1947 George was involved in a mining accident that cost him his left hand. He was operating the motor when the brakes stuck, causing him to be thrown to the ground. His left arm was caught under the motor and his left hand was cut off. Andrew Hall brought him to the Ford garage where Harold was just opening for the day's work.

Harold quickly transported him to Doc Sutherland's where the ever faithful Emma (Mrs. Doc) wrapped his arm in a sheet, did what she could to stop the bleeding, and Harold rushed him on to the hospital.

George continued on with his work until retirement. In 1957 the Powers home was flooded by the terrible waters of the Russell Fork, as were all the homes along the river side of the road in Fork Bottom. The family saved, salvaged and cleaned what was possible (as did hundreds of others) and continued to live there. In 1960 George suffered a stroke and he died in 1965. Pinkie sold the property in 1969 and moved to the ridge where she lived until her death in 1989.

George and Pinkie Powers were fine people, a caliber that we need more of. The family remembers George as a man of honesty and integrity, a man who desired to do what was right himself and see others do the same. He loved people and loved to be around others. "Always pleasant and always a gentleman," is how his daughter-in-law, Katy, remembers him.

They all recall how he loved the outdoor life. Hunting and fishing were a way of life to him, and Harold recalls that he took his vacation in hunting season instead of July.

"He had a big tent and always wanted his family to go with him, besides 14 or more others who would go along. We had a great time and Dad was a great sportsman in every sense of the word.

"Well, to sum it up," Harold says, "Mother was a wonderful person and Dad was more than a Dad to me. He was my friend and companion." What a blessing to be able to say that !

Our special thanks to Harold, Katy Jo and Juanita Powers for taking the time for these interviews.

Old-Time Christmas Memories

Harold and Orba Rush are two of Dickenson County's outstanding citizens, and I plan to do their story a little later on, but right now we're focusing on their Christmas memories.

Fix yourself a cup of coffee or tea, turn on the Christmas music, and let's take an armchair trip up to the eastern part of New Jersey across the Hudson River from New York. We'll share Christmas with Harold in the place where he was born and grew up.

"Oh, golly, I was very young when I remember my first Christmas. My father was raised on the French-German border. He was German and my mother was French, and our Christmas customs were a little different from what they are now. For instance, my Father never allowed us children to see anything pertaining to our Christmas until Christmas morning," Harold recalls.

"After we children were in bed my parents put up the tree, decorated it and placed the presents underneath. Later on, when I was a little older, I remember my mother taking us children to church where we sang the Christmas carols and the minister read to us the Christmas story from the Bible.

"The Sunday before Christmas our Sunday School had a Christmas program and we children all had to take part. It was very nice. On this particular Sunday each class sat with their teacher. If a child had a question to ask about what the minister was saying, he or she could ask the teacher and the minister would stop and give the teacher time to answer."

On Saturday nights Mrs. Rush would take the children to the movies, and it was here on the "Pathe News" (usually at least a week old and on the old time news-reel) that Harold saw the "real" Santa Claus on the Macy's Thanksgiving Parade section. This newscast was narrated by Lowell Thomas.

Also, when Mrs. Rush would go into New York to shop, she would take the children to Macy's where they saw the "real" Santa in person and many of his "helpers" who were dressed like him. These helpers were highly respected because, after all, Santa had to have help.

Harold recalls New York and New Jersey as a "melting pot" of many nationalities who were migrating into this country. With them came their family traditions and national customs. At Christmas there was a mixture of St. Nicholas, Kris Kringle and Santa Claus, as well as other differing customs, but it seemed that everyone was working together to make it a beautiful and joyful time.

The cities were beautiful with their decorations and there were carolers from the different schools and churches. As they walked down the streets, singing, folks would join in with them, sometimes walking alongside them.

"And summing it all up, what are your best memories?" I asked.

"My best memories?" Harold smiled. "I've told you of our Sunday School and Church. Also, on New Year's Mother took us to church to see the old year out and the New Year in. Sometimes, as a little fellow, I would stretch out on a pew and go to sleep. I just couldn't stay awake.

"But I remember our tree. It was beautiful with many unique decorations, and I remember the morning when I was about six years old and woke up to find a bike under the tree! My uncle helped me learn to ride.

"Sometimes we would get together with my aunts. They lived about 17 miles out in the country. One of my aunts made homemade bread. She would knead it on Friday night and bake it Saturday morning in her coal and wood stove. We would have big Christmas dinners. I have many happy memories of Christmas and still love this time of year."

Dickenson County 60 years ago was quite different from New York and New Jersey, but bear in mind that we were just coming out of our "pioneer" days. The modern conveniences of the city were almost totally unknown here.

In fact, as Harold said, "Seventeen miles outside of New York the coal and wood stove was still in use. Out there, it was country. Back here, it was country throughout the entirety of Southwest Virginia, with the exception of a few little towns dotting the landscape, but even they were country and we celebrated Christmas country style."

Orba has her memories, and best of all, she still has her Mom who made so many of these good memories possible.

Shared By Rushes

Pictured are Orba rush, left, and her sister, Allene, ages five and six. Note the little black stockings and homemade dresses.

Pictured is Harold Rush at age five or six. Harold's father was a professional photographer in New York and New Jersey and this is one of his pictures.

Orba recalls, "We looked forward to Christmas and were excited at the thought of what it would bring. There would be fruits, nuts and candies that were rare for any other season of the year. Our Christmas trees were cut from our own property and decorated, for the most part, with homemade decorations.

"Santa was a big part of our Christmas. Our Santa, in looks, did not totally resemble the Santa pictured in most of our minds. True, he had Santa's face (of course), but his clothing was different. He wore a jump-jacket and overalls, and strangely enough he had shoes like our dad wore! Something funny is that we children never questioned the fact that our Dad always had gone to gather in the wood just before Santa came to the door!

"I remember Mom saying to us children, 'Listen! I hear someone at the door!' We'd get very quiet, and suddenly there would come a sound of knocking. One of us would run and open the door and there he was! It was Santa with a sack over his back with a toy for each of us along with other goodies!

"In those early years we girls would get a doll. You know, they were the kind of material that would fall apart if they were left out in the rain, which sometimes our brothers did! I suppose there were other small gifts, but the dolls stand out in my mind. (Orba still loves dolls and, I believe, has a collection.)

"We also had jack-rocks, homemade from pieces of crockery. The boys would get capbusters and firecrackers along with small trucks and cars.

"Back in those years there were chestnut trees in the woods, and we would gather them and roast them in the ashes of the fireplace. There was also a supply of hazelnuts, walnuts and beechnuts gathered earlier in the fall. I guess, in looking back, I can still feel the excitement that a child has at Christmas, but now I also realize that

See ANITA, Page 10-B

Anita ————————————

Continued From Page 1-B

it was a family time, a time when we all got together.

"One of the things that stands out in my mind is the cooking and baking Mom did, especially her cakes. There was the big chocolate cake with candy sprinkles on it, a beautiful white cake decorated with big red cinnamon drops, and the gingerbread or molasses cake with homemade applesauce, made from home grown apples, between each layer and over the top! I can still remember standing by the table looking at those cakes!

"Christ was always a part of our Christmas. When we were very little Mom took us to church, and then when Miss Jenson, Miss Shoemaker and Mr. Mowbray came into the area, they were faithful to teach us children. The church at Haysi also gave us children Christmas treats. We grew up when times were rough, but we were a close family (we still are) and Christmas was always an exciting and wonderful time!"

And what about now? Harold, Orba and their two sons, Bruce and "Binky" have always been a very close family and Christmas has always been, and still is, a very special time. Not only do they share as a family and with all their relatives, but they are on hand for community activities and wherever they can help.

They have always been a big part of the Christmas parade, announcing events and sharing their musical talents and equipment. Their home and lawn decorations add to the beauty of the season, while the big star behind their home has become a traditional Christmas landmark.

One other thing I want to say about Harold, Orba and the boys is true throughout the year, but especially at Christmas. They are a very giving family, and whatever they give or share comes from the heart.

I mustn't forget! Have you ever tasted Orba's Russian tea? Well, there's nothing better on a cold Christmas Eve, and it usually comes complete, steaming hot with a Christmas ribbon attached!

Our special "thank-you" to Harold and Orba for taking time out, just before they went to New Jersey and New York for Thanksgiving, to share their Christmas memories with us!

Harold and Orba Rush are pictured shortly after they were married. Orba and Harold's anniversary is Feb. 12, and her birthday is Feb. 13, preceding Valentine's Day on Feb. 14. Orba says those are three great gift days coming all at one time!

Stanley Recalls Logging Adventures

For the next several weeks, readers of *The Star* are going to enjoy some interesting history and stories as related by Stanford Stanley and his wife, Irene.

Stanford Stanley of the Foxtown section of Clintwood is the son of James Jackson (Jim Jack) and Florence Fleming Stanley. James' parents were William F. and Jane Mullins Stanley.

Florence was the daughter of Sarah and Wilburn Fleming and, insofar as Stanford Stanley knows, all these earlier generations grew up in and around what is now the Clintwood area of Dickenson County.

The only grandparent Stanley knew was his grandmother, Sarah, who was "a tall, slim, black-haired lady, and who to the best of my memory," he recalls, "wore long black dresses and those little black, button-up boots.

"She wore her hair in a bun at the back of her neck and she was a serious, quiet-natured lady. My grandfather died before I got a chance to know him, but I understand he was a farmer."

Jim Jack and Florence Stanley lived in the Longs Fork area of the county. Stanley was a farmer and sold Singer sewing machines, carrying them on his back when making deliveries. He also sold tailor-made suits for the Stone Field Company, "and they were fine suits" Stanford Stanley recalls.

In his later years he did carpentry work and was a Regular Baptist preacher.

"My mother enjoyed her home and her children, and I remember her always holding my hand when we went anywhere. She was a good mother.

"I well remember when some of us children went to Arkansas with Dad.

Stanford Stanley and his wife, Irene, taken at a memorial meeting.

My uncle drove us in a big flat-bedded truck. He, Dad, and another man rode up front and us kids rode in the back.

"When we come to a toll bridge the man was just going to charge for the ones up front, but about that time all us kids raised up and let out a big yell. 'What's going on back there?' my dad asked. Anyway, the man at the toll gate took another count of heads!"

"What kind of work did you do when you reached Arkansas?" I asked.

"Well, we had heard there was good work out there but we didn't find it that way. The only work avail-

See ANITA, Page 4-B

When He Was Seven

Anita ——

Continued From Page 1-B

able was wood cutting and it was slow, hard work. We were cutting Arkansas Spruce and the resin was bad to clog up the saw teeth.

"We had to keep a bucket of coal oil (lamp oil, we call it now) on hand, to brush the resin off the saw so the teeth wouldn't drag through the wood."

"Did you help with this work?" I asked.

"Oh, yes, I pulled my end of the saw-well. That is, me and my brother, Emmerson, pulled one end of the saw while Dad pulled the other end."

"How old were you?" was my next question.

"Well, I was about seven. Emmerson was a little older."

"How did it happen that a little boy of seven was doing this kind of work?" I queried. "Did you consider this work, or did it seem more like a game to you? Did you look forward to getting up in the morning or did you dread it, knowing what the day held?"

His answer came after a moment's thought. "Oh, it was work — hard work and hot work. Sometimes it was so hot you could have fried an egg on a rock. The mosquitos were bad there, too — especially in the low, swampy places.

"But anyway, sometimes I dreaded to go to work with that saw, but I knew we had to. We cut one rick of wood per day. A rick is a space eight foot long and four foot high, measured off with stakes. We cut the wood in 10-12 inch lengths for cook stoves and heaters."

Stanley's knowledge of hard work and its necessity didn't stop with the use of the cross-cut saw. At the tender age of seven he was also plowing bottom land for raising cotton, and hillsides for garden produce.

"I plowed with a turning plow and our old mule," he relates. "The bottom land wasn't too hard but the hillsides weren't too easy!"

"How much cotton did you raise?" I asked.

"The one year that we really raised it, we had about four acres. It was a slow, time-consuming job from start to finish. You plant cotton just like corn — three or four seeds to the hill (the seeds are pretty small) then when it comes up, you plow and hoe it just like corn — thin it, too.

"Then when it's harvest time you strap a nine-foot 'toe' sack across your shoulder, letting it drag behind you in the back so that both your hands will be free to pick two rows at a time. In a day's time we might pick 10-12 pounds of cotton because it's so very light with no weight about it.

"Some people could pick 15-20 pounds a day, but that was about the limit. When we were finished picking, we sold it to a man who owned a cotton gin that removed the seeds. Until the gin was invented the seeds had to be removed by hand.

"We were paid 50 cents per hundred pound for our cotton, the same amount we were paid for a rick of stovewood."

During this time the family was living at Calico Rock, Ark., near the White River. One day the little boy Stanford decided to take a break and have some fun. That White River looked like just the place for some real enjoyment.

When his folks found him, he was having the time of his life.

Even now, many years later, Stanford has a place in his heart for those boyhood days spent swimming in the White River where, he says, "in those days it was a wonderful place for a boy to swim."

When Stanford was about 10 years old, he and his brother, Emmerson, came back to Clintwood to his sister Bonnie's home, and his mother got word that they had arrived. ("You know, we didn't have any fast ways of communicating with each other back then — it was mainly word of mouth," Stanley reminded me.)

"Anyway, I'll never forget. I saw Mother coming up the hill to see us. She had a red apple in her hand for me and when she saw me, she started crying. She hugged me and said, 'It's been a long time — I've missed you. It's good to see you.'"

The feeling was mutual. Stanford was glad to see his Mom and the other folks again, and now he was ready to start another phase of life — school at Clintwood!

Pictured left to right, the mother (Florence) holding baby Emmerson on her lap, Jim Jack (father) holding Joe, then Ruth. Back row, left to right, Delsie, Pearl, Loretta, and Bonnie. Brother Earl didn't get in the photographer's view except for his arm. Neither can you see Stanford. His mother was expecting him at that time! One other child, Dallas Lee, was born after Stanford. All in this family are deceased now except Stanford, Ruth, and Dallas.

Stanley Passes Love Of Music To Children

MOUNTAIN ECHOES

WITH ANITA A. BELCHER

If you have been following the Stanford Stanley story for the past two weeks, you know exactly where to pick up on this one. This week, though, if you listen with your heart while you read, you will hear an intermingling of music, childish voices, and the steady, encouraging words of the wife/mother.

Let's begin as both Stanford and his wife relate the following.

"We were still living at Darwin when our first child, Ronald Stanford, was born. He was a beautiful baby, but evidently was born with a defective heart. He died when he was only seven months old and that was a great loss to us."

God has promised that "joy will come in the morning" when we trust him, and so it was with the Stanleys. A little less than a year after the death of their son, they were blessed with a daughter, Regina Kaye, and then another son, Ollie Jay.

About this time, the Stanleys moved to Lockard Flats (Foxtown area) and here their other children, John Jackson, Demus, Elizabeth, and Harold were born.

During these years Stanford got back into the music world, forming his first band, "The Clinch Valley Boys." It was made up of Stanford, who played the guitar and did most of the singing, Curt Branham playing the banjo, Jack on the bass, and Ollie Jay on lead guitar. Charles Lovell (Pee Wee) played the mandolin.

"My first appearance was over WDIC radio," Sanford recalls. "We played every Saturday between 11 and 12 o'clock. From that point we began to spread out, playing at WLSI, Pikeville, at Whitesburg, Kentucky, then we played on closed circuit T.V. at Blackie, Kentucky.

"We did appearances at Big Stone Gap at the 'Lonesome Pine Jamboree' and at Pioneer Days as well as

'Bristol Country Music Days' and Mountain Empire's 'Home Craft Days.'" (These are just a few of the places and events where Stanford and his band played.)

At most of these appearances, Regina Kaye traveled with them, performing the "flat-foot" dance and also acting as treasurer for the group. Inevitably, it seems, bands "split up" and once again, Stanford found himself forming a new band, "The Blue Grass Cut-Ups."

By this time, bluegrass was the music which Stanford loved to play and sing, and that is the type of music which he and his sons and family enjoy most today. But let's back up a little.

Back in those early years when the family was growing up, music was a part of their everyday life. By the time the boys were seven or eight years old, they were learning to play some kind of musical instrument.

During the day, while their dad was at work, their mother taught them chords. And at night, they and their dad would play and sing. The new band was made up of Stanford and his sons.

Ollie Jay played lead guitar, Jack played guitar and bass, and Demus played the banjo (he can play about anything he picks up, I'm told). Harold also played lead guitar and banjo, and Steve Brown, son-in-law, played mandolin.

Stanford played the guitar and did most of the singing, although the boys also added their voices. I have used the past tense "played" here, but the band "still plays on" when they can get together.

It's nothing new. Mrs. Stanley relates, "I well remember the boys waiting at the door at night for their dad to come home so they could tell him what new tune they had learned that day, and then they would gather

'round in the kitchen while I cooked supper.

"They would sing and play music. After our children have grown up, they love to think back on their childhood. Their memories are good."

This is Stanford's first band, The Clinch Valley Boys, made up of, front row, Stanford and Curt Branham, back row, Charles Lovell (Pee Wee), Ollie and Jack (Stanford's sons).

Stanford has played with Ralph Stanley on stage, and at his Bluegrass Festival at his home. He has also played with Bill Monroe, once singing–

See ANITA, Page 6-B

Stanford Stanley is pictured here with Ralph Stanley and Ralph's granddaughter at the Ralph Stanley Festival about four years ago.

Continued From Page 1-B

ing on stage with him and hearing Bill say, "Well, uh, you got a bigger band than I did!"

He has also recorded two 45 albums, "She's Long, She's Tall," and "Truck Driver's Luck," written by Mrs. Stanley.

Stanford Stanley has been recognized by several of the organizations for which he has performed. He has certificates from Mountain People and Places, Pioneer Days, Home Craft Days, Bristol Country Music Days, and a trophy from the United Mine Workers.

Many, many events and benefit shows have been performed by this wonderful musical family. I cannot express the feelings of his family adequately, so I am going to share a letter from his daughter, Elizabeth, who beautifully speaks for herself and the feelings of her sister and brothers.

She writes, "My father is a special man. He is a retired coal truck driver whose dream and ambition was to make it good in the field of bluegrass music. In the late 1960s and up into the '80s he played music with sell-out crowds to listen to him play.

"He raised six children on a truck driver's pay, and my Mother and he

raised all the food we ate. Four of his children received a high school education and one a college degree, but there is no competition for our father's love for his children.

"He loves us all equally and was always there for us, no matter how tired he was at the end of the day. I well remember sitting on his lap and feeling the warm embrace of his big, strong arms. Often I went to sleep listening to him sing.

"My father is very family-oriented. He was proud of us children and took us along on his show dates. Music, you might say, was born in our blood, and dad recruited his own sons to follow along with him. My four brothers are very talented and can play any instrument they can lay their hands on.

"Musicians county-wide know the contribution my father has made to society, and though I am not looking for fame and fortune for my father, I do wish he could have one walk through the county paper's Hall of Fame!"

These words were too beautifully written to file away in my records and, Elizabeth, your wish has been granted. Your father has walked down the "Hall of Fame" in the county paper, and next week your mother will do the same!

171

Music Led Stanford Stanley

As we continue with stories about Stanford Stanley, he recalls his own life, and life in general when he was a boy, a teen-ager, and a young adult.

Last week he told of his life in Arkansas when he was just a little fellow, doing a man's work, and then of his arrival back home and the joy it gave his mother to see him again.

This week we were going to begin his story as he entered school at Clintwood, but actually his school days began earlier than that.

"As I got to thinking back on those days," Stanford told me, "I realized that I was leaving out my first years of school. I was just a little tyke when I started in the Primer, probably five or six years old. This was at Honey Camp, and Cora Hawkins was my teacher.

"I next attended the Georges Fork school and Zella Swindoll was my teacher. These teachers were very good — strict, but good, wanting us to learn the things they were teaching. I still remember my Dick and Jane reader.

"When I was living in Calico, Arkansas, I attended the school there and had two good teachers, Miss Hattie Combs and Miss Jean White. While attending school at Calico I had to walk three or four miles, a good part of it consisting of railroad tracks.

"There was this big, high trestle we had to cross over, and when I came to it and looked down I just 'froze.' Someone would have to come and help me over. It's funny," Stanley continued, "how that little incidents

MOUNTAIN ECHOES

WITH ANITA A. BELCHER

stand out in one's memory.

"I will never forget going to school one cold morning and this red-haired Arkansas boy walked up to me and said, 'What makes your nose so red?'

'Well,' I answered, 'I don't know, but tell me, what makes your hair so red?'" Nothing more was said and both little boys went on their way to school.

School at Clintwood was his next adventure in education and he enjoyed it, but about this time he began to work on a "subject" which he found much more enjoyable.

"My brother Earl was a musician, playing mostly the guitar, and sometimes he would go out to this little knoll there at the old home place and play and sing. One evening I walked out to where he was and asked him if he would teach me to play.

"'All right,' Earl answered, 'set down here and I'll teach you three chords — G, C, and D. Now you can play anything with those three chords

but you'll have to learn to change positions, because different songs are sung in different keys.'"

After this initial lesson, Stanford went to work teaching himself. For the next few years he went on practicing, playing the guitar, and singing. "Most of the time in those days," he relates with a laugh, "I was my own audience!"

"Where did you get your first guitar?" I asked.

"Velden Vanover gave me one that he owned. He knew I had an interest in music and he gave me one of his. Later I bought one from one of the hardware stores at Clintwood. I think it was a Stella. They don't make that one anymore."

By this time, Stanford was a young man and doing a good job with his music and singing. His brother Earl, who was living in Arkansas, sent for him to return to Calico so the two of them, with the help of two fellows living in the area, could form a band.

Back To Arkansas

March 15, 1997

This is Stanford when he was a little boy, eight years old, in a Clintwood Elementary School picture.

Stanford and Irene Mullins Stanley a short time before they were married.

Once again, life's path was leading Stanford back to Arkansas, only this time it was over a different route. "What was your means of transportation this time when you returned to Calico?" I asked.

"Well. I got up at 4 o'clock that morning, picked up my suitcase and guitar, and walked to Clintwood. There I caught a ride with the mail carrier — Fitzhugh Buchanan, I be-

lieve his name was — and I rode with him to Fremont. I think he drove one of the early Chevrolet cars.

"I caught the train at Fremont, had a lay-over one night in Memphis, Tenn., and next day caught the train to Calico. Once there, Earl, the two fellows who lived there, and me formed our band which we named 'The Arkansas Ramblers.'

"We had a good time playing and singing. Back then we were strictly 'country' and we loved it. We mainly went to people's homes for get-to-

gethers, and would play and sing 'til way up in the night. Those Arkansas people love to dance and play music. They have some great fiddlers.

"One night we had to come back home in the pitch dark — didn't have a light. That wouldn't have been so bad but part of the trip was in an old boat, crossing the White River, and that could have been dangerous."

During these days several "good ol' country boys" were making it good

See ANITA, P age 7-B

Continued From Page 1-B

in country music. In fact, those early musicians paved the way for those who would come later. One such group was Jim Ed Brown and his sisters, Bonnie and Maxine.

The Browns contacted the "Arkansas Ramblers," asking them to join their band. "But somehow," recalls Stanford, "we talked about it but just never took any action on it."

"We kept bumping into each other every time we were in Clintwood," recalls Mrs. Stanley, "but our first date was when I was working in Radford, and Stanford and I met at a friend's home. From then on we dated steady and were married about a year later."

"Where were you married," I asked, "and do you remember what you wore?"

When Stanford was about 22 years old, he returned to Clintwood. While at the bus station in Norton one day, he saw a beautiful girl in whom he was immediately interested.

When he asked about her, he learned her name was Irene Mullins, and that she, too, was from the Clintwood area. Though he wanted to catch the bus she was on, he decided not to, hoping for another chance to get to know her.

"Oh, yes, we were married behind the Longs Fork Post Office. It was a terribly hot day (June 9, 1947) and Stanford's dad, who was the Postmaster and a preacher, performed our ceremony. He said, 'Let's step outside where it's cool' and that's what we did.

"There was a big crowd of people there. I wore a pretty gray dress, and Stanford wore brown dress pants and a white shirt. Mother cooked us a wedding dinner and it was very good."

"Where did you start housekeeping?" I asked. Both Stanford and Irene joined in this part of the conversation.

"Our first home was at Darwin, a three-room plank house with a shingled roof. Our floors were bare because rugs, even linoleum, could not be bought then because of the war [World War II]. We bought a bedroom suite which we still have and still use."

During these early years, Stanford continued working in the mines and becoming a family man. For the time being, music had to be put on the "back burner" so far as playing for the public was concerned.

But when he came home in the evening, a part of what he looked forward to was relaxing with Irene and playing his guitar!

Tune in next week to learn about some of the best country and Bluegrass music you could ever hear! You'll enjoy the story, but you really need to hear the music!

Irene M. Stanley Shares Memories Of By-Gone Days

March 19, 1997

MOUNTAIN ECHOES

WITH ANITA A. BELCHER

Irene M. Stanley is a soft-spoken lady who has a wealth of memories of by-gone days to share with readers of *The Star*.

She is the daughter of John A. and America Elizabeth Crabtree Mullins, and the granddaughter of John Wesley and Alice Mullins Crabtree and Isom and Rachel Hamilton Mullins.

The parents and grandparents were raised in what is now Dickenson County, with the exception of Rachel Hamilton, who was born in Bland County and was also three-quarters Cherokee Indian.

Mrs. Stanley, who was born May 7, 1921, recalls her first home.

"The first home that I can remember was in Jenkins, Kentucky. My dad worked for Consolidated Coal Company and at the time he was only getting one or two days a week. He saw hard times coming and he moved his family back to the old homeplace on Lick Fork.

"One thing I remember about living at Jenkins was how this family of foreigners would come to our springhouse where Mommy kept the milk, and gather the snails off the walls and cook them. To these folks the snails were considered a delicacy.

"I was about seven years old when Dad made the move to Lick Fork, and I remember very well stopping at Jim Fleming's store at Red Onion Gap. We had probably traveled by wagon that far and we had to walk the rest of the way, probably about 2-1/2 miles.

"There was six of us children; the baby was about two years old. Mommy and Daddy had lost two babies while living in Kentucky. One had died with pneumonia (a little boy) and a little girl from unknown cause. I remember that there was a glass cover over her body in the casket to prevent any spreading of anything contagious.

"The house that we moved into at Lick Fork had been built by my grandfather, Isom. He had raised his family there, and then sold out to Clinchfield and went to Missouri where he had heard that work was so good you 'could pick the money off trees.'"

Mrs. Stanley still laughs over this oft-repeated story and remarks that "all the money had been picked when grandpa got there!"

Mrs. Isom (Rachel) Hamilton Mullins at age 16 is wearing a dress she made. She was the grandmother of Irene M. Stanley and was three-quarters Cherokee Indian.

"Grandpa had built a nice home. In fact, in those days it was called a 'fine home.' It was a large, three-room, weather-boarded house referred to as an "L-shaped" structure.

"Dad rented his old homeplace from Clinchfield for $25 a year and even that much was hard to come by, but it was home.

"I forgot to mention that a porch ran the entire length of the front of the house, and (at this point Mrs. Stanley's smile reflects her feelings) today the Lick Fork tipple sits in what used to be the old frog pond.

"The house sat just below it, and we would sit on the porch and listen to the frogs. I wonder how they ever drained that place! It was so marshy and swampy."

Mrs. Stanley grew up knowing what it was to work hard. "Every child had to come with its share of the work," she reflects, "and we all knew what was expected of us.

"One big reason that Poppy wanted to move back to Lick Fork was because of all the land there was to farm, for he knew that even if work was bad he could feed his family with the food we could raise, and we surely did raise the food.

"We never knew what it meant to get out of 'the first weeds' in the corn patches (all you farmers know exactly what "the first weeds" means) for we planted one patch of corn right after the other so it would keep coming in until frost.

"We raised beans by the bushels, and I don't mean just a few bushels! It would make your eyes pop to see them piled up. We ate our farm produce all during the growing season, and of course Mommy preserved much of it for winter.

"She dried beans behind the cook

See ANITA, Page 4-B

Anita —————

Continued From Page 1-B

stove and then hung them on long strings behind the table where we ate. She used them in mixed pickles, and made pickled beans using 60-gallon barrels to hold them.

"Mommy always kept her barrels of pickled food on the back porch and once, (here Mrs. Stanley's eyes began to twinkle, and she told me this well-known family joke which she wanted to share with *Star* readers) my brother, Otto, heard someone getting into the barrels of pickled beans (he had gotten out of bed early to start the fires) and he ran in the house and grabbed his gun."

His mother, knowing his intentions, yelled at him, "Don't shoot, don't shoot! You'll hit some of the kinfolks!"

Farming didn't stop with raising corn and beans. (By the way, there was no sweet corn then, only field corn, but it was as delicious to the taste back then as sweet corn is to us today. It was hard to wait until those first "roast'n ears" were ready!)

Besides eating fresh corn throughout the growing season and using it for pickling, the corn was used to feed some of the stock, and it was also taken to a mill to be ground into meal.

"We took our meal to Crabtree Hollow to the Jarvie Mullins grist mill," Mrs. Stanley recalls. This must have been a wonderful farm with a farmer who knew how to manage it, and I can see it almost as if I were there, as she continues.

"We raised lots of pumpkins, cushaws, and squash. Mommy dried a lot of them and they were so good when cooked with butter and spices. Poppy also fed them to his cows.

"I remember once, when Poppy was fattening up a cow, that she got choked on a piece. She was standing just above a rock ledge, and Poppy told Otto to grab hold of her tail and make her jump over the ledge.

"Otto did, and the piece of pumpkin popped out of her throat and mouth, but she kept on running with Otto holding her tail. By the time they had made two or three trips around the house, Otto was pretty well winded!"

In addition to the farm produce which was raised and harvested, there was a large orchard on the old home place.

"Grandpa had stuck apple trees all over the place," Mrs. Stanley relates, "and there was so many different kinds that I can't remember all the names.

"I know there was a Winesap and a Roman Beauty and an early June apple that we fried for breakfast, and when you have a breakfast from those early June apples with hot biscuits, butter, and milk — well, you've had a breakfast!

"I don't think any of the old trees are left. There used to be some with the briers and vines tangled over them, but I guess they're gone now.

"I remember that Poppy had one or two trees set out in a kind of an incline —late apples — and he holed them up under the house and covered them with fodder. They were what was called 'good keepers,' and I can still taste them."

These are the simple stories of life as it was 60, 70, 80 years ago — stories of how men watched the sky and depended on God to send the right amount of sun and rain, stories of working from sun-up until sun-down, with bits of down-to-earth humor in between.

The stories you've just read picture much of our early county history, and Irene Stanley tells it well because she lived it and because she is a good story teller!

We'll continue our visit with Irene Stanley the week after Easter.

Irene Mullins Stanley Tells

MOUNTAIN ECHOES

WITH ANITA A. BELCHER

If you were going to write a book about your life for future generations to read, what would you include?

No doubt you would mention your place of birth, your parents and your grandparents back as far as you could trace them, and you should certainly mention any notable event which happened to you or any of your kin.

But having written that, what would you write next? Let me give you a suggestion.

Write those things which many people shrug off as not "being important" or which "nobody would want to hear," for oddly enough, those are exactly the things which people want to read and which future generations will treasure.

Write about the "small" things as well as the outstanding happenings of your life. Write about those things which have helped to shape you, to make you uniquely you! That's what Irene Stanley has been doing and continues doing for another week or two.

Mrs. Stanley's memories of her growing-up days at Lick Fork are almost inexhaustible, and they flow smoothly as she relives those days with her parents, and sometimes her grandparents, her brothers and sis-

ters, at the old homeplace.

With a smile on her face and her elbows resting on the table, she says, "I've told you about the farm, now let's talk about raising bees and honey.

"Poppy had a lot of bees and probably 10 or more bee hives. We had lard cans full of honey; we never run out.

"Poppy would 'rob' the bees twice a year ("rob" is the terminology for taking honey from the hives) and besides giving some to the neighbors, we used it to eat and for sweetening.

"There are different flavors of honey, you know. You can look at it, if you have been around it long enough (and are interested), and tell what kind it is.

"Poppy could taste it and tell you

exactly what kind of tree it came from, but the color and taste runs pretty well like this: lynn and sourwood are white and mild in flavor, poplar is the reddest with a stronger flavor, while locust and clover are medium in color and flavor.

"At least, that's the way I remember it. Some people feed their bees sugar, and if they do, the honey they make will turn to sugar. Pure honey won't do that.

"Oh, I must tell you a funny story about Poppy and the bees! There were two kinds of birds that set on the limbs of the trees, waiting for the bees to come out of the hives. Then they would dive down and eat them, and wait for the next ones to come out.

Of Everyday Happenings

Left to right are Wesley, Otto, Carnegia and Irene Mullins. Shirts, pants and dresses were all hand-made by their mother. The picture was made at the homeplace at Lick Fork.

"Well, my brothers, Westly and Otto, had gravel shooters, and they would try to shoot the birds. One day Poppy came out and said, 'Boys, let me show you how to do this!'

"He took one of those sling shots, drew back, held his thumb up, and

said, 'Now see here! See my thumb? I use it to sight with, like this!' He took aim, let go with that gravel and, ping! It hit him right on the thumb nail.

See ANITA, Page 10-B

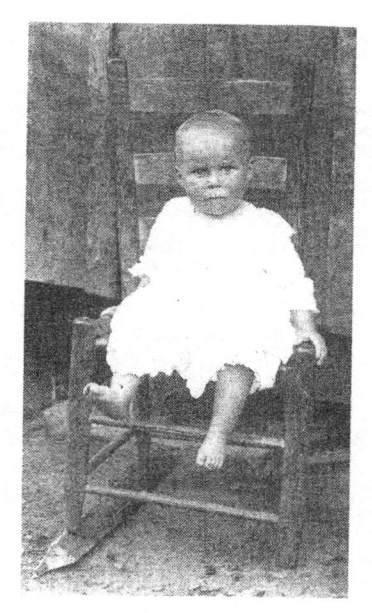

April 02, 1997

Irene Mullins Stanley, when she was a baby. Note the beautiful dress hand-made by her mother. This picture was made while living in Kentucky.

Continued From Page 1-B

"Well, Poppy didn't try to give the boys any more lessons in gravel shooting, and his thumb nail eventually turned black and came off.

"Yes," Irene replies in answer to my next question, "yes, we raised cane and had big stir-offs each fall, probably in October. Of course we did it in what is now called 'the old-time way.' Then, it was the only way!

"We used the mule to pull the guide pole around the cane mill, his end being lighter and longer than the opposite end. I've fed cane into the mill many a time, and I well remember that I had to duck each time the heavy end of the pole came around, or I would have gotten knocked in the head!

"By the way, that guide pole was a log, a hickory, I suppose. Mommy would usually 'judge' the molasses, which meant she would say when they were ready to take off.

"Well, one fall Poppy told Mommy she was letting them come off too thin and he'd judge the next batch. He did so, and when they started pouring them into the cans, they turned to taffy!

"We ate taffy for a long time that year. We'd take a stick and wind it around and around in the can and bring it out taffy-coated! We used

molasses for eating and some for sweetening, and of course, Mommy made molasses cake.

"Mommy would also 'fry' molasses. She'd put a little oil in the pan and some soda in the molasses and stir it all together until it reached a boil, and it was very good that way. At least we thought so!"

Mrs. Stanley continues, "Speaking of food, the Lick Fork area was a natural place for berries to grow, especially blackberries and wild strawberries. Mommy would can them in gallon cans for dumplings and cobblers.

"We always had a lot of company at our house to eat, because everybody around knew how good a cook Mommy was.

"Well, it was my job, along with my sister, Carnegia, to wash the dishes. That was a big job when we had so much company, and I would stack the plates up real high and carry them to the kitchen.

"Poppy told me one day that I was going to drop them, and if I did, I would get a whipping. I told him I wouldn't drop them, I knew just how to carry them.

"Then, just like you might know, it happened! I dropped the whole stack and every one of them broke! I got my whipping, and we had to eat out of bucket lids until Mommy and Poppy

could get some more plates!

"Another thing I'll never forget is how that after dinner, when the weather was cold, everyone would gather around the fireplace and talk. They'd talk about everyday happenings, and then they'd tell stories, jokes and riddles.

"I remember a lot of the riddles, and I'll tell you one of them. 'Six set, seven sprung, and out of the dead the living come.'"

Can you guess the answer? I couldn't! Can any of you readers? We'll tell you the answer next week!

"There was something kindly funny about those times when we set around the fire," Mrs. Stanley continued.

"We just had those bark-bottomed chairs, you know. There wasn't any couches or anything like that.

"Well, sitting around the fire talking, folks get thirsty. Someone would say, 'I'm thirsty. Would somebody get me a drink?' Nobody would move. Why? Because nobody wanted to lose his seat by the fire!

"You see, some of us would be standing there waiting for an empty seat! I liked those times, though. There was no radio, much less a television. None of the violence and vulgarity that we hear and see today. Just sharing. It was better that way!"

Continued next week.

Irene Stanley Shares Winter

This week Irene M. Stanley shares some bits of "Americana" which take us back to the grassroots of our area. No doubt these are some of the "fireside" stories which were told on long winter evenings, or perhaps while sitting together on the porch at the close of a hot summer day.

Let's begin with a couple of ghost stories. Mrs. Stanley is our narrator.

"My Aunt Pearly Crabtree, who lived on Lick Fork, raised a lot of beans which she peddled over in Jenkins, Kentucky. She went by the way of what we now call Red Onion Gap and where Jim Fleming had his store in a low 'cut' there.

"Well, there was a bottom, a piece of land called 'The Sarah Bottom' there at Lick Fork, and when Aunt Pearly would reach that bottom, this big black thing (it looked like a bear) would climb up behind her and ride to the 'Meek Bottom' where it would disappear.

"One evening, Mommy sent my brother, Westly, to Jim Fleming's store to get some coffee, at least I suppose it was coffee, for Mommy and Poppy couldn't do without it, and on the way back from the store that 'thing' climbed up behind Westly.

"It like to have scared him to death! He rode that mule hard into the yard, jumped off his back, and into the house he came, closing the door behind him. Poppy told him he'd better put the mule up, and Westly answered that he wasn't going back outside that

MOUNTAIN ECHOES

WITH ANITA A. BELCHER

house for anything! ·

"Brother Otto had to put the mule in the barn. No, Aunt Pearly wasn't afraid. She said she'd never done anything to hurt anyone and there was no reason for her to be afraid!"

Irene's husband, Stanford, had been listening to her story, along with my daughter Becky and me, and he remarked, "You know, your Dad saw a ghost over at the old coke ovens on Tom's Creek."

"Oh, yes," Irene replied. "I've heard Poppy tell that story many a time. Poppy and Uncle Trig was working at the coke ovens there at Tom's Creek (you can still see where they were) and one night they walked down the road to get some water.

"Suddenly, right in front of them, was this ghost. Poppy started running, with Uncle Trig hollering, 'Wait, Johnny! Wait for me!' Poppy didn't wait for anything. He just kept on running with Uncle Trig right behind

him!

"I guess what they were thinking of was a girl that had been killed there, and other people had claimed to see her ghost."

Mrs. Stanley's eyes began to twinkle and I knew another story was in the making.

"Poppy decided he'd make a little whiskey to help out with the finances, so he and his nephew, Garnie, had a still in the woods which they worked at night.

"One night they heard steps coming through the leaves, and they thought it was the revenue officers. 'Run, Uncle Johnny, run,' yelled Garnie, and Poppy yelled right back, 'Don't call me by my name, Garnie. They'll know who I am!'

"The 'revenue officer' turned out to be a dog!"

Speaking of dogs, here's another interesting story.

"Aunt Hulda lived over in Bur-

180

'Fireside' Stories

Isom and Rachel Hamilton Mullins, paternal grandparents of Irene M. Stanley.

John Westly and Alice Mullins Crab-tree, maternal grandparents of Irene M. Stanley.

dine, Kentucky, and she had this big bull dog that the neighbors started complaining about. She asked my Dad if he would bring him over to our house and keep him.

"Poppy said he would, and after he'd kept him for several months, Aunt Hulda decided she wanted him back. Poppy took him back and — guess what? In no time that dog was right back at our house!

"He had traveled all the way from Burdine by himself, and that's not all. From that time on, that dog traveled back and forth between Lick Fork and Burdine whenever he wanted to.

"Oh, yes, there's another funny story I want to tell you about Poppy," Irene said with a jolly laugh.

See ANITA, Page 3-B

Anita ——————————————

Continued From Page 1-B

"One night we heard something in our chickens, and Poppy said it was an owl, and that it was in the big oak tree that stood right in front of our house.

"Mommy said that her guineas were roosting up in that tree, but Poppy said it was an owl, but 'be it guinea or owl it's coming down,' he said. 'Go get my gun, Otto,' he told my brother.

"'I believe that's my guineas, John,' Mommy said, but Poppy pulled the trigger and shot right into that tree. Well, you might know what fell out was one of Mommy's guineas!"

As we talked, there would be little "side glimpses" of by-gone days, of the older folks who continued to be an important part of the home until they were no longer there, and even then their influence remained.

"I well remember," Mrs. Stanley reminisced, "how that Grandpa Crabtree would tell us about walking many a day from Wolf Pen at Darwin to Tom's Creek at Coeburn where he worked at the coke ovens for $1 a day.

"Another thing I remember," and here she chuckled at the memory, "is how that when Grandpa and Grandma Mullins (Isom and Rachel) came back from Missouri, they spent a great deal of time with us.

"They had their favorite place near the fireplace, and here they would sit and talk, and argue about who was going to die first. Grandma was sure it would be her, and Grandpa was emphatic in his belief that it would be him.

"Well, Grandpa won the argument. He died several years before Grandma."

Ten Sisters Learned Manners

For the next three weeks, you are going to enjoy stories told by one of the area's best storytellers, who has a vivid memory, a keen sense of humor, and a heart of compassion.

You'll hear (or rather you'll read) stories of 10 girls raised on a mountain farm, of a grandpa who was a "jolly old fellow", and of parents who opened their heart and home to anyone who was in need.

Here's one other thing to "whet your appetite"!

You know we've all heard the younger generation talk about their "sleep-ins" or their "sleep-overs"? Well, I doubt if any of them ever experienced the kind or the number which our storyteller recalls, but I'm going to keep you in suspense on that story for a week or two!

Now lean back in your chair and relax as Beulah Lyall takes us back down (or maybe down for the first time) over a well-worn path where no foot prints can now be seen, but where memories linger.

"I was born on Nealy Ridge, one of 10 girls," Beulah says with a smile. "No boys, just us girls! Can you imagine 10 girls growing up together?

"My parents were Floyd and Lucretia Yates Arrington. Paternal grandparents were Brice and Polly Ann Stinson Arrington, and maternal grandparents were Jeremiah and Polly Yates.

"I remember my grandpa Arrington very well. He was a jolly old fellow who sat around and sang funny little songs for us children. He never scolded us or told us to get to work.

MOUNTAIN ECHOES

WITH ANITA A. BELCHER

Beulah Lyall, our story teller for the next three weeks.

Grandpa Brice Arrington

Sometimes he would sit, holding his cane in front of him, and "nod off" to sleep.

"Grandpa Yates was a tall man and very industrious. He was very neat and wanted us children to be the same way. 'Now, wash your face and brush your hair,' he'd say.

"He thought the world of my mother and always wanted us children to help her all we could. 'Now go tote that wood in for your mammy,' he'd tell us. Both my grandfathers

visited in our home often, but my grandmothers died before I could know them."

Home for Beulah was on Nealy Ridge, where she says, "I remember our first house. It was part log, part plank, with Daddy adding on rooms as he could. I guess Uncle Tom Singleton built the log part, for so far as I know he was the first person who lived there.

"Some of my best memories are of the board walk that led from the front door of the log house to the gate in the paling fence. I played on that walk when I was real small, for hours at a time.

"We had a pretty yard to play in. There were about six big locust trees and a weeping willow which we sat under on hot days. It was shady and cool there, and the willow was so pretty.

"Mother raised lots of flowers. She had roses growing alongside the fence, Rose of Sharon bushes, lavender li-

lacs whose fragrance was wonderful, old time snow-ball bushes, and peonies.

"Outside the fence was a lane, which was fenced on both sides and which led to the main road. Folks traveled this road on their horses, and when visiting us they hitched the horses to the paling fence posts.

"Right in the middle of this lane stood a big chestnut tree, the biggest

See ANITA, Page 10-B

185

From Their Mother

Anita —————————————

Continued From Page 1-B

I've ever seen, with the best nuts I've ever eaten. Funny thing, though, the nuts were small. During those years everyone let their stock run free, and when those chestnut started falling we had to beat the pigs to them!

"Let me tell you something else about our yard," Beulah said. "You know my Dad worked at many things and worked hard in his community and county. He was a fire warden, postmaster, a school board member for years, and it seems to me that he was on the jury for half his life!

"He was also a Justice of the Peace, and during the summer he would hold court in our yard under the trees. We children were allowed to hear a lot of the cases, but some of them Daddy wouldn't let us hear.

"Many cases were settled there in our yard. People sometimes were found guilty and fined or sent to jail. Of course, sometimes thy were found 'not guilty.'"

Beulah loves recalling past days and events, and she has no trouble recalling even the smallest details.

"Inside our home there was no living room as such," she recalls, "because with a family like ours there had to be beds in every room except the dining room and kitchen.

"However there was one room that was different. I guess it was the 'front room,' but there was still a bed in it."

"Then what made it different?" I asked.

"Well, that was where Mommy and Daddy slept, and that's where the Post Office was located. Did I tell you that Daddy was instrumental in establishing the Post Office at Tenso and then the one on Nealy Ridge? He was Post Master for a long time at Nealy Ridge.

"Anyway, in that room was the old crank-type telephone and a big fireplace. In the winter time, when people came to get their mail (usually the men), they would sit in front of the fire and talk about their work and swap stories. There was a lot of good storytellers back then.

"But let me tell you about our beds! We had straw ticks on all our beds, and feather beds on top of the straw ticks. Every year we changed the straw (it smelled so fresh and clean) and washed the ticks and boiled them.

"Mommy was a very clean person. With all the hard work she did, I never saw her dirty. I have heard it said that she was a beautiful girl in her growing-up days.

"I know she was a good mother. In fact, when we got spanked, Mother was the one who did it, but she was very kind.

"That's one of the things I will always remember about Mommy and Dad: they were strict but they were kind. They were hard workers and kept us girls busy on the farm there on Nealy Ridge.

"All of us, us children too, had to work, because the farm had to provide most of the food we ate. But," and here Beulah leans forward and smiles, "we had good times growing up as a family there on the Ridge, and we had good neighbors.

"We got to spend time with our friends and cousins who lived in the area, and the boys who lived around us were good boys. They never said or did anything out of the way. Though they were full of fun, they treated us with respect.

"Yes, I remember who they were. Just to name a few, there was Uncle 'Hop' Counts' boys, Uncle Tilden, Uncle Noah, and 'Aut' Counts who all had boys, and there were the Hale boys and the Arville Deel family. All of them had fine boys.

"Also (and here Beulah's smile is one of sweet remembrance), we girls were taught how to act. We never left home without our mother first talking to us about how to act, how to conduct ourselves as young ladies.

"Usually she and Daddy or an older sister went with us, but even so, she counseled with us and would say, 'Now girls, if you need to go outside for anything, have the lady of the house go with you, for that way nobody can talk about you!'"

What an example this mother set, and what a pattern for mothers of today and mothers of tomorrow to follow!

Continued next week.

Front row, first gentleman is Jeremiah Yates, Beulah's maternal grandfather. Back row, second from left, Uncle Bob Arrington, fifth from left, Andy Yates, John Yates and David Yates, all sons of Jeremiah.

Lyall Tells Of Pioneers Who Made Local History

For the past two weeks, Clynard and I have enjoyed visiting with Beulah Lyall and "seeing" local history unfold before our eyes, as we listened to her describe how life used to be, and as she shared memories with us of some of the pioneer people who helped make that history.

Last week she spoke of her grandparents, her parents, and her early life. This week she continues with some additional information about her parents and how "things were back then."

"My parents, Floyd Monroe and Lucretia Yates Arrington, came from honest, God-fearing, hard-working people. My father was born on Backbone Ridge, September 15, 1870, and my mother was born on Edwards Ridge above Sandlick, November 9, 1878.

"Mother and Daddy grew up only five or six miles apart and married April 22, 1896. They first lived on Mill Creek (Tenso) and then they moved to Nealy Ridge where they spent most of their lives.

"My sisters often went back to the place where Dad was born and loved it very much, and so did I, but I also dearly loved the homeplace where Mother was born.

"Clarnie Lyall lives there now, and you probably know that it's near to the old Nicey Anderson homeplace.

"My mother and Aunt Nicey were childhood friends, playmates, and loved each other very much. My sister Margaret and I used to visit the neighbors and relatives on Edwards Ridge, and were often in the home of

See ANITA, Page 7-B

Floyd and Lucretia Arrington, Beulah's parents, at home on Nealy Ridge.

188

Anita —

Continued From Page 1-B

Uncle Dave and Aunt Melvina Yates.

"Uncle Dave was my mother's brother, and one of his children was Delphia. She married Stanford Anderson, and I'm going to tell you something."

At this point in our conversation, Beulah stops to reflect a few minutes as she thinks back on those days when she and her sisters and their friends were young, with life spread out before them, and her memories are good.

"You know, I'm going to tell you. Delphia Yates Anderson was one of the prettiest girls I've ever seen. She had dark curly hair and deep blue eyes.

"Many of those girls were beautiful. There was Mae Edwards Colley and her sister, Polly Ann, and also Lucille Counts — and my own sisters were pretty, too."

"Miss Beulah, you grew up in a large family of girls, and you had many cousins and friends. What did you young people do back then for recreation?" I asked.

"Oh, I have wonderful memories of growing up," was her quick response. "My parents were hard-working people, and they taught us to work as soon as we were big enough, but we were allowed to have fun, too.

"One of the fun things in our life was that we were allowed to have our friends in our home. I can't remember when we didn't have company, both young and old. Mother always cooked for our friends as well as the older folks and relatives, and I never heard her complain."

Suddenly a thought came to my mind. "You are talking about cooking and it makes me wonder. What did you young folks do for snacks back then, since hamburgers and chips were unheard of?"

Miss Beulah answered that one with a hearty laugh. "Well, there was usually food cooked, but I remember in the summer time we'd go out to the garden and gather fresh corn to boil, or find a big ripe tomato and make us a sandwich. Now that was good eating!

Pictured are the 10 Arrington girls at their home in 1928. Left to right, seated, Willie, Beulah, Margaret, Bonnie and Norma. Standing, Carrie, Polly, Maxie, Stella and Maude.

Pictured front row, Joe Arrington, Bob Arrington, Floyd Arrington and Jim Arrington. Back row, Ellen Arrington Owens, Melissa Arrington Singleton, Nannie Ellis, Caldonia Counts and Emeline Rose.

"There weren't many restaurants in those days and 'fast food' places hadn't been thought about, but we thought our food was wonderful!"

Miss Beulah and I agreed that fresh corn-on-the-cob and a ripe tomato with a biscuit couldn't be beat, but before we made ourselves too hungry, we got back to the subject of fun times in those long-ago days.

It's funny, but it's wonderful how those "fun times" and home responsibilities were so closely related that it was hard to separate them, but isn't that the way it should be? Listen as Miss Beulah tells me about it.

"I helped to do all the chores on the farm and in our home. I learned to clean, cook, and can, to churn and mold butter. I helped plant our crops, helped tend and harvest them.

"We had lots of apples, cherries, and peaches. I would climb the trees and pick the fruit. I can remember hauling a whole crop of corn from the field and never stopping until every ear was stored in the corn crib.

"And the fun? Well, after the work was done, we had corn-shuckings and bean-stringings, and then we would have a square dance! We had some fine musicians in our community, so we never lacked for music!

"We had ball games on Saturday and Sunday afternoons (well, most of Sunday was at church and feeding the folks afterwards) and in the fall we gathered chestnuts and other nuts and wild grapes.

"We had grapevine swings, and I can still feel the thrill of swinging on them. We also did a lot of horseback riding, and that was a lot of fun.

"I could handle a horse very well from the time I was 14 or 15 years old. I could saddle it for riding, or put its work rig on it just the way Dad taught me.

"My sisters and I shared the fun and the work. They helped me with everything I did, and by the time I grew up, several of them had married and had children. I spent a lot of time at their homes helping them, and I learned a lot about caring for children in those days.

"You know my daddy and mother were the parents of 12 children, two of whom died in infancy. One of these was the only son they had. They raised 10 girls to adulthood before Mother's death, February 16, 1948.

"These children were Carrie Mullins Counts, Polly Ann Mullins, Maxie Counts, Stella Deel Baker, Maude Hay, Willie Hay, Beulah Harlow Lyall, Margaret Reedy Mullins Hillman, Bonnie Dickerson, and Norma Buchanan.

"The ones living now are Maude, myself, and Norma. Daddy died at the age of 93, February 6, 1962.

"I was blessed to have a wonderful family, and my Daddy and Mother were exceptional parents, always setting a good example for their daughters. I thank the good Lord for them.

Continued next week.

Note: The large picture of last week needs a correction. The gentleman in the front row, seventh from the left, is Beulah's grandfather, Jeremiah Yates. If anyone can identify any of the others, please call 926-6011 (Dick Troyer) in the afternoon. If there is no answer, please leave your message on the answering service.

Beulah Lyall Creates Pictures Of The Past

For the past three weeks, readers of *The Star* have had an opportunity to "visit" with Beulah Lyall. And I have certainly been privileged to spend quite a few hours with this lovely lady, listening to stories of our early pioneers and how they lived, and how they worked from "sun-up to sundown" to make a living for their families.

Through her stories, I have watched a child sit on a board-walk and play in the sun, I have watched teenagers walk through the dewy grass of early morning to gather chestnuts in the lane, and I have seen honorable young men courting beautiful young girls.

I have closed my eyes and listened to the music of the fiddle, guitar and banjo, and watched the young folks dance after a hard day's work on the farm while the "old folks" kept a watchful eye and sometimes joined in the fun.

I have heard about the grist mill run by Beulah's father, and how the men would bring their grain to be ground, and how they would visit and swap stories while waiting for their meal.

I have "watched" her mother round up the sheep, herd them into the barn and shear them, and then I have watched her hands, never idle, spin and knit the wool into clothing.

"And Mother could sew anything," Beulah recalls. "She could look in a catalog and pick out a dress she liked, and cut out one exactly like it from her material."

There were other stories handed down from the older folks, such as a fire put out with a churn of buttermilk at Uncle John Barton's house, and the chilling ghost stories that Uncle Tom Perrigan told, stories which made your spine tingle and made you afraid of the dark — and yet, you wanted to hear more!

MOUNTAIN ECHOES

WITH ANITA A. BELCHER

Beulah and friends from Bristol who perform at various functions throughout the area.

Anita

Continued From Page 1-B

"I'm 85 years old now, and I hope the Lord blesses me to keep my health so that I can continue what I'm doing for a good while to come.

"I've also been blessed to travel quite a bit in these last years. I've been to Hawaii three times, to Spain, Northern Africa, and old Mexico. I've traveled in several of our states, including a trip to Alaska, since I've been living in Bristol. I enjoy traveling very much."

"Do you think the way you were raised had a big influence on your life?" I asked.

"Oh yes," was her quick response. "The way I was raised had a great effect on my life and still does. I remember my mother saying, 'Children, if you draw nigh unto God, he will draw nigh unto you.'

"On summer evenings we would gather together on our porch and sing the old hymns, and we children learned to sing them.

"My mother asked my little niece, Terri, who was then about three years old, to sing 'Jesus Reigns' to her shortly before she died, and Terri sang for her."

The evening was fast drawing to a close, and it was time for Miss Beulah and me to "close our history book" and get on with the present. What better way could our conversation have ended than with these heartfelt words spoken with deep emotion:

"I thank God every day for my health and for good friends and family. Glenn and I had two lovely daughters, Glenna and Lucy.

"Glenna married Harry Widener of Abingdon and they had two sons, Patrick and Mitchell. Lucy married Dick Troyer of Harper, Kansas, (they live in Clintwood) and they have two daughters, Melissa and Sabrina.

"I know I have been blessed and I thank God for every good thing that has ever happened to me. I have a great hope of meeting all of God's children someday in that great beyond, where we will all be like Jesus and be satisfied if our trust is in him.

"I love all my friends, everyone, no matter what church they're in, as long as that church is preaching the truth. My faith is in Christ and I'm looking forward to the day when I will be in heaven."

Thank you, Miss Beulah for the time you have spent with me, and thank you for making me laugh.

Thank you for those moments when we didn't laugh, those times when we spoke of our parents and grandparents, who had a deep trust in God and who were determined to make a living "by the sweat of their brow," and to raise their children to be fine, hardworking, God-fearing people.

Clynard and I both want to also thank Billie Mullins and Elva Moore for their hospitality while we were visiting with our story-teller and historian of the month, Beulah Lyall!

Note: One thing I was about to forget was the "sleep-ins" I promised to tell you about. Miss Beulah was telling me how her parents always welcomed friends and relatives, and how there was usually company dropping by or spending the night, but those times were nothing compared to "Association" week.

During that time there would be 70 to 75 people from church staying at their home.

"Where in the world did they all sleep?" I asked.

"Oh, in beds, on blankets on the floor, in the hay-loft, and down at the mill," was her answer.

"Did you feed them all?" was my next question. Beulah laughed as her mind went back to those days, and she could visualize as well as if she were there those busy, happy mornings.

"Yes, indeed, we fed everyone. We bought 25-pound bags of flour, and mother fried bacon and sausage and ham. She made some fresh corn. We had all kinds of jams and jellies. Everyone had a good time and mother never complained about the work."

Correction: In the May 7 story about Beulah Lyall, her surviving sisters should have been Norma and Margaret.

There were other stories handed down from the older folks, such as a fire put out with a churn of buttermilk at Uncle John Barton's house, and the chilling ghost stories that Uncle Tom Perrigan told, stories which made your spine tingle and made you afraid of the dark — and yet, you wanted to hear more!

Then there is the bit of what is now history, but what was at that time the future: of how young Doc Tiv Sutherland rode his horse to court young Emma Yates, who was boarding at Beulah's home while teaching school at Nealy Ridge!

There are the precious memories which are dear to Beulah. "Mother and Daddy took us to church from the time we were small. When we were real small, Mother would make little gingerbread cakes and take them to church in case we got hungry.

"You know Mother and Daddy were charter members of what is now the Lick Creek Primitive Baptist Church. There were others, including Uncle John Deel and Aunt Sarah and Uncle Stonewall Rose and Aunt Leah.

"When first organized, they met in .the old Nealy Ridge school house, then moved to the church house now used by the Freewill Baptist, then Lawrence and Maxie Arrington Counts gave property and were instrumental in building a new church building where it now stands on Lick Creek.

"Rean Singleton was Moderator there for a number of years, and the first deacons were John Deel, Stonewall Rose, Patton Edwards, and Floyd M. Arrington, my father. There may have been others, but I know that all these men served as deacons until their death.

"Later on, Lawrence Counts, Fred Yates, Bascom Deel, and others served in the same office. Frank Viers became the moderator, and in 1949, I joined the Lick Creek Primitive Baptist Church, and I'm still a member there.

"I had four other sisters who were members, Carrie Mullins Counts, Polly Anne Mullins, Maxie Counts, and Maude Hay. (Maude is still living.)

"Stella belonged to the Puether Chapel Freewill Church, Willie was a member of the Turner Old Regular Baptist, and Bonnie was a member of the Clintwood Baptist. I love my church, but since moving to Bristol about four years ago, I don't get to come back and attend like I want to."

"Miss Beulah," I said, "you've lived a long time and you've enjoyed life very much, but you have also gone through a lot of sorrow. Tell me how you have managed to keep such a good attitude and have such a cheerful outlook. It's uplifting just to be around you."

Beulah thought for a minute before giving me an answer. "I always look on the bright side of things and I dwell on the good memories. Then I stay busy.

"After moving to Bristol I became a part of the Slater Senior Citizens

Beulah Lyall today.

Center, and for the last three years I've been involved in their exercise program, which they offer five days a week.

"I also belong to an out-reach program for seniors called 'The Golden Goodies.' There are now eight in our group, and we visit other senior citizen organizations, nursing homes, retirement homes, and lots of other place.

"We do a lot of 'senior-cising,' which is exercising to music, and we try to show other seniors how it helps to keep active. We perform at parades and fairs, and dress according to the theme and season.

See ANITA, Page 10-B

Engie Rose Exemplifies

By ANITA BELCHER

We've done a lot of traveling in the past few weeks, so let's rest up a bit before we fly over the Grand Canyon, cruise Powell Lake, drive over the Great Divide in a blizzard or watch the elk and bighorn sheep in the Rockies!

There's a lot more for us to see, but if you're like me, you're ready to take a break and have a good old visit with some of our folks right here in Southwest Virginia, for after all, that's where our heart is! Right?

We'll resume our travels later, the Lord willin', but this week we're going to visit with a beautiful young lady who, until a few "long" months ago, was the picture of health and energy.

Then without warning, cancer struck in a very unexpected way. Now these days, Engie Ramey Rose, who is still beautiful, presents a picture of courage and faith.

MOUNTAIN

ECHOES

Some of you will read her story several times, because not only will it tug at your heartstrings, it will also encourage those of you who are traveling down the same road to "keep walking," to trust in the Lord and not give up.

This story will be in parts, so I'll give you some of Engie's family background first, which will no doubt cause some of you to find out that you're "a-kin" to her. Others of you will recall working with her dad, Ersel, and her uncle Clarence Ramey.

Engie is the daughter of Ersel and Faye Elswick Ramey, both now deceased. Her paternal grandparents were Charles and Elizabeth Wallace Ramey and her maternal grandparents were John and Hettie Shortridge.

Mrs. Elswick was a native of Buchanan County where her husband's people also settled, but the father of Mr. Elswick came directly from England.

The Elswick grandparents were farmers. The Ramey grandfather was a regular Baptist minister and a miner for several years. He and his family lived in the Tivis section of the county.

While living there, twin boys, Clarence and Ersel, were born to the Rameys, and that is where they spent the first three years of their life. Then

Courage, Faith In God

the family moved to Kentucky where Mrs. Ramey died.

The boys and their sister, Oma, then went to live with their grandfather, Issac, of whom they had good memories throughout their life.

The twin boys had a good time "being twins," especially when they reached courting age, but there came a day when they got serious and both of them met the girls they wanted to marry.

Clarence married Ester Willis and Ersel married Faye Elswick. Ersel and Faye started housekeeping at Splashdam and this was where five of their six children were born.

These children were Ann (Sweeny), Engie (Rose), Johnny (deceased), Charles Clinton (deceased), and Patricia Carol (deceased). Ersel died in 1971 and Faye died in 1982. Now that you've gotten somewhat acquainted with the family, let's visit with Engie.

Life began for this young lady at

Engie Ramey Rose

Splashdam (then a booming mining camp) and she was delivered by our famous Dr. T.C. Sutherland.

Everything went fine and the family continued living in Splashdam

until Engie was about three years old. At that time Ersel and Faye decided to move to the old Will Branham place on Big Ridge, where Engie spent her growing-up days.

I suppose that is where her brother, Dexter, was born. (I could find that out for sure next time, but I didn't want to take the chance of omitting Dexter's name.)

Engie recalls the day when the family made the move to Big Ridge.

"There was a big snowstorm at the time," she says, "and I remember standing on the porch and falling into a snowdrift up to my waist. That was a scary experience for a little girl but my daddy rescued me!"

Growing up as a little girl was fun, and some of Engie's greatest memories are those of playing with her cousins, (and there were lots of them) and with the neighbor children, especially the Cumbos.

We'll continue with Engie's story next week.

Rose Recalls Brother

By ANITA BELCHER

This is part two of Engie Rose's story and there will be a part three.

As was mentioned in the first part of our interview with Engie, her memories of growing up at home with her brothers and her sister, Ann, as well as cousins and neighbor children, are good ones.

It seemed that her second home was with the Clayton Cumbo family, and Janice Cumbo was her very best girl friend, but when all was said and done, it was her brother, Johnny, who was her biggest buddy.

"I guess one thing was that I was older and bigger than Johnny, and I was always defending him and taking his part because he was smaller than all the boys at school, but he was always 'there' for me, too. We were a team.

"I remember when we attended the Music School and were turned out for recess, how that most of us headed for the old water pump out in the yard and Johnny didn't stand a chance to get a drink because of the bigger boys.

"Well, I'd take his part and then sometimes get punished for doing so. Sometimes it meant standing in the corner and sometimes it meant a spanking. The worst thing about it

MOUNTAIN ECHOES

was that when I got spanked at school I got another spanking at home!"

The Music School children were transported to Haysi when Engie was in the third grade.

Some of the children were sent to the high school building while others, including Engie, were taken to the old black tarpaper building referred to as "the temporary building."

Her class continued to attend there until they were ready for high school. Engie recalls her school days with fondness and there are no bad memories at all.

She loved her teachers and classmates and well remembers the old-fashioned games which were still popular a few short years ago, such as jumping the rope.

High school days also made for wonderful memories and, strange as it may sound to some young people today, the best memories are centered around the Bible Club and the many activities connected with it.

"It was just 'the thing' to be in Bible Club in those days," Engie recalls. "We learned so much and had fun. There was no opposition from anyone. Those were good days and the more I think back on them, the more I realize how good they were!"

It was in those high school days that Engie became aware of a young man by the name of Kelly Rose. She had heard about him from an older friend who was playing "cupid," telling Engie that Kelly "liked" her and also telling Kelly that Engie "liked" him!

Then one day they met in front of the lockers at school.

Engie recalls, "I was so impressed by him. He was good-looking and wore the neatest clothes, and even his shoes were 'spit and polish' clean! We started talking and walking around at school together and then he started coming over to my house.

"We'd sit on the front porch swing together and talk. We weren't really

Was Her Biggest Buddy

dating — just good friends. Daddy was very strict with me about dating. He was very careful about where I was going and there was certain places that were off limits. Daddy wanted me to do what was right.

"I remember one night he told me that my skirt was too short and I would have to change it. It was really just barely above my knees but that was 'too short' in Daddy's opinion.

"I went back to my room and changed to one that came just below my knees and Daddy said that one was all right."

While we were talking, Kelly, Engie's husband, came in from work and joined the conversation. I asked him how he felt about Mr. Ramey's attitude.

His response was, "It's a good way for a father to be. It makes a boy feel a lot more responsible for the girl he's taking out."

Next week we'll continue Engie's story and share with you how both she and Kelly have coped with her unexpected invasion of cancer.

The Ramey family, front row, left to right, Johnny, Ann and Engie. Parents Ersel and Faye in back.

Rose Loves Joy Of Everyday Living, Being With Family

By ANITA BELCHER

Engie and Kelly began dating seriously before they graduated from high school and were married on June 6, 1969. Their first home was a small house which Kelly had built close by his parents, Steve and Emma Rose.

They still have some of their original furniture, a four-poster bed with chest and dresser for which Kelly had paid "cash down," which Kelly laughingly remarked was "a lot of money back then."

The rest of their furniture, at least their appliances, were bought from Laura and Pridemore Viers who owned a hardware store beside the Haysi Farm Supply. Steve and Emma gave them their first table and Emma was also the "role-model" cook in the family.

"Mommy was one of the best cooks in the world," says Kelly. "Everything she cooked was good, especially her vegetable soup."

"And I couldn't cook anything," Engie laughs.

After many trials and some errors the cooking problems disappeared, and Kelly now says, "Engie has to be one of the best cooks anywhere. I've never tasted cold slaw as good as what she makes."

While they were living at the little house, two of their children, Rachel and Brian, were born and, of course, this brought added happiness to the young couple.

"Those were happy days," they told me, "in fact, maybe what was some of the happiest days of our life."

In the late 70s Kelly and Engie built a nice home on a piece of family property and another blessing was added to their family, a son, Joshua. Kelly and Engie's home became a gathering place for family living away from the area.

"After mommy and daddy died we were the only ones left in the place that used to be home for all of us. We had family gatherings, especially during the holidays, and had the most fun, just being together.

"Kelly's family was always a part of our get-togethers because my brothers and sister loved his brothers and sisters and we were always just one family. We still are."

"As you think back over those years, what are the things that stand out most in your thoughts?" I asked.

"Well, as I look back I guess it was just the joy of everyday living. Kelly and I were together with our family, we had the children, we enjoyed our gardens and the hay fields, we had a quiet life, just the way we liked it.

"I enjoyed walking and exercising. In fact, I enjoyed life! One of the things I enjoyed most, along with my family, was my church. Going to

MOUNTAIN ECHOES

Kelly and Engie Rose today.

church was always a joy to me, never a burden.

"I have never understood anyone who complains about going to church. To me, it's such a joy.

"Some of the greatest people I have ever known and who have influenced me most have been those faithful men and women that attended church with me when I was a child and continued through my teenage years.

"Many of them have died now, but their influence and training, their sweetness and faithfulness is still an influence in my life.

"A few of these folks are still living, but if I start naming them, I'll leave someone out, so I just want to thank God for all them who have gone on and those who remain."

In April of 1997, Engie and her family were shocked and grieved by the sudden death of her brother, Johnny. Shortly after this happened, Engie began having trouble swallowing.

After a trip to the emergency room when a pill wouldn't go down, she decided she must make an appointment to find out the cause.

At first she was assured that there was nothing wrong except maybe tension as a result of her brother's death. After another examination, a tumor was discovered, lying just behind and against the esophagus. I well remember the night at church when Engie told us about it.

"It's not that serious," she said, "it's just a benign tumor that surgery will take care of, but it must be removed or it will cut off my breathing."

We were all concerned but thankful that the outcome looked good. We had our time of hymn singing at church that night, and for some reason I remember how much Engie enjoyed it.

She had a beautiful voice which always added to the congregational singing, and she's using it again, getting a little stronger all the time!

When Engie made her next trip to the hospital, she and her family, the church and all her friends underwent another shock. The tumor was malignant and the only hope was chemotherapy and prayer.

The doctors started the chemo and Christians everywhere who knew Engie began praying, praying fervently and continually. Kelly was constantly by her side.

Things didn't look good and then

See ANITA, Page 5-B

198

Anita

Continued From Page 1-B

suddenly, we got the good news! The tumor was gone! I well remember that day because we were in San Diego, Calif., and were having our anniversary dinner when I got the call about Engie.

As soon as everyone was seated around the dinner table, I said something like this: "As happy as this occasion is, I have something to tell you that is going to make it happier," and then I gave them the good news.

Right there in the middle of that big dining room there were tears and prayers of thanksgiving!

In talking to Engie this week, I asked her if she could in any way describe her feelings over the past few months. My question was not asked out of curiosity, but I knew that whatever she said would be of help to others who are facing the same situation.

"No, there is no words to describe how you feel," she answered. "First there is the shock, then the disbelief, then the feeling, 'this can't be happening to me.'

"You think about your family and how they need you and how you just can't not be there for them. You think about life and you think about death and then you begin to struggle to live.

"I just can't understand why people don't want to live and will even take their own lives when there are others of us who are trying so hard to live. I know prayers have been answered for me and I feel that God put me into the hands of exactly the right doctors.

"There has been a reason for all this and though we wonder about it, neither Kelly nor I question God."

"What advice do you have for others that may be going through this?" I asked.

"Well, I am not much on giving advice but I've learned a lot that has helped me. You cannot allow yourself to get depressed. If you start thinking about what might happen, it will take you right on down.

"You have to face reality, but do it in a positive way. I have a lot to live for, but my greatest comfort is in knowing that I belong to God and that whether I live or die, I'm in his hands.

"I think on the positive. I think on Bible verses and I love the one that says, 'whatsoever things are lovely, whatsoever things are good, think on these things.'

"The way I look at it is, even the person in perfect health has no promise of tomorrow. Our future is in God's

hands and he is going to do whatever he knows is best. We just need to trust him.

"Yes, if it's his will, I'd like to live and see my son Josh and my little granddaughter, Kayla, grow up. I'd like to see Brian settled into his own home and spend time with Rachel. I want to be active in church again.

"I want Kelly and I to grow old together. I want us to sit on the front porch together again."

Vance Treasures 'Working The Ground' On Mountain Farm

By ANITA BELCHER

MOUNTAIN ECHOES

This is our last "arm-chair" visit to the Vance farm and this time we are going to look at it, and the man who owns and operates it, from a different perspective.

Instead of just seeing the pastoral beauty of a mountain farm, we're going to look at what it takes to make it beautiful and find out if it can also be productive.

We have read in our history books (and some of us who are older can recall first-hand) how our parents and grandparents pushed back the wilderness to provide a home and a farm.

They wanted a place which would provide the necessities of life for their children, and a place where their children and grandchildren could grow and send down deep roots.

That's what Gary Vance and his wife wanted, and that's what they have been, and still are, working toward.

When they bought the old Yates farm, the Yates home was still standing and the barn was pretty well intact. There was land cleared for gardens, hay crops and grazing, but not enough for what Gary was envisioning.

He intended, with the blessing of God, to make a living from his farm, and not only a living, but a profitable one.

He set to work to make his vision a reality. He began by clearing more land, cutting trees and hauling the marketable ones to the saw mill. Then all the under-brush had to be cleared out and the lane seeded.

(It took me less than a minute to write these sentences, but hours and days and months went into hard labor to do the actual work. Isn't it interesting how little time it takes to tell about something which took so much hard work to do?)

Each year Gary continues to clear more land and there are now about 75 head of cattle grazing there on the farm.

Just the cattle alone is a big undertaking, but then there are the clearing and seeding, fields of hay to be mowed at exactly the right time for drying and baling, a tobacco allotment to be worked, and dozens of day-by-day chores which arise unexpectedly, as well as the usual ones.

It's a beautiful scene there on the mountain but it doesn't happen without a lot of hard work and honest sweat, and there are the disappointments and frustrations.

When I first visited the farm, there was a newborn colt that nuzzled its nose under my arm while I stroked its shiny coat.

The next time, when Cly and I went back with our daughter Judy, granddaughters Emily and Christian, and two little great-grandsons Miach

See ANITA, Page 2-B

Anita

Continued From Page 1-B

and Jacob, the little colt had died without any warning. We all wanted to cry and I'm sure some of us did.

Then there are the predators who like the taste of corn-fed geese and chicken, and the day on which the farm equipment tears up when it's needed the most!

These are just some of the hurts and frustrations, but Gary is a patient man. He has the heart and mind of the early American pioneer who carved a home from the wilderness and felt closer to God while working in his own "Garden of Eden," rough though it might be!

His wife, Joyce, is an encouragement to him, as are his sons and daughters.

Yes, by hard work and prayer, Gary sees the farm as being profitable with the opportunity of becoming more so, but besides that, he will tell you that "there is just something special about working the ground and seeing the results of your labor."

I think I understand what he means. In a sense it's like being in partnership with God!

I hope you have enjoyed the time we've spent at the Vance Mountain Farm as much as I've enjoyed taking you! Thanks, Gary and Joyce, from all of us!

Arrington Played Role In Securing

By ANITA BELCHER

This was to have been the last of my interviews with Haskell Arrington, but after the visit I decided to ask him if he would be one of our "historians on call." That simply means that if he or any of you recollect a bit of history or an interesting occurrence which took place years ago, just give me a call and I'll get with you.

The following is an example of what I'm talking about.

Mr. Arrington, Clynard and I were eating lunch at the Rhododendron Lodge and Restaurant and one of us remarked what a beautiful facility we were blessed to have in this area.

Mr. Arrington, glancing at the ceiling, asked, "Do you have any idea where those large overhead beams came from?" We had to admit that we didn't.

"Well," he said, "I was on the original Breaks Park Commission Board, also on the Building Committee, and our first undertaking was to build the restaurant which would serve as a meeting place for the various boards.

"Anyway, we wanted a nice place and we special-ordered those beams from California. They were supposed to have been delivered on a certain day but there was a one-month delay which threw our building plans off schedule by that much ... but they're beautiful, aren't they?"

He continued, "After the restaurant was completed we had the first two motel units constructed. I saw a lot of progress during the eight years I worked with the Commission.

"Yes, I was there at the official

MOUNTAIN ECHOES

ribbon cutting ceremony when Vice President Barkley and Governor Weatherly of Kentucky officially dedicated the area as the Breaks Interstate Park.

"That was an exciting day and much work had gone into planning. Many people from all walks of life were involved in this great undertaking and each one became a part of its on-going success."

Speaking of progress, Mr. Arrington shared a recollection with us which will be of great interest to anyone who has ever lived in this area.

We were talking about the early days of Haysi and I asked Mr. Arrington if he would describe those days for me. I wanted to know about the business places and the folks who worked and lived there. At another time I will share that story with you, but I think this one takes precedence.

As we talked about the various businesses, Mr. Arrington suddenly smiled and with a chuckle shared the following bit of history.

"You know when I returned from military service I went to work at the Cumberland Bank. The bank was one of the four places in town that had a telephone. The other three were owned by the Ford and Chevrolet dealerships and by Doc Sutherland. The phone number at the bank was 7K24 and Doc's was 7K25.

"There was a need for more telephones. Bart Mullins was the Mayor of Haysi then and I was on the town council. I recall some of the other council members at the

Local Telephone System

time as being Alex Arrington, W.H. Arrington, Riley Bartley, A.J. Mullins and E.J. Rose.

"Being a council member and having easy access to a phone, I called C&P and discussed with them the need for more phone service in the area. They informed me that they were not interested at the time. Bart Mullins also received a letter from them and he brought it to the bank for me to read.

"I decided that the only other option we had was to contact the Bluefield Phone Company which already had a line extending to the mouth of Greenbrier. Arthur Owens, who was deputy sheriff in Buchanan County, had the last, and probably the only, phone on that line for many miles.

"Anyway, when I called Bluefield they told me they were definitely interested in locating in Haysi. I informed C&P of the situation and they immediately decided to extend their services into the community.

"We called a town council meeting (we met·in the old jail behind the bank) and we voted to use C&P since they were already established in the town." So, now you have the story of how our phone system was obtained!

Mr. Arrington would like to end this interview with some of his fondest memories and reflections. "I am thankful that I have had this sketch of my life written. It has brought back many memories that I never would have thought about otherwise.

"It has brought back precious memories of my parents and has caused me to realize how much I loved them. As I read these stories over they bring me joy and comfort. I want everyone to know what my Christianity means to me. It means my life. Nothing else would matter without that.

"Then, I have been blessed to know some wonderful people in my lifetime. There were my parents, friends, loved ones and business associates. I have been blessed to have two wonderful marriages. First, there was Dorothy and then, several years after her death, there was Julia.

"Julia and I had more than 50 years together and had four wonderful daughters — Sue, Martha, Elizabeth and Teresa. Our sons-in-law are fine men and I will always appreciate them.

"We are also blessed with four grandsons, David Arrington, Scott Farmer, and Bradley and Brandon Bacon. David and Scott have graduated from college, Bradley has graduated from high school and has a scholarship to any college of his choice in Tennessee.

"Brandon is in the 10th grade, plays football, is a wonderful musician and loves to drive grandpa's tractor. I am very proud of these boys and am very thankful for my family.

"I want to share one little story with you about our two girls, Martha and Sue, when they were small. When I came home from work at night they would get me to sit in my easy chair and they would work on my hair. They said they were being just like Vivian Kiser, Julia's beautician.

"They would pretend to give me a permanent and use Julia's curlers to curl my hair. One night they said they were going to give me some 'spit' curls and I guess I dozed off to sleep while they were working on me.

"I woke up to hear them spitting on the curlers that they were putting in my hair! Needless to say, I didn't go to sleep anymore when the girls were playing 'beauty shop'!"

That's a good ending to a series of wonderful stories as told by Haskell Arrington. Let him know how much you have enjoyed his recollections and we'll look forward to hearing from him again in the near future, the good Lord willing!

Haskell and Julia Arrington

Mullins To Share Lifetime Of

By ANITA BELCHER

The stories that I will be writing for the next three or four weeks have been a long time in the making, in fact over a hundred years!

The lady who is sharing them with us is Maude Fuller Mullins who was born at Bartlick, Jan. 5, 1902. She is the daughter of Richard Morgan (Uncle Dick) and Rosa Belle Compton Fuller and is the last living member of her family.

To acquaint you with, or re-acquaint you with, Mrs. Mullins and her family, I want to give you some background information that will perhaps help you as you work on your own family tree. It might also be of help to some of Maude's family as they are tracing their roots, so let's go back a few generations.

Maude's father, Richard, was the son of Jacob and Margaret Jane (Pud) P. Fuller. Margaret was a daughter of Richard (Fighting

MOUNTAIN
ECHOES

Dick) and Crissie Counts Colley. Richard (Uncle Dick) was named for his famous grandfather.

Maude's mother was Rosa Belle Compton Fuller and she was the daughter of Shadrack and Mindy Owens Compton.

Here is where the Uncle Crockett Owens family enters the picture, for those of you who might be interested.

Because this is an old family connected with other first settler families, with roots that are far-reaching, I will give you the names and marriages of each of Uncle Dick's (Maude's father) brothers and sisters:

Christina (m) Matthias Owens
Henry Hawkins (Uncle Hawk) (m) Elizabeth Kiser
Mary "Polly" Anne (m) Jim Sutherland
James II (Uncle Jim, also a Baptist Minister) (m) Christina Hicks
Didema (m) James Manuel (Red Jim) Owens
Martha, Lurinda and William Walter died as infants
Margaret Jane (Aunt Marg) (m) George Owens
Richard (Uncle Dick) (m) Rosa Belle Compton
Noah Calhoun (m) Belle Stanley
George was unmarried (b) 1872 (d) 1952

Now, here are the names of Maude's own brothers and sisters:
James (Jim Fuzz) (m) Aurora

204

Historical Recollections

Mullins
Dora (m) Cleve Wallace
Flora (m) Arvil Mullins
Dewey (m) Vada Counts
Margie (m) Dee Mullins
Fred (m) Goldia Counts
Maxie (m) Pridemore Mullins

Maude married Jim Mullins, brother to Aurora, Arvil, Dee and Pridemore. Vada and Goldia also were sisters.

Now, maybe some of you have suddenly realized that you have some kinfolks in this list of names, and hopefully it has also been a help to some of Maude's family who are interested in tracing their roots.

Having laid this groundwork, let's get back to the lady who is kind enough to share so many "upcoming" stories with us. Let me just tell you a little about her as she is today.

Maude Fuller Mullins is a beautiful, quick-witted lady. She has a sharp memory and a keen sense of humor inherited from her father, to whom she refers as "Poppie."

It was my delight to visit with her and two of her daughters, Sallie and Sharon, one day last week, and the time simply flew by. I am looking forward to more visits before they have to return to Ohio.

I'm not going to tell you any of Maude's recollections this week, but I will tell you this: Maude grew up on Bartlick when it was a community of water mills (a full flowing creek) and country stores.

It was during the time when the fields were all tended and lumbering, along with the "dinkey railroad," were a big part of the economy. It was a time when the school and church were "front and center" of community activities.

Next week we'll "tour" old Bartlick through the eyes of an eight-year-old girl who has now turned 100-plus. I can hardly wait! I will tell you this: Maude has that old-time hospitality. She hugs you when you come in and no one should leave her home without eating. I'm saving up on both counts for my next visit!

Mullins Considered Her

By ANITA BELCHER

This week we continue with memories and recollections of our "centenarian historian," Maud Fuller Mullins who was born 100 years ago, Jan. 5, 1902, at Bartlick (Bessie). Her parents were Richard Morgan and Rosa Belle Compton Fuller and, as I mentioned last week, Mrs. Mullins holds a high regard for her father and mother (Poppie and Mommy).

Repeating what I said last week, her great respect, her tender memories (oftentimes mixed with humor) and her undying love for them "runs like a silver thread in an every-day garment." Now, let's continue with those "home-grown" memories. Most of these are in regard to her mother.

Mrs. Mullins recalls, "Like I told you last week, Mommy, though not well, was a hard worker. She and Poppie had an orchard and Mommy loved to work in it. They had most of the usual fruit trees - apple, pear, peach and cherry.

"I remember that Mommy would dig around the base of the peach trees to kill the worms (borers, no doubt). Mommy and Poppie had a kiln where they dried much of their fruit."

"Did your Mother do much quilting?" I asked. "Oh, yes," was Mrs. Mullins' quick response. "Mommy made quilts lined with 'outing' (flannel) and filled with cotton bat-

MOUNTAIN

ECHOES

ting. She had so many quilts that they were stacked to the ceiling in one of the upstairs bedrooms.

"You see, not only did Mommy work on her quilts by herself, but back then we had "quiltings." That's when some of the neighbor women would come in, bringing their own needles and thread and sometimes a kettle of food, and they would work on quilts together.

"The quilt they were working on would be fastened to a quilting frame which was anchored to, and hung from, the ceiling.

"On the days when Mommy had a quilting, Poppie would have a 'working.' There were different kinds of workings but the ones I remember Poppie having were when the men would come in and help clear up a 'new ground' for next year's crops.

"The larger trees which they cut were sawed into lumber at Poppie's sawmill and the smaller ones, along with the brush, were burned. At these quiltings and workings, dinner was always served and was an occasion that had been well prepared for.

"Usually you could count on chicken and dumplings along with 'shuck' beans and, of course, plenty of coffee. We also had bean stringings and corn shuckings which were lots of fun. After the work was finished we had music and dancing which sometimes lasted 'til pretty late into the night, and that was fun, too."

"Weren't you awfully tired after all that hard work and staying up so late?" I asked. Mrs. Mullins laughed. "If we were it didn't bother us," she said. "We were having such a good time together."

Last week as I wrote Mrs. Mullins' story I overlooked one of her recollections that should have been included in the "sheep shearing" that she recalled her Mother doing. Because of the important part that flocks of sheep played in the life of the early settlers I want to share this piece of history with you.

Mrs. Mullins relates, "Lots of people had flocks of sheep back in those days. I remember Uncle Wash Mullins who married Aunt Rend (Poppie's sister) would drive his flock of sheep by our home and on into Grassy. He probably took them on into Elkhorn City, Ky., where he lived, but I'm not sure about that.

Mother Her 'Best Friend'

"You know, it's a funny thing about sheep. They will stay in the woods and graze until they get hungry for salt, then they'll come into home, probably about once a month. We lost quite a few sheep to sheep-killing dogs.

"Some of these dogs were just running wild, maybe in packs, but sometimes a good farm dog would get a taste of a sheep's blood and when he did, he become a killer. People had no use for sheep-killing dogs and would kill them if they were found to be guilty."

I (Anita) can vouch for that. My grandmother Fuller had a flock of sheep and one night when I was staying with her, I awakened to the sound of a gun being shot at intervals. When morning came there were some dead dogs, so I was told, lying on the bluff above the school house.

Raising sheep was a serious business, more so for the wool than the meat, though mutton was an important part of the diet for some families. Also, the tallow was almost a household necessity.

One thing's for sure: one of the worst things anyone could say to someone they were angry with was, "You're as low-down as a sheep-killing dog!"

Another memory before we end for this week came when I asked, "Did your mother like flowers?"

"Oh, yes," she said, "Mommy loved to work with old-time flowers. She loved morning glories, marigolds, zinnias, touch-me-nots and the old-time roses.

"And Mommy loved to cook, too. At Christmas she cooked and baked special dishes. We had turkey (we raised turkeys), pork and, of course, chicken and dumplings. She baked what we called a fruit cake, but it was what we now call a molasses cake or stack cake. It was delicious!

"She also baked apple and peach pies, using the fruit she had canned or dried from her orchard. My Mommy was a wonderful woman...she was my buddy...she was my best friend.

"I loved her so much and she died when I was only 11 years old. I stayed right by her side, bringing her drinks of water or doing whatever I could to help her while Poppie was at work. I loved her very much...I still do."

What a wonderful mother this lady must have been, to have created so many memories in such a short space of time...just 11 short years. What a legacy she has left...a legacy of faithfulness unto death to her husband and children!

What a testimony Maud Mullins shares with us, with all mothers, when she can say, looking back over 100 years of life, "My mother was my best friend!"

Continues next week.

Mullins Tells Of 'Snipe-Hunting,' Chewing Tar

By ANITA BELCHER

MOUNTAIN ECHOES

I believe many of you are clipping out the Maud Mullins interviews so maybe it will help you to know that this is the sixth one. There should be about three more.

I am hoping that when Mrs. Mullins returns to her home on Big Ridge for a visit, we can have another opportunity to talk and share together, for not only is she a delightful person to spend an evening with, she also has so much knowledge about the history of our area and about the roots from which we grew.

Her mind is so clear and her memory so good. We are blessed to have her share with us. Now let's continue:

Maud recalls, "I come from a big family and we had a good family life. The other kids in the family gave me a pretty 'rough' time in a teasing way. I'll never forget the night they sent me 'snipe-hunting' down near Uncle Noad's (Noah Fuller) house.

"They gave me a big sack to carry the snipes home in and left me standing under a big tree, holding my sack open for the snipes to fall into. They all went back to the house. After standing there quite awhile I realized there were no snipes and I went back home in the dark by myself. I never did tell Poppie on them for he would have 'skinned them alive'!"

Another story: "I remember there was a board on our stairway that made a funny noise when I beat on it. I would wait 'til the other kids weren't around and then I would make a racket with it. The others would come running to see what the noise was but they never did find out!

"There was a loose board on our stairway which I could lift up and hold in place while I dropped down to the next floor. This was my secret 'hide-out.' Nobody could find me when I did this."

Maud's eyes twinkle as she tells these stories and she enjoys the memories of them as much as, if not more than, we enjoy hearing them for the first time - and that's a lot!

And here's still another story. "You know, not long after Mommie died, our home burned down. It caught fire from the kitchen stove when one of the children left a stick of wood burning that fell to the floor."

(I, Anita, believe that's correct. I'll check with Mrs. Mullins again on this information).

"Me and my sister would probably have burned up in the house had it not been for our brother, Jim, who pulled us to safety. Anyway, when Poppie and some men were building our new house, Beauty Senter came to spend the day with me. She was Mitchell Senter's daughter by his first wife.

"They lived down on the creek, near to where the Fields families live now. We were about 12 years old at the time and were having a wonderful evening together. We climbed up in the loft of the new house and saw the 'gooey' tar that was being used and decided to chew it."

(Was this pine rosin, or actual tar? We'll have to find out as I didn't make a note on it.)

"We chewed it all evening, until bedtime." I couldn't help but ask, "Why in the world did you chew something like that? It could have made you sick, or worse."

Maud laughed again at the memory. "We thought it was good, I reckon, and we didn't get sick over that, but Beauty got into trouble over staying too late. Sometime after

Anita

Continued From Page 1-B

dark, I remember it was pretty late, Beauty's dad came for her. She was supposed to have gone home while it was still daylight, but I guess time just got away from us and we were having such a good time together.

"He took her home and I suppose she got a whipping the next day for not obeying, and she didn't get to come back again. I remember that Mr. Senter had some other children whose names were Virgie, Eva, Bowles and Bruce."

There's one more little story: "I went to my first school in a building down next to where Vesta Cochran lives now. It was a one-room building built from hewed logs. I was in the Primer that year and can remember the pot-bellied stove and split log seats with holes for the legs to fit in.

"I remember the poem that I recited for my teacher, Avon Sykes. It went like this:

'I had a little dog and his name was Ring,

Around his neck I tied a string.

I tied it so tight his eyes turned blue, Now old Ring, I'm through with you!'"

All of us listening shared in Maud's laughter. In my mind's eye, I could see this little five- or six-year-old girl, proudly standing in front of a room full of students, bravely reciting her four-line poem, which just maybe one of her brothers had taught her!

At any rate, her teacher Avon Sykes must have liked it and liked her because he bought her "box" at the next box (pie) supper!

Little Sister Cared For Newborn

By ANITA BELCHER

In my column last week I shared some of the stories with you that graduates of Haysi High School (the '40s) told me at the reunion which was held at the Breaks Park Sept. 20-21.

I have another one or two for you this week, but first let me correct two awkward-sounding statements that I made last week.

In Glenna R. Patton's story it sounded as if she had carried two 20-gallon crocks up the hill from the spring. It wasn't quite that bad. She carried water from the spring and filled two 20-gallon crocks!

In Faye Minga's story, I left out an important word. When she told me of the deaths of both her husbands and her son, she added, "In spite of all that has happened, I've had a simple, but good life." Faye can say that because her trust is placed firmly in the Lord who grants us peace in the times of storm.

As I corrected those two statements, it made me think of one of the most humorous ones that has ever occurred in my column. This time it was not my mistake — it was a typesetting error and it happened like this.

I was writing the stories that Woodrow Rasnick told me, and at one point he carefully explained how one Christmas his dad had made him a wagon, fashioning the wheels from the wood of a black-gum tree.

After his dad had it all finished he told Woodrow's mother to "grease" the joints of the wheels with some of her homemade soap.

When the next issue of the paper came out, Woodrow called me and laughingly said, "Anita, I

MOUNTAIN ECHOES

loved my story, but my mother did not grease my wagon wheels with her homemade soup! It was soap!"

I joined in his laughter, the mistake was corrected the next week, and everyone who noticed also had a good laugh! I assured Woodrow that I had used the correct word; however, it's not impossible for me to use the wrong one.

It's amazing what one little letter can do to a word, isn't it? I thought you might enjoy that little side story. Now let's go back to the reunion.

I think we were all disappointed that so many of our classmates didn't attend this year, but maybe many of you did not know about the time or date.

Haskell Arrington had planned to come but was not feeling well that day. B.T. Quillen wrote that he would love to come but he doesn't drive now and thought it better to stay home. We missed both these fine gentlemen.

Several others who planned to come later called or wrote to say they were hindered at the last minute (so to speak) by personal or family sickness, some of it quite serious. We need to pray for one another.

I am sorry I could not capture Thelma Miller Ullom's story on paper, but she was rushing out the door even as she spoke, so as to show some younger family members who had traveled with her and Glenn some points of interest, especially the old family cemetery.

I'll try to catch her next time because she has a real gift of remembering and telling how "things used to be."

Now, I will share with you another story that Homer David Willis told me to share with you. You may read this one and then read it again to be sure you read it right the first time!

Homer relates, "I was born in Bryson City, N.C., Jan. 17, 1927. My father, Eddie F. Willis, worked in the mines and was not home when the big flood of '27 hit Bryson City. It was like the floods that have washed Haysi almost off the map.

"Well, it washed out the bridge that connected our home to the city and so everyone was stranded. In the meanwhile my mom realized that she was about to give birth to me and there was no one to help her.

"My sister Edith (Bartley) was about 10 years old at the time. There was no way to even inform anyone of Mom's situation and so she did what she had to do! She delivered me by herself!

"She cut the cord and cleaned me up and put me in the arms of my 10-year-old sister, Edith, and told her to care for me. My mom then developed pneumonia and was so very ill, delirious for most of two weeks.

"She had planned for the baby

When Mother Could Not

Seated, left to right, are: Frankie Massie and Alice? (friends of Kathleen Holbrook), Glenna Rae Patton, Ada and George Wallace. Standing in the first row, left to right, are: C.C. Belcher, Norma Minga (friends of Faye Turner Minga's sister-in-law), Faye Minga, Anita A. Belcher, Katy Jo Arrington Powers, Joe Patton, Genola Taylor Youngblood, Fayetta Davis Campbell, Maple Belcher Edwards, C.P. and Elsa Williams. Standing in the back row, left to right, are: Grey Campbell, Glenn and Thelma Ullom, Kathleen Holbrook and Homer David Willis.

to nurse, so there were no bottles in the house, and still no bridge across the river to make connections with doctor or husband and, of course, no phones.

"Little Edith took over and did the only thing she knew to do about the new baby's food. She cooked green beans and mashed them to an almost liquid state, cooked potatoes and mashed them and used her mother's canned applesauce to complete his diet.

"She also milked the cow and fed the new baby fresh cow's milk from the tip of a teaspoon, as there were no bottles!"

Homer continued, "When a makeshift bridge was put in and the doctor and dad came, they found mom very weak but better, and the baby was doing fine. You know, for a long time, I though

Edith was my mother because she continued to care for me as if I were her own, even though mom was there for me."

How can we thank Homer enough for a story that is so dear to his heart, and won't we all realize more than we have ever done before that we have a great God who cares for us when we are not able to care for ourselves?

And folks, won't we all realize more than ever that our children and other children are capable of doing far more than we give them credit for, when they are put to the test?

Right now, even though all of us who have known Edith Willis Bartley over the years have loved and respected her, I think a new dimension has been added. I think when I see her now, I will see a

little 10-year-old girl, holding and caring for a new-born baby brother who otherwise could have died!

Before ending this column I want to mention that Glenna Rae Patton gave me the book *Haysi, Virginia Community and Family History* compiled by Dennis and Diana Reedy, to present to the Haysi High School Library in memory of the deceased members of the class of '45 and in honor of the members still living.

Glenna wishes this book to be presented to the high school as a gift from the remaining class members of '45. Glenna, I will personally carry out this request for you and your classmates.

Doc Sutherland's Dedication

By ANITA BELCHER

I have a letter I want to share with you this week which contains interesting information. It's a letter from Lottie Sarlouis of Elmira, Mich., and was dated in November 1998.

I read Mrs. Sarlouis' letter and enjoyed it very much, but then I misplaced it, finding it only this past week. I believe I mentioned her recollections of Doctor Sutherland in an earlier issue of *The Dickenson Star*, but it is doubtful that I printed her entire letter which is filled with bits of local history, and deserves to be recorded for future generations.

I hope that Mrs. Sarlouis, daughter of Hawk and Polly Bowman, is still living to read this, and I hope I will hear from her again. If she isn't living, I hope to hear from her daughter with whom she made her home. Her letter reads:

"I have been reading your stories in

MOUNTAIN ECHOES

the Clintwood paper for a long time and they bring back a lot of memories to me. I was born and raised in Dickenson County except for two years when we lived in Buchanan County.

"Your story on Lottie Lyall when you and she walked up Fall Branch

and rested on a big rock under a big beech tree ... well, that was the very place my brother and I rested when we hoed corn all below the road there. As I read your story I could almost feel the cool breeze at Buckeye Hollow. I spent my happy teen years in the Fall Branch area.

"I ate many a good Sunday dinner at the table of Mrs. Cynthia Mullins. Her children and some of her grandchildren and I were teen-agers together. I also attended the little tent Bible School in Tom Bottom. It was conducted partly by the Rev. T.K. Mowbray and Eula South of Haysi.

"I attended the new Pound school the first year that it opened in 1930 and I was on the basketball team. If Jessie Lyall is still living, she and I are the only girls left who played on that team.

"Later my parents moved across the river to a big log house, then later to Ramsey Ridge. When I married Frank Melton we lived in the log

Revealed In Sarlouis Memories

house where my first two children were born.

"Now here is a story about our good Doctor Sutherland. I was sick when we lived at Fall Branch and Doc Sutherland came to see me. He had to park in Tom Bottom and walk up Fall Branch.

"Afterward, I went to his office many times over the old Raleigh Sutherland drug store. Then when we lived in the old log house across the river from Tom Bottom (after I was married) I remember it was time for my second child to be born.

"It was about 10 at night and it came a big rain storm. Doc had to park at the water tank (by the railroad) and walk a long way around the hillside, and the water was running down the little path from the road to the house. Doc came in with his pant legs rolled to his knees and his shoes in hand.

"He looked at me and told me that I had 'picked a mighty bad time to have that baby!' Afterward when we were discussing what we would name our baby, I was for calling him Oscar, but Doc said, 'My name is Tivis Lee so give him the Lee part of my name and he will grow up to make a fine man!'

"So we named him Oscar Lee and he did grow up to be a fine man like Doc said! I moved back to Tom Bottom in 1941 and had an asthma attack. Doc Tiv came to see me and pointed his finger at me and said, 'If you want to live to raise these babies, lay them cigarettes down!' I did what he said and have never smoked a cigarette since!

"My dad worked for W.M. Ritter Lumber Company much of the time and so we had to move a lot. I can relate to many of the good stories that you write as I look back over my own life. I will be 82 years old on Nov. 24 and I am now living with my daughter in Michigan."

Mrs. Sarlouis ended her letter with, "I can't write very good and I can't use a pen at all." I am amazed how well her letter was written. At age 82 her writing was better than many a high school graduate!

As I said, I hope Mrs. Sarlouis is still living and that we will hear more from her. If I have printed parts of her letter before, I won't apologize, for many of you would not have seen that issue of the paper, and anyway, it's worth reading twice!

Broken churn pieces make

Laura Wood Viers was born May 1, 1928, on Backbone Ridge about a mile from Martha Gap. Her parents were Harrison and Judy Wood and brothers and sisters were Robert, Ayers, Toy, Swanson, Andy, Englin, Elmer, Pearl and Gertrude. Out of that large mountain family there are five still living: Andy, Englin, Elmer, Gertrude and Laura.

Laura looks back over the years and recalls, "Our family lived in an ordinary five-room boxed house furnished very much like many of the mountain homes. The beds were the old time iron bedsteads with featherbeds to sleep on. I don't believe we had mattresses back then.

"Our chairs were bark-bottomed and our kitchen table was homemade. We had a fireplace in the front room and another in one of the bedrooms. A wood-burning stove for cooking was in the kitchen and mom used the ashes to spread around certain plants in her garden. (Ashes are excellent to spread about blueberry bushes and azaleas and several other shrubs and plants.) Mom also had a spinning wheel in one room which she used in making some of our clothing."

"Did your mom have sheep?" I asked. "Because if she had a spinning wheel it stands to reason that she had at least a few sheep."

"Oh, yes," Laura replied. "Mom had a flock of sheep which she sheared once a year. Once the sheep were sheared, we had to clean the wool, picking out the big stuff like burrs, then we had to card it."

(A "carder" was like a big comb that one had to pull through sections of wool.) Laura agrees that carding wool was not an easy or pleasant job. At this stage it did not smell good and left one's hands oily and rough.

"After the carding was finished then mom spun the wool

Mountain
ECHOES
ANITA BELCHER

into yard which was dyed different colors," Laura recalls. "Mom then knitted the yarn into sweaters, caps and socks. I call still see mom's long knitting needles."

Laura worked hard growing up but enjoyed her big family of brothers and sisters. She and her sisters played with paper dolls cut from mail order catalogs, and built play houses in old outside buildings.

They played with jack rocks, but not the kind children play with today. Let Laura tell you about them!

"Our jack rocks were made from broken pieces of old churns, hammered out to just the right size. Our jack rock ball was made of yarn as was the ball we played outside games with. We never had a store-bought rubber ball." She laughs as she recalls some of the moves that were made playing jack rocks.

I (Anita) remembered that there were the "ones, twos" and right on up to ever how many jack rocks we were playing with, but Laura recalls "the real test came in 'putting the beans in the pot,' 'ponies in the stable,' 'pickin' berries,' 'cuttin' the cake,' and 'kissin' the baby.'"

There were other intricate moves, the grand finale being "pittie-pat" but that's enough to start everyone thinking and remembering good times at

home and school.

There was the daily housework and those were the days when every week had a "wash day" and other designated days. Laura recalls, "Wash days consisted of building a fire in the furnace built on the outside with rocks separated just enough to set a tub of water on with a fire underneath.

"White clothes were put in hot water with lye soap and allowed to boil, being punched down and turned over occasionally with a paddle or a broom stick. When Mom considered them clean enough, they were carefully lifted out and put into another tub of water and scrubbed on the wash board with lye soap. Then they were once more lifted out and into the final tub of rinse water.

"When rinsed thoroughly, they were wrung out by hand and hung on the clothesline."

Laura and I both remember that in the summertime, although this was back-breaking work, it could be very pleasant with the smell of the hot, soapy water, the clear, cold rinse water, and the fragrance of clothes drying in the sun and wind ... picture perfect!

It was different in the wintertime. One could almost freeze over a tub of boiling water, and hanging clothes on the line was a test of endurance. Sometimes an article of clothing could freeze before it was fastened to the line and once it got there it froze hard as a brick.

Talk about red hands! Ask someone who lived back then how cold their hands got while trying to fasten clothes on the line with clothes pins. Laura laughingly recalls, "That was the reason why clothes got really dirty in the wintertime. We couldn't change them every day like people do now and we didn't get a bath everyday either.

"When we did get a bath in

old-time jack rocks

Laura Viers is pictured here as a young woman.

Laura completed the seventh grade at Turner School and would have loved to continue her education but did not have that opportunity. She continued living at home helping her folks, and admits that she preferred outside work to house work.

"I guess I was the tomboy in the family," she laughs. "I had rather be outside helping dad or the boys, cutting or sawing wood, building or fixing a fence or whatever else they were doing. I'm just an outside person, I guess, or at least I was back then."

Laura and Pridemore (Pride) Viers had gone to school together at Turner and had been good friends. When he went to the Navy she hated to see him go and missed him. They kept in contact by letter, and when he returned home they renewed their old friendship and it developed into a love and marriage which has lasted almost 61 years—the way God intended marriages to last.

Next week we will travel down those 60-plus years with Pride and Laura.

Also, next week I will include some additional information on the Wood family which Elizabeth Edwards, wife of Cephas Edwards, sent me. Cephas is the son of Benjamin Howell Edwards and Margaret Wood Edwards, daughter of Dack and Sarah Wood.

Thank you so much, Elizabeth.

the wintertime it was in a big galvanized wash tub in front of the fire with one side of us freezing and the other side too hot!"

Along with these memories, Laura recalls that her folks made lye soap and hominy but doesn't recall the recipe. Do any of you remember? If so, let us know.

Laura also attended Turner School. Her teachers, as she recalls, were E.H. Anderson, Walter Carty, Flora Swindall Willis and perhaps John Turner. Her best friends were Theda Hay Artrip, Juanita Turner Mullins and Boone Turner.

Valentine's Day was an important holiday when everyone exchanged cards, and Easter (Friday) was a special day when there was an Easter egg hunt.

Thoughts on 'home' shared from ancient borrowed book

This was supposed to have been the conclusion of Pride and Laura Viers' story but once again we were interrupted by circumstances beyond our control.

There were funerals, and we grieve with those who are grieving, and pray that the God of all comfort will sustain each family who has lost loved ones. Even as I write this I have heard of two other dear families who have lost a loved one, and my heart aches for those left behind.

I cannot help commenting about the picture of Laura Viers in last week's paper. Even though I saw the original and sent it to the paper it was not as clear as when printed by *The Star*. Indeed, Laura Wood was a beautiful girl and the sweetness of her countenance just gripped me.

As I thought back, I recalled pictures of other girls who were taken during those war-torn years and there was a certain mature look on the faces of some of them that was beyond their years.

I think the knowledge of the war (WW II) that our country was fighting, and its far-reaching effects, affected all of us, the way we looked and the way we lived. However, as true as all that is, we still must admit that Laura Wood was a beautiful girl. She is still a beautiful lady.

By the way, as some of my older readers have already noted, Laura's picture was taken at Raleigh Sutherland's studio, the one and only of its kind in the area. Do you recall where it was? I think I do.

It was in a little nook between the old Exxon station and the Pizza Factory. He had different background curtains to use for certain occasions. Let me know if I am wrong about the location.

Pride and Laura have been receiving many phone calls and comments about their stories. She has given me permission to print their phone number: 276-835-9301. We may have to wait another week for the conclusion of the Viers' memories as I am

ANITA BELCHER

in Atlanta for my doctor appointment.

In the meanwhile, I want to share with you two or three paragraphs from an old antique book that Regina Barton had in her Mountain Treasures shop and her husband, Jason borrowed it.

I borrowed it from him, not knowing what a treasure I was about to open. I am a collector of old books but I have to be content with the opportunity of borrowing this one. Thanks, Jason.

Now, are you ready for this? This book was written in 1873 by Alex M. Gow and copyrighted in 1901 for use as a public school book, much like the old McGuffy readers. I think this was for sixth and seventh graders. The following is one paragraph out of the chapter on "Home."

"Home, sweet home. A beautiful poem has been written by Mrs. V.S. French, entitled, 'Mother, Home and Heaven.' The delightful idea it coveys is that the mother is the ministering angel of the home, and the home as it should be is the nearest earthly resemblance to heaven.

"It is sad that all homes are not happy, but the reason they are not is often seen in the restlessness, impatience, irritability, and un-charitableness of its members. Children are frequently negligent in duty, careless of obligations and unreliable in promises.

"Is it a wonder that homes in which perpetual discord occurs are unhappy? Every well-ordered family must have its rule of government, which must be observed by each of its members, or trouble will surely follow.

"How important, then, that the young should learn that easy acquiescence (obedience) which renders them able and willing, habitually, to prefer the wishes and comforts of their parents and the happiness of their homes, to their own convenience and selfishness.

"Many children are in constant opposition to parental influence and government, thereby making themselves unhappy and the family miserable.

"They are not always responsible for the wretchedness of their homes, and yet they may do much by the exercise of care and kindness, prudence and forbearance, love and charity, to make them better. It is worth the effort of any one in the family to attempt such a reformation if it is needed."

Well, did you enjoy that and don't you wish we were using those books with our family and children today? I will share other "bits and pieces" of these wonderful, almost forgotten, "treasures" with you from time to time.

I am sure you are all looking forward to the next Pride and Laura story — so am I! In the meanwhile, may God bless and guide you, each one.

In Touch

with Dickenson County Family, Friends & Neighbors

'Mad-stone' claimed special powers

'I had heard about this remarkable stone from the time I was a child and was fascinated by the stories I heard.'

ANITA BELCHER

THE DICKENSON FORUM, PART II

I hope you enjoyed last week's column with the news items from the old 1937 *Forum*. I cannot resist sharing the same old paper with you at least one more time and I believe you will appreciate and enjoy it. Now for the lead story.

Many of you may recall when I used my column to write about the "Mad Stone" used back in the late 1800s and early 1900s. I had heard about this remarkable stone from the time I was a child and was fascinated by the stories I heard, but it was not until I worked with Mary Cain on a program out of Virginia Tech that I was able to get the complete picture.

Mrs. Cain was a well-educated woman, very knowledgeable and very practical, who had experience with this stone and believed it to work.

What she told me was much like the story on the front page of the 1937 *Forum*. It was titled "'Mad Stone' on Display Here; Miraculous Cures Claimed." The story:

"Many citizens of Clintwood had their first view of a 'Mad-stone' today, and a great deal of interest and curiosity was aroused by it. The mad-stone is owned by Aunt Louisa Kiser of near South Clinchfield, and it has achieved quite a reputation in that community.

"The mad-stone was brought here by Noah Powers, Commissioner of Revenue, to whom it was loaned by Mrs. Kiser. It is a small stone, almost circular, and about three inches across the widest point.

"It is of a peculiar soapy formation, reddish mottled in color, and weighing in all some 10 or 12 ounces. It appears to be porous, and this quality is said to give it the strange 'sucking' power attributed to it.

SEE ECHOES, PAGE 5B

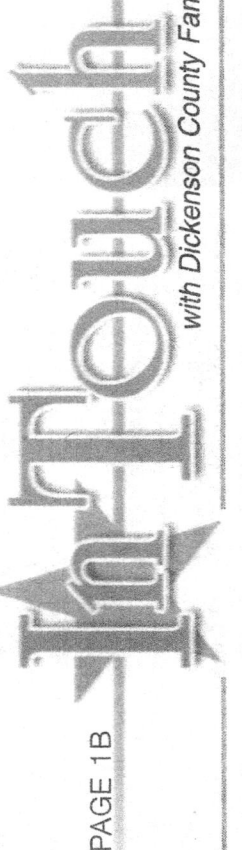

CONTINUED FROM PAGE 1B

"A large number of mad-dog and snake-bite patients have been treated with this stone. It is claimed that in case of poisoning either by a venomous snake or a rabies-infected dog, the stone, when applied to the wound, will cling and draw out the poison.

"R.C. Miller Jr., a student in the local high school, claims that he once saw this mad-stone in operation. His family was living in South Clinchfield at the time, and he stated that he had heard of this mad-stone many times but had never seen it.

"Then one day a little girl was bitten three or four times on the hand by a copperhead snake which she had picked up. The father of the child rushed her to the mad-stone.

"Upon application of the stone, after having been immersed in sweet milk, according to young Miller, the stone clung tightly to the wound, and when it dropped off and was replaced in the milk, a greenish substance colored the milk to the approximate tint of pea-soup.

"The child seemed to be in much better condition and the father went his way rejoicing after having paid a fee of 50 cents.

"Tradition, coming down from the Indian days, has it that these mad-stones, of which there are several in the country hereabouts, are formed in the stomachs or spleens of deer and elk.

"The stone exhibited by Mr. Powers has a small hole through it, whether this was natural or not was not explained."

So there you have just read one of the leading, front-page stories in the local newspaper, Nov. 12, 1937.

My mother had told me about some of the horrible deaths that were caused by rabies back in that era, for there were no vaccinations to prevent or cure that terrible disease.

I was probably about eight years old when some kind of rabid animal bit a rooster belonging to my Fuller grandparents at Bartlick. As I recall, the rooster was killed but it pecked my grandmother.

If I remember correctly, all the adults that were present at the scene had to travel to Clintwood to get the newly-discovered shots which were given in the stomach. I believe they had to go for several weeks. I remember I was really awed by all the excitement.

Since I have written this much about the "mad-stone" and rabies, let me suggest that you watch the movies *Old Yeller* or *To Kill a Mockingbird*. There you can see the concern about a rabid animal, but I'll end on a sort of funny story.

When our children were growing up we had lots of stray animals "set off" at our house. Most of them were hungry, all of them wanted a home and we tried to feed the poor things until they would just disappear, to who knows where.

Anyway, one evening a big grey cat appeared on the scene. He looked healthy but acted wild and I warned the children to stay away from him, all to no avail. One of them, and each one thinks he or she was the one, reached down to give him some food and immediately got a big scratch from a snarling cat.

I called the health department and they said I would need to cage the cat for 14 days to see if it showed any signs of rabies. I managed to get him into a cage of some kind and for the next 13 days we fed and watered him as if he were our favorite pet (which he wasn't).

On the 13th night, somehow, when I went to feed him, he slid out the door of that cage and was gone like greased lightning.

I'll never forget that night. It was dark, but so foggy it was hard to se the darkness for the fog. I got a flashlight and one of the children (they all think it was them) went with me to hunt a wild, grey cat on a cold, dark, grey November night.

You may think it's funny, but I prayed, "Lord, please help me to find that cat and catch him. My child's life may depend on finding that cat." Suddenly the child (whichever one it was) shouted, "Mom, Mom, I saw him over there in the weeds," and he/she pointed their finger.

"Stay right here. Don't you move," I said, and, like a feminine Sherlock Holmes I slowly and carefully edged my way toward the roadside weeds, parting them gently as if they were a rare plant species. Suddenly, I saw him, yellowish-green eyes glowing like a neon sign. "Now, Lord, help me get him," I prayed.

"Come on, good fellow, come on, let's go home and get some food." He looked at me quizzically from those yellow-green eyes but didn't move as I reached out my gloved hand for him. I picked him up and with a fast beating heart I carried him to the car.

He seemed mesmerized. He didn't move. I popped him into the cage on the back seat and my child and I offered up a prayer of thanksgiving. Call it what you will, I still refer to it as a miracle.

On the 14th day I called the health department and they asked all the usual questions and then said we could turn him loose, which we thankfully did.

Had it been 70 years ago we would have been calling Louisa Kiser or Mary Cain for the Mad-stone!

Memories, photos, honors shared at class reunion

Members of the Haysi High School Class of '43 and other 1940s class members are pictured above. Seated, from left, are Barbara Morris (visitor), Lois W. Yates, Maple B. Edwards, Anita A. Belcher, Glenna R. Patton and Kathleen H. Puckett. Standing, from left, are Betty Belcher Long, KatyJo Powers, Vivian F. Owens, Merle T. Powers, Clayton Belcher, Lucille T. Belcher, Merle G. Fuller, Faye T. Minga and Thelma M. Ullom.

219

Mountain ECHOES

ANITA BELCHER

The Breaks Rhododendron Lodge was again the scene of the annual reunion of the Haysi High School class of 1943 and other classes graduating in the 40s.

Although there were not many folks attending this particular get-together this year, it was a day of Haysi class reunions, as there were three other groups meeting at the same place, same day. It was good to get to talk to several of those "younger folks" who had graduated after our classes of the 40s.

Our reunion began on Friday night, Sept. 14 in the dining room of the lodge. It was a joyous occasion just to be together again. Those attending the dinner that evening from out of town were Thelma Miller Ullom and daughter Patty Eckert, Glenna Ray Patton and Evelyn Steele Gilbert.

Those living in the Haysi area who attended the dinner were Lillian Price Hay and friend, Carrol Baker, Merle Gilbert Fuller, Vivian Fuller Owens, Katy Jo Arrington Powers (teacher), and Clynard and Anita Belcher.

Needless to say there was a lot of sharing and laughter as well as some serious moments.

Joining us the next day for lunch in the banquet room were Kathleen Holbrook Puckett and friends Alice Strood and Frankie Massie, Faye Turner Minga, Lois Willis Yates, Maple Belcher Edwards and sister,

Betty Belcher Long. Betty graduated from Haysi High School and was hoping to see one of her favorite teachers, Homer David Willis, but for reasons I'll explain later, he couldn't come.

Frankie Massie, Alice Strood, Patty Eckert and Barbara Morris are all visitors and have been "adopted" by the 40s class as "one of us." Later in the afternoon we were happy to have Clayton Belcher and wife Lucille Taylor Belcher, along with Merle Taylor Powers, stop by and visit with us for a while.

Our food was delicious, and after prayer we all settled down to enjoy each other's company and the beauty of the day. The views from our windows were wonderful. Turning one way we could see The Towers and from another angle The Chimney Rock was picture-perfect.

There were pictures inside, too ... maybe not perfect, but reminiscent of other days. Believe it or not, all of us used to be kids, then teens, then there were the high school days, graduation, jobs, military, marriage, children, grandchildren and yes, now, great-grandchildren. There were pictures of it all, though not enough time to look at all of them!

Also, inside, as a centerpiece, was a vase of red roses, although we didn't have to be reminded that some of those we love are no longer with us and some are in ill health. Our prayers of sympathy are with those of you who have lost loved ones, and our prayers for better health go out to others. "God is our ever-present help in times of trouble."

Clynard Belcher carried on the business of the group with the help of Kathleen Puckett. Anita Belcher spoke of the efforts being made in the town of Haysi to clean up and beautify.

Each member of the group had something to add to the conversation and perhaps it was the mention that Haysi had acquired 20-some acres of land in the old Splashdam community that the '57 flood washed away, which

stirred up memories of the community that used to be there, and just where each place was located and where the school was and who taught there.

When school was mentioned, of course our thoughts turned back to the old Haysi High School and, interestingly enough, someone brought something to our attention which others of us didn't remember.

How many of you recall that the stairway at the high school went up on both ends of the entrance, front and back? One end was exclusively for the boys and the other for the girls.

How many of you remember the little "store" that was underneath the stairway for the "Ag" boys to manage for a project they were doing? (Haskell Arrington was treasurer). How many of you recall when the high school burned and what other event happened at that time which changed the course of history?

One other item we didn't discuss because probably none of

220

us knew about it and maybe none of you who read this will recall it ... but then again, maybe someone will.

In the old 1937 newspaper, The Dickenson Forum, sent to me by a gentleman in Kingsport, a short column on the front page reads, "Haysi seniors to present a play, a comedy/drama, 'Up the Hill to Paradise.' The cast includes Fay Deel, Maxine Compton, Delphia Turner, Rausja Rasnake, Gay Mullins, Lake Arrington, Alpha Rasnake, Nolan Kiser, Oscar Mullins, Bruce Wright and Gorman Yates."

I (Anita) knew several of those cast members, though I was very young.

Now, back to the present. As we talked about the loss of the old high school building and events following, Betty Belcher Long shared a bit of interesting history with us.

She wrote the following down for me, "The Pennix Construction Company out of Gastonia, N.C., took over the building of the new high school.

Imogene Stanley began as their bookkeeper and worked until the job was half finished. When she left, I (Betty Belcher Long) took her place and worked until the job was completed. They were a great company to work for."

Thanks, Betty, for sharing that with us. That's the way we record history.

One last thing ... I mentioned that Homer couldn't be with us and now I'll tell you his reason. It's one we can all share with joy and thanksgiving. Here is his letter to Clynard and me which we shared with the class, and now with the rest of you, although Homer didn't request that we do this. Hopefully, he won't be upset.

(I'm not printing his entire letter, just the part that you'll want to hear). "I'm sorry that I won't be able to make it to our class reunion this fall. I must be in Richmond as the honored guest of the Commonwealth Club.

"Virginia Commonwealth University is naming a conference room in the new business building for me and have set up

a scholarship in my name, so I've got to be there. Give every-one my love. Homer (Dave)"

Homer, we are so proud of what God has blessed you to accomplish and the fact that you as a person and a teacher have been recognized in such an hon-orable manner. How proud your mother would be of you, as well as others who are gone and those still living. Your class of '43 is happy for you, and also your many students.

Your "mountain folk" are proud of you and will again speak with respect and honor of another of their "sons" who, by the grace of God, has done exceedingly well and been faith-ful to his heritage. Plan to be with us next year.

Fields born in house with intricate gingerbread scrollwork

For a long time I have wanted to sit and visit with Helen Fields of Bartlick and listen to the memories she could share and record bits of "grassroots" history that only she has knowledge of. Memories shared make history, and we need history for the generations to come to build on.

Helen is the daughter of General Jackson and 'Tilda Sykes Mullins. Mr. and Mrs. Mullins were from the Pound River, the Skeetrock area of the county, and were related to many of the Dutton and Mullins families who lived there.

Her grandparents on her mother's side were Vol and Polly Mullins Sykes, and grandparents on her father's side were Doc and Sally Salyers Mullins.

The General Jackson Mullins family made their first move from Skeetrock to Bartlick just before Helen was born so that Mr. Mullins could work the rich, productive soil there for a livelihood for his own family as well as hiring out to other farmers. Wages were small, but back then a dollar was a lot.

Helen was born at Bartlick, May 31, 1917, in the house that came to be known as "The Bud House." This was because Bud Fuller, his wife Fronia and their family lived there for a number of years.

I have written about this house in other stories and still wonder who was the original architect and owner because it was of an unusually beautiful design, with an arched entrance which boasted a gingerbread scroll design.

One room was designated as the "music room" which was also unusual. Before my uncle Bud lived there, a Preiody family and a Lee family made the house their home, but I honestly believe that my great-grandfather, Jacob Fuller, was the original owner because the hollow that divides the two mountain sides, where the house was, is referred to as Jacob's Branch.

No, I haven't forgotten that this column is about Helen Fields. This is one of the things that she and I sat and talked about, and if anyone has any further information about the old place, let one of us know.

Anyway, sad to say, all traces of the home and farm are gone now and a big mining operation has taken in that whole area. Two more interesting memories of the old place are a large building that stood on the outskirts of the lawn. Was it a small store or just a storage house?

Helen remembers that up the hollow was a big chestnut orchard that bore chestnuts by the bushels. "The ground was covered with them, and they were never wormy back then," she recalls.

After living at Bartlick for four or five years, Mr. Mullins moved his family to Richlands to work in the mines. They traveled by train, and to reach the depot they walked over "Bone Ridge" on a path directly across the creek from where Helen lives now.

This trip was made by both parents and three children: Cholie, age 10; Helen, age five; and Johnny, age three. All the family furniture was also moved by train. This was a very awesome trip for Helen and, I imagine, for the other children as well.

After about two years the family moved from Richlands to Marrowbone, Ky., where Mr. Mullins again worked in the mines. This trip was again made by train, leaving the depot at Doran.

After a year or two at Marrowbone, the family moved back to Bartlick where their home would be up in the "Parkis Hollow" where uncle Wiley Hay had lived.

Just a note here that many of you will understand and others need to know: Back in those days there was not any "public work" or anything a man could go "get a job" at. This was a part of the country that was being settled — it was new and raw. The only work was farming and logging and most of that was done by individual families.

Mining, which was often a "killer," was dangerous to the body from mining accidents, and affected their health in the deep underground environment. Yet, this was about the only other job a man could get for a little income, so men moved their families from place to place, following the mines.

If a man didn't work in the mines he might work all day for a 25-pound sack of home-ground meal or a quart of corn-meal mush or molasses. "Then why did you dad leave the mines at Marrowbone?" I asked Helen.

"I really don't know," she answered, "but I imagine it was because he was so tall and the coal was so low that he just couldn't handle it." I took another look at the picture of Mr. Mullins and I could see what she meant.

"Tell me about the Parkis Hollow. I've heard about it all my life, but haven't been up there, so I'm eager to hear about it," I said.

"Well, uncle Wiley Hay had lived there and had built a big log house. It had two large rooms downstairs and one upstairs. The one upstairs was empty except for a big spinning wheel. On rainy days my sisters and I loved to go there and play.

"The downstairs was used for everything we did as a family, except eating. The kitchen was a room that had been built onto the side. In what we called the front room was a huge fireplace and the chimney was made with rocks, some being so large that it's a wonder how anyone ever got them up there."

Helen continued, "To reach the house and farm one had to walk about three miles up the hollow by the creek to where the land leveled out, and there it became a big level bottom that reached as far as the eye could see.

"On the left side of the house and creek (over which there was a foot log) there was a big barn where we kept the horses, cows and pigs. We also kept ducks and chickens and it was fun hunting eggs, especially the duck eggs.

They would lay them beside the creek and sometimes lay them in the middle of the creek.

"The duck eggs were very different from the hen eggs. The shell was harder to break and the yolk darker yellow and richer. My mother used some of the feathers from the chickens and ducks for pillows."

"Did you have any problems with wild animals destroying your crops and livestock?" I asked. "No, not at all," was Helen's ready answer. "I suppose it was because Dad always kept dogs. He was never without a good 'coon dog and fox hound."

"Did he do a lot of hunting?" I asked. "Not much," Helen replied. "We had plenty to eat and dad stayed too busy working the farm. He worked some for other farmers, too, for a little additional money ... not much, for there wasn't much money then.

"You asked about hunting? Well, the dogs did most of the hunting. They would sometimes be gone for days on their 'hunting trips' and return home after the chase was over."

"And what did you girls do?" I asked. "Well, we had our work around the house and we had time to play, but when we were older we also worked for other people if they needed us. All of us, my dad, brothers and sisters would work in the fields or wherever there was work to do. I would help the women with their children and with the washing and ironing.

"Five dollars a week for a hard week's work wasn't much but we were thankful to get it. I only wish that children and young people today could know what it means to really work and

appreciate what they have."

Next week we'll mention the names of Helen's brothers and sisters and who they married. I think you will find this quite interesting, especially as you realize how many of them or their family members you know.

Also next week, and very appropriate for this season of the year, Helen is going to share with us some stories about "foddering" and the fun of dodging the little stinging worms that make their homes in the hayfield.

Now, to end this week's story, first let me say what a joy it was to visit with Helen. It's a shame that many of us who live only a mile or two apart seldom see each other until there's a funeral. We need to leave off something and visit our neighbors. Neither we nor they will always be around to visit.

Now, having said that, let me share with you one of Helen's stories which I wish I could have been a part of.

"I want to tell you about the Sugar Tree Bottom," she said. "It was below the house and full of sugar maple trees. In the springtime, papa would take his ax and cut a slot about eight to 10 feet high on each tree. He would make a spout and work it into the slot at just the right angle. Then we would set buckets under the spout and the sap would begin to drip into the bucket.

"The drops seemed to drip very slowly but by morning, the bucket would be full. Then Mommy would take the liquid and boil it down until we had pans of maple syrup, and yes, it was fun and it was good."

As I said, I wish I could have been there — don't you?

Family raised crops to support themselves

Helen Fields is surrounded by flowers at her 90th birthday celebration.

Helen Mullins Fields: Part II

This week we are continuing with stories and memories that have been a part of Helen Fields' life and that she now shares with us.

In last week's issue of The Star, Helen Mullins (Fields) and her family were living in Parkis Hollow where they continued to live until Helen was about 10 years old. At that time her dad had the opportunity to buy about 20 acres of land from Doc Mullins on Camp Branch.

This land was, and still is, in the stretch of bottom land (left-hand side of the road toward the Breaks Park) above the two homes that are now built there. Just below these homes in another piece of bottom land, and just before the entrance to

ANITA BELCHER

The Garden Hole, was the Camp Branch School which we'll write more about later on.

There was an unfinished "boxed" house on this piece of property which Mr. Mullins had to work on as well as fencing in a piece of his bottom land for a

garden. A part of the land which Mr. Mullins bought was used for a corn field which provided food for the family, grain for the mill and corn and hay "fodder" for the livestock.

Reading about this corn field will provide some of you fond memories which you'll talk and laugh about, and others of you who have grown up away from the mountains will read it and say, "How did they do it?"

Helen recalls how it was done: "Dad had to clear the timber off the hill side, maybe an acre, maybe more. Then, of course, the fallen timber had to be removed, and that left the stumps to deal with. Most of the stumps were left ... too many and too time-consuming and almost impossible to remove them."

SEE ECHOES, PAGE 7B

224

"Did you dad plow this field before planting the corn?" I asked. "If he did, what about the stumps?"

"Yes, dad plowed the field using either a horse or mule. He just had to go around the stumps."

After Helen told me this, I got to thinking — today we have to dodge traffic, especially in the cities, and I smiled as I thought about some of today's drivers who handle the traffic quite well. How would they do dodging stumps on a steep hill side with a big turning plow and stubborn mule? Time have changed!

Now, back to Helen ... "When we moved to the Parkis Hollow all our family except me, my sister Chloie and Johnny were married and had homes of their own. All the work around the house and the farm had to be done by my dad, mother and us three children.

"At first Johnny was too young to help out, so us girls had to work with our parents. Mom would work in the field until it was time to go to the house and get dinner. I can still see her pulling off the ears of corn and carrying them to the house where she would shuck them, then grit them into meal for bread."

"Explain to me about gritting the corn. How was it done?" I asked. "Well, the old folks made their own gritters," Helen replied. "They would take a coffee can, flatten it out and make holes in it with a nail. Then they would nail it to a board, sharp side out, and that was their gritter.

"The corn had to be at a certain stage...not too milky...not too hard. When it was gritted it was not like meal. It was doughy. Mommy would add the usual ingredients and bake it into cornbread. It was wonderful. I can taste it now. Yes, I could bake some if I had the corn at the right stage."

Pictured are the parents of Helen Fields, General Jackson Mullins and Tilda Sykes Mullins.

"Did your folks plant beans with the corn?" I asked. "Yes, they planted the big white hasting beans," Helen answered. "I don't believe that some of the beans that folks think are hasting beans really are. These days we have the purple tip, blue tip and pink tip, but they aren't hastings.

"The hasting bean was a long full green bean that would run to the top of the hickory cane corn and it had a flavor that other beans didn't have. Mommy always saved her seeds from her beans and everything else. We never bought seeds from the store."

Since this is the fall of the year and people are gathering in their crops or going to produce markets, I thought it would be interesting to know what crops were raised and "gathered in" 80-some years ago, so I asked Helen.

"We raised about everything," was her reply. "The usual garden stuff which mommy canned, pickled and dried. Earlier in the year she had already made jams and jellies and now (October) was the time to finish up with the garden produce.

"We had a cellar out back of the house, back in the hillside. Only the front was visible. Here was where mommy kept her canned vegetables and fruit as well as the Irish potatoes and pumpkins and crocks of pickled corn, beans and kraut.

"Sweet potatoes were kept in a closet in the house close to the fireplace, and each one of them was individually wrapped in paper. Of course we had strings of dried beans. We didn't dry the pumpkins. They were kept in the cellar 'til mommy would bake them with brown sugar and butter.

"(Some people would cut and slice pumpkins in the fall and dry them for winter-time use).

"Speaking of pumpkins, we also raised watermelons and musk-melons and mommy raised a special kind of musk-melon called the banana melon. She planed the seeds in the sweet potato ridge and the fruit was absolutely delicious.

"Yes, we also raised the old-time artichoke. They grew out by the fence and we would dig them in the winter for a special treat."

Maybe you who are reading this column have noticed that we have been privileged to have an inside look at a mountain farm from the time the land was cleared until the time of harvest.

Now, we'll take a look at one of the last jobs the farmer and his family had to accomplish before winter set in, so far as farming was concerned. Again, for some of you this will bring back old memories; for others, it will be something new that you haven't seen or experienced.

Helen explains, "When the corn was fully ripe and the fodder (corn blades) was dry, it was time to do the 'foddering.' That means that we went into the field and stripped the fodder off the stalk up to the ear. We then took what we had stripped off and stuffed it behind the ear of corn to dry a little more.

"A few days later we would go back, remove the fodder from behind the ear and tie it into a bundle with another blade of fodder. This was repeated until the whole field of fodder had been tied into bundles and ready for the barn loft for winter feed.

"I didn't like this job, not because of the work but because of a little stinging worm called the pack saddle which lived in the fodder. I don't like worms anyway and I hated the sting of the pack saddle which raised a big whelk that itched and hurt for what seemed like a long time."

If those of you who are reading this already feel tired from the hard work Helen has described, well, you still have several days of hard work ahead to read about. Now, the tops have to be cut!

Once again Helen explains: "When the fodder was all gathered in, the men had to go back and 'cut the tops.' The women didn't usually work at this, though some did. This was really men's work as they went from stalk to stalk with a big butcher knife or whatever knife that worked best for them.

"Each stalk was slashed just behind the ear of corn and gathered into bundles until there was enough for a 'fodder shock.' Soon the field would be dotted with shocks of fodder ... more food for the livestock for the coming winter. A beautiful sight achieved by hard work."

The last of the field work would be the gathering of the corn and hauling it to the crib. Then later the stalks would be cut to the ground and the field prepared once more for the spring planting.

"When you look back on those times just how would you describe them?" I asked Helen.

"They were wonderful times," was her ready response. "It was hard work, but there was something there that I wish we had today. Maybe we looked more to the Lord back then." I agree with her, don't you?

The next time you drive to the Breaks Park, glance over at the strip of bottom land just before you get to the entrance of Garden Hole. Visualize this old mountain farm and share some thoughts about the story you've just read. Helen would like that.

Look for Helen's picture in next week's Mountain Echoes.

October 24, 2007

School did double-duty

Helen Mullins Fields, Part III

This week's column was to have been about the meeting and marriage of Helen Mullins and Mack Fields, but that will be next week's column.

I didn't intentionally change it but when Helen and I began discussing last week's column, it revived so many memories for both of us, and we began making so many connections with people and places, that we simply ran out of time.

Some of the local history that Helen recalled is too important, especially for children and grandchildren (and generations to come) to leave out. Also, friends and relatives are already contacting Helen, eager to know more about the people and places that she remembers.

But before we go further, just one simple but important recollection — "You know," Helen relates, "I imagine some of Mommy's old roses are still growing along the side of the road over at the Camp Branch place. They were the old rambling kind and not long ago some were still there."

When we spoke of the Camp Branch home, I remembered that I had promised to ask her about the school there.

"I don't recall as much about that school because I only went for a short time. I believe the teacher at the time was a Miss Blanche Neel. I wanted to quit school and go stay with my brother, Jim, and his wife, Maude, and help with the children, but I do remember going to the Bartlick school when we lived in the Parkis Hollow."

I (Anita) didn't want to leave out this memorable phase of Helen's life, so even though it changed our planned schedule, I asked her to tell us about it. I think all of you will enjoy this. Remember this is before the Camp Branch days. We are just "back-tracking" a little.

Mountain **ECHOES**

ANITA BELCHER

Helen recalls, "we walked out of the hollow to school ... had to walk almost through the yard of uncle Noah and aunt Belle Fuller's home and cross a bridge (probably built by Uncle Noah) to get across the creek. Uncle Noah had a country store and that is where I got my first piece of candy!

"He and aunt Belle were a real inspiration to me because they were so kind to us children. I remember as a child thinking to myself that they had what I called 'smiling faces.' I still see some people like that and it's so nice!"

"What else do you remember about the school?" I asked. "Well," Helen laughingly replied, "I can still see aunt Belle's geese sunning themselves at the edge of the school

yard and I think they were waiting for us! Anyway, as soon as we crossed the bridge they stretched their necks and started after us! I don't know what they would have done but we were afraid of them and ran."

"And what about the schoolhouse itself?" I asked. Helen recalls, "The schoolhouse at Bartlick was set on a big piece of bottom land that Mr. Fuller and his wife gave to the school board to use as long as it was used for a school. It was a two-room school with a set of steps going up to the porch.

"On each end of the porch was a cloak room ... one for the boys and one for the girls. That's where we put our lunches and hung our coats, sweaters and boggins. Inside there was a potbellied stove and a partition that would roll into the ceiling in the center of the room.

"On Friday evenings we would have spelling matches or other activities and the dividing partition would be rolled out of sight. It was the same at Christmas when we had special programs."

E.H. Anderson was the teacher of the "big room" and June Priode the teacher in the "little room." (June Priode is the aunt of Vickie Silcox and Mickie Branham and is still living. In fact, not too long ago she sent me (Anita) some pictures of students at the Bartlick School while she and Mr. Anderson were teaching there. Maybe we'll print one or two of them later.)

Both Helen and I thought it was Judy, a sister of June, who taught, but Mickie, her niece, says that though Judy might have taught there at some time, it was June who was teaching during the days we're writing about.

Also, Blanche Neel, who was teaching at the Camp Branch School, was another sister of June and Judy. These were daughters of Lucien and Carri Priode, a wonderful couple who were probably one of the first families to live in the "Bud House." Thank you so much, Mickie, for this information.

Helen continues, "When I went to school there, Ada Counts Fuller was one of my best friends and continued to be so until her death not long ago." Another thing Helen recalls, "You know, Anita, the road used to make a big sweep or bend around the creek. Where the road is now was all hillside and we children played there. The girls built playhouses."

Though there were no natural gas wells back then, there was evidence of the hidden wealth lying dormant. Helen recalls, "In back of the schoolhouse, a well had been dug for water but it was never used because of the gas seepage.

"If a match were dropped into that well the flames would shoot right into the air. And, " she relates, "in the middle of the creek directly in front of the Arville Fuller house was a little island where the natural gas collected and could catch fire."

What do you remember about some of the homes or the people who lived back then?" I asked. "Well, I remember the uncle Dick (Richard) Fuller home. He was married to aunt Rosa Belle Compton. They had a nice home and a nice family. They were a fine old couple.

"Then there was uncle Noah and aunt Belle and uncle Allen Willis and aunt Rena who had a daughter, Rena. She was a another one of my best friends. I would spend the night with her and listen to someone play their organ. I loved to stay there."

I (Anita) remember the old Allen Willis place. Another of the Willis daughters, Delma, was one of my mother's best friends and she also loved to go there with young friends and listen to the organ music.

Helen and I recalled the Mitchell Senter home and the many family connections that centered around it, and then there was the uncle Bennie and aunt Mary Edwards place. "Some of the Edwards girls were my good friends," Helen recalls, "but I believe they are all gone now."

Perhaps the home that intrigued us as much as any was the uncle Jeff and aunt Betty Cochran place that stood in the piece of bottom land beside the creek where 611 and Route 80 now intersect.

"It was a fine, two-story house with a porch running the full length of it," Helen recalls. "Uncle Jeff and aunt Betty were two of the kindest people one could ever meet and they had the nicest family. One of their daughters, Francis, who had very red hair, was one of my very best friends. We built playhouses along the creek and had the best of times!

"Francis grew up and mar-

on Friday evenings

At left is June Priode (Hawks), who taught in the 'little room' at Bartlick School when Helen Mullins (Fields) attended it. Mrs. Hawks is still living at Hopewell. Below is E.H. Anderson, who taught in the school's 'big room.'

ried Wess Farmer. There was another daughter, Bertha, who married Whet Mullins and then a son, Corbett, who married Vesta Edwards, daughter of uncle Bennie and aunt Mary Edwards."

The old Cochran property is still there but the house no longer stands. The dirt road that ran between the house and the creek was changed to bypass the Cain place and a stiff curve became a part of the new road, directly across from the old Allen Willis workshop and the home that Helen loved to visit.

What's left is one of the few old steel bridges across the creek where the dirt road used to run and, of course, there's the mem-

ories of the playhouses built by two little girls under the trees and along the creek banks.

Of course all of you have noticed that we have called all these older folks that Helen remembers by the title of "uncle" or "aunt." As most of you know, it was simply a term of respect and endearment. We still do that back here in the mountains. You don't have to be "blood-kin."

Thank you, Helen, for another look into the past. For many, you have shared stories that oth-

erwise would never have been known. Even now, some folks are saying, "Well, I didn't know that!" and don't be surprised if they call you.

Now, just a note: in last week's column, I called the hillside across from the Fields home "Bone Ridge." The correct name is "Bone Hill." Also, Helen believes that the Mullins grandmother was a Reed, not a Salyers.

Fields' marriage spans

HELEN MULLINS FIELDS
PART 4

An old-fashioned pie supper was the setting for the meeting of young Helen Mullins and Mack Fields of Bartlick back in 1932, but before going any further with their story, I'd like to share with all you who read this column the memories that Helen and I have shared about those pie suppers of years ago.

We had a lot of fun re-living those days, and I think it will recall many memories for most of you and will be a source of information for those of you who didn't live "back in those days."

Helen and I pieced our memories together and they were too good not to share with the readers of *The Star* ... and, of course, they set the stage for Mack and Helen's friendship, courtship and marriage.

Just what were "pie suppers" and why did we have them? First of all the county schools needed money for essentials which the county couldn't afford or only partially pay for.

Coal was a big item, and other schoolroom necessities such as coal buckets, shovels, oil for the floors (twice a year), and other every-day needs which the teacher would have to pay for out of his or her own meager salary, unless he or she could come up with a money-making idea.

(Helen reminded me that the boys were "excused" from classes for several days in the autumn to gather firewood, so there was no expense for wood, and those were happy "holidays" for the boys.)

Having a pie supper, usually in the fall of the year, proved to be the most successful venture for financial help. This was not only a solution for the teachers, but it gave the mountain people an opportunity to get together, a chance to share the good and bad news of the community, a chance for the men to proudly escort their wives and daughters to a social function, and for the women and girls it was the proving time of their pie-making abilities.

There was usually some music provided by local musicians, (Helen recalls the banjo in particular; I seem to remember the fiddle), sometimes some dancing and always the bidding off of cakes and especially the "pretty girl" cake.

For a girl entering her cake in the "pretty girl" category was much like a young lady these days being willing to be a contestant in a fall festival. It was a great honor to be the winner.

One of the unspoken, but well understood, rules of the pie supper was that whoever bought a pie had the privilege of eating it with the lady who brought it. Husbands made sure they were prepared to buy the pie that their wife brought, and young ladies, down deep in their hearts, hoped that certain young man would be there and buy their pie.

On the other side of the coin, young men came, hoping the girl of their choice would have brought a pie that he could buy and share with her, thus getting acquainted.

Helen recalls that on this particular night of which we write she and her sister, Chloie, attended the pie supper at the Camp Branch School. Helen brought her pie, an egg custard.

She recalls that she had seen young Mack Fields around in the community from time to time, but had thought nothing of it. On the night of the pie supper she saw him across the room and thought to herself, "There's a good-looking young man. He's the man I want to buy my pie. I hope he does!"

Well, he did, and of course, following the rules, they sat down together and that was the beginning of an acquaintance that led to a life-long marriage.

Helen wanted me to add one more thing that she still laughs about and she thinks her friend Emma Jean Lyle (Phillips) will get a laugh out of it, too.

It was the occasion of another pie supper, this one at Lower Bartlick, the Pound school. Sometimes when a fellow knew that his friend, married or unmarried, was bringing his wife or girlfriend, he would purposely run the bidding up for her pie, knowing that the husband or boyfriend would keep bidding regardless of how high the bidding went.

Mike Lyall and his wife, Lottie, good friends of the Fields family, were there that night and Mike decided he would bid on Helen's pie. The bidding got pretty high. Finally one of the men gave up and the pie went to the highest bidder.

Helen Fields (center front) is surrounded by her children. In the second row are Wilson and Barbara .In the third row, from left, are Joy, Stony and Tommy. In the fourth row, from left, are Roger, Hank and Earl. Helen and Wilson are holding a photo of husband and father, Mack Fields.

Mack and Helen Fields met at a pie supper in the early 1930s, and ended up spending nearly six decades together.

nearly six decades

Helen laughs as she recalls, "We all sat down together and ate it!"

Now, back to the beginning. Mack's family had lived on Ramsey Ridge and had recently moved to Tom Bottom, the Fall's Branch area. Helen recalls, "After our meeting at the pie supper, Mack and I continued to date almost every weekend for the next two years. Even though he was only 21 years old he was working steadily at the Splashdam mine."

"How did he get back and forth to work?" I asked.

"Well, in those days there was a hotel in Haysi and he stayed there through the week," Helen replied. "I think he only paid about $1 a day for room and board. I remember the hotel very well. There was a porch that ran the length of it with rocking chairs all the way across. Big red geraniums hung across the front."

Mack and Helen's wedding day was Dec. 26, 1934. They were married in Clintwood with Lee Stanley performing the ceremony. Helen recalls, "I wore a brown dress, belted in the back with a V-neckline. Mack wore blue pants, a white shirt and jacket.

"Mack's brother, Kemp, and sister-in-law, Bessie, went with us for our wedding. Afterward, Kemp and Bessie left with his sister, Daisy, to visit her husband who was in the hospital. Mack and I spent our honeymoon at their house, caring for their children."

"Where did you set up house-keeping?" I asked. "Our first home was in Tom Bottom in a two-room house on the right-hand side of the old Alex Mullins place which, of course, is gone now."

"And what did you start out housekeeping with?" was my next question. Helen replied, "We ordered a stove, a wardrobe and a dresser from Spiegel, and Mack bought a couch and two straight-back chairs from somebody ... I don't remember just who.

"We bought our bedroom furniture from the Haysi Hardware and that was how we got started. I still have the wardrobe and Barbara has the dresser. We were very happy there and that's where our first daughter, Joy, was born."

In 1937 the Fields family moved to Bartlick to the house where Helen now lives, but there have been changes. At first there was one window and two doors in the front, and one window on the side. Now it has been remodeled and an upstairs added.

The outside has changed also. When Mack and Helen first moved there, the creek ran in front of the house and the road was on the far side of the creek where houses are now located. It was a very quiet community with mostly the same neighbors that were mentioned in last week's column.

Mack continued working in the mines until he got the position of mail carrier on a mountainous route. He left with the mail at lower Bartlick (the commissary housed the post office), on to the Breaks, from there to Haysi, then on to Splashdam. From Splashdam he traveled to Tarpon then into Clinchco.

At Clinchco he waited for the incoming mail and on receiving it, traveled back over the same route. During this time, several logging jobs opened, so Helen carried the mail while Mack worked at logging for a period of time.

Helen recalls some of the postmasters: "At the Breaks the postmaster was James Raines. At Tarpon, Inis Mullins, at Haysi, Ireland Baker.

"As I recall," Helen says, "after the logging business went out, Mack went back to the mines at Splashdam. This was also in the early days of small truck mines and tipples were a pretty common sight along the roads. It was about then that Mack bought a truck or two and started hauling coal, probably short bed trucks, as the big tandems had not come into this part of the country.

"He did not get into the trucking business big time but I guess that's where the boys and even some of our grandsons got their love for trucking. They grew up with it and they still drive and maintain their own trucks."

The Fields family had grown during these years. After Joy's birth, the next child was Stoney Mack, and then a baby girl, Trula Mae, who was still-born. Afterwards, sons Roger Lee and Wilson, a daughter, Barbara, and two more sons, Hank and Tommy.

All the children are married now and have settled with their families close by Helen where she is surrounded by their love and that of grandchildren and great-grandchildren.

Mack died as a result of an automobile accident in 1992. Their marriage had lasted 58 years and Helen has nothing but good memories of those years.

"Anita, as I look back over my marriage, there isn't one thing I would change about it, except I wish I had been a Christian during those years, serving the Lord. I had a good marriage."

"And what is your advice to young people or to anyone who is thinking about getting married?" I asked. Helen did not have to think of an answer. Her reply came quickly and with deep feeling.

"My advice to young people (or any couple) is to stay together. That is the way God intended it. The vows we made are sacred. They are made before God and should not be taken lightly. That is what I pray for."

These are the words of a Godly mother who is one of God's dear children. What a different world we would be living in if her advice were taken! Thank you, Helen.

Note: A correction—Blanche Neel who taught at the Camp Branch School was the aunt of June Priode, not her sister. She was married to Noah Raines from the Breaks. She later moved to Clintwood, married and taught in the school system there for several years and retired as a school teacher. Their son, Bob Raines, was superintendent of Washington County Schools.

Also, thank you to Jean Edwards, a manager at the Southern Heritage Inn at Clintwood, whose friendly cooperation assisted us in helping someone in a needy situation.

Last, but not least, a special greeting to Graham Compton of Johnson City and to Banner and Carma Sykes who look forward to receiving *The Star* each week.

Also, special prayers for Roger Counts in the hospital at Bristol Memorial, and David Hay in the hospital at Johnson City. May God bless each one of you.

Sharing random memories of mountain life

Mountain ECHOES

ANITA BELCHER

Helen Mullins Fields: Part 5

The visits I have had with Helen Fields over the past month have been like a cool drink of water on a hot day! They have been refreshing to me, and I'm sure many of you feel the same way as you have shared her memories.

I am sorry that this will be our last "newspaper visit" with her until Christmas when I include her memories of what Christmas was like when she was growing up, but that will be something to look forward to.

In the meantime, my column today will be stories and bits of family history that we couldn't squeeze in before, but stories which are too interesting and informative to leave out, like going huckleberry pickin' back in the Cumberlands or, as some say, "back in the south of the mountain."

Helen recalls, "Anita, when we want huckleberry pickin' we had to prepare for the trip the day before, because you see, we went to spend the day, camp out that night and come back the next day.

"On this particular trip it was my dad, Jim "Fuzz," Chloie and me who were going. Aurora, my sister, sent me and my brother, Arville, out to catch and kill a chicken and get it ready for frying as part of the food we were taking.

"Well, we caught the chicken and Arville laid it on the chopping block where I was supposed to hold its head still. When Arville lowered the ax I turned my head and the chicken got away! We had to catch it again.

"I don't recall exactly the other food we took but I know it included some meat and bread and probably some stuff from the garden. I also remember that if dad got the chance he would shoot a rabbit and roast it over the fire!"

"Was it a long trip back into the mountains?" I asked. "And how did you get there ... was there a path or trail of any kind?"

"Yes, it was a long way to where the huckleberries grew and there was a trail that others had made over the years. We rode our horses, but we were tired when we got

PLEASE SEE **ECHOES**, PAGE 3B

233

CONTINUED FROM PAGE 1B

there. When we reached the right place we hitched our horses, ate our dinner, then got to work pickin' the berries.

"The bushes were low ... maybe three feet high ... these were the old time bushes, you know. We would pick until our buckets were full and the buckets didn't fill up fast because the berries were small."

"Did you leave when you had filled the buckets?" I asked. "No," Helen replied. "When we had picked all the berries our bucket could hold, dad made bark buckets for us.

"He 'circled' the bark of a birch tree however tall he wanted the bucket to be, then slipped the bark off (he had circled it all the way 'round on both ends), then he bottomed the bucket and fastened it on the side by weaving strips of bark in and out from the bottom to the top.

"We filled those buckets, too, until we had enough to fill the sacks we brought. When we finished we got our supper and made a camp fire. We could sit around it and talk until time to go to sleep."

"What was it like spending the night back there in the mountains? What did you use to sleep on and did you take a blanket or something for cover?" I asked.

Helen laughed as she recalled, "Spending the night was all right. We didn't see any wild animals or snakes. We slept on the ground. We were young back then and by the end of the day we were so tired we could have slept anywhere!

"We didn't need a blanket because berry-pickin' time was in hot weather. Next morning we got up, fixed our breakfast and rode back home. Mommy or my sisters would can the berries and use them for pies, jellies and jams."

Now, for all of you who trace your genealogy through some of these articles, you may be helped by studying the Fields family through a couple of generations.

Of course the parents of this particular family were Jim and Alifair Fleming Fields. Children were as follows: Edith (m) Bill Bailey, Alma (m) Ben Hall, Julia (m) Willard Stanley, Osie (m) Joe

Pictured are Helen Mullins Fields and some of her brothers and sisters. In the front row, from left, are Dona Mullins Colley, Tilda Sykes Mullins (mother), Helen Mullins Fields, Dee Mullins and Aurora Mullins Fuller. In the back row, from left, are General Jack Mullins (father), Jim "Zeke" Mullins and Arville Mullins.

Fleming, Alice (m) Arron Phillips, Itley (m) Evins Mullins, Atley (twin to Itley) (m) Gladiola Belcher (other marriages?), Bill (m) Vergie Stanley, Leon (m) Osie Lee of Camp Branch, Kemp (m) Bessie Sharder, Mack (m) Helen Mullins, half-brother Rice (m) Una?, half-sister Daisy (m) Charlie Hill.

Sisters and brothers of Helen were Dona (m) Noah Colley (he was a brother to Preacher Howard Colley and their parents were Josh and Liddy Colley), Dona (m) second time - Spencer Carrol, Lieum (m) George Cochran (son of uncle Jeff and Betty Cochran). Lieum died at age 32 probably of aneurysm since two others in the family have died from that cause.

Arville (m) Flora Fuller (daughter of uncle Dick 'Richard' and Rosa Belle Compton Fuller, Dee (m) Margie Fuller (daughter of uncle Dick and Rosa Belle Fuller, Jim (m) Maude (daughter of Uncle Dick and Rosa Belle Fuller), Pride (m) Maxie (daughter of uncle Dick and Rosa Belle Fuller), Aurora (m) Jim "Fuzz" (son of uncle Dick and Rosa Belle Fuller), Early (m) "Phil" (daughter of Dora Fuller Wallace, Chloe (m) Tom McCowan (son of Steve McCowan and ?), Helen (m) Mack Fields,

Johnny (m) Leona Hamon (daughter of Emory and Mary Hamon). Johnny was killed when his car stalled on the railroad tracks.

Inis died as a newborn and Noah died age 12 of what was then known as the "flux," actually diarrhea and vomiting.

In these days a simple treatment of I.V. fluids would probably have saved him, but back then, if blackberry juice didn't work, death was almost inevitable. (Helen and I both recalled the blackberry juice cure.)

Helen recalled her folks opening cans of blackberry juice for sick members of the family. I recall my mother doing the same for me, but what I remember most is mom telling me how this remedy was used during the awful outbreak of flu and flux when so many people died. It was their only hope and often worked.

I was amused several years ago when I picked up a magazine and turned to the page where "news of medicine" was printed. Across the page was a picture of a blackberry brier with beautiful blooms and underneath the caption something like this: "The blackberry fruit and its juice have just recently been discovered to be helpful in cases of vomiting and other stomach disor-

Helen Fields' sister, Chloie Mullins McCowan

Helen Fields' brother, Johnny Mullins

ders."

I couldn't help but smile, thinking back to how the older generation had made that discovery long ago.

Now, for Richard (uncle Dick) and Rosa Belle Compton Fuller's family. I think you will find this interesting if you compare the Mullins and Fuller family. Keep in mind, they were no kin until they married.

Dewey (m) Vada Counts, Fred (m) Goldia Counts, Jim Fuller (m) Aurora Mullins, Dora (m) Cleve Wallace, Flora Fuller (m) Arville Mullins, Maude Fuller (m) Jim Mullins, Margie Fuller (m) Dee Mullins, Maxie Fuller (m) Pride Mullins.

Dora Fuller Wallace had a daughter "Phil" (mentioned above) who married the youngest of the Mullins boys, Early, a fine-looking young man, as most of those boys were. Dora also had a son, Fran.

Helen recalls the price that families paid, and that many of the men paid for working in the mines. "You know, Anita, I had two brothers, two brothers-in-law, and one nephew killed in the mines, all at Splashdam. Both Pride and Early were killed there and brothers-in-law, Noah Colley and Carrol Spencer, and Noah's son, Monroe

Colley. Also, Dora's son, Fran Wallace."

If you read back over the above paragraph, you will see that not only did Helen and other family members suffer a great loss, but her sister, Dona, lost both husbands and a son in the mines.

Let's end on a pleasant bit of Helen's childhood memories along with a precious possession. She still has her first grade reader, "tattered and torn," that she used at Bartlick school. The covers are secured with strong cord, stitched by her mother's hands, which makes the little book more precious!.

"Helen, God has blessed you to be 90 years old now and not as active as you used to be, but how do you spend your time?"

"Anita, I have quite a bit of pain from arthritis but I don't want to give up. I embroider pillow cases, quilt squares and table scarves. Joy and I make quilts (and Helen shows me the latest baby quilt,

beautifully embroidered, hand-stitched). I also have a loom that I use to make 'boggins for children or anyone who likes to wear them."

"What do you enjoy most at this time in your life?" I asked. Helen's answer was potent with deep feeling: "Seeing all my family together ... that's what I love best. There's never a day that I don't see some of them, but Thanksgiving and Christmas are those special occasions when they all come and that is my most enjoyable time."

Helen is a Christian and member of Splashdam Freewill Baptist Church. She can't attend at this time because of the painful arthritis, but she loves her church and the members there. In fact, I think Helen loves everyone.

"Just how important is Christianity to you and what part does it play in your life?" I asked.

"It means everything to me," Helen replied. "God is very real to me. I couldn't get up in the morning without him and I don't know how anyone else does." I'll never forget her answer. I hope all you who read this will remember it and meditate on it: "He has my heart," she replied.

Helen, thank you so much for these visits and all you have shared with us. May God bless you and those you love!

Note: At any time any of you find a mistake in names or places in any column I write, please let me know. Over the years people spelled their names differently, and it's a blessing that certain places and events can be recalled at all. In an article *like this we* cover *more than* 100 years of local history, but we want to be as correct as possible.

This week, our apologies go to Earl Fields for not listing him in Mack and Helen's children, but Earl, you are listed in the picture. Also, I believe, Stoney Mack is a grandson and Stoney Fayne is the son.

I had *an interesting letter from* Sallie Compton of Liberty, S.C., in which she made connections with certain people in last week's column. Mrs. Compton, I so enjoyed your letter! Please write and tell me who your parents and grandparents are, as several people are very interested.

Story threads unwind in tale

Mountain ECHOES

ANITA BELCHER

Many of you who see the name "Lucille Browning Sutherland" will recognize the lady I'm writing about, but some of you, for different reasons, will not.

However, all of you will be interested in the history Lucille provides us with, beginning with her great-great-great-grandfather, David (Deal) Deel who landed in America on Sept. 5, 1785, along the east coast of Virginia.

As we go along, we will pick up on the ancestors in between David Deel and "Uncle" Andy Floyd Deel, who was Lucille's grandfather, and was born, lived and died in the Prater Creek community of what is now Buchanan County.

With that much of a preface, now I'll explain how I came into this story and how it all came about. Actually, it started back in the 1950s, now that I think about it. That was when I would take my grandfather, Charles Anderson, to see Uncle Andy Floyd Deel.

I loved to be around my grandfather and it was a special treat when I took him to see "Uncle Floyd." That's what he called him when talking to me, but when talking to him, he just called him "Floyd," and Uncle Floyd called grandpa "Charlie."

The one time that stands out in my mind was one evening, probably late fall, maybe early spring, when Grandpa asked, "Nita, would you take me up to see Uncle Floyd?" "Sure," I answered, and picking up a light jacket, we walked together to my car.

On arriving at Uncle Floyd's, he met us at the door and even their greeting stands out in my mind. Both were a trifle heavy (not fat), both wore bib overalls, and grandpa's silvery-white hair, as usual, was curling around the old railroad cap he wore.

"Howdy, Floyd," he said, and Uncle Floyd replied, "Howdy, Charlie," and both reached out a work-worn hand to the other in greeting. I stood watching, never once thinking that some day I would write this story. How thankful I am that I remember it. "Come on in, Charlie," Uncle Floyd said, and his smile included me.

Once inside the house the two old gentlemen talked on several subjects while I sat and listened. Suddenly Uncle Floyd asked, "Charlie, would you like to see my casket?" Grandpa nodded in agreement. "That would be good, Floyd," he said.

They walked across the room to a doorway where a heavy curtain hung. Uncle Floyd pushed it aside and we all three entered what perhaps had been the living room. Now the only piece of furniture in it was a beautiful handmade casket, resting on some kind of stand.

Both old men looked it over carefully, ran their hands over the outside, speaking of the smoothness and admiring the handiwork in general. The inside also passed their inspection.

"Well, what do you think of it, Charlie?" Uncle Floyd asked. "It's a good piece of work, Floyd, a fine piece of work," Grandpa answered.

We went back through the curtained doorway and the two old friends resumed their conversation until time for us to leave. Grandpa and Uncle Floyd parted with another handshake, another smile, and a "Come again, Charlie."

I don't recall one word that Grandpa and I said on the drive back home, or even if we talked, for we were re-living his visit with his old friend and I was thinking about Uncle Floyd and the casket and how good he felt about having it ready when it was needed, and how proud he was of the workmanship, and how calm he was about the prospects of death.

Neither he nor Grandpa seemed the slightest ruffled about the certainty of dying. It gave me something to think about, not only then, but over the years, right up until now.

There was one other thing that I wondered about, and I think I asked Grandpa

# of generations

to explain why he and Uncle Floyd were so close in their relationship. He answered me, but somehow, his answer got lost, and over the years, I've been left to wonder.

At last, I've found out the answer — it came through Lucille Browning Sutherland and my cousin Bill Anderson, who is going to fill in some missing pieces.

That will be another story in another column, but this much I will tell you now, so you'll know how Lucille Sutherland fits into the picture. Indeed, if it were not for her, I wouldn't be writing this at all.

Several years ago, Lucille and her husband, Bill, saw Clynard and me somewhere. Both of them loved to read *The Star*, and one of them said to me, "Anita, you need to come and visit us. We have something you'd like to see."

Of course, I had to ask what it was and they told me that when Lucille's grandmother died, she left a trunk to Lucille that had belonged to her great-grandmother, Sarah.

Inside the trunk, along with other items, were little pieces of rolled-up paper tied with thin sewing threat. Inside the rolls of paper were — guess what? Should I wait until next week to tell you?

No, that would be too hard to wait for. I'll tell you now. Inside each piece of paper were locks of hair cut from the head of family members when they died. The date of death and the name of the person were written there. I believe the oldest date is 1851.

Well, several years passed by and several events took place in our family that made it impossible for me to write for a while. Also, Lucille was going through some very hard times. She and Bill had suffered the loss of a son, then Bill became ill and passed away (not too long ago), and Lucille herself has been, and still is, battling cancer.

When we parted after this interview she was leaving for more tests and I haven't heard from her since. We pray that God's hand of mercy is on her and that another victory has been achieved.

But, isn't it odd how things happen sometimes? I didn't know if I would ever get with Lucille again with so much going on in both our lives, but one day I got a phone call (on my answering service) from her niece, wanting to know if I had any information on her grandmother, Sarah Anderson.

I knew that my grandmother, Sarah Anderson, was not her grandmother Sarah, so I called Lucille and she invited me to her home for a visit where we began to untangle threads that went back many generations.

Those threads keep unwinding up to the present generation and beyond. It's amazing and very, very interesting. If you find it interesting, too, join me next week for another "unwinding" session.

In Touch

with Dickenson County Family, Friends & Neighbors

Deel family tree roots interesting

Mountain ECHOES

ANITA BELCHER

I want to give credit to Bonnie Owens, a former teacher in the Haysi area, for most of the information in this week's column. Bonnie worked diligently over the years on the Deel family history and had planned to publish a book, but serious health problems prevented this.

Bonnie's husband, Linkous (Link) was a son of Andy Floyd and his wife, Martha. We'll publish this in honor of the hard work Bonnie did, and I thank Lucille Browning Sutherland for loaning me the material. Lucille is a granddaughter of Andy Floyd and Martha Deel.

There are many folks throughout the country who are working on their genealogy, and this column, along with next week's, will be of great help to those of you who find that you are a "limb" of the Deel family tree.

David Deel (Deal) landed in America on the east coast of Virginia on Sept. 5, 1785. He was of German descent from Hamburg, Germany. He moved from the east coast of Virginia to Washington County, then to Russell County and from there to Buchanan County on the Levisa River.

David married Elizabeth Coleman who was probably from Tazewell County. David and Elizabeth had at least one son, Benjamin, who married Polly (Mary) Stigner.

SEE ECHOES, PAGE 7B

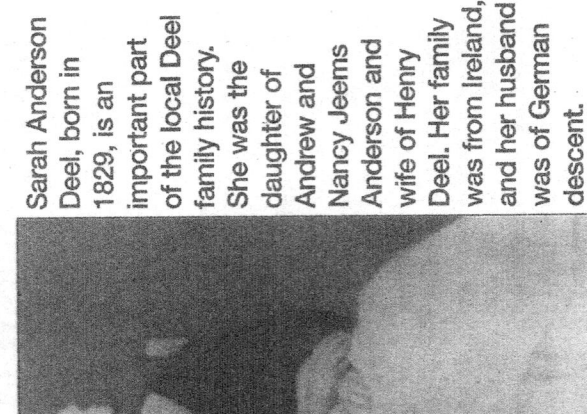

Sarah Anderson Deel, born in 1829, is an important part of the local Deel family history. She was the daughter of Andrew and Nancy Jeems Anderson and wife of Henry Deel. Her family was from Ireland, and her husband was of German descent.

Polly, who was sometimes called Mary, was the daughter of Charles Fredrick Stigner who was born in Hamburg, Germany, of Jewish descent. After the War of 1812, Charles changed the name "Stigner" to "Stiltner," which is the name used today.

Benjamin and Polly had 13 children, nine of whom grew up, married and had families. The nine are: David, born in 1816; Fredrick, born in 1817; Sarah (Sally) born in 1820; Henry, born in 1823; James Harvey, born in 1823; Jacob, born in 1828; Pricey Jane, born in 1832; Alexander, born in 1834 - served four years in the Confederate Army, 21st Virginia Cavalry Co. E.; and Benjamin Franklin, born in 1838.

Benjamin and Polly were married in 1814. Benjamin was born in 1790 and died in 1845 of typhoid fever. He was buried in the old Colley Cemetery at Sandlick. (Note: As I understand it, the old Colley Cemetery was plowed up and used as a garden. I hope I'm wrong.)

Benjamin's wife, Polly, was born in 1793 and died sometime later than 1860. She was buried in the family cemetery near the Shumate Grove Church (now moved up on Greenbrier Creek and called the Russell Prater Regular Baptist Church).

Henry Deel, a son of Benjamin and Polly, was born in 1823. He married Sarah Anderson, daughter of Andrew and Nancy Gemes (Jeems) Anderson. Nancy's people had migrated to America from Ireland and lived for a while in Maryland. They then moved to Virginia to the Copper Creek area in Russell County.

Andrew and Nancy Gemes Anderson had at least nine children: Isaac, born 1812; Nancy, born 1813; Samuel, born 1818; Winnie, born 1820; Matilda, born 1823; Elizabeth, born 1826; Sarah, born 1829; Polly Jane, born 1833; and George Washington, born 1834, who served in the Confederate Army, 29th Virginia Regiment, Co. G.

He was wounded near Richmond, losing a part of one arm. He came back into this area and became the first public school teacher in the Sandlick community.

Henry and Sarah had two sons. The first died at birth and the second was Andy Floyd, who my (Anita's) grandfather, Charles, referred to as "Uncle Floyd." In next week's column, there will be more information about Andy Floyd, but right now let's continue with Sarah Anderson Deel, as many people want to know just who she was.

It's easy to confuse her with Sarah Raines Anderson, wife of my grandfather, Charles. It's very interesting — Sarah Anderson Deel was the daughter of Andrew and Nancy Gemes Anderson which made her a sister to George Washington Anderson, father of my grandfather, Charles H. Anderson.

No doubt his name was Charles Henry Anderson which means he was named for Henry Deel, Sarah's husband, who was the uncle of Grandpa Charles.

Just a little more very interesting insight into the life of Sarah Anderson Deel. After the death of her husband in 1884, she earned a living by teaching school in the kitchen of the log house where she lived. She had nine pupils, her son Andy Floyd being one of them.

She got $1 a month for each student, usually a three-month term. She taught reading, writing, spelling and arithmetic. She was 85 years old when she died on Feb. 17, 1917.

We are told that she was a very neat and precise lady. She sewed her wedding clothes by hand which she wore three times — when she was married, when she was baptized and when she was buried.

There is more to tell about Sarah and other members of her family but we'll continue next week. I would love to have been in her classroom and had her for a teacher. Come to think of it, I think I have learned a lot from her, just reading this material and talking to others.

Note: If I have made a mistake in any of this, please let me know. Genealogy can sometimes become a hard thread to untangle.

Lucille Sutherland continued family tradition of teaching

Mountain ECHOES

ANITA BELCHER

I know that many of you are interested in the contents of Sarah Anderson Deel's old trunk, but first let me introduce you to the lady who made this column possible.

I spoke of her in the first column when I wrote about the Andy Floyd Deel family, but that was several weeks ago. I need to bring you up to date with a little of her life's story that I hadn't written about, and some which I had, just to give you a complete, though a condensed picture.

Lucille Browning Sutherland was born and grew up on Prater Creek, the daughter of Thelmer and Sarah (Dolly) Deel Browning. She had one brother, Harold, who is now deceased.

Mrs. Browning, daughter of Andy Floyd and Martha Clevenger Deel, was a teacher in the Buchanan County School and so was her sister,

Bertie, who is now 99 years old. Bertie was married to Montague (Tyra) Kiser.

Another sister to Mrs. Browning, Flora, was married to the well-known and highly-respected educator, Clyde Reedy, from Clintwood (Reedy Ridge).

(Read this and be able to communicate to people that many of our pioneers of 100 years ago back here in the Appalachian Mountains

believed in education and encouraged their children in that direction.)

As you comprehend Lucille's background (remember, Grandmother Sarah was also a teacher, as was her brother George Anderson) it shouldn't be surprising that from childhood, Lucille wanted to become a teacher.

She recalls that when she

SEE **ECHOES**, PAGE 7B

Lucille Browning Sutherland is pictured here about the time she graduated from college.

240

CONTINUED FROM PAGE 1B

attended the Lower Greenbrier Elementary School, she would gather a group of children together to play school and she was always the teacher. She also recalls that her mother and her aunts attended this same school when they were children and were taught by "imported" teachers from Richmond.

(I, Anita, for many years have been aware of the fact that many of our early teachers were not local, and have often wondered what influenced those who came here from the outside world to come into this remote mountainous region. Most of them were great teachers who loved the mountain people and inspired their students to continue their education. Many of you who read this column will remember some of those teachers, as I do.)

Now back to Lucille. Her teachers at Greenbrier Elementary were Kelser Deel, Alta Hagy and Arnold Clay. After finishing elementary school, Lucille attended Grundy High School and by the time she was 16, she knew she wanted to become a home economics teacher. Her reason why?

"I felt that I and other girls needed to know more about home-making," was her simple answer and that continued to be her desire throughout her teaching career. Lucille attended Radford College and graduated in 1948. Her first job as a Home Economics teacher was at Haysi High School and she recalls her 10 years there with much pleasure.

The trips to FHA camps are memorable and some of her students who came to mind while we were talking were Jane Carpenter, Patsy Kilgore, Lois Ratliff, Rita Wright and Betty Sutherland. Those years hold fond recollections for Lucille and all her students were very special to her.

In 1952, Lucille met Bill Sutherland on a "blind date" worked out by Jean Wright (Matherly). She had seen him driving his coal truck, but had never met him personally. On this particular day she, Jean Wright and Juanita Powers met at the Haysi Drug Store (Tigers Den) and Bill "happened" to stop by.

The three girls rode with him to Clintwood in his new yellow convertible where Bill got out and bought each of them a candy bar. "Who rode in the front seat with Bill?" I asked.

"I did," replied Lucille. "I drove back to Haysi where I had parked my car and then went on home. I didn't see Bill again for some time, then we met again and began dating.

"We were married on the last day of school before Christmas, Dec. 19, 1952, by Lee Stanley at Clintwood. I recall that the mines where Bill worked closed down for our wedding.

Bill and Lucille first lived in an apartment over the Farm Supply in Haysi, then bought a house up on Prater Creek where they lived for about six years. From there they moved to the Honaker side of Big A Mountain where they bought a farm which Bill named Shady Valley Rest Farm and it is beautiful place.

Lucille continued teaching until she retired — 10 years at

Haysi, six in Lebanon and 23 at Honaker.

During that time the Sutherlands had three sons, Paul Allen who is a doctor and lives near York Town, John Ross who is a mining engineer and lives near his mother and Mark Lynn who was killed in an automobile accident in 1991.

Mark had finished two years at college at East Tennessee State and was home for the summer. He came to Haysi to pick up a camcorder to video the graduation services at Honaker.

On the way back, he met a car whose driver did not dim his lights and Mark, who was blinded by the lights, went over the hill between two sections of guard rails. He was killed instantly. Many of us remember that tragic time and our prayers went out to the Sutherland family.

Bill died on March 30, 2006, after a lingering illness. However, he was blessed to see four wonderful grandchildren, all of whom are in college.

Ross is a nursing student at Southwest Virginia Community College and lives with his grandmother, Taylor attends Mountain Empire, majoring in international relations which gives her the opportunity to travel to many different countries, Heather is a senior at Longwood College, majoring in art, and Megan attended Canterbury College in New Zealand but is now attending William and Mary as a music major.

All the grandchildren visit Lucille as often as they can and she is thankfully proud of them.

Lucille works with "Friends of the Library" at Honaker and is involved with church work at the Finney Baptist Church where she attends. She is a deeply sincere Christian.

Please keep her in your prayers. In 2003 the doctors discovered cancer in her left eye (melanoma) and since then it has spread to different organs of her body. Right now she is taking chemo treatments for her lungs. The Lord has given her victory so far but let's unite in prayer for Lucille who loves the Lord and extends that love to many people.

I've just realized that if this column gets in the paper in time to be published, I cannot continue with the "Grandmother Sarah" story which I had intended to write. However, so you won't be disappointed, I will tell you about some of the contents of the trunks and will describe them for you next week, the Lord willing.

Here goes ... Inside the trunk are little rolled-up pieces of thin paper, tied with what appears to be a sewing thread. Inside these little rolls of paper are locks of hair cut from the head of a relative at the time of their death. Yes, there are some names and dates.

Also, there are some old tax tickets dating back to when Sandlick was a "township" and I will also describe some of these for you next week. I think you will find all of this very interesting.

I first thought I could include Lucille's story and that of her great-grandmother, Sarah, all in one column, but I found that I could not if I were going to do justice to both stories. I hope you understand, and I believe you do.

Mountain ECHOES

ANITA BELCHER

Sandlick Township tax assessments interesting

I think you folks who live in the Sandlick area will find this week's column especially interesting, although I have no doubt that everyone who reads it will think back to the years of which I write and be astounded at some of the differences that have taken place.

In the year of 1871, Henry Deel was living in the "Sandlick Township" of Russell County. His township levy on personal property and free school was 83 cents, and the tax on his land was 54 cents, bringing the grand total to $1.37.

On another ticket his township levy was 42 cents, tax on his land was 28 cents and the capitation tax (poll) was 25 cents. This is a tax that was levied on persons rather than on land to have the right to vote, and in later years was declared unconstitutional in the United States. The name of J.H. Duty, Treasurer, is signed on these tickets.

It's very interesting that there is a ticket (or tickets) for Mr. Deel in 1871 in Buchanan County. Evidently he had land in both counties which later became a part of Dickenson County.

I did not think to ask Lucille about that part of the story because I was so interested in the old tickets themselves that I let that information slip by. Maybe some of the younger generation in this great family (or older) would like to take it on as a project in history to unravel "The

PLEASE SEE ECHOES, PAGE 5B

Pictured, from left, are Flora Edwards Deel; son, Woodrow Deel; Vicey Clevinger Reece; Melvina Clevinger; and Martha Clevinger Deel.

243

Echoes

CONTINUED FROM PAGE 1B

Mysteries of the Old Trunk." I would if I had time.

Anyway, the tickets for the Township of Sandlick, Buchanan County were $2.88 for value of 144 acres of land, property income tax was $4.39 cents and the poll tax was $1.

Clynard, Lucille and I tried very hard to figure out the signature of those tickets and I copied it the best I could. It looked something like "Ab LS? Adener." There were no periods, it was written in cursive and each letter was carefully drawn out.

This gentleman was the treasurer and one can almost visualize him, studiously signing his name on these important documents. He never dreamed that they would be preserved for more than 100 years.

I hope you have enjoyed that bit of our "grassroots" history and we are indebted to Sarah Anderson Deel for preserving it for us and to Lucille Browning Sutherland for sharing it.

Now, about the picture you are looking at. We have Bill Anderson to thank for sharing this picture, and I'm copying the information for you that's written on the back of the frame.

From left, you are looking at Flora Edwards Deel. She was Bill's aunt, sister of his mother Verna. She married Charlie Deel, son of Andy Floyd and Martha. Charlie and Flora had two sons, Woodrow and Charles. Woodrow is in the picture sitting next to his mother.

Both sons died, Charlie Jr. at birth and Woodrow when he was five or six years old, and the father, Charlie, died at age 20 or 21. (I cannot resist noting how beautiful Flora was.)

The lady next to Woodrow is Vicey Clevinger Reece and next is Melvina Clevinger. The third one is Martha Clevinger Deel. Melvina was the mother of Vicey and Martha.

(Note the aprons that the women have on. They were considered part of the necessary dress in those days. Many times they were worn to church. Martha's is checked, probably red or blue.

I have often told our grandchildren how our grandmothers would turn their children over their "red-checked apron" for a spanking, and several of our own grandchildren love to think they got a spanking over my apron like this.

Also note Martha's pretty string of beads. Our older generation of ladies liked to look good for picture-taking and church, even though many of them worked in the fields and garden throughout the week.)

The following was written by Bonnie Owens when she did a family history for the Andy Floyd Deel descendants. Bonnie wrote this about Melvina Clevinger:

"Melvina was a midwife for about 30 years, delivering most of the babies in the area. She kept a record by putting a straight pin in a piece of red flannel cloth. This cloth was about 10 inches wide and 18-20 inches long. The pins were in rows.

"She would ride behind the father-to-be on horseback or she would walk. She served the area 10-15 miles in all directions from her house.

"After her death, Martha served the women in the area in the same way. There was one young man who, when he got old enough to work in the mines and received one of his first paychecks, came to Martha and said that he wanted to pay his father's debt for the babies she had delivered for him and his wife. He paid her $5 for each of the children in his father's family."

There is so much more that could be written about the history of David and Elizabeth Coleman Deel and the many generations that have descended from them, and there are stories that should be told which some of their descendants remember personally, or they remember the stories that have been passed down to them.

If you are one of those people, then you should write down those stories and preserve them for future generations as Sarah Anderson Deel did.

244

Wright's advice survives beyond the grave

Mountain ECHOES

ANITA BELCHER

There is a verse in the Bible pertaining to Abel, the second son of Adam and Eve, that pertains to many people I have known in my lifetime.

The verse is *Hebrews* 11:4, in which God tells us that Abel offered a more excellent sacrifice than Cain (his heart was right before the Lord), therefore showing forth a witness of righteousness which caused the Lord to have this testimony recorded of him: "He being dead yet speaketh."

None of the people of which I speak were in the exact category of Abel, but I ask you how many times have the wise words or deeds of someone you used to know come to your mind, even though that person may have been dead for years?

Certain situations arising in several communities in the past few months made me think of this Bible quotation. Though I thought of many people whose wise words would have fit the occasion, my thoughts stuck with Walter Wright and one of the stories he told me, which I published.

First, let me tell you what's been happening and then I'll retell one story that Walter told me. The problem is stealing or theft in several communities and just recently in Haysi. Several things have been stolen, some of the most recent have been flowers that merchants have placed on the sidewalks to help make the town look more attractive.

Why would anyone want to steal flowers? As one merchant said, "I would gladly give some flowers to someone who needed them ... they wouldn't have to steal."

Now, let's go back to about 70 years

PLEASE SEE **ECHOES**, PAGE 14B

245

CONTINUED FROM PAGE 6B

ago. Walter Wright was a little boy who grew up in, or nearby, an area of the county known as the Middle of the World. Like most mountain families, they lived by hard work and had little money for any "extras."

Walter was happy in his world surrounded by mountains and woodland. He was part of a very close family and had many friends, boys about his age. One thing he didn't have, though, and he desired it more than anything else in the world.

He wanted a pocket knife so badly, as the saying goes, "he could taste it." Other boys and men had one and he looked at pictures of them in the Sears Roebuck catalogue, but there was no money to make the purchase.

One day, his mother sent him down off the mountain to the Pendland Country Store and post office at Bucu. When Walter reached the outside of the store he saw a rare sight — one of the early model cars parked in the yard with the owner somewhere inside the store or office.

As any little boy would do, he looked the car over carefully, then made his way to the store. Suddenly, he glanced down at his bare foot and there right in front of him lay a pocket knife! Words cannot describe the joy that filled his heart. At last, he had a knife!

He hurried through the business that his mother had sent him for and then made his way toward home. Now and then he would feel in his pocket for his precious knife and could hardly wait to get home to show his folks.

All at once, something happened. He began to think, "That knife doesn't belong to me! Somebody lost that knife! I should have gone in the store and showed the merchant and have given him the chance to find the owner."

He turned his steps back down the mountain. It seemed that now the knife was burning a hole in his pocket. He just wanted to get rid of it — it wasn't his.

When he reached his hand in his pocket to pull the knife out, it wasn't there. Walter was sick at heart. Her retraced his steps homeward, looking in the path and on both sides. There was no knife to be seen.

I can still feel the sorrow in Walter's heart as he wrote me the story. He said, "Mrs. Belcher, I was so sick I thought I would never make it home.

"When I came to the fence and crossed over to where mother was hoeing potatoes, she looked at me and said, 'Walter, what in the world is wrong with you? You're white as a ghost.'" He answered, "I'll be all right, mother. It's just a hot day and a long climb."

Walter told me that he never told his parents this story. He said, "I didn't want to bring the shame on them to know that I had taken something that wasn't mine. Even though I wanted to give it back, I still felt guilty and ashamed. It bothered me all my life."

Years later, when Walter was in military service on special assignment with some of his buddies, in Italy I believe, they were to take over a small town and search out any hidden enemy forces that might be in hiding.

Walter was assigned to search a huge barn filled with hay. He cautiously entered and, having made certain no one was in the downstairs section, he slowly mounted the stairs, with his bayonet ready. No one was in sight.

To make sure no one was hiding beneath the hay, he would plunge his bayonet into the heaps and stacks. Suddenly he hit something solid.

Raking back the hay, he saw a good-sized bag and on opening it, he was amazed to find it filled with money — lots of money. He closed it quickly and ran with it to the officer in charge. The officer took it and several weeks later called Walter into his office.

"Wright," he said, "The owner of this money can't be found. It's yours. Send it home and put it in your banking account. You deserve it."

"No sir," Walter said. "It isn't mine. I just found it."

Walter's letter to me continued, "Mrs. Belcher, I still remember what happened when I found that little knife that wasn't mine. I remember the awful feeling, the guilt. I never again wanted anything that I hadn't worked for. I didn't want anything that wasn't mine. Fifty dollars a month Army pay wasn't much, but it was mine by honest work."

Mr. Wright has passed on now. He made a remarkable name for himself in service and became a Christian, and was a great witness for the Lord as long as he lived.

I wonder just what's going through the minds of people who steal. They're not stealing for food or clothing. Almost anyone would help them in that case. Do they think it doesn't matter, or that, after all, it's not that much?

Well, it's according to how good your math is. One big pot of flowers cost $16, which amounts to about two hours' wages for some people, plus the labor and the time. That's not cheap. But that's not the point. There are more expensive items being stolen, but that's not the point, either.

The point is the principle of the matter. To steal is wrong whether it's a car or a pot of flowers. And here's the bottom line: Thieves may steal when the policemen are in another part of town and can't see them, but there's an Almighty Eye that is in every part of town all the time.

He's never off duty and he never sleeps. We have good law enforcement officers but they can't be everywhere at once. But God can and in some way, some day, he will require at your hand what you have stolen, plus interest.

Heed God's word and heed the advice of Walter Wright, now dead but yet speaking: "I don't want it. It isn't mine. I don't want anything I haven't worked for."

Bartlick School pictures spark cherished memories

In 1946 I was a young high school graduate wondering what to do with my life. I didn't want to get married, there were no community colleges then, college away from home was more than a dream away and leaving home for a job in Michigan was unthinkable. So what was I to do?

This story goes back farther than 1946 or what to do with my life. It touches on the lives of many people and centers around one community and the school there and its teachers.

I'm speaking of the "upper" Bartlick School, but let's go back a little farther than that. Some pictures I received this week from one of my former students at Bartlick made me want to share this bit of local history with you and I hope you enjoy it. Ready?

At first, as in most communities, there were no schools there, but the citizens of the area wanted their children to be educated. The first school was taught in the old Harve

Mountain ECHOES

ANITA BELCHER

Colley house (close by where Kaye Owens now lives), while another old house further down the creek was also used for school purposes.

Uncle Hawk Fuller from Colley was one of the early teachers. In the early '90s a schoolhouse was built on the Harve Colley place. It was small, built of logs, with a dirt floor and a fireplace at one end. After being used for four or five years the school board condemned it as being too small.

(I, Anita, have seen the pictures of that little school, and I think it was still standing back several years ago. It really was small. My mother was too young to go to school then, but went a few times as a visitor with an older brother, and she told me about it.)

Many things happened between the years of 1900 and 1912 amongst the citizens of several locations in the county and the school

PLEASE SEE **ECHOES**, PAGE 7B

board. To the credit of these citizens, let it be said that they were eager for a school building in their own community, and as my father noted in his notes on the Bartlick School, there was "warm competition" between some of the communities.

Finally, in 1912, a location was agreed on for the building of a schoolhouse that the school board felt would be ideal for all the patrons in the Bartlick area. This was a big flat bottom midway between the home of uncle Wiley Hay, who lived furthest up the creek, and uncle Lige Counts who lived farthest down the creek.

Uncle Noah C. Fuller and his wife, Belle, owned this excellent piece of property and did not want to sell it, but with some concessions, turned it over to the school board "for as long as it was used for school purposes."

A very neat, one-room building was erected here, complete with a porch, cloakroom and full-size windows on two sides. A pot-bellied stove heated the room.

In 1915 the number of students became so large that the school board added on another room, as nice as the first one. For several years this building also served as a church and a voting place.

As remote as the area was (just a narrow, winding dirt road leading into it) the school attracted some of the finest teachers in the county, probably in the state. One of the first was Dr. Ira Mullins, then Tom Colley, Avon and Frank Sykes, Pharaoh and Bryan Burchett, Perry Gilbert, Stanford Colley and Perry Anderson.

Granville Colley also taught here. Some of his students were Jim K. and Jim C. Fuller, Cora Elswick, Dora Wallace, Fred Priode, George Counts, Bowles Senter, Grady Belcher, Dixie Mullins and Kilby Cochran.

Other teachers who taught here were Kate LeFelle Childress, Lilla Mullins Artrip, Alice and Nantz Callaway, Taulby Colley, Crissie Colley, Vertie Owens Arrington, Judia Priode, Frank Kelly, Bruce Stanley and E.H. Anderson.

In the years after Mr. Anderson left (the pre-war years) teachers were scarce. Men were being called into service and women were leaving for the factories up north. The small country schools were being left behind. Lack of transportation, bad roads and a place to stay caused teachers who came, to remain only a short time and leave.

It was at this time that I graduated from high school and with my dad's encouragement, I applied for the position of teacher at the now one-room school at Bartlick. James M. Skeen, school superintendent, was amazed that I wanted to teach in a one-room school with all seven grades and no upgraded facilities.

I recall telling him, "Mr. Skeen, I know all those folks. Most of them are my kin people. It isn't far from my house, I can easily walk the distance and if the weather gets too bad I can stay with my grandparents."

Mr. Skeen knew my grandparents. They had given the property for the school house and most of the former teachers had boarded there. Among those who boarded with them was Bruce Stanley, a fine man and an excellent teacher.

When we would go visit my grandparents, Mr. Stanley was always kind to me and treated me like a little lady. I will always remember him for those characteristics and now added to that, I have him to thank for the picture or pictures you are looking at today. Mr. Stanley took them while teaching at Bartlick.

Now, to continue with where I came in, I got the job as teacher and it was one of the best years of my life. It was a "Little House on the Prairie" scenario: the one-room school, pot-bellied stove, wooden ink-well desks (well carved on) and all seven grades.

The seventh graders were as tall as I and the boys were much stronger than I and some of them as old. There were 68 students in all and I loved every one of them and still do.

There were large families back then and often I would be teaching five or six out of the same family. That was the case with the Sam Jones children. I'm not sure how many there were but I taught one in each grade.

Jack was my fifth grader and it's to him that I am indebted for these pictures that Mr. Stanley took. Jack and his wife, a daughter and a granddaughter stopped by to see me on a trip down from Ohio, and knew I would be interested in pictures of the school, some made years before I taught.

Yes, I was very interested and it was those pictures that inspired me to write this history of the Bartlick School.

I also thought that with our own schools just now starting, this would be an interesting column for teachers and students alike.

There was something special about those old schools taught 30 or 40 years ago. We started the day with prayer and the Pledge of Allegiance. The children were taught to obey at home and they supported the teacher, for the most part, when discipline was necessary.

We teachers could discipline. I had a paddle on my desk and a beech tree switch in the corner, but I had love and concern in my heart for the children and they knew it. But they knew, too, that I could discipline and I didn't have to ask permission first.

I only paddled one child that year, one of the best boys in school, but it was a matter of sticking to my word and the children knew it.

The paddle was used for pecking on the desk for attention and the switch was used as a pointer, but nevertheless they were there if needed.

Another thing that I loved about "those days" was that students wouldn't have dreamed of calling a teacher by the first name, not even if we were a-kin. It was always Miss, Mrs. or Mr.—a show of respect that we need from young people of every generation.

Another important thing about those schools was that we could talk about God and his creation and have a Bible on our desk. Thank you again, Jack and Mary, for your visit and sending me the pictures.

At left is the Wildcat Fire Tower, which Noah C. Fuller kept during the months when forest fires were possible. The photo was taken during a school outing when Bruce Stanley was teaching. The photo above is from the Jack Jones collection of Bartlick School students. Pictured in the front row are Jack Jones, Angeline Stanley, Lexie Fuller and Ola Fuller. In the back row are Paul Cochran, Fred Fuller and Kemper Fuller.

Baptizing hole once marked

Mountain ECHOES

ANITA BELCHER

Part 2 of 2

From last week: A swinging bridge once spanned the river where the Noah Yates Bridge is now, and in times of "high water" the river would splash through the bridge floor. Children liked to watch the raging waters roar between the banks and eventually overflow them.

We had a flat-bottomed boat which we used to travel back and forth across the river, and on one occasion I recall my dad stringing a cable across the river (when it was at normal flow) from a tree on each side to help stabilize the boat when the flood waters came. However, when it was really flood stage, the boat was useless.

I have wondered if Haysi was ever flooded in those years, for I never heard it mentioned. It would seem that in the year when the high water mark was about halfway up on the door of the Uncle Tom Colley home (where the mobile home of Clyde and Ruby Colley is now located) that Haysi would have had a lot of water.

Before leaving the subject of the river I want to mention that in the sum-

Sandlick bridge

mer it was the joy of adults and children alike for swimming and fishing.

I hardly ever drive up the road to Sandlick that I don't glance over at the "big rock" on the edge of the river behind the Victor Mullins used car lot but what I recall again the times we went fishing there.

Mom took biscuits with ham in a brown paper bag and we made cups from the broad cucumber leaves to drink water from the spring flowing into the river. By the way, that rock was

PLEASE SEE ECHOES, PAGE 9B

251

Echoes

CONTINUED FROM PAGE 6B

a "high water mark" for folks living in the area.

Also, when we needed to cross over the river to the other side or when my sister and I just wanted to skip rocks or jump from rock to rock, the "shallows" down from the culvert at the hollow beside the Colley home was a perfect place. We caught minnows there, too.

Two other things I will mention about the bridge at Sandlick and the river: How many of you remember the mulberry tree that grew at the end of the bridge on the highway side (dirt road back then) and how many of you recall the baptizing hole at the far end of the bridge (school house side) where the Primitive Baptists used?

I remember both. The mulberry tree was just out of reach even when we climbed on the railing of the bridge, and it's a wonder none of us fell and broke our neck trying to get the mulberries.

The baptizing hole, where new members were immersed and the sound of the attending congregation singing the Old Baptist hymns were an unforgettable scene, after all these years is still vividly recalled.

Jean wanted to know something about the people living in the area at the time any of us remember, and who stands out in our mind. Well, I've already mentioned my mother, my aunt Verna and Hazel Adkins.

Two of them stand out because they were near and dear to me as my mother and my aunt (there were many other reasons) and Hazel because of her unique cheerfulness and hospitality. Taken together, they represent our mountain women together and individually.

The next people I recall with fond memories are the Tom Colley family. Mr. Colley was not living when I was a child, but his wife, aunt Nicey, and two daughters, Frances and Polly Jane, lived at the home place that I mentioned earlier.

The old Colley home was beautiful and should have been preserved as a historical landmark. On entering from the porch into the living room, guests went directly into the dining room (if it were lunch time) which nowadays would be considered a "sun room." It was beautiful, with a long table facing a wall of windows.

I had the privilege of eating there once and aunt Polly and Francis treated me with much thoughtfulness. They were very dignified ladies but very kind. (It's funny — Polly was always "aunt Polly" while Francis was "Francis" or "Mrs. Colley".) Aunt Nicey was old and not well.

The last time I was there my mother took me so she could sit with the daughters to help and comfort them while their mother was dying. I well remember ... I sat on a bench under the huge pine tree that was in their yard, watching butterflies swarm over a big butterfly bush and wondering what it was like to die. (I was about five at the time.)

While I was sitting watching the butterflies and thinking, aunt Polly came out with a saucer of cookies and a glass of lemonade. Those ladies stand out in my mind — they were to be admired for many reasons. There were other daughters in the family, and two sons.

I never knew Fred who was killed in WWI, but I knew Stanford and he was an outstanding gentleman in many ways. For one thing, he was one of the best "scribes" in the entire area. His writing was beautiful and if you ever see his signed name, you will know what I mean.

The Colleys owned the Sugar Maple bottom across from Paul and Betty Anderson's house and I understand they were successful in harvesting maple syrup. They also owned the "Uncle Tom Colley" field, which was a beautiful piece of property where mother would take my sister and me to play while she picked berries.

The field had grown up with several crabapple trees whose blooms gave off a fragrance which only the wild crabapple can do. I can still close my eyes and breathe in their perfume. The old field is gone now, stripped away to obtain the wealth that lay under it.

Well, Jean, this may not be exactly what you wanted, but it's a start of what I remember about my growing-up days at Sandlick, and I hope you like it. I will write probably several other columns about this community as I recall it for historical purposes, and out of sheer enjoyment of sharing my memories and to help you in your project.

I will need to do some interviewing in between these columns, but while people are busy with harvesting and canning, it's a good time to do some "free lance" writing.

I hope all of you who have read this have enjoyed it, and that it has renewed many of your own memories of where you grew up, and my guess is that many of you have roots right back here in Sandlick or in one of the small communities that was similar.

I will venture a guess that many of you have folks living here even now. Well, that's the making of history and a reason for reunions.

Family cemetery restoration becomes labor of love

Mountain ECHOES

ANITA BELCHER

The restoration of the Elam-Puckett Cemetery was a work of love, commitment, dedication and hard work. Diana Kilgore Reedy shares the full story with us and shares it so well that I don't need to add anything except a brief preface.

My first knowledge of this old cemetery was just before or right after Clynard and I were married. The cemetery is situated on a piece of sloping ground behind the community of McClure Bottom in Haysi, and very close to where Winnie Puckett Elam lived when her infant daughter died in March 1920.

"Aunt" Winnie owned the land so it was only natural that she establish a family cemetery nearby.

Clynard and I did a lot of walking in the pre-WWII days, as well as when he came home from service, because cars were not yet available to the general public. Your name had to be on a long waiting list.

We would visit his parents and other relatives living in McClure Bottom, including his aunt Winnie and uncle Charlie Elam.

Their family cemetery is also where Clynard's grandfather, John W. (Uncle Johnnie) Puckett is also buried. "Uncle Johnnie," as he was known by the local folks, owned one of the first stores in the area, situated above one of the tunnels that runs through McClure Bottom. In fact, my mother bought her first pair of dress slippers from Uncle Johnnie's store.

All the folks who worked so faithfully on this cemetery or contributed to the cost are related to Uncle Johnnie and others buried there.

I never thought at the time when I walked through the old cemetery that our first little son, Clynard Terrance, would be buried there. I was still in the

PLEASE SEE **ECHOES**, PAGE 9B

CONTINUED FROM PAGE 8B

hospital at the time and visited the little grave afterward.

We put up a small marker with a fence, but time and weather took their toll. We will now put up a permanent marker. Shortly after our little son was buried there, a town ordinance was passed which prevented anyone else from being buried in the old cemetery.

As Diana mentions in her story, that problem no longer exists, thus the son of Winnie and Charlie, Sheldon, a WWII Air Force veteran, could be laid to rest in a cemetery that reflects the love and dedication of many family members.

Clynard and I want to personally thank Merle Fuller for continuing to work toward getting this work done and encouraging us all to get busy before "it was too late" for some of us. We want to thank Diana for being a "first responder" and, along with Merle, getting the work actually started.

Diana shares a beautiful story with us, but the story she doesn't tell is amazing. You cannot imagine the time and back-breaking work that went into this project. This cemetery was full of vines, bushes, small trees, uneven terrain and fallen headstones. Now it's beginning to look like a small park.

May this story be an inspiration to all of us, to make the resting place of our loved ones more beautiful.

Thanks, Merle, Diana, Dennis and all the grandchildren and cousins.

Now, to Diana's story.

I received a phone call from Merle Fuller at the end of May. She said, "Diana, I've decided to make it my goal to get the cemetery cleaned up and the headstones reset. I would like to see this done before I die."

I told her we had a couple more work days but after that I would assist in any way I could to help her realize her goal.

Merle began collecting donations from family members to pay for getting a tree cut down, hedges trimmed, headstones reset, etc. She had talked with a man who said he would help with some of this but kept putting her off.

We finally decided to get my son-in-law, Bucky Kiser, to cut the tree and trim the hedges. Along with Bucky came two of my grandsons, Austin and Donovan French, to help

with this project.

As with most projects, once you get started you see the need for more to be done than you

originally thought. The hedges were trimmed, the one big tree cut, then several smaller ones, too. Austin and Donovan worked hard in helping to move the cut trees and brush to the far back of the lot.

Merle called Earl Dean Yates to come look and give her a price on cleaning headstones and resetting the ones which were loose or had already come off. He was very busy and couldn't come right away. Being the impatient person that I am, and knowing we didn't have much money to hire this done, I took my garden sprayer filled with pure bleach and began cleaning the stones.

Merle and I both were pleasantly surprised at how white the stones came with pure bleach, a scrub brush and lots of elbow grease. Merle very graciously supplied me with bucket after bucket of clean water to rinse the stones.

During this first phase of work in the cemetery, Dennis had been involved in a different project. Once his other project slowed down he became very involved in helping with whatever I wanted or needed done.

Merle, Dennis, Austin, Donovan and I worked a little most evenings, grubbing and burning the brush we had put in back of the cemetery. The old wire fencing and trash were bagged and set out for trash pickup.

As brush and trees were cut, burned and cleared away, this old cemetery, which had been hidden for many years, was now open for all to see. Few people even knew of its existence.

Dennis talked with an old friend, Ivory Steffey, who had once helped with setting headstones and received lots of good information on materials and procedures for doing this. With this information, my husband and I reset our first headstone, which marked the grave of a baby.

A couple of the stones were too large for the two of us, so I called my brother, Joe Kilgore, for help. As we were leaving the cemetery that day, Joe looked at the cemetery and then me and said, "Mother would be proud of you."

Tears came as I replied, "I wish she could have seen it." For you see, her mother — my grandmother — is buried there.

Next week: The cemetary restoration continues and includes a visit to the land owner.

The photo above shows what the cemetery looked like when the project began, while the one below shows the finished project.

Restoring old family cemetery lots of hard work, but rewarding

Last week: Diana Kilgore Reedy began sharing her story about the restoration of the Elam-Puckett Cemetery. It was a project of love, commitment, dedication and hard work. This week, Reedy's story continues.

To some, restoring an old cemetary, might seem like a gruesome, unnerving job, but to me it was very rewarding.

I had made a promise to Merle Fuller, my relative, friend and neighbor, that I would help her attain her goal and with God's help I would see this job finished.

I have to say it wasn't all hard work. We would take a break, sit down and talk about our relatives. Merle has a way of telling a story that makes it come alive. She confirmed many questions about family members to both Dennis and me and revealed things we didn't know.

Throughout the entire project much laughter was shared. Each night as I went to bed, tired and sore, I couldn't wait to get back the next day to work and visit with Merle.

Throughout the project each of us would express our opinions on things we wanted to do — cut this tree or leave it, put up a fence or not. Neither of us ever got upset with the

ANITA BELCHER

other and in the end pretty much agreed on all that was done.

One of our main concerns was to keep peace with the neighbors. To us they never voiced any negative feelings toward this project.

After partial fencing was decided on, Dennis and I took off to Lowe's. We looked at different types, styles and prices of fencing before making our decision. It became our choice because at this point there had not been enough donations from family members to pay for fencing.

We made our choice, paid the cashier, loaded up and headed for home. Now my mind was whirling with thoughts of no money to pay someone to put up the fence.

The two of us had tried at one time putting up three panels of vinyl fence around one end of a porch and I had gotten so frustrated that I had called my son, Marty, to please come and help.

I knew it was going to be a difficult job, but neither of us realized that the lay of the land determined the outcome of the fence. When Dennis told me that each panel would have to be stepped up, I could only imagine how horrible this would look.

When we explained this to Merle, she was even more horrified than I. As usual, though, after thinking it over, she said, "You all do what you think best." Putting up fence, for me, was one of the most difficult jobs. I just couldn't get my mind geared in that direction.

Dennis did all the figuring and cutting and together we managed to get the job done and still remain together. One day my grandson, Austin, helped with the fence and let me do the grubbing. I was so thankful for that break from fencing.

On the way home that evening, Austin told me he thought Dennis was too particular. I replied I understood how he felt, but being particu-

PLEASE SEE **ECHOES**, PAGE 11B

Echoes

CONTINUED FROM PAGE 6B

lar and wanting a job done right was a good thing, although a bit frustrating to the helper.

It was about this time I decided to call the owner of the cemetery, Sheldon Elam. He and my mother were first cousins and during her life had always kept in touch, but I had never met any of his daughters. I spoke with him on the phone and told him we were cleaning up the cemetery.

He seemed very pleased and promised he would have his daughter, Marilyn, call me. True to his word, I received a call that very evening. The two of us had never met, nor talked, yet spent at least two hours on the phone. Since then we have talked many times.

Dennis and I decided we wanted to see Sheldon and talk with him in person. On Aug. 5, I called Marilyn and set a date to visit with her and her dad. We arrived at Sheldon's, below Asheville, N.C., around 1:30 p.m. on Aug. 7.

Although Sheldon's health was very poor, his mind was extremely sharp. He was able to answer many questions and confirm many things we had been told by others about family members. Marilyn brought old pictures of family and made copies of some we had never seen.

We stayed several hours and had a wonderful visit. Little did we know it would be the last time we would ever see Sheldon. Within a few days he took a turn for the worse and exactly two weeks from that day he departed this life.

Sometimes it's ironic how

Merle Fuller, right, is credited for getting the ball rolling to restore the old cemetery. She is pictured with Joe Kilgore.

things work out. None of us had any idea when we began our project of helping Merle attain her goal in cleaning up this little family cemetery that anyone else would ever be buried there.

Sheldon had told his family, and even mentioned to Dennis and me during our visit with him, of his desire to be buried in the Elam-Puckett Cemetery upon his passing.

The cemetery was established in March 1920, when an infant sister of Sheldon's was buried there. He also had an infant brother buried there in June 1921.

Others buried in this cemetery are:

■ Gurvis Burnett, August 1920

■ my grandmother, Rebecca Alice Epling, August 1927

■ her dad, John W. Puckett, 1932

■ two children of Earl and Almeda Gross who died in a house fire in the old Haysi mining camp, c. 1930s, no original marker, a homemade one was constructed and put up by my husband, Dennis Reedy

■ Guy A. Burnett, father of Gurvis, March 1942

■ And the last one buried there was an infant son of Clynard and Anita Belcher, Clynard Terrance Belcher, August, 1948

By the time my great-grandmother, Martha Puckett, wife of Johnny Puckett, passed away in 1952, there was an ordinance preventing anyone else being buried in this cemetery due to families living near the cemetery having well water. Sixty years later that is no longer a problem because of the public water system.

On Aug. 24, 2008, Sheldon was laid to rest in this little cemetery beside his infant sis-

ter. There was a beautiful graveside service with family and friends gathered around, military rites, my nephew, Matthew Fuller, sang a song, read a few scriptures and had prayer.

Merle Fuller's goal has been achieved and an old man's wishes fulfilled. I can only say, "Thank you, Merle, for allowing me to take part in helping you reach your goal. It was a project that I enjoyed and could hardly wait to get back to see the progress that each day brought and to hear more of your jokes and family stories."

Lastly, we have decided to contact the remaining grandchildren of Martha Puckett in hopes of getting their permission to move the remains and headstone of Grandma Puckett from the Patton Willis Cemetery on Big Ridge and place them beside her beloved husband, Johnny Puckett, in the Elam-Puckett Cemetery where she had originally wanted to be laid to rest.

Diana Kilgore Reedy stands with her husband, Dennis, left, and brother, Joe Kilgore, in front of her grandmother's tombstone at the Elam-Puckett cemetery.

Haysi classes of 1940 hold reunion

Mountain ECHOES

ANITA BELCHER

It was a cold day on Dec. 17, 1983, when the Haysi High School class of 1943 met for their first reunion since their graduation on the evening of April 26, 40 years before.

That day in December 1983 an important decision was made by those attending the reunion — a decision that every year the class of '43 would continue to meet as long as there were any members willing and able to attend.

That was 25 years ago and every year since, the class has faithfully met at the appointed place. Only one change has been made and that was to include all members of any class graduating from Haysi High School during the 40s, along with spouses and friends.

This year (2008) the time and place was Oct. 10 and 11 at the Breaks Park Lodge. Several of us met Friday night for dinner and just a good time of fellowship and relaxation.

Those in our group included Merle Gilbert Fuller, Vivian Fuller Owens, Katy Jo Arrington Powers, Juanita Turner Powers Mullins, Evelyn Steele

Gilbert, and Anita and Clynard Belcher.

Besides enjoying each other, we enjoyed meeting other folks from different parts of the country and talking with them. October is whitewater rafting month on the Russell Fork, and many come to participate in or to watch the activities. It was a great

PLEASE SEE **ECHOES**, PAGE 16B

From left, Maple Belcher Edwards, Clynard C. Belcher and Kathleen Holbrook Puckett represented the Class of 1943 during a reunion for those who graduated Haysi High School during the 1940s.

CONTINUED FROM PAGE 7B

time to promote our area.

Saturday morning saw the dawning of a beautiful day, with foliage at its peak. The late summer sun and early autumn chill seemed vying for first place. By early afternoon, jackets or sweaters felt comfortable, making us more aware of the changing season, but it was refreshing.

The staff at the lodge had the banquet room in perfect readiness for us and when we added flowers and pictures it was beautiful. A very special "thank you" from all of us to those who worked so hard to make us feel "at home."

Now, for some information about those who attended the reunion on Saturday, Oct. 11. First of all we were disappointed to have only three of the class of '43 there. Those who represented that class were Maple Belcher Edwards, Kathleen Holbrook Puckett and Clynard Belcher. Others of that group had various health problems or family responsibilities.

I did an update on members of each class represented and for those of you who could not attend and for others who are interested, this is what's going on in their lives.

■ Maple Belcher Edwards is now 82 years old and "pert as a cricket!" She takes no medication except a baby aspirin and she walks an hour each morning, five days a week. Maple and her husband had two daughters and she now has one granddaughter, five grandsons, eight great-grandsons and three great-granddaughters.

Maple loves to travel and takes every opportunity to see different parts of our country. She is faithful in her church and wants to see her community progress.

■ Kathleen Holbrook Puckett still has the same quiet personality and is still the "behind-the-scenes" leader. She had to leave to get back to Bristol before dark so I didn't have the opportunity to ask about family and other interests. I liked what she said as she was leaving, "I've got to go but mainly what I've got to say is that every day is a blessing." How true.

■ Clynard Belcher has retired from the insurance business but stays busy with church and civic affairs. He and Nita still love the outdoors and traveling even short distances to photograph the scenery and pick huckleberries.

They have four children, two sons and two daughters, and are blessed with 18 grandchildren, 12 great-grandchildren and one more on the way. Clynard is an Elder in the Haysi Presbyterian Church and a veteran of World War II.

■ Betty Belcher Long (class of '53) lives in Ohio. She and her husband had four children and she now has six grandchildren and one great-grandchild. Betty's school days memories revolve mostly around sports and the teachers who worked as coaches.

She fondly recalls L.G. Robinson, Kathleen Beverly, Robert Arrington and Homer Willis. The most exciting happening in her life this past year was becoming a great-grandmother. She is also very proud of her son and son-in-law for forming a race car team in the late model car division under the name of GARMAC.

■ Barbara Morris is Betty's friend from Ohio and she simply says that having grown up in the "flat lands" that she loves the mountains here and the scenery.

■ Juanita Turner Powers (class of '44) was glad to return home and be with friends and loved ones. It has been hard adjusting to the death of her husband, Erdman Mullins, but Juanita is a strong woman and looks constantly to the Lord for strength and courage.

She continues working with a charity program, Faith in Action, and teaches a ladies group in the Sinking Springs Presbyterian Church in Abingdon. She has four children, six grandchildren and six great-grandchildren.

■ Vivian Fuller Owens (class of '47) spent a good part of her summer with her daughter who had serious surgery. When she's home she keeps busy with her house and lawn. You might also find her by the river which runs close by her house, re-channeling the water.

This is serious business to Vivian. Her home has barely survived the last two floods, her garden was washed away and her lawn damaged. The river is choked with refuse from various sources and Vivian has seen the disappearance of wildlife from this beautiful section of the Russell Fork.

With that pioneer spirit which many mountain folks have, she continues to work a little at a time to beautify this area and make it safer when the water is high. Vivian also helps out in Bible school at Dickenson First Presbyterian Church where she is a member.

■ Merle Gilbert Fuller (class of '44) worked as a cosmetician for 25 years and then retired to a quiet but busy life at her home in Haysi. She loves outdoor work and divides her time between her Haysi home and the one "on the mountain" where she grew up.

This summer she spearheaded the effort to get the little cemetery across the road from her house cleaned up. She, too, is a faithful member of Presbyterian Church in Haysi.

■ Evelyn Steele Gilbert (class of '46) is a faithful member of her church in Bristol and is also active in civic affairs. She is very involved in the interests of her young great-grandson, Lucus (I think that is his name; correct me if I'm wrong).

His great interest lies in photography (I believe I'm correct in saying he is only four years old). His mother entered four of his pictures in a photography contest and he won two blue ribbons.

One picture portrayed town

buildings with some of the windows opened and others closed. He simply named his picture "Opened and Closed." He did another of several guitars and appropriately named it "Guitars."

I believe these two were the ribbon-takers but Evelyn was impressed with another of a dragonfly which he titled "The Dragon has Landed." I believe we're looking at some future talent there.

■ Katy Joe Arrington Powers (class of '40) came back to Haysi and taught for 35 years after she graduated from high school and college. Those years were all in Home Economics except two when she taught science.

Katy suffered the loss of her husband, Harold Powers, this year but she has continued to be of great help to her church and community. We wonder what we would do without her. She serves on several committees in the county and town and worked faithfully with Bible school, with the Autumn Fest and the Dickenson County Fair.

Katy recalls going to Clintwood this summer and finding several of her former students working at responsible jobs. Her biggest surprise was going on a bus tour into Amish country and finding that 13 of those traveling with her were also her former students. A big surprise to everyone.

■ Alice Stroad is a friend of Kathleen Puckett and has attended our reunion for several years. It was good to have her back again and we missed Frankie Massie, another dear friend of Kathleen. She is battling cancer and our prayers are with her.

Here's a little information on those we heard from who couldn't come. Homer Willis is having a hip replacement but he managed to travel in Europe this summer before heading back home for surgery. His travels were so very interesting that I hope we will see him next year and hear about them "firsthand."

Virginia Anderson Treadway's health is not the best but her faith in the Lord is strong. Fayetta Campbell's husband, Grey, is in very bad health. We need to pray for them. Marie Arrington's husband, Doug, passed away this summer and Marie has been spending quite a bit of time in Abingdon close to her children.

Irene and Boone Sutherland were not up to coming but sent their good wishes. We could not get in touch with Thelma Ullum or Glenna Rae Patton and missed them along with others who have been so faithful to come.

I do not want to end on a sad note, but all of you who graduated with Jean Wright Matherly, or perhaps you are a former student, need to call her. Her husband, Stacy, died this past week and she was able, with the help of the former Gail Viers, of Sandlick, to get in touch with our daughter, Becky, and her husband, Joe Morecraft.

Neither of them realized it, but they were only a few miles apart. Jean taught Beckie in school and encouraged her in singing. When Stacy died she thought of Beckie and wanted her to sing at his funeral, and asked Joe, who is a Presbyterian minister, to hold the services.

Beckie relates that it was a sad but precious time and she was thankful that she and her husband could "give back" a little to one who had given so much for so many over the years.

Jean is not in good health and I know she would like to hear from old friends. Call me and I will give you her phone number or you can get it from directory assistance, Atlanta area.

Please try to come to the class of '43 and the '40s next year. It will be held at the Breaks again, probably the first week of October (Oct. 9 and 10, we hope). Everyone left before the date was decided on and the lady who does the scheduling is off, due to surgery. Watch the newspaper (The Star) or call us.

If anything in the "update" is not exactly right, just remember that I had to get information in the middle of conversations and folks coming and going. Anyway, I think you have a pretty good idea of what did and who was there. If you were there, you know we had a wonderful time. If you weren't there — we missed you.

InTouch

with Dickenson County Family, Friends & Neighbors

Whitner thankful for many blessings

Mountain ECHOES

ANITA BELCHER

The Rev. John Whitner and his wife Gerry, in the back row, are pictured with their children and grandchildren. Rev. Whitner has spent four decades serving his church and the community.

I think you will enjoy this week's Thanksgiving column because it's about a man who has dedicated a good part of his life to the people of the Sandy Basin area of Dickenson County and to regions around and beyond this particular area. I had intended to write only about his Thanksgiving memories but when I found that he was willing to take the time to share other memories, I was delighted. Many of you who read this are not members of the churches he has pastored, but he has touched the life of most of you who know him. His love and compassion are not limited to the members of any one church, but he reaches out to all who need him.

Many of you have called him in the early hours of the morning to help transport a family member to the hospital or just to come and pray with you. Others of you have asked him to conduct a funeral for a family member or perform a wedding ceremony. He has taught your children, and visited and preached to men in jails and prisons, bringing them a reason for hope. His love and concern for the unsaved is evident as he seldom misses an opportunity to tell them of the salvation found only in Christ. He is a humble man who walks with the Lord and his life bears testimony to this fact.

PLEASE SEE **ECHOES**, PAGE 9B

Who is this man? He may be one of many that you know and that I've just described, but I'm speaking of the Rev. John Whitner who came here with his family in the early 1960s to serve the Presbyterian churches in the Haysi, Sandlick, Bartlick and Big Ridge sections of the county. He has served the churches well, but his love and service have reached far beyond these four churches. He is a man of God who loves the Lord and the people of the Appalachian Mountains.

Mr. Whitner shares some of his memories with us as well as some of his present day activities. He relates, "I grew up in a Christian home in the northern part of Atlanta, Ga. Our membership was in the Central Presbyterian Church located across the street from the Georgia state capitol. Every Sunday morning we would travel 10 miles to Central Church for Sunday School and worship. When we three children got older, my brother would take the car and drive us to youth meeting on Sunday night. We would pick up some other young people on our way. Then on Thursday night I would catch the trackless trolley into town for church night supper, and would then stay for choir practice at the church.

"I was well-grounded in my Christian faith, but when I started attending Georgia Tech to get a degree in Electrical Engineering, I found my faith being tested. I began to wonder how I could know that I was right in what I believed when there were so many intelligent professors and students who were smarter than I and who had a different set of beliefs from mine.

"The crisis of my faith reached its peak in my second year of college when my parents thought it would be a good idea for me to stay on campus. I became very uncomfortable with my roommates because I could see how widely we differed in what we believed. When I talked to my mother about this she and I went to talk with a godly seminary professor whom we had known for many years.

"Besides using his Bible, this professor told me the story of the great French mathematician, physicist and philosopher who made great contributions to the world of science in his day (1623-1662). He constructed the first digital calculator and the first hydraulic press which was capable of an enormous magnification of force. This led to the modern day hydraulic brakes in cars and trucks. He laid the foundation for the calculus of probabilities which is the basis for figuring insurance premiums. A modern day computer language called 'Pascal' is named for Blaise Pascal, because he laid the mathematical foundation on which it is based. In 1654, Pascal had a personal conversion experience and from that time on he committed his life to defending the Christian faith against skeptics. His argument became so well-known and effective that it became known as 'Pascal's Wager.'"

Mr. Whitner continued, "After spending time in God's word with this godly Bible professor and hearing the story of this brilliant scientist I determined to live my life for God as He is revealed in the Bible. I have never regretted that decision, and because I know God's word is true, I know I have eternal life through Jesus Christ my Lord."

Mr. Whitner's testimony regarding his early years made a deep impression on me. First, it made me realize anew how important a godly foundation

is for children; secondly it proved the importance of a good family relationship; thirdly, I think it will make us all think more seriously about the dangers our young people face when they leave home; and, fourthly, I thought how great it was that there was a wise and godly man to turn to for help. Another thing that impressed me was that this professor was wise enough to use the example of a great Christian mathematician to help this young electrical engineering student. If he had used an example about hunting elk up north, the illustration would probably have fallen flat, but he knew that this young engineer could relate to the great mathematician. What a blessing wise counsel is!

Mr. Whitner had written some of his information down for me and I'm going to reprint it just as it is written, and those of you who know him will say, "That sounds exactly like Mr. Whitner." Now on with his story.

He wrote, "I graduated from Georgia Tech in 1954 with a degree in Electrical Engineering, and immediately got a job with Lockheed Aircraft Corp. outside Atlanta. I was barely able to get settled into my new job when I received my draft notice to report for basic training in the Army at Fork Jackson, S.C. Upon completion of basic training I was stationed at Redstone Arsenal in Hunstville, Ala., where I was assigned to the Rockets and Missles Division.

"One Sunday evening after I got settled on base I drove around looking for a Presbyterian Church that had an evening service. I found a small one whose pastor was a minister by the name of Ben Wilkinson. I liked the church and found that the pastor was also holding Sunday afternoon services at the jail. He invited anyone that wanted to help to come along and I decided to attend.

"In the car, on the way back from the jail service, the pastor asked a young lady, Gerry Jones, to tell me how she came to be in Huntsville. Part of her story included the fact that she had attended King

College in Bristol, Tenn. This surprised me because my sister had also graduated from King a year or two before and Gerry knew her. It didn't take Gerry and I long to discover that we were meant for each other. Some time later we were married in the small church where Rev. Wilkinson was pastor. That memorable date is February 22, 1958. We have just celebrated our 50th wedding anniversary.

"When I received my discharge from the Army, I got my old job back with Lockheed Aircraft, and Gerry and I moved into our own little house near the plant. My parents were nearby, we enjoyed visits with them and we were also busy helping to organize a new Presbyterian Church in our area where I was elected deacon. Life seemed to be just perfect. God blessed us with our first son and I loved my job. Who could ask for more?

"Well, after a period of time the government contracts Lockheed had were running out and they started laying off workers. They kept the engineering staff on as long as possible, but one day my supervisor called me into his office and told me that a new layoff was coming soon and that would include me. However, he said Lockheed had a new opening at the Polaris Missile base at Charleston, S.C., but I would have to let him know that afternoon if I wanted to accept the position."

Mr. Whitner continued, "Gerry and I sold our home and moved near Charleston. Years before, I had made a vow to God that if He would open a door for me to go into foreign mission service I would leave everything and go. The opportunity hadn't come, but now Gerry and I began to make application for mission service. First, I checked into going out as an industrial missionary and then I looked at the educational mission field. I was deferred until I could get my credentials as an education missionary, so I resigned my job with Lockheed Aircraft Corp., then we packed up our family and moved to Decatur, Ga., where I could attend Columbia Seminary and prepare for what-

The Rev. John Whitner and wife, Gerry are surrounded by their children. From left are Jerri Anne (now deceased), John R., Steve and Rick.

In Touch

with Dickenson County family, friends & neighbors

'Christmas tree' article brings memories for Deel

■ Part 1 of 3

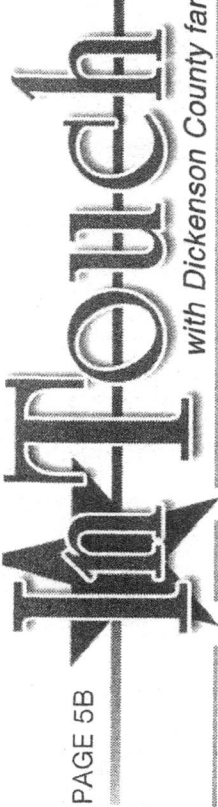

Mountain ECHOES

ANITA BELCHER

I was just getting ready to write my New Year's column for *The Star* when the doorbell rang. I heard my husband greet someone with great enthusiasm. This in and of itself was not unusual because Clynard gives all our visitors a hardy welcome, but there was just a little something different in his greeting this time.

I thought that perhaps one of our "far away" grandchildren had managed to get home for the holiday season, so I stepped to the family room and there, to my great surprise and delight, stood Trooper Tim Deel.

Even as I write the words, "Trooper Deel," I smile because I knew Tim in his high school days when he and our son, Kerry, were

Virginia State Police Officer Tim Deel stands in the living room of Anita and Clynard Belcher's home.

best friends.

We invited him in and we three sat at the kitchen table, reminiscing. Tim had read my "Searching for a Christmas Tree" column and it had recalled memories for him.

"Many times," he remarked, "as I've gone by your house, I have wanted to come in and visit you all, so today as I was finishing up my work, I decided to stop by and talk awhile."

Reading about our search for a

cedar tree at Christmas brought back fond boyhood recollections for Tim. He tells a favorite memory.

"It was one Christmas when several of us in the family went to look for a tree — I think it was me, Brent, Randy, dad, and yes, grandpa was along. Back then (and maybe they still do) at the holiday seasons a lot of men and young boys would take along their guns, just in case they saw some kind of game to shoot at.

"I think dad had his shotgun and I had my .22 rifle. We walked 'til we came to an old Clinchfield strip job, thinking surely we would find what we were looking for there. However, there were no cedar trees around in that area, but what we did see was a covey of quail.

"Of course they scattered in all directions when they saw us, but one of them flew into the forks of a tree standing nearby, thinking he was safe. I took aim with my rifle and shot him. He fell, not to the ground, but on the top of an old 'mash barrel' which in times past had been used in

PLEASE SEE ECHOES, PAGE 11B

265

Echoes

CONTINUED FROM PAGE 5B

the making of moonshine whiskey."

Tim continued, "Grandpa had a little white feist dog at the time and I thought he was going to get my quail, but he didn't. I carried it home and mom or grandma fixed it for dinner. Yes, it was good eatin'."

That was the beginning of our story exchange and at this point Clynard recalled a story that had happened many years ago when his folks were visiting us at Thanksgiving.

While dinner was in the final cooking/baking stage, Clynard and his dad decided to walk around the hillside where the Don Kenny water tower is now located. At that time it was all woodland.

As Tim had mentioned, most men carried a gun along when they walked through the woods at certain seasons of the year, so it was just the normal thing for Cly to take along his .22 rifle.

He and his dad saw several squirrel nests and Clynard said to his dad, "Do you suppose that squirrel would be in one of those nests?" Well, naturally the only way to find out was to aim and shoot ... which Cly did.

Immediately a squirrel fell to the ground, shot dead center.

Now, back to Tim. On his long drives as a trooper, he has a lot of time to think, and at this season of the year there was a lot of thinking about Christmas.

He recalls, "I remember another year when Brent, Randy and I decided we would go looking for a Christmas tree. We started walking, got an old gas line road and kept walking 'til we came out somewhere on Nealy Ridge. I guess we went farther than what we realized and it got dark on us.

"In the meantime we found a Christmas tree, but we also found something else that we knew would be important to our dad. You see, dad liked to start his garden plants early by planting the seeds in a container. He would use old tubs that were no longer useful for holding water, fill them with garden soil and plant his seeds in them.

"Well, while we boys were looking for a cedar tree, we found two old bottomless tubs and we said, 'We'll take those for dad.' We hadn't gotten too far back toward home when we heard dad and uncle Barney hollering for us and saw their flashlights.

266

In Touch

with Dickenson County family, friends & neighbors

Grandparents important in Deel's memories

■ **Part 2 of 2**

Last week, we featured the first part of Anita Belcher's column about Virginia State Police Agent Tim Deel and his recollections about searching for a Christmas tree as a young boy. The story left off as Deel and his two brothers found two bottomless tubs which their father could use to get an early start on his garden plants. Before they could go much farther, they heard their dad and uncle searching for them.

"I know they were worried about us but I think they were pretty mad, too, at having to come out on a dark,

cold night looking for us. Right then we felt real good at having found those two old tubs for dad to use, not only because we would need them come spring, but also they were our 'peace offering.' Hopefully they would keep us from being in too much trouble."

Tim continued with his thoughts of Christmas, "You know we still go Christmas-tree hunting every year. When I moved into Lee County in 1988 I thought I had moved into Christmas tree paradise. In Dickenson County cedar trees are scarce but they grow just about everywhere over here. The old fields are full of them and

ANITA BELCHER

they grow by the roadside.

"Most property owners are glad to get rid of them, so my son Brandon and I loaded up, took our ax and went looking. We found one growing on the bank beside the road, located the land owner,

got his permission, cut the tree down, took it home and got it decorated. That's a tradition for our family."

I switched the conversation back to Tim's growing-up days.

"What did you most enjoy about Christmas when you were a boy?" I asked.

"Going to my grandparents'," he replied. "Grandma, in fact both grandmas, fixed all sorts of good food during the holidays. Grandma Lillie and Grandma Ethel were both good at fixing all the good things they knew we boys liked. I remember the cakes, pies and popcorn balls made with molasses. It was just great! Just being with my

grandparents was special — I miss them a lot."

"What was your favorite gift?" I asked. His quick reply was, "A sled! We boys used that sled 'til it fell apart, and we would put it back together again with bolts and nails. We seemed to have had more snow back then, and we had a certain place where we tromped the snow down hard to make for good sledding.

"Sometimes we would pour water on the snow and let it freeze over so we could go faster. It's impossible to say how much skin we lost during those sledding days but that didn't seem to matter,

SEE **ECHOES**, PAGE 7B

267

CONTINUED FROM PAGE 6B

we had fun.

"My two sled-riding buddies are grown up, too, now. Brent is a teacher at Haysi High School and Randy is a loss prevention officer at Lowe's in Wise. They may be grown up but they still cherish their memories, too."

It was hard to believe, as we sat at the table and talked, that 30 years have gone by. It seems but a few months ago that Tim, Kerry, Walt Belcher and Tim Hayes, along with one or two other close friends, were just boys, enjoying being together and just "goofing off."

High school days were mentioned and some of the activities that took place. In the midst of the laughter, Tim remarked, "You know, we were good kids ... not bragging on us, but giving credit to the way we were raised. Our parents held us accountable for what we did, they knew where we were and basically what we were doing.

"They taught us the meaning of respect, accountability and honesty and our grandparents expected the same standards from us. Sure, we were full of mischief but nothing that was bad or harmful."

Maybe some of you are wondering whey I didn't wait until next Christmas to publish Tim's story. It would have been a great one for Dec. 1, 2009. Well, there are several reasons why I didn't wait.

For one thing a lot of things can happen between now and next year — such as the notes that I scribble down on note cards and pieces of loose paper just might get lost in the shuffle. However, the honest reason is the way our conversation ended. When I asked Tim a routine question, the answer he gave me was totally unexpected and I had to blink away the tears.

The question was, "Now that we've shared all these stories about Christmas, tell me, as you think back to your growing-up days, what is it that you miss most, now that you're grown up with a family of your own?"

Without a moment's hesitation, his answer was "Grandparents ... I miss my grandparents ... they were a big part of my life and my Christmas."

The answers to the next questions couldn't lie dormant for another year either. They should strike deep into the heart and mind of everyone who reads this column. "Tim," I asked, "as a young man with a family and a very responsible job, what advice would you give to anyone living in today's world?"

Again, there was no hesitation as he answered. "The number one priority, above everything else, is to do God's will. That's the most important thing in life. Number two is family.

"When I was growing up families were close. Nowadays, many families live a loose, almost disconnected lifestyle. Many are dysfunctional, without discipline or accountability. There are not the high moral standards we used to have.

"Number three is country. As a young boy and then as a young man, everyone loved America. There was no flag burning; we loved our flag. There was no question about what the primary language of the country should be and there was no question about our Christian religion.

"Sometimes I get to thinking — if we went to another country to live, would they change their religion or language to make us happy? We know they wouldn't. We need to get back to the America we used to know and the standards we used to have."

Tim is in a good position to discuss all the above questions. He grew up in a close family with brothers, Brent and Randy, and two fine parents, Dean and Sandra Deel. His father also served as a State Trooper, a DMV investigator until his retirement.

268

When Tim was still a young fellow, I (Anita) had several delightful visits with his grandparents, Lester and Lillie Deel, when I was doing their "life story," and those visits are still very memorable.

(Tim adds a little to their story by mentioning that his uncle Hubert now carries the mail over the same route that his grandpa used to carry it when times and roads were much rougher.)

Tim himself has a close family. He is married to the former Sharon Rasnic, a registered nurse from Mulbery Gap, Tenn. He has one stepson, Billy, who is a part-time student at Mountain Empire Community College and is employed by the Office of Surface Mining. He and

Sharon have one son, Brandon, who is a freshman at Lee High School.

Tim is a Christian, a member of the Jonesville First United Methodist Church and a member of their choir. When it comes to facing the reality of serious declines in our country, especially those pertaining to morals and family life, that's not a matter of choice for Tim. It's his responsibility.

He works as a Senior Trooper with the Virginia State Police with the Sex Offender Investigative Unit, Region 4. His is a serious business that makes him responsible for a large area of our region, including the following counties: Lee, Wise, Scott, Dickenson, Buchanan and Russell, along with the cities of Norton and Bristol.

Before we got any farther along in the new year, I wanted to share Tim's evaluations of life with you. Think of the value he places on a close family and family traditions, think of the importance he places on God and the Christian religion, on love of country and loyalty to all that our flag has stood for over the years.

Think of his concern for children and young teenagers — yours and mine. Maybe all of us need to "take a page" from Tim's book and re-evaluate our personal family calendar and see if we're on Tim's page or if we need to make some adjustments, especially in regard to our children and grandchildren.

Tuck his Christmas memories away until the first of December 2009 and focus in on his views on God, family and country. Those are the reasons I wanted to write this column now. Hopefully Tim's story will give you encouragement for the year ahead.

Just as Tim was leaving he remarked, "You know I stared working in '87 and I do a lot of traveling in my working or on vacation. I like to travel and I like to visit, but it doesn't matter where I go, I always want to get back home. Sometimes we take our mountains for granted, but there's no place like them — they're home. This is God's country."

We're proud of you, Trooper Deel. You and many of your school friends have done well and have made responsible citizens for the very reason you have mentioned.

In Touch

with Dickenson County family, friends & neighbors

Couple's love story unique in many ways

Mountain ECHOES

ANITA BELCHER

It will not be difficult to write this third column about Stacy Matherly because it was at this phase of his life that he became a part of our church family, and a close personal friend to just about everyone in the town of Haysi and surrounding communities — young and old alike.

However, I cannot write about Stacy without writing about Jean, his wife of 54 years, whom he would say was "the love of his life."

Stacy's story would be incomplete without some memories of Jean woven into it, even as his life would have been incomplete without her. Theirs is a unique love story, and with her permission I'll share it with you. You'll enjoy following the threads of their life.

Jean was born at Birchleaf (Sandlick), one of nine children born to Will and Emma Colley Wright. Her home was on Crooked Branch, nestled between two mountains with the dirt road and creek in between. The nearest neighbor "just down the road a piece," was the Hiram Anderson family, and "over the hill" were the E.H. and Victor Anderson families.

On down the creek was the John Davis home and across the road John's son, Hatchel Davis, and his family. A bridge spanned the Russell Fork River, and from that point the community spread out to include general stores, a church, a school, and the homes of some of the finest pioneer settlers who

SEE ECHOES, PAGE 10B

CONTINUED FROM PAGE 5B

ever migrated into the mountains of Southwest Virginia.

In between the two Davis homes was a little white church built after the coming of a missionary lady, Miss Helga Jensen, who started a Bible class which was attended by a number of adults.

Within a year after the coming of Miss Jensen, a Scotch-Irish Presbyterian minister, the Rev. T.K. Mowbray, came into the community and helped organize a Presbyterian Church. The first Elder of this church was E.H. Anderson, a school teacher who lived and taught at Sandlick and other schools in the area.

It wasn't long before another missionary lady by the name of Elizabeth Shoemaker settled in the Haysi community. Miss Shoemaker worked with adults and young people and had a great and godly influence on families in both Haysi and Sandlick. It was through her generosity that several of the young women in the area were able to attend college.

You might wonder what all the above had to do with Jean and Stacy. Jean would answer your question by explaining to you that the whole course of her life, and the lives of many others, was dramatically changed by the teaching and guidance they received in the small Presbyterian church at Sandlick.

Then she would go on to tell you, with her contagious enthusiasm, how it was that the men and women who taught there brought her and many others to understand the teachings of the Bible, to love and obey God and to believe on the Lord Jesus Christ as Saviour.

The teaching Jean received there as a child, and as a young adult, never departed from her mind and heart, and influenced the decisions she made the rest of her life, including her work as a teacher, her decision about marriage, and her life as a wife and mother.

She remarked, "You know, Nita, from the time we were little, we didn't know any other way but the way we were taught. We lived in a community like you don't find any more. The people who lived there cared for each other. It was like we were one big family and we were all there to help one another. Then when the church was built and we children were taught the Bible stories and how to love and obey God, we were truly blessed."

Like many mountain children, Jean had a love for music. She loved to sing and quickly learned the hymns that were sung at church and the songs especially written for children. Deep inside her was the desire to play a musical instrument such as the organ or piano.

Her family didn't own either, but she heard that "Chief" Richardson and his wife, Mae, owned an organ. Jean would walk from her home to the Richardson home, regardless of the weather, to hear Chief play. She learned the notes from him, but had nothing to practice on.

Then she heard that Mary Coyle and her son, Bobby, who lived at the old Tom Colley place, could play the piano. Jean recalls, "That was back when we wore 'half socks,' those that came up to our knees, and I would walk from my house down to the old

Colley place to hear the Coyles play and sing.

"Mrs. Coyle played the more simple songs but Bobby could play classical music and he had a wonderful voice. I watched them and memorized more notes, and though I didn't know what they meant, I knew I could use them if I had a chance. Many times my legs would be frozen red and stiff but what I heard and learned was worth it."

Like many mountain children, Jean Wright Matherly loved music, and in addition to singing she wanted to play a musical instrument. Her family didn't own one but she would walk to hear neighbors play.

Later on in life Jean had a piano, and sure enough, she remembered the notes and with more teaching she became an expert pianist, using her music and her voice to glorify God and train many young people. She little realized at the time that she would marry a man who loved to sing and play the guitar, and that the two of them would spend many happy hours together, each enjoying the music of the other.

Jean finished elementary school at the beautiful school building at Sandlick, then graduated from Haysi High School. There she played basketball and continued with the sport at King College and ETSU.

Coming back to Haysi she began her teaching career in elementary grades. One night she and a friend attended a basketball game at Ervinton High School. A young man by the name of Stacy Matherly was taking up tickets.

After the game was over she walked by Stacy at the door and laughingly said, "Let's go to Haysi." To her surprise he answered, "Wait 'til I've finished up here and I'll go with you." Thus began a lifelong "friendship."

One evening after they had spent some time together, Stacy left without saying anything. The next evening she looked out the window and saw him parked in his convertible beside the road. Jean walked to the car and he asked her to get in — he wanted to talk to her.

He finally hesitatingly asked her if she would consider being engaged to him even though he didn't have a ring for

---

her at the time. Of course her answer was "yes," and within the month he presented her with a ring.

Jean and Stacy were married Dec. 26 at Fairmont Presbyterian Church with her brother-in-law, Rev. Tinsley Bradley, performing the ceremony. They both continued their teaching careers at Haysi while living in an apartment over Haysi Farm Supply.

Within a short time after marriage the Matherlys adopted a little girl, Mary Jay. When asked what he felt he could offer the child, Stacy replied, "Not a whole lot monetarily but a lot of love and a Christian home."

While living at Haysi, the Matherlys attended the Presbyterian Church there. Rev. E.H. Anderson was the pastor and he was a man who believed in visiting his flock, as well as the unsaved.

He had a deep concern for children and every year he and others willing to help would teach Bible schools, not only at the Presbyterian churches but in every community school or out in the open. Miss Shoemaker was one of the faithful helpers, always taking her little portable organ along, but Jean was also one of the leaders of the team of teachers.

272

By this time she was playing the piano and she led the children in the Bible school songs. One year Rev. Anderson held 16 Bible schools (I believe I'm correct). Jean well remembers the year she helped him conduct 10 Bible schools.

During all this time, Stacy was learning more about the Bible and understanding the need to become a Christian. Jean tells this next story in her own words: "One night Mr. Anderson was preaching, and during the last hymn he asked if there was anyone there who wanted to profess Christ as their Saviour.

"Someone told me afterward that Stacy was gripping the back of the pew until his knuckles were white. Then he suddenly let go of the pew and almost knocked Tommy Anderson over in his rush to get to the front of the church and profess his love for Christ and his desire for church membership."

You know, Tommy loved Stacy and was always wanting

---

to sit by him. Yes, I, Anita, recall my brother's love for Stacy. In fact he was going to visit Stacy, and the two of them were going to find a Christmas tree when Prater Creek was flooding, running through the floor of the bridge across to the old William Arrington home.

Tommy looked down at the raging water and saw a tiny little hand above the surface. He thought it was a doll that had been swept downstream but suddenly a little face appeared.

Tommy dived into the water and was able to grab the child, Stevie Fuller, just before he was swept around the bend at the NYC building. I imagine the Christmas tree search was postponed but thankfully both Stevie and Tommy survived.

Stacy became a member of the church, serving in Haysi for eight years, College Park Presbyterian Church for 10 years, and Ben Hill Presbyterian Church for 11 years. He served as elder, deacon and choir member. His great desire was to serve God by serving others, helping anyone he could who was in need.

As Stacy Matherly learned more about the Bible he understood the need to become a Christian. He was a church member and elder, deacon and choir member in various churches. He served God by serving others.

Stacy left a great family and he left many good memories for them. In addition to his wife Jean, he left a daughter, Mary Jaye Harrison; grandsons, Ryan and Eric Harrison; great-grandson, Ben; sister, Lois Kennedy; brother, Jay Matherly; and many other close family members.

Again, I quote Jean, "Stacy and I had a wonderful marriage. We had so many good times together. We shared a lot, we laughed a lot. We played music

---

together and sang together. We went to church together and shared our Bible reading and prayer together at home.

"Stacy always led in prayer. Toward the last when the tumors in his head were causing him to become forgetful I would say, 'Stacy, do you want me to finish praying?' He would answer, 'No, I will ... just give me a little time to think.'"

As I said at the beginning of this column Stacy and Jean had a unique marriage, the kind you don't find much anymore.

Even at the time of Stacy's death, God worked out some very "unique" circumstances. Stacy and Jean had moved and not settled into a church, and knew no minister in the area.

Suddenly it came to Jean's mind that our daughter, Rebecca, whom she had taught in her children's choir at Haysi, lived somewhere around Atlanta. She called Gail Viers Haviland, living in Atlanta but originally from Sandlick, to ask if she knew where Becky lived. Gail didn't know but called me (Anita) for her phone number.

in the time of great need, it was the "home folks" that God brought together to share the sorrows and joyful memories and the knowledge that Stacy is with the Lord.

Jean says that Stacy was somewhat of a poet. He loved writing poetry to her and leaving it around where she could find it. The following was written to her on Valentine's Day, 1994:

Love is like a waterfall
A thirsty traveler finds
As he travels through a weary land
And reads its many signs.

An accident some may say it is
And Fate, some others cry
But I think love's a gift,
Like the rainbow in the sky.

Like the water builds an oasis
In the arid desert bleak
But the love that comes to me from you
Is like the sunlight at its peak.

My love (for you) was like the water
That sparkled from the wall
But now it gushes from its peak
Like a giant waterfall.

— Always be my love,
Stacy

Jean's great desire was for everyone to know how much Stacy loved the Lord and his family, and how much he loved everyone he knew, and of his desire to help anyone in need, and to "bring out the best in them."

Thank you, Jean, for sharing these memories with us. Truly Stacy's is an inspiring story that will live on and be of great encouragement to others, even now.

On calling Beckie it was unbelievable that she lived only a short distance away. She immediately drove to Jean's home where she assured her long-ago choir teacher that she would sing at the funeral and yes, she knew someone who would play the guitar, Stacy's favorite instrument.

Another problem was soon solved. Beckie's husband, Rev. Joe Morecraft, Jean knew, would conduct the services, with Jean's nephew, Bradley Long, assisting. God worked it all out and Jean says, "Everything was beautiful, just as Stacy would have wanted it."

Doesn't it amaze you that after the passing of so many years and living in a city as large and complex as Atlanta,

In Touch

with Dickenson County family, friends & neighbors

Sutherland exemplifies worth of older citizens

ANITA BELCHER

Probably one of the most respected men in Dickenson County is Benjamin Fulton Sutherland, Attorney at Law. It might surprise him to hear this because he is a quiet man who goes about his daily work, not looking for praise or applause from anyone.

In the past months while interviewing him, I have learned much of his past history and have come to admire the sound principles on which he has built his life and his sensible world view.

I have listened intently to stories of

early settlers going back to his grandfather Jasper's time up until the time that Ruben Wright drove a taxi in Clintwood. I will not share much of that information with you this time because I want to focus mainly on Mr. Sutherland himself for a very special reason.

This is his birthday month — almost his birthday, so we'll wait for another time to share his stories of others, perhaps in a few weeks when the weather "moderates." Today is Mr. Sutherland's day.

Mr. Sutherland was born in

Clintwood, the first of the family of children to be born in the house which his dad had built for his wife and children. The house still stands on the hill directly across from Wachovia Bank. The same rock wall still stands in front of the house which was built by Guy Pizzuto, a stone mason from Sicily. (More about that later).

Mr. Sutherland grew up in Clintwood in the '20s and began his law practice

PLEASE SEE ECHOES, PAGE 9B.

Echoes

CONTINUED FROM PAGE 5B

there in 1949. He recalls, "I grew up in Clintwood when it was still a frontier settlement. Every family had their own garden of which they were very proud.

"There were at least 50 gardens from one end of the street to the other, not counting the ones you couldn't see, and neighbors loved to stand and discuss the condition of their crops and exchange ideas. Every family had their own milk cow and every one had a hog for slaughtering in the fall.

"Of course there were no sewer systems, so everyone had their own outhouse. An automobile was a novelty. Walking, horses, or wagons pulled by horse and mule team were the modes of traveling for the most part."

Mr. Sutherland's grandparents had a great influence on his life. Like many of the early set-tlers they carved a home and a farm out of the wilderness. They were farmers, cattlemen, blacksmiths, storekeepers, and soldiers. They did what needed to be done and performed each day's task with fortitude and determination.

Mr. Sutherland's father, Holiday, was also an inspiration to him. He recalls, "My father was a prodigious worker. He came to his law office at 8 a.m. sharp, worked until lunch time, then worked until 5:30 p.m., at which time mother would have dinner prepared.

"At 7 p.m. he returned to the office where he worked until 10:30-11 p.m. I assume Grandfather Jasper's work routine on the farm set a pattern for both my father and me."

I was fortunate enough to know Holiday Sutherland when I met him on the street or side-walks of Clintwood. I had heard the older folks speak well of him, so I felt honored when he recognized me with a smile or a tip of his hat.

I knew his son, Ben Sutherland, much better and have always respected him, but have come to know him better for the man he really is as I have sat across from him at his desk.

Over the past two or three months, as we shared the history of the county (indeed the nation) up to the present day, I have learned, as the old saying goes, "Sometimes still water runs the deepest."

He is a great historian, knowledgeable, clear and concise, and he's a capable commentator and evaluator of today's political, spiritual and economic status.

Mr. Sutherland is also a vet-eran of World War II and was part of the company of men who built the bridge over the Rhine River in Germany at a crucial time in our nation. (More on that later, also).

I will end this column by mentioning that Mr. Sutherland is one of the few of "the old school" left, and is thankful for his training. Many of the young people "raised" back then developed a strong work ethic, honesty, integrity, commitment, correctness of dress and appear-ance as well as a code of thoughtfulness and good man-ners, dependability, fairness, and justice.

A life built on the foundation of love for God, country and family was a pretty common thing back then. Mr. Sutherland is a man of strong principles, though he would be the first to admit that he isn't perfect.

Today and in the days to come we need to develop the "old school" philosophy in our young people, or our nation may cease being the nation we once knew.

In a sense of the word, under God, our children and our young people are our greatest asset. But stop and think. These young people need the wisdom and guidance of our older folks. If used to their fullest potential, the worth of our older citizens cannot be measured.

As I watched Ben Sutherland walk across the street one day, I said to myself, "There goes a great story." Then another thought quickly replaced the first one. "No," I said aloud (though no one was listening). "He (Mr. Sutherland) is not a great story, he's a book of stories. He's a walking histo-ry book filled with a variety of subjects ready to be shared with great insight and wisdom."

And then I thought, "We must not let him slip away with-out knowing and appreciating at least some of the things he can so richly share with us."

Thank you, Mr. Sutherland, for taking time out of your busy schedule to talk with me, thus sharing with many hun-dreds of people.

Folks, all our older citizens are treasures, but they should not remain "hidden treasures." Record their stories and use them in your everyday life while sharing them with others.

Every time I write some-one's history I am thankful to God for allowing us to know that person better and to know that much more about our roots and our history.

Today we want to thank God for allowing Benjamin Sutherland to live and go on working for 91 years, and for sharing his life with us. Happy birthday, Mr. Sutherland, from your many friends wherever they may be.

In Touch

with Dickenson County family, friends & neighbors

Mountain ECHOES

ANITA BELCHER

Many things different 'back then'

Last week I did a "Happy Birthday" column for Ben Sutherland, Attorney at Law of Clintwood. Mr. Sutherland is the son of Simpson Holiday and Pearl Harrison Rush Sutherland, and his paternal grandparents were Jasper and Louise Dyer Sutherland.

This week I am focusing on the grandparents for the simple reason that their story is so interesting that it bears repeating.

The Sutherland grandparents lived at Hatchet Branch, in the Nora area where Jasper Sutherland continued to live until his death. Mrs. Sutherland lived on at the old homeplace where she died a year or two later.

I asked Ben Sutherland about his grandparents' home, their farm, and their way of life. His memories were very vivid as he recalled, "My grandparents lived in a white frame house, somewhat above the average for those days. There was a huge dining room with a long dining table. I remember that people were always coming at mealtime. I don't know where they came from, but they came.

"No one was ever turned away, as everyone knew

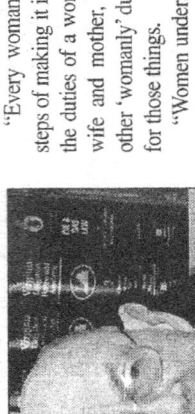

Ben Sutherland

they were always welcome. Grandfather worked his entire farm all four seasons but needed more help at harvest time. Grandmother cooked for the hired help as well as for others who came."

"What was the actual role of your grandmother in the home?" I asked. "Well, you have to understand that in those days it was a man's world. There was this thing about women getting an education. Women were supposed to get married, bear children and be a mother to them.

"Every woman could card wool and follow the steps of making it into clothing. It was understood that the duties of a woman was limited to that of being a wife and mother, of cooking, canning, sewing and other 'womanly' duties. They didn't need an education for those things.

"Women understood this. Life was hard back then and their time was consumed with these responsibilities. My grandmother, Louise, was head of the domestic household, but in other categories, grandfather was the decision-maker."

My next question: "Mr. Sutherland, the mountain people who settled in this area have always been very intelligent. Why do you suppose that a few generations, or at least many people, even into the early 1900s, couldn't read or write?"

Mr. Sutherland gave the question thoughtful consideration, then answered, "It is my theory that in those early days there was no time for book learning. To survive, entire families had to work from daylight until dark. If any reading was done it was after dark by the light of the fire.

"My grandfather Jasper couldn't read or write, but my grandmother Louise could. She read to him at night from the Bible which was the only book they owned."

Things were certainly different back then. The main source of food was the farm, the only things "store

PLEASE SEE **ECHOES**, PAGE 7B

Echoes

CONTINUED FROM PAGE 5B

bought" were things you couldn't grow. Even some shoes were homemade though a man occasionally would buy a pair of boots.

Shoes were repaired at home, clothing for the most part was made at home, as was much of the medications. But what did folks do when they had a toothache?

Mr. Sutherland smiled. "Grandfather was elderly when I knew him and had reduced his farming activities, but he was the neighborhood dentist. When anyone needed a tooth pulled, they came to Grandpa's.

"You see, Grandpa was also the neighborhood blacksmith. He was a very strong man, and along with his other tools he had a set of forceps. He kept a keg of apple brandy on hand as a pain killer so getting a tooth pulled at Mr. Sutherland's blacksmith shop had its enjoyable side, too."

Hopefully, next week we'll be hearing and reading more interesting stories about those early days that few people remember or have a record of.

Thank you, Mr. Sutherland, for sharing history with us that we would never have known otherwise.

Storybook wedding fascinated young girl

Euna Hay was married the first time to Milford O'Quinn from Prater Creek. Let's hear the story from Mrs. Hay herself.

She recalls, "I met Milford at the home of my best friend, Thelma Singleton, daughter of Rene and Erie Singleton. Milford asked to take me home but I refused. I was afraid that Thelma might get mad at me, but she told me later that Milford was just a good friend and that it was fine with her if we dated.

"I didn't want to do anything that would hurt the Singletons because they were such fine people and best friends with our family. Erie was such a wonderful woman and would never let me leave her home without seeing to it that I had a good home-cooked meal. She was like a mother to me.

"Anyway, Milford and I started seeing each other and of course, he came to our house up on the mountain. In the fall of the year we did a lot of walking around the farm just looking at everything, and I guess gathering some nuts. We were never by our-

ANITA BELCHER

Mountain ECHOES

selves — my folks wouldn't allow their girls to go out with a young man by themselves.

"My older sisters had their brothers with them but I was the baby girl. The rest of the family had grown up and married except Verna and Cecil. Verna was the sister next to me and Cecil was my younger brother. One of them always walked along with Milford and me."

"If you dated for almost a year what did your family, Milford and you do on the long winter evenings?" I asked.

Mrs. Hay thought for a minute and then smiled. "We sat in front of the big fireplace ... you know I told you that it took up most of the front wall. Did I tell you that it had a mantle all the way across it?"

I couldn't resist the question: "Euna, what was on the mantle?" A look of surprise came to her face and she recalled something that there had been no reason to think of for years.

PLEASE SEE **ECHOES**, PAGE 9B

Mrs. Euna Hay O'Quinn poses with her first husband, Milford O'Quinn, on their wedding day in the summer of 1936.

278

279

CONTINUED FROM PAGE 8B

"Why," she answered, "there was a big clock that set right in the middle of the mantle. Dad had to take it down once a week to wind it. We had no electricity, you know, so we also used old oil lamps. And another thing I remember, Anita, was the big black telephone that hung on the wall by the mantle."

I told Euna that I, too, recalled the same kind of phone that hung by my grandfather Fuller's door. I believe that these phones were in the homes of people who were somehow connected with the forestry service.

Euna continued her memories of winter evenings at her home on the mountain. "I've just remembered, Anita, that many nights we would pop corn that came from our garden. Mother always had a popcorn patch and we enjoyed popping the corn at night. Sometimes we popped it on top of the cook stove and other times we held it over the fireplace.

"We also roasted potatoes in the ashes. Mother and Dad sat up for a while and then they would go to bed. Their bed was just behind us there in the big front room."

Milford and Euna were married in the summer of 1936. I know because I was there. Let me tell

you about it. I was about 7 years old and like most little girls I was fascinated with fairy tales and stories of weddings and brides and what they wore, how they looked and what the groom wore and did they look happy and would there be flowers ...

I think that's a part of being a little girl, but actually I haven't changed much in that regard. I still love weddings.

Anyway, my mother and Euna's sister, Verna, were sisters-in-law, having married brothers. The two families were very close, so of course our family was invited to the wedding. We walked together down from our little houses on our mountain to the highway (dirt road) down to the Hadley Road where we crossed over the branch and began the climb up the path to the Edwards home.

It was a hot day and I well remember Cecil (Jack) picking me up and carrying me "piggy-back" on his shoulders 'til we reached the top.

Everything at Euna's home that day was centered around her wedding. The yard was pretty and green with aunt Alice's (Euna's mother) flowers bordering the paling fence and aunt Alice, slender and spry, busy moving in and out of the kitchen, seeing that everything was in order.

Uncle Dave (Euna's father), handsome in his

dark suit and white shirt, gave the bride away, with the admonition to the groom after the ceremony, "Son, you take care of her or you'll have to answer to me."

Of course after the wedding there was dinner set out on long tables and those of you who have attended a "mountain dinner-on-the-ground" for any occasion can imagine what a feast it was.

For some reason I remember the green beans but it was the chicken that had me worried. There were so many people there, the kettles and pans of chicken kept disappearing and I wondered if there was going to be any left for us children. You see, in those days children had to wait for the grown-ups to go first.

The wedding itself was beautiful, held on the lawn, with all the surrounding beauty of a mountain farm. Milford looked very handsome, dressed well for the occasion. The bride was so beautiful she could have stepped out of one of the fairy story books.

She was dressed in all white with a saucy white hat, earrings and bracelet to match. Somehow, though, as you look at her picture, you'll see an inward beauty there, reflected on her face, that is still there today. That's the most important thing.

I'm glad that I, a little seven-year-old girl, was there that day. I didn't know it then, but I was in the middle of a living history book. There were the older generations that had helped settle this area, their faces registering both pride and humility, patience but determination.

I saw how beauty and productivity had been carved out of the forest, how that a large family had been raised on a mountain farm through good and bad times, I saw a gentle mother who taught her children in the ways of the Lord and I felt her kindness.

I saw neighbors coming for miles to share in the joyful occasion — I saw people dressed in their best and I saw that special thoughtfulness and sincere politeness that is a unique quality of a true mountaineer. I saw respect for older people from the younger generation and I saw children being obedient to their parents and grandparents.

That day I saw the future being "turned over" to the next generation.

I saw all this and much more, only then I didn't realize it. It took living and looking back.

That day my eyes were riveted on the bride. She was beautiful ... she still is.

Family collected clothes so needy

This week's column is the last in the series of stories that Euna Hay has shared with us about her growing-up days as a child, teenager, a young woman, a wife, mother and grandmother.

At our last visit she told me of her marriage to Silas Hay after the death of her first husband, Milford O'Quinn. Milford died in 1946 and Euna was left with four children to raise by herself. In 1948 or 1949 she met Silas and they were married in 1950.

Euna recalls, "Silas was working in the mines at Clinchco when we started dating and when we decided to get married we went to a minister's home in Grundy for the ceremony. I remember that I wore a tan-and-brown outfit and Silas wore a nice suit."

Silas and Euna started housekeeping in her home at Abner's Gap where she and Milford had bought property. I was interested in the location of the home because Abner's Gap was good way from Prater where Euna had lived much of the time during her first marriage.

Today as I met with Euna's sons, James, Darrell, Gary and Charles, together they told me the story of the property and the home at the gap.

"Why?" I asked, "did your mom and Milford decide to make a move from the Prater area to a place on Route 80, close to the highway?"

"Because," the boys told me, "they wanted to put in a store and they felt like the piece of property, close to the road, was an excellent place for that kind of business. They bought property at a good price and were getting ready to stock the store when Milford was killed.

"This was a two-story building with living quarters on the first level and the store on the second level. This was because the living quarters were on the ground level and the store came out even with the highway."

I was interested in the fact that when Euna was married the first time, she and Milford had gone into the store business and I asked how that happened to come about, as I didn't remember any of Euna's people running a business of that kind.

I think it was James who answered my question. "Grandpa James O'Quinn always had a store so that was the business that my dad grew up in, and it was just natural for him to go into the same kind of work."

As the boys shared these memories, other recollections came to their minds and I have included all these for future generations to know about.

They told me the following: "When Milford and mom bought

Silas and Euna Hay

the Abner Gap property there were big hemlock pines growing there. Uncle Arthur, mom's brother, cut the trees down and a man who lived up the hollow at the 'gravel pile' sawed the lumber 'on the halves' for them.

"After the house was finished, aunt Verna and uncle Victor stocked the store and ran it for a time, but then decided to go into the restaurant business at Clinchco (Riverside)."

As Euna told us in last week's column, when she and Silas were married, the highway department told them they would have to move the house back farther from the road. Silas rebuilt the home and that is where he and Euna lived and raised their family. That is still "home" to the children and grandchildren and others who love Euna.

When mining slowed down at Clinchco, Silas went to work as a deputy sheriff in the county. The boys didn't recall exactly how long, but they remembered very well when he went to work as the first truant officer in Dickenson County. Euna had told me about this time in their life and the sons filled in the details

They recalled, "Dad's job was to go to the home of families whose children were not attending school and find out what the problem was. As he visited those homes, he found that many of the children did not have proper clothing to wear."

He took it upon himself to personally go to business places and individuals to ask for help for these needy families. He would gather the clothing and take it to the homes where it was needed. Finally he put an ad in the local newspaper asking for

could attend school

help for these families.

The ad caught the attention of the *Bristol Herald* newspaper, and they ran it as a "human interest" story. From there it went to the *Roanoke Times* and the result was phenomenal. Clothing came from various organizations, including a church in New York which sent tractor trailer loads to Abingdon.

The county had a flatbed truck which Silas used to haul loads of clothing to his and Euna's home. The boys all remember those days. I believe it was Gary who went with his dad on some of these trips.

One of the boys recalled there were "tons" of clothing, so much so that the porch of their home broke through and Silas had to build a new one, this time using concrete! All the clothing was packed in heavy burlap with metal bands securing each unit.

Darrell recalls that "home began to look like a mail order catalog distribution center as orders began to come in from schools and other organizations who knew of needy families."

The boys recalled that the burlap and metal bands were hard on the hands, but they were all proud of their dad and mother for the work they were doing in the community. Euna told me that many nights she and Silas would stay up until 1 a.m., packaging clothing, and Silas would deliver it as soon as he could.

The boys recalled the strong work ethic that Silas lived by. They spoke of how he dug the post holes and put up the chain link fence for the softball field at the Kiwanis Park. Gary was with his dad much of this time. They recalled the hard work they did while growing up.

They told me, "We had a big garden at Abner's Gap and dad rented the big bottoms on Frying Pan Creek from Clinchfield. We had fields of corn and beans as well as other crops, and we all worked. Mom worked right with us. We walked from home to Frying Pan, carrying our lunch with us."

As we talked about gardens and crops, one of the boys laughingly said, "You know, mom thought something was wrong if she didn't have 700-800 cans of food stored up for winter!" When I talked to Euna, she said, "Yes, that's the way it was ... and that was besides all the pickling I did."

It was exciting to talk with this fine family of brothers and listen as they shared stories and memories of their growing-up days. As you notice in my first sentence of this column I said this was the last in the series of Mrs. Hay's stories — but it isn't!

There are stories you want to read, about "music on the mountain" when Euna was a girl growing up, about the fiddle that hung over the mantle and who played it, and Bill Anderson's story, along with Gary's about gigging for bullfrogs, and about Grandpa Lum Hay's Christmas surprise.

Thank each of you boys, James, Darrell, Gary and Charles, for taking the time on a busy morning to talk with me, and thank you, Charles, for sharing your office space with us so we could have a place to talk.

Your mom will be thanking you, too, for helping record her story of which you all are an important part.

In Touch

with Dickenson County family, friends & neighbors

Dog tags 'come home' after six decades

Mountain ECHOES

ANITA BELCHER

The following true story has been recounted in two or three newspapers and featured on at least one television program, but somehow it never made its way back to the hometown of Oscar Mullins, a young man who gave his life for his country and his buddies during World War II. Oscar was the son of General and Lillie Epling Mullins and the family lived in Haysi, Va.

The story came to me through Becky Mondrage, who I believe is related to the Mullins family by marriage, and she desired very much to have it published in our local newspaper. I agreed that the story should be shared. Perhaps, as you read this story you will feel that, in a sense, at last Oscar Mullins has come home via his county newspaper.

Much of the information in the following story I'm writing comes from an article published in a South Carolina newspaper, "The Aiken Standard," and written by Carl Langley. I could not change the story to make it my own, because facts are facts and they don't change to suit the fancy of the writer. However, I did

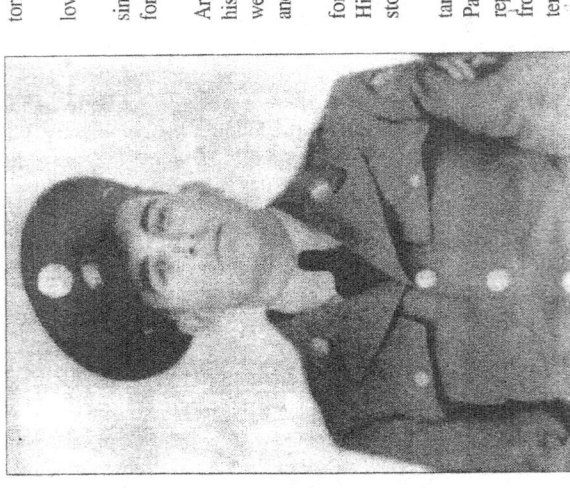

Oscar Mullins

call Mrs. Opal Mullins Wright, sister of Sgt. Oscar Mullins, for an interview to get the information firsthand and not just be copying someone else's work. Basing my column on the account given by "The Aiken Standard" and approved by Mrs. Wright, here's what happened.

For nearly 64 years, Sgt. Oscar Mullins' dog tags rested in a Belgium forest where one of the most his-

toric and bloodiest battles of World War II was fought. Mullins was the oldest of eight children and deeply loved and admired by his family.

The young man was only 26 when he killed during single biggest and bloodiest battle for American ground forces in World War II, the Battle of the Bulge.

Also recorded as the Battle of the Ardennes or Ardennes Offensive, the battle was among the most historic events of WWII. German losses in the battle were critical in ending the war and leading America and its allies to victory six months later.

The Ardennes Mountain region covered a huge forest in Belgium and in the final months of 1944, Hitler sent nearly 30 divisions there in an attempt to stop the Allies.

On Dec. 26, 1944, Mullins and the four men in his tank crew had just finished breakfast when German Panzer tanks opened heavy fire on them. According to reports, Mullins removed two badly wounded men from his tank and sent the other two to cover. He reentered the tank and began firing at the Germans. Mullins had destroyed or disabled nearly 12 enemy tanks before the ammunition in his tank exploded, offering him no chance to escape, according to reports.

The tank burned for two days, so little was left inside. All of his personal belongings were destroyed in the explosion, including a family picture that he carried in his shirt pocket.

Oscar's brother Ira was in a tank about a mile away

PLEASE SEE **ECHOES**, PAGE 9B

Echoes

CONTINUED FROM PAGE 7B

during the battle, but was unaware at the time that Oscar had been killed.

Upon hearing news of his death, Oscar's entire family was devastated by the loss. They were proud, however, that he gave his life for his country while helping free millions who faced enslavement by the Nazis. Mullins was awarded the Distinguished Service Cross posthumously, but Mrs. Wright says some of his fellow soldiers believe the Medal of Honor should have been awarded since her brother not only died for his country, but specifically for his tank crew.

Mullins' dog tags were thought to have burned during the explosion that killed him. That wasn't the case, however. On May 21, 2008, Mrs. Opal Mullins Wright received them through the mail. Now they were protected by and displayed inside a frame.

It is now believed the force of the explosion that destroyed Mullins' tank blew the tags a short distance away.

It would be many years later that a man searching the battlefield for relics would find them.

Mrs. Wright relates that the dog tags would have ended up for sale at a Netherlands flea market had it not been for a man named Niek Hendrix. Mrs. Wright considers it a miracle that her brother's dog tags were brought to the attention of Hendrix, who regularly searches battlefields for historic remnants. Hendrix is a member of the Liberators, a group of Dutch and Belgian history buffs who help care for a military cemetery in the Ardennes where many of the Allied soldiers, whom they hold in reverence, are buried.

Hendrix, according to Wright, lives in a little village in the Netherlands and is among WWII survivors. He is involved in the upkeep of the cemetery and war memorial on the battlefield where an estimated 19,000 American and British soldiers were killed.

Wright said the man who found the dog tags had shown them to Hendrix. The man told Hendrix he had found the tags on the battlefield and planned to sell them at a flea market. Hendrix reportedly offered to buy them, telling the man that they belonged to a family who had given a son for their freedom.

Hendrix then began a search to find the Mullins family. It would take him four years to do so.

He first went to the archives in the Ardennes and found Oscar's name on a memorial wall. However, no other information available. So he took his search for Oscar Mullins' family to the Internet.

It was a niece by marriage of Oscar and Opal's sister, Shirley, who found Hendrix on the Internet. The niece knew of Oscar's death during the war. While doing a search for the Mullins name on the Internet, she learned of Hendrix's mission to find a name to go along with the dog tags.

The niece told Shirley what she had found. Shirley contacted Opal's son, Ronnie, who then found Hendrix on the Internet.

Ronnie made three trips to the Ardennes for information about his Uncle Oscar and he carried the story through to the end, said Wright. Ronnie and Hendrix then began a correspondence.

Ronnie gave him Opal's telephone number and Hendrix call here. "Niek called me and we talked a long time. He said that it was meant to be that he had come across the dog tags and was able to find our family," Opal recalls.

Opal — whose husband, Bruce, is a WWII submariner who retired from the Navy as a chief petty officer — says having the dog tags returned brought a measure of comfort to Oscar's brothers and sisters.

Mrs. Wright continues, "My mother and father always grieved because my brother's remains could never be recovered."

She said at least her son was able visit the battlefield and see his uncle's name on the memorial wall.

I (Anita) knew the Mullins family very well. I walked by their home every day as my Dad and I walked to school. One or two of the children were near my age. My husband knew Oscar and he, too, fought in the same battle further south.

Opal was a "blonde beauty" and married handsome Bruce Wright, brother of Jean Wright Matherly and Mary Wright Ratliff. She told me last week that she and Bruce eloped when he was home from the Navy and that his brother, George, and sister-in-law, Catherine, helped them with their plans and accompanied them to their wedding. Opal says that George paid the minister five dollars for their wedding fee and Bruce told him that was the best five dollars he would ever spend!

Other children in the family besides Oscar, Opal, Ira and Shirley are Betty (deceased), Gene (deceased), Forster (his son, also named Forster, was among best friends of one of our sons, Hugh Belcher) and Ruby. I believe I taught Shirley and Ruby in school and dad taught most of the Wright family.

Opal speaks of her Christian home with her parents belonging to the Old Regular Baptist Church. Miss Elizabeth Shoemaker influenced Opal to start attending the Presbyterian Church. Miss Helga Jensen and the Rev. T.K. Mowbray, along with the Rev. E.H. Anderson, had much influence on Bruce. Bruce recalls with laughter the poem "Touser Shall be Tied Tonight" that Mr. Anderson recited to his students. The Wrights are a precious Christian family and they asked for our prayers as neither of them are well.

Their love is still with the mountain people and they have heartfelt memories of growing up here. "It's still home and we're still plain old mountain people," they say.

Opal recalls the closeness of their family. "We still get together when we can and pray for each other," she says.

She recalls the kind, gentle mother and the good hard working father. "Dad's main work was carpenter work ... Did you know that after fire destroyed most of Haysi that Dad rebuilt or helped rebuild most of the homes and business places that had burned to the ground?" Opal said.

"No," I said. "But I knew he did the work on our Presbyterian Church in Haysi when we added on extra rooms."

We still grieve with the Mullins family over the loss of Oscar even as we grieve with thousands and thousands of others who gave their sons that we might live in peace and freedom and we should not forget those who return home maimed by the horrors of war. What a blessing that after 60 years God worked in such a way that the Mullins family received the dog tags belonging to Oscar and Niek Hendrix will forever be dear to the family, as will also family members who helped Niek in his search.

Thank you, Becky Mondrage, for bringing this story to my attention and thank you, Opal, for sharing your personal knowledge and memories about your brother. May God bless you and those that are dear to you.

This is the month when we especially remember those who have died for our country. Let us remember them with thanksgiving and continue to pray for those who still fight for our freedom.

Branson shares fond memories of grandparents

T.G. Branson, residency administrator for the Virginia Division of Transportation for Wise and Dickenson counties, was kind enough to take time out of his busy schedule to have an interview with me. I thank him very much for this, and I thank my husband for accompanying me.

Although Branson holds a very important position in our two counties which actually has a far-reaching effect, I wanted to begin our interview with a background of his recollections of those early growing-up days, his parents and his grandparents. So that is where we begin.

ANITA BELCHER

Branson is the son of James Everett and Ethel Josephine (Vance) Branson, who lived in Castlewood, though T.G. Branson believes his mother was born in Mitchell County, N.C.

The Branson grandparents, William Henry (known to everyone as Will) and his wife Rachel (White) also lived in Castlewood, though Mr. Branson was born in Washington County.

T.G. Branson's paternal grandparents, William Henry and Rachel White Branson.

PLEASE SEE **ECHOES**, PAGE 14B

284

CONTINUED FROM PAGE 6B

"And what did these grandparents do for a living?" I asked. "As I understand it," Branson replied, "Grandfather worked on the railroad and farmed while grandmother stayed home raising their family." Branson does not have many memories of his grandfather who died while he (T.G.) was quite young.

Of his grandmother there are many fond memories. He recalls, "Grandmother Branson was a very kind woman, deeply religious. She attended a little church in Castlewood but I don't know what name it went by. She was a quiet woman, in other words not loud and forward, but she enjoyed being around people.

"She loved to come and visit our family and share ghost stories with us children at night. She and grandfather lived in a plain, frame, two-story house in Castlewood. Downstairs was the kitchen, the dining area and the big pantry where she kept her home-canned food, nothing store-bought. The upstairs rooms could be reached by an outside stairway to a porch.

"Grandmother must have loved flowers because I remember the old-time rambling roses that grew around her back yard and porch. She must have been an excellent cook – she taught my mom how to cook though mom's mother was one of the best in that category.

"I recall, too, that my grandmother, Rachel, had an old-time pump organ which she kept in one of the upstairs rooms. Maybe she played it when she was young but I'm not sure. I heard her brother Henry play, mostly religious music. I have many good memories of my grandmother Rachel."

"And what about your other grandparents?" I asked. "My Vance grandparents, Tillman and Elizabeth (Yelton) Vance, lived in St. Paul. Grandpa worked some in the mines in the Wilder area and in the summer time they would go back to North Carolina to do some farming.

"Grandpa was a small man and I remember he always wore a hat. When his health was such that he was unable to work anymore, my grandmother Elizabeth (Lizzie) told him that if he would build her a boarding house she would run it, board those needing rooms, and serve them meals. Grandpa agreed, and in 1929-30 Elizabeth's boarding house was built across the street from the present Oxbow Center.

"This was a two-story building with the dining area, or as we would call it today, the lobby, on the road level. Here the boarders had their meals and drinks (nothing alcoholic) and did their visiting. In this room was a long counter, marble topped, where folks sat on bar stools to eat their meals.

"In the dining hall was also a large glass case containing candy, cigars, etc., and an old-time drink machine where the drinks stayed cold by setting in cold water.

"Three steps up from the dining room was the kitchen with the living quarters on the same level. Here, also on the same level, were the rooms for boarders, each with a number above the door. I believe there were eight or 10 rooms."

"Did your grandmother have help in running this business and who were the people back then that needed to board away from home?" I asked.

Branson replied, "So far as I know, Grandmother didn't have help — maybe someone local would come in when needed. She kept a clean place and served good food, some of which was grown locally and sold by 'peddlers.'

"The folks who stayed there were just traveling people who needed a room for the night or possibly longer. A few miners and, no doubt, a few drummers."

Branson recalled that when business was slow, paying guest were invited up to the kitchen to eat with the family instead of eating in the big dining hall.

"Sometimes," he remembers with a smile, "a man would come in who'd had too much to drink and grandmother would give him a meal and lecture him on the evils and dangers of drinking, and when he had sobered up, send him on his way. During the Great Depression, she saw to it that no one went away from her place hungry."

"Mr. Branson," I commented,

T.G. Branson

"you remember your grandfather Branson as being a hard-working farmer and railroad man, and your grandfather Vance as being a miner and a man, who in ailing health, would see to it that your grandmother had a business to run. What are your outstanding memories of your two grandmothers?"

Branson thoughtfully considered my question and then replied, "I think my Grandmother Vance was a typical mountain woman, born and raised in the mountains of North Carolina. She was kind-hearted, practical, and cared for the needy who came her way.

"One of the things I remember about her (and here Mr. Branson's smile turns into a chuckle) is that she always gave us kids enough money to go to the movies, buy popcorn and one drink. I'll always remember that."

"My grandmother Branson was so very, very kind-hearted and good — so considerate of others. I guess it was her deep, heartfelt Christianity and her desire to help others that I will always remember best."

Work and play part of memories from boyhood

T.G. BRANSON
PART TWO

Last week when I interviewed T.G. Branson, I did a brief history of his grandparents. This week we focused on his parents and his early childhood beginning with his earliest memories.

He is the son of James Everett and Ethel Vance Branson of Castlewood. When James Everett Branson finished high school he began working as a mechanic in St. Paul. While working there he met and married Ethel Vance who lived in St. Paul.

You will recall from last week's column that it was Elizabeth Vance, Ethel's mother, who ran the boarding house in St. Paul which was known as The River Front Café. After the young couple were married, they moved to what is still known as Old Castlewood.

Shortly after moving to Castlewood James Everett Branson started working with the Department of Highways as a guard at one of the several convict camps located throughout the region.

(Many of you reading this column will recall the convict camp at Sandlick in 1950-51. It was in the long bottom where the Sandlick Elementary School is now located and a huge persimmon tree stood about mid-way the bottom on the edge of the river bank.

ANITA BELCHER

Rev. T.K. Mowbray and Rev. E.H. Anderson held church services at this camp. The land was owned by John Davis whose house stood where the school buses are now parked. Davis was boss over the WPA work force in the area, and his home was directly across the road from the little white Presbyterian church that was lifted off its foundations in the 1957 flood and came to rest on the end of the bridge.

This bit of information is given to better acquaint Mr. Branson with our community, and to help each of us to understand his position better. As Residency Administrator for the Virginia Division of Transportation in Wise and Dickenson counties, he is very familiar with our communities, highways and bridges and he has a personal interest in their history.)

SEE ECHOES, PAGE 11B

Echoes

CONTINUED FROM PAGE 7B

Now back to his father's story.

Branson believes his father worked in either Dungannon or Tazewell as a convict camp guard, then at some point he began doing road maintenance work. When he retired he was Superintendent of the Lebanon Area Headquarters for the Virginia Department of Highways.

Though Mr. Branson's work called for time away from home, and much travel, he, his wife and family continued living at Castlewood throughout their life.

T.G. Branson, who was the youngest of seven children, remembers his early growing-up days at Castlewood. He recalls, "I must have not been more than three years old when a wind storm came through Castlewood. I remember my mother picking me up along with my sister to carry us out of the house.

"When she opened the door she must have realized she wouldn't be able to stand against the wind. Sections of our roof were blowing off. She took us back into the house where, thankfully, we were safe."

Branson also remembers when the Castlewood High School burned. "I must have been about five years old then," he recalls. "Our house was about 100 foot below the school on the opposite side of the road. Mr. Maynard Salyers had a country store directly across the road from the school.

"When the school started burning, Mr. Salyers feared the heat would melt his candy and ice cream so he got help to move both cases over to our front porch! I had my fill of ice cream and candy that day!"

"How did you spend your free time during those growing-up days?" I asked.

"Probably like most of the young boys in those days," Mr. Branson replied. "We played marbles and, of course, cowboys and Indians was a favorite game. Some of my friends had an old flat-bottom fishing boat back then and we did a lot of fishing in the Clinch River, and that's where I learned to swim.

Above right are T.G. Branson's parents, James Everett and Ethel Josephine (Vance) Branson. Above left is the old family homeplace at Castlewood.

"We had responsibilities, too. There were the fields and gardens to work and other outside chores which we children were expected to do. Yes, Christmas was a special time. We always cut our own tree, a cedar, to decorate."

Branson continued, "I guess one of the most interesting and memorable things we boys did was working a paper route. My oldest brother, Bobby, began it. He started out just locally, delivering *The Roanoke Times* and *The Bristol-Herald Courier*. He would walk or, as a usual thing, ride his bicycle.

"This route was handed down to each of us boys, and as time went on it kept expanding. By the time I took it over I was delivering 300-350 papers."

"Mr. Branson," I asked, "What was home life like? Were your parents strong disciplinarians? Did you children show respect for them?" Of course I knew what his answer would be.

He smiled, but answered seriously, "We had great respect for our parents. They were loving and kind but we knew they would discipline if necessary. We obeyed and even the thought of 'talking back' didn't enter our mind. I think I got one whipping from my dad and my mom could use a switch when necessary.

"My mom was a fine lady... an avid reader. She was a person who went by the old saying, 'You might be poor but you don't have to be dirty.'"

An example of this stays with Branson until this day. He relates, "My mother knew a family that was very poor. Even their patches were patched, but they were one of the cleanest families around anywhere. She admired this family and taught us to be like-minded."

Thank you again, Mr. Branson, for taking time out of your busy schedule to share bits of history with us that we would never have known otherwise. We'll continue next week down the highway of past history leading up to the present.

In Touch

with Dickenson County family, friends & neighbors

Surveying job led to VDOT administrator post

Mountain ECHOES

ANITA BELCHER

In this week's column, once again we're going to walk down the road of recollections with T.G. Branson, beginning with his first day in elementary school, keep traveling with him through high school, and continue with him until his first job and marriage. Next week, we'll finish our journey with him, but thankfully, Mr. Branson will keep traveling on.

"How old were you when you started school and what was it like?" I asked.

He replied, "I was 7 years old when I started and the first day of school was not very different from any other day, except for the scheduled routine. I knew most of the children ... most of us lived in the same community and our house was close to school, so there was nothing really traumatic.

"I remember very well that after the high school burned, the county constructed several small buildings to house the elementary school children. We children fondly called these small buildings 'chicken coops.'

"We didn't take a lunch to school with us. When the high school burned down, there was a building close by that did not burn. It was used for a cafeteria and the grade school children were allowed to eat there.

"We went to grades one through six in elementary school. The seventh grade had been added to the high school. During those days, Carl Vickers was my best friend and reading was my favorite subject, although I had a great interest in math. I enjoyed those years in elementary school very much."

SEE ECHOES, PAGE 9B

Pictured are members of T.G. Branson's family from North Carolina. His grandmother, Elizabeth Vance, is seated second from the left. All these children belonged to the old couple, William Yelton and Phoebe G. Yelton, seated on the end of the front row.

Echoes

CONTINUED FROM PAGE 7B

I asked, "How old were you when you entered high school?"

"I was about 13," Mr. Branson replied, "and it was my first year to ride a school bus. I still loved reading, but now my favorite subjects were literature and world history.

"No, I didn't plan my subjects around what I planned to work at in life because I wasn't sure just what that was going to be. I planned on entering college after graduation, but, instead, I started working for VDOT in the surveying department.

"No, it wasn't because my dad had worked for them. It was just that a job came open and I applied for it. When I got the job I started planning my education around my work. I took college courses, some by mail, in surveying, math, highway engineering and computer programming courses, and computer information systems.

"After working in surveying for about three years, I was promoted to inspector of new roads construction which I enjoyed very much."

"When did you meet your wife?" I asked.

"Well, there used to be a drive-in restaurant, 'Steak and Shake,' in West Norton. One day, this pretty girl and I happened to be there at the same

T.G. Branson's grandfather Tillman Garfield Vance is on the left. Mr. Vance's wife, Elizabeth ran the boarding house. Will Wright, holding the catfish, was a visitor. Could he be the Will Wright from Sandlick?

time. We started talking, I found out that her name was Brenda Sue Dorton, and I asked her for a date. She accepted my invitation and close to a year after we met, we were married."

"Do you recall what year that was and where you were married?" I asked.

"Yes," Mr. Branson replied.

6"We were married July 8, 1968, at the home of a Rev. John E. Davis, a Methodist minister who lived in Greendale near Abingdon. I recall that I wore a slate grey suit and she wore a white dress.

"We spent our honeymoon in the Smokies and started housekeeping in a rented house in Wise. Later we bought a home in Tacoma. We had three children, one is deceased, then we have a son, Tilman Jr., and a daughter, Kristie Leigh."

Mr. Branson continued to work as road inspector for some time, and was then promoted to project engineer. His work in that capacity included both Wise and Dickenson counties.

From the position of project engineer, he was promoted to assistant resident engineer over the work in Jonesville, Lee and Scott counties. In 2004, he was promoted to residency administrator for Wise and Dickenson counties, a position which he still holds with a friendly dignity and efficiency.

Thank you again, Mr. Branson, for your time and the delightful insights you have shared about your family and the work you accomplish for the benefit of the traveling public. We are all looking forward to next week, when we take another trip down your road of recollections.

289

In Touch

with Dickenson County family, friends & neighbors

Branson discusses his different roles

Mountain ECHOES

ANITA BELCHER

LAST IN A SERIES

This week I will share my last scheduled visit with T.G. Branson, resident administrator of Wise and Dickenson counties' VDOT activities. These visits have been both delightful and educational for me and I will share with you some of what I have learned.

"Mr. Branson," I asked, "exactly what is your job as resident administrator of Wise and Dickenson counties?"

Mr. Branson replied, "I am the contact person for all the VDOT activities. Directly under me is my assistant, Jackie Christian, who fills in for me when needed, but who is also very proactive in overseeing VDOT activities. He does an excellent job, as does Mr. Harmon Kilgore, who is over the maintenance crews."

Mr. Branson speaks highly of these two men, as he does of all the employees under his supervision.

"As the contact person for VDOT, what kind of calls are you likely to get?" I asked.

Mr. Branson smiled, "I receive calls of almost every nature. Almost anything you can think of pertaining to roads, bridges, drainage, curves, right-of-ways, guardrails, mud slides, trees that have fallen across the highways, and a number of other things.

PLEASE SEE **ECHOES**, PAGE 9B

Echoes

CONTINUED FROM PAGE 7B

"In most of these concerns, a call to the area headquarters would be sufficient, but I try to answer every call and try to help out where I can. If the problem turns out to be a major one, the area supervisor will let me know.

"The headquarters for Dickenson County is at Fremont, and in Wise County there are three locations, Glamorgan, East Stone Gap and Coeburn."

Branson continued, "If there are concerns or complaints of a higher level than what our department handles, then they will be reviewed by higher-level departments of VDOT. Many public concerns are much more involved than meets the eye of the individual or individuals who are concerned.

"For instance, removing a curve, widening a place in a narrow road or putting in a drainpipe might seem simple, and sometimes it may be. Other times there are many issues to be dealt with, such as what would be the negative effect of what is being asked for?

"There are times when certain citizens might want a road widened but a land owner might not want to give up the property it would take. It might mean that widening that road would mean taking someone's front yard or garden spot....

"There are many issues that must be addressed. Sometimes it simply means that certain concerns and requests do not meet state regulations. That can cause a knotty problem which we try to unravel, but we still have to work within the state rules and regulations.

"Then there is always the question of money. There is money allocated for the secondary roads and then that which is allocated for primary roads.

"When you hear us talk about the six-year road plan,

we are talking about these allocations. We have strict state guidelines that we must adhere to. There are many things we would love to do, but sometimes circumstance or finances do not permit it being done at that particular time."

These visits with Mr. Branson made me realize that anyone who is truly interested in understanding what is going on in our highway department should ask for an appointment to meet with our residency administrator.

He will see you if at all possible. Ask him in the quietness of his office how the whole system works. It doesn't take him very long to give you a general overall view and then he will cover intricate details.

You will leave feeling much better, more knowledgeable, perhaps less "hot under the collar" about some of your concerns, and with better understanding than when you came.

I know, because during my interviews with him, I mentioned some things that I thought needed doing. He made a note of them, promising to look one or two over, suggesting that I call Mike Gulley at Fremont on one or two others, and explaining why two or three of my concerns were of the nature that needed to be reviewed by a higher level of VDOT.

Branson also attends the meetings of the board of supervisors where he give his report, takes input from citizens and the board, and endeavors to answer questions and comments. I believe we are very fortunate to have a man of Mr. Branson's caliber to hold the position of residency administrator in our two counties.

Not only is Branson the residency administrator of Wise and Dickenson counties, he holds another important position of which many people are probably unaware. He is also a minister of the Gospel,

T. G. Branson is shown with his wife, Brenda Sue.

pastor of the Rose Hill Church of God, 16 miles west of Jonesville.

Branson spoke of some of the ways God has worked in his life from the time he realized that, although he was happily married, had a good home and family and a good job, there was still "something missing" in his life.

He had been raised in a good moral home but he knew very little about the Bible or salvation, and somehow he felt that these were the missing parts.

It was amazing to hear how God worked in his heart and life to develop the plan that he had for him. Because his spiritual journey is personal, I think it is best to leave it to him to share on whatever occasion he thinks best, with whom he feels led to share it.

One experience he shared ties in so well with both his position at VDOT and his spiritual life and I believe you will appreciate hearing about it. With his permission, I will share it with you.

He relates, "I was driving to Clintwood for an appointment the morning after Halloween night. This was before I was a Christian and I had prayed that God would show me what to do to have peace in my heart with him.

"As I was driving I came upon a roadblock that had been put there the night before by Halloween tricksters. I parked, got out of my car and began removing the roadblock.

"As I worked, the Lord was also working, by speaking to my heart and mind, telling me that I had roadblocks in my life that needed to be removed. I finished my work and got in my car, praising God for his answer to my prayer."

From that time on, Branson began to study his Bible, attending different churches until he found the one in which he felt he was called to serve. He has studied faithfully "to show himself approved" as he serves the public as VDOT

administrator and as he administers the word of God to a needy people

While we talked I had written a word on the edge of my notebook. "Mr. Branson," I said, "when we first started these interviews and I was writing about your parents and grandparents, you gave heartfelt descriptions of each one. However, there was one that stood out particularly in my mind.

"Do you recall saying that your grandmother Branson was a devoted Christian and was a great believer in prayer? Do you believe that her prayers for you were perhaps a part of the reason you became a Christian?"

Mr. Branson smiled. "I was just thinking about that," he said. "Yes, I'm very convinced of that."

So was I. The word I had written on my note pad was "grandmother." Praying grandparents are a great blessing to any family for generations to come.

I have always respected Mr. Branson from the few brief encounters I have had with him in regard to concerns about roads in the county. That respect has deepened as I have come to understand his Christian outlook and activities as a pastor and to see how seriously he takes his position as residency administrator of Wise and Dickenson counties.

Thank you so much, Mr. Branson, for the work you are doing as a pastor, ministering to the physical and spiritual needs of the people you come in contact with. And thank you for your time and patience in explaining the intricate details of our highway system to me.

I learned much and I hope others who read this have also gained a better understanding of your work and responsibilities, and the efficient way in which you handle them.

May you know the blessings of a job well done as you continue down the highway of life.

In Touch

with Dickenson County family, friends & neighbors

As an 8-year-old, Anita Belcher, shown above in a childhood photo, worried fiercely about how her family would get a Christmas tree for their little grey house at Sandlick. At right is a tree from a modern day Christmas at the Belcher home.

Young girl yearns for Christmas tree for mountain home

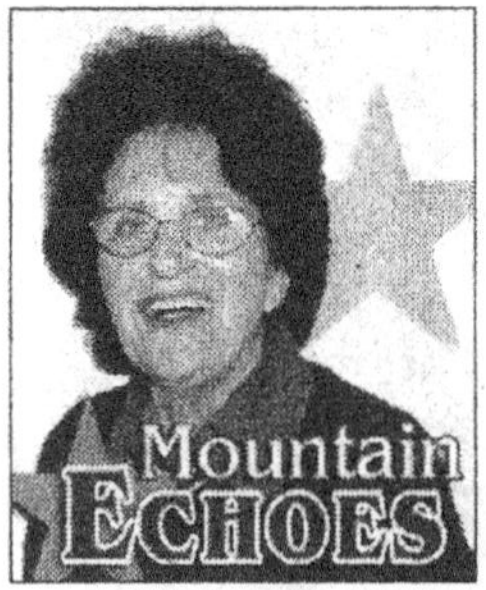

Mountain ECHOES

ANITA BELCHER

This is the story of Nita, a little girl who was born in 1929 during the Great Depression, when even a little seemed a whole lot. It's mainly about her love of the Christmas season, her desire for a Christmas tree and the anxiety mixed with the hope that somehow Dad was going to get one. But how, since none small enough grew nearby?

Nita (myself) has other memories of those childhood years but at Christmas time, the longing for a Christmas tree was never far from her mind. If you were 8 years old living back in those years, this story will bring many memories to your mind, and you who are younger will find yourself somewhere in this story.

This was first published about 30 years ago for our first "batch" of grandchilden, who were Anne, Emily, Joey, Jennifer, John Calvin and baby Jon-Isaac.

Then the second round came along, Mercy, Jordan, Grant, Christian and Ariane. By this time, the first grandchildren were having their own families. Their children, some now teenagers are Jane, Anita, Jessica and Mary Piper Scarbarough; Micah, Jacob,

SEE ECHOES, PAGE 8B

CONTINUED FROM PAGE 3B

Emma Claire and Noah Patton Laughlin; Emily Lealand, Owen Cly and Anderson Barnes; Izalou and Asa Raines Morecraft; Charlie Morecraft; Boston Neal Belcher; and Eli Kendall Rogers. And there's a new one on the way.

Besides all these, we are blessed to have a new set of grandchildren: Ben and Joe Mitchell, Fern and Anna Mitchell; and Kris and Cameron Dotson. This story is especially dedicated to each of these children, but is also lovingly dedicated to your children and grandchildren. If they love stories, sit down and read them the story of Nita's Christmas!

Nita lived in the small community of Sandlick, which is nestled deep in the heart of the mountains of Southwest Virginia. There were many things for the children living there to think about and participate in starting back in November.

There had been the Thanksgiving program at school with plays, songs, poetry, special art work with which to decorate the windows and walls, and yes, the Bible reading was a part of the day. We learned the Ten Commandments, the Lord's Prayer and other key verses in the Bible.

We children loved to have programs where we could be "actors" and, of course being chosen for the major parts such as the Indian chiefs Massasoit and Powhatan, along with the leaders of the colonies, Governor Bradford, John Smith and others who were of vital importance. Whichever girl was chosen to be Pocahontas was looked upon with great admiration and, no doubt, envy to some degree. I might add here that appropriate costumes were not a problem. Boys and girls in those days were just as creative as boys and girls are today and had much less to work with. A wing feather from an owl or the barnyard rooster added much to the dignity of the schoolboy Powhatan with his blackened, painted face.

As exciting and rewarding as all that was, it was in a sense overshadowed by the greater occasion of Christmas. It all started at school on the first of December when the Thanksgiving decorations came down and Christmas decorations began to go up!

At Sandlick, we had a beautiful school building that was located on top of a high hill above the community. With its tall windows, winding stairs which led to the second floor, and the big pot-bellied stove, the rooms were just waiting to be decorated.

It was a beautiful scene! The ceilings were high and some of the men folk in the community brought in a huge spruce pine for our Christmas tree. The warmth from the stove brought out the fragrance of the tree, a fragrance that no other tree can match! Happy boys and girls cut, colored and drew the decorations, plus a few that were store bought, no doubt by the teachers. By the time it was all finished, the room resembled a picture from a story book and the Christmas tree shimmered and glistened in the warmth of the old pot-bellied stove.

Nita enjoyed every minute of all the activities, but something kept bothering her. She didn't have a Christmas tree at home and Christmas just wouldn't seem like Christmas without a tree. She knew their small grey house, painted by time and weather, wouldn't have room for a very big tree, but just a small one would do. But where would it come from? No little ones grew nearby, and as the days passed with fluffy white snow flakes falling, Nita really became anxious. Daddy didn't seem worried, but Nita was afraid that with his work as a farmer and a teacher, he just might forget their discussions about a Christmas tree.

It helped to relieve her mind a little when some big boxes of mixed flavors of stick candy arrived as treats for her dad's students and she, along with her sister, Ginnie, got to fill the bags with the colorful candy. "Be careful," Daddy would say, "you may eat the broken pieces, but don't break any!" What a temptation, but, no, we didn't break any!

But as the days kept passing, Nita grew more worried — still no sign of a Christmas tree to brighten up the little grey house on the mountain.

At church, in the little white building which later the Flood of '57 washed away, we had a precious time together. The Anderson girls, probably with the help of their brothers, brought a tree for Sunday school to place the treats under. It was a beautiful tree, though not as large as the one at school. At church and Sunday school, we heard the sermons and stories about the real meaning of Christmas and sang the beautiful Christmas carols that many of us still sing today. It seemed to be snowing a little more every day, and after the last evening Christmas service at church, Nita and Ginnie walked home with Dad and Mother up by the old Hiarm Anderson home, across the hill by the cemetery and then down the hill to the little grey house where there was a bright fire and warm food — but no Christmas tree!

By this time, probably about a week before Christmas, Nita was worried! Snow was thick on the ground, and the ice on the river was frozen hard enough to walk or skate on. The trees in the forest stood stark and bare, their limbs outlined with snow. The little stream that usually gurgled and sang it's way down the hollow, moved slowly now, between the ice-crusted stones. To Nita, everything seemed bleak and bare and the weather was too bad — too cold to even think of hunting for a Christmas tree, even if there was one to hunt.

Feeling like crying, Nita walked to the window in the kitchen to look outside. The window was frosted over, so she took her finger and rubbed the frost off so she could look out. Dad was out at the back of the house where there was a big chopping block, chip yard and wood pile. Nita could hear the sound of his steady chopping. She watched him wedge the axe into the block while he picked up and piled the wood he had chopped.

Then suddenly she heard another sound and she saw another person coming through the snow riding a mule. Nita's eyes grew big. Behind that person, on the mule was ... a Christmas tree! It was Grandpa Anderson, who had ridden all the way from the Breaks to bring his two little granddaughters a Christmas tree.

Nita forgot how cold it was. Out the door she ran straight to Grandpa. He caught her up in his arms, wrapped his big lumber jacket around

her and carried her into the house. Daddy just looked at Nita and smiled a big smile. He had known all the time.

Once in the house, Grandpa set Nita down and moved close to the fire. Steam began rising from his jacket, and the white hair that ringed his lumberman's cap curled in frosty white curls around his neck. He rubbed his hands together as he held them over the warmth of the fire, and finally he moved back a few steps, smiling at Ginnie and Nita.

"Come here," he said, "and put your hands down in my pickets." Ginnie and Nita eagerly reached down into the depths of the big pockets to bring up handfuls of peppermint drops. Grandpa smiled. "I thought my little gals would like some candy for Christmas!" he said.

We snuggled up in his lap and felt the warmth of his love. Thanks, again, Grandpa. To this day, I have never forgotten the effort and love it took to bring happiness to two little girls I have never forgotten the love of two parents who planned it all. I have never forgotten the love that Christmas tree seemed to radiate throughout our humble little home.

Most of all, when all is said and done, and the memories are all sorted out, I will never forget that God, our heavenly Father, made plans for the first Christmas, and it is the love of Christ, the coming of Christ that made it possible. May our hearts

radiate His love as we enjoy the blessing He has provided.

I hope each one of you have a beautiful Christmas and, if you or your child desires a Christmas tree, I hope you will have one. In years to come, you and your child will remember, even as I does.

And now from our house to your house, across the miles and over the mountains, our prayers go out to you and yours for a blessed Christmas and a peace that only comes through Christ.

Matherly remembered for many outstanding characteristics

ANITA BELCHER

This is a column I write with mixed emotions, both joy and sorrow. Joy because I had the privilege and pleasure of growing up with Jeanne Wright Matherly, and sorrow because she is no longer with us. But again, joy that she is with the Lord whom she loved so much.

Many of you knew Jeanne when she was a girl growing up at Sandlick. Many of you who read this were her "best friends." Many of you are close family or related in some way, while others of you were just friends or friends of the family. Some of you will recall her activities in school — her love of basketball and her outstanding participation in the Glee Club. Any of you who knew her at all will always remember her for your own particular reasons, but I think that her genuine love of the Lord and people were her outstanding characteristics, while her enthusiasm and vivaciousness won the hearts of all whose lives she touched.

PLEASE SEE **ECHOES**, PAGE 7B

Echoes

CONTINUED FROM PAGE 4B

The following is the obituary that Jeanne's sister, Mary Elizabeth, prepared for me to publish:

Jeanne Wright Matherly was born Jan. 17, 1925, and died Jan. 12, 2010.

She was preceded in death by her husband, Stacy Matherly. Her memorial service was held at Woodstock Funeral Home, Woodstock, Ga., on Jan. 22 at 11 a.m. Interment was in the Georgia National Cemetery. The service was conducted by the Rev. Robie Hembree with Rebecca Beicher Morecraft providing the eulogy and music. Jeanne was born in Birchleaf, Va., daughter of Will and Emma Colley Wright. She was a teacher in Dickenson County and Atlanta, Ga., for many years. She is survived by a daughter, Mary Jaye Harrison of Acworth, Ga.; two grandsons, Ryan and Eric Harrison; two great-grandchildren; a sister, Mary Wright Ratliff of Atlanta; and brother and sister-in-law, Bruce and Opal Mullins Wright of Aiken, S.C. Jeanne is also survived by several nieces and nephews.

A lifelong member of the Presbyterian Church, Jeanne was always happy in her service for the Lord wherever she was. She taught Sunday School, Bible School, and did the music for the Haysi Presbyterian Church before moving to Atlanta. At the time of her death, she was a member of the College Park Presbyterian Church, College Park, Ga. Jeanne grew up in the Sandlick Community and, like many others, her material things were very meager but there was always a lot of love. Her church meant everything to her and she taught us to always remember who we were. She would say, "Remember your good name. If you lose that, you lose everything." We always remembered what she and the church taught us. When we went on a date, Mom would tell us if we lost that good name, we had nothing! That was something we never forgot!

Jeanne said she and Mary spent many happy hours together, playing paper dolls, making doll houses out in the woods, double dating and going off to college together. They were so close that at one time Mary introduced herself as Jeanne and Jeanne as Mary. Neither of them ever corrected the blunder and they had many laughs over it! Jeanne and Stacy, Mary and Kenneth finally moved to Atlanta where the two sisters grew even closer in their love for each other

Mary closes her note with this thought, "All of us who knew and loved Jeanne have received a personal blessing from knowing her."

Crooked Road is boost for region

For the past several years, a lot of good things have been going on in Southwest Virginia that many folks are not aware of. Perhaps even if you have heard discussions or read articles about tourism and economic growth that would affect at least 19 counties of Southwestern Virginia, you might have just dismissed it as another political move or at best another dream that would never come to fruition.

I know those feelings. I think it's been over 30 years ago that I and a few other faithful folks took on the job of trying to clean up and beautify Haysi. We met with some success, mainly through much hard work and determination. There were no funds available, but we still kept working and hoping. So before I tell you about some of the good things that are happening, and how you can become a part of these ongoing projects, I want to tell you some interesting little stories that have helped keep me from falling into the "depths of despair."

The first big inspiration I had happened when we made a visit to Helen, Ga., about 20 years ago. We were visiting with some of our family and they planned a "tourist" trip for us to this little town that existed over the years mainly because of its timber. When it was "timbered out," the town began to die. Only the "town fathers," a few families and a few basic buildings were left. The men of the town met and came up with a plan. They would use their mountains as a background for an Alpine village. The plan worked. Helen, Ga., became known as one of the leading tourist attractions in the nation and abroad.

Those folks used what they had and that put me to thinking. What did we have more of in Dickenson County than any place around besides coal? Then the thought came. Potatoes! Helen, Ga., had an October fest, so why couldn't we have a potato fest? With the help of several others (I recall Rocky Barton in particular), we organized the Potato Fest and it was a huge success, bringing folks in from around the country. Later it was replaced by the Autumn Fest, but the whole point is, we used what we had, and it worked.

When the Dickenson County Chamber of

Mountain ECHOES

ANITA BELCHER

Commerce was formed, it was, and still is, a blessing to the entire county. Under the leadership of Rita Surratt, good board members and the cooperation of county officials, the Chamber has helped to bring about some of the good things that are happening now.

When the chamber was organized, one of my jobs was that of beautification and litter control. Jordan, our granddaughter who was so badly hurt in an automobile accident, was about 8 or 9 years old then and she was my buddy in cleaning up and beautifying. You'll see later why I mention her in this particular part of this column.

Anyway, the work of the Chamber continued with each of the committees making progress, and I well remember when Clynard, as the Chairman of the Tourism Committee, would introduce himself to people and discuss with them how that in a short time tourism would be the number one income for Southwest Virginia even though we would still depend on coal as long as it lasted. He did a great job as "ambassador" for tourism in our region, but frankly, I was embarrassed for him because, after all, as much as I loved our mountains, who was going to believe his tourism message? How were we going to compete with the well-groomed rolling hills and broad valleys just 30 miles beyond us?

As is being seen more and more these days, he and many others who had that vision of tourism for our part of the state were right on track while my worries were needless.

Clynard continued his "advertising" of our area wherever we went and unknown to us at the time, there were other men and organizations besides our own local citizens and officials who were working on showcasing our part of the country.

In the meanwhile, Cly and I were traveling quite a bit, always looking for ideas for our county and town. We found a lot of pros and cons, in other words, positives and negatives, but one I have used many times is the example of an old hardware in Floyd County that was going out of business because business was virtually non-existent. The owners decided to close it with a Friday night jamboree, and that night there was standing room only. As I understand, a business continued on in the old hardware and I'm told that the Friday night jamboree attracted people from other countries as well as local folks. I do not know what has eventually happened in that situation, but at that time just simply taking advantage of what they had brought success when it was needed.

Strangely enough, my fir knowledge of anything h pening that would attract sitors to Southwest Virginia vas when I was sitting in a cold room adjoining the uma imaging room of the ottish Rite Hospital in Atl a, Ga. Jordan's accider had occurred, and to r / knowledge there was not physician who attended he (and there were many) whc elieved she would live — t unless they believed in mi cles. Yet they continued try g with all the knowledge f y had to save her life.

That particular day, she was having a scan that would take over an hour, and I waited with my feet wrapped in blankets and sound proof covers over my ears. I stared at blank walls and wished I had brought something to read that would help divert my mind from both the noise and silence around me. Suddenly my eyes lit on some old dog-eared magazines on a table in the corner and I picked up the one I was most familiar with, The Reader's Digest.

Flipping through the pages, I came to the section where various attractions are listed for different states. I wasn't really that interested because none of them related to us, "not even Virginia," I thought, "because so much of the time what you read and hear about the Appalachians

and Southwest Virginia is negative."

Imagine my surprise when I read in that little space allotted to each state about The Crooked Road: Virginia's Heritage Music Trail winding through 19 counties in Southwest Virginia, including Dickenson. Then the article that described briefly how the idea of The Crooked Road and its purposes came into existence sent warmth to my blood and hope to my heart. I asked if I could have the magazine and as soon as I could, I told Jordan about it. Even though she was still in a partial coma, I knew she would want to know. I showed the ad to many other people and told them about the wonderful place we live and invited to come for a visit and many already have.

The Crooked Road was just the beginning of a new phase of what had been in the making for many years by many people. It has put us on the map and is called by USA Today as one of the "must see" locations and is one of the most visible attractions in Southwest Virginia. Yes, it has boosted our economy and has seen more than 40 new businesses along its route, while tourism along with increased access to high-speed telecommunications have created hundreds of new jobs for the area. I wish I had the time and space to describe at length about the impact The Crooked Road has made and is making on our area, but I don't, however you can find out by asking for material, brochures and by talking to some of our county officials or by contacting the Chamber of Commerce.

Next week, I am going to continue this column by giving you information on other great things that are happening in our area, but most of all, I'm going to tell you some vital ways you can be a part of these "great happenings."

Just now, as I end this week's column, I'll give you some homework. Let me know if any of your family fought in the Civil War (War Between the States), and anything you know about them, such as their name, rank, what company they were with and where they fought. Any stories you know or have heard about that time in our history would be greatly appreciated.

December 10, 2010

Otto Good recalls frigid European winter of war

Mountain ECHOES

ANITA BELCHER

I have known Otto Good of Sandlick since I was a little girl, but it's an odd fact of life that sometimes neighbors who live within a 10-mile radius (or less) of each other find that time has slipped away and over the years they've hardly seen each other.

I've thought of Otto often and have talked with some of his family in recent months, but I think it was when I did the columns on old textbooks, and added the notes from Tolby Anderson's letter, that I decided I must visit Otto. Tolby and Otto were schoolmates along with a host of other students.

Usually when I visit someone for an interview, I begin by asking them about their parents, grandparents and back as far as they have any information. I do this because many people who read these columns sometimes find an

PLEASE SEE ECHOES, PAGE 9B

ancestor they've been looking for and who fills in a missing link.

With Otto it was different, but first let me introduce him to you. Otto was born Sept. 5, 1920, the son of William Malcolm and Pearl Owens Good. His father's family lived in the Jenkins, Ky., area and his mother's parents, David Crocket and Sallie Wallace Owens, lived at Sandlick where Otto was born.

We'll talk more about genealogy later but I will mention here that Otto is a Southwest Virginia boy and proud of it.

He relates, "I was born and lived all my life at Sandlick with the exception of one year, seven months and 28 days spent in military service and seven years in Detroit, Mich. I went

Otto Good is shown as a young soldier in 1944.

CONTINUED FROM PAGE 6B

there to get a job and make some money for our family, but I missed my home in Virginia.

"We traveled back and forth a lot and finally one day after a close call in a traffic accident I decided the dangers of traveling and the home sickness wasn't worth it. I brought my family back home."

This particular evening when I visited Otto, he had his mind on days spent in military service and I'm going to try to tell his story exactly as he told me. I was fascinated as I "followed" him through the icy cold and snow of the European winters, the loneliness and dangers of living in a foxhole, frozen rations for Christmas, and always the uncertainty of life. Now for this part of his story as he relates it:

"After I graduated from Haysi High School I went to work at the Red Jacket Mines. I was married and had two children, Roger and Patsy. I was drafted for military service and sent to Fort McClellan in Aniston, Ala., for my basic training. From there I was sent to France, then into Germany and Austria."

Otto was a gunner in a machine gun squad. He says, "The only time I ever carried a rifle was in basic training. The rest of my time in service I carried a 30-caliber machine gun and a 45-caliber pistol. I had an assistant who carried the tripod for the machine gun and anoth-

er who carried the extra ammunition.

"Our squad was in foxholes in France during the Christmas holidays of 1944. That had to be the coldest place I was ever in. When the cooks brought us Christmas dinner of turkey and stuff-ing and maybe a piece of pie, it was frozen but we managed to eat it.

"The closest I ever came to being killed or wounded was when we were trying to cross the Siegfried Line in Germany. (This line was a sys-tem of heavy fortifications built before WWII on the western frontier of Germany.)

"A cannon shell landed within three feet of me but didn't explode. We were trying to get through that fortified line, crawling on our stomachs, when I realized that my package of cigarettes in my front pocket was taking up space. I reached down and moved them to my back pocket so I would be that much closer to the ground.

"As we were trying to make it through this for-tified line, it fell dark and we crawled back out-side the line and waited for daylight. We couldn't believe it when daylight came, there was not a German in sight—only empty pillboxes (fortifica-tions used by gunners).

"We came through the Siegfried Line without any problems and advanced on into Germany until we came to Munich. There on the outskirts of that city was a concentration camp filled with Jews ready to be killed and buried, or buried alive. A bulldozer had already dozed out the trench the

width of the dozer blade for their grave.

"I was the first member of our squad to enter the camp, and those poor people fell down to the floor and kissed my muddy boots. They did the same as the rest of our men reached the inside of the camp. We gave them all the food we had including chocolate bars.

"You have never seen starvation unless you saw what we had seen. It's hard for people to believe, but I really mean it when I tell you that these people were simply bones covered with skin. If you have heard on the news that such places did-n't exist, just ask us who have seen them."

On the lighter side of his experiences, though disappointing, was the realization when he looked at the sign-in book at a USO center in Marseilles, France, that he had just missed seeing Junior Sutherland, Doc Tiv's son from Haysi. It was still good to know that there was somebody close to home that was nearby.

Sometimes, if you listen, really listen, there's a big heart-touching story in a short sentence. I heard that story when Otto made the simple remark, "Sometimes when I was in service I would look at the moon and think, 'That same moon is shining back home.'"

Otto was very interested in the lifestyle of the people who lived in the countries where he served. He observed that most of the German peo-ple were very friendly and their lifestyle was much like ours in America.

The French people were somewhat different. He was especially interested in how they built their barns attached to their homes and didn't have to walk very far to do their barnyard chores! Otto was in Austria when the war ended, head-ed for Italy. On leaving Austria his squadron was transferred to a little town, Uem, on the Danube River. Soon he would be receiving his discharge papers and heading back to America—to Southwest Virginia and home—the dream of every soldier!

Otto Good is a quiet man but very knowl-edgeable. There is an old saying, "Still water runs the deepest," and I have found as I inter-view people that the old saying is very true. Much history is never recorded, and even fam-ilies are not aware of the history of their own parents or grandparents.

Many times we think these older folks don't want to talk, but the truth is, they're wait-ing for somebody to be interested in what they've got to tell.

I recall interviewing an older man several years ago and his son was listening very closely. Finally the son spoke and said, "Why, dad, you never told us any of those things." The old gentle-man replied, "Son, none of you ever asked me."

Think how much we would have missed if Otto had not taken the time to share with us, and I'm sure that all of you, like me, are looking for-ward to my next visit with him.

In Touch

with Dickenson County family, friends & neighbors

New Year a time to remember, forget

ANITA BELCHER

In 1849 Alfred Lord Tennyson wrote the following poem: "Ring out the old, ring in the new; ring, happy bells, across the snow; the year is going, let him go. Ring out the false. Ring in the true. Ring in the valiant men and free; the larger heart, the kinder hand. Ring out the darkness of the land. Ring in the Christ that makes us free."

Unless you can find a book (or books) dedicated to the theme of the New Year, it's a somewhat difficult subject to write about, leaving us to rely a great deal on our own knowledge. As for preparing for this very important event, I think we're all so tired from the many Christmas festivities that we just gently ease into the New Year, hardly realizing it's here until we start writing our next check!

All this is true, but now start reading the next sentence to get the other side of the story.

However, having written all that, I need to make some amends, for even as I write I recall poetry and prose pertaining to New Year's snuggled in between Christmas and Valentine's Day.

I believe I have read that the well-to-do people of England celebrated the coming of the new year with much festivity, while the working class had a much humbler celebration.

I am sure that other countries had their own customs of greeting the New Year also.

In America, the New Year was celebrated according to the region one lived in. During the Victorian Age, 1837-1901,

PLEASE SEE **ECHOES**, PAGE 10B

Echoes

CONTINUED FROM PAGE 5B

named for Queen Victoria of England, Christmas and the New Year were celebrated with much pomp and splendor by the well-to-dos.

A Christmas tree for these families would stand 10 feet tall or more. It would be anchored in a heavy stone crock, filled with sand and water and decorated with real candles.

These candles would be lit only twice during the holiday season, once on Christmas morning and again on Christmas eve, before the coming of the New Year. There were 30 candles per foot of the tree and each one must be placed so that no branch was directly above the flame. A bucket filled with water, and a long stick wrapped in a rag, sat close by.

In country and farming areas, both Christmas and New Year's Eve were celebrated in a much less pretentious way, but just as joyful.

I'm trying to remember if our family and neighbors did anything special on New Year's Eve and then, on New Year's Day.

I feel pretty certain that our church had a special service on New Year's Eve, and Mom would fix a New Year's dinner. Just like at Christmas, that dinner would all come from food canned in the summer, cooked and baked in the wood stove.

I think for men, it meant that all the outside work and chores must go on, with maybe a day or so for hunting.

One thing I know for certain is that when night came, Dad had us gather around the fireplace and read from the Bible, thanking God for the blessing of the past year and asking for His guidance in the year to come. An unforgettable memory!

We've come full cycle now. Because of television and the Internet, we can join in New Year's celebrations in our own country, and even other countries. We can talk to our families via telephone, e-mail, Facebook and even instantly send pictures. It's an amazing world.

What would the past generation think of all this modern technology? I can hardly take it all in myself. In fact, I can't.

Here in Southwest Virginia, and I'm sure throughout the nation, but especially in small rural areas and close knit communities, we do celebrate the coming of the New Year.

Some of us gather in one of the family homes, while others meet at their church for worship, prayer, praise and food.

For me personally, the New Year is a time for reflection, of looking back as well as looking forward.

I look back at all the blessings that have been ours. The little things that are really such big things — eyes that see, ears that hear, muscles that move, food to eat and the ability to eat it. A home to live in, enough income to meet our bills, a car to drive and the ability to drive it.

A place to openly worship God without fear of a terrorist attack. A place where we still have the freedom to say "Merry Christmas" instead of "Happy Holidays." Faithful ministers, and our men and women guarding our country.

I thank God that even at our ages, Cly and I are able to toil the ground, make gardens and preserve the produce.

Like you, how thankful we are for family and for friends.

Have you ever thought about how many dangers you have come through by God's grace? How many bad roads you've traveled and made it home safely?

And a big one; just to be able to get out of bed each morning, fix your own food and have the ability to think and make decisions for yourself or others who may need you.

All of you who read this have, like me, been blessed to live another year and to see the beginning of a new one.

The New Year is both a time to remember and forget. Remember the blessings and forget the offenses. Christ, who has preserved our life over the years and is our hope for the future, would have us do this. After all, when all is said and done, He is the greatest blessing of all. Everything we are blessed with comes from Him, the rain, snow and sunshine!

Let me close with a passage from one of my favorite authors and artists, Eric Sloane. In his book, "Once Upon a Time," he writes, "Logically, yesterday is gone forever, yet spiritually, whether two centuries or two minutes ago, it is still an important part of the present.

"Once upon a time,' even though a thousand years ago, gave birth to what we are today. If we can mark time, along with our scientific progress, long enough to let the old morals and spirits catch up, we shall be all the better for it.

"The heritages of Godliness, the love of hard work, frugality, respect for home and all the other spirit of pioneer countrymen, are worth keeping forever.

"What we do today will soon become 'once upon a time' for the Americans of tomorrow and their heritage is our present day responsibility!"

Let us remember the words of Mr. Sloane and begin the New Year with a fresh realization that the way we live affects not only ourselves and our family, but reaches out in some unforseen way to affect our nation.

In the same way, the way we live, the decisions we make, sets the pace for the America which is to be when our generation has become a part of history.

May we all face the New Year with the courage and determination to do that which is right in the sight of God and man.

301

Made in the USA
Monee, IL
22 May 2025